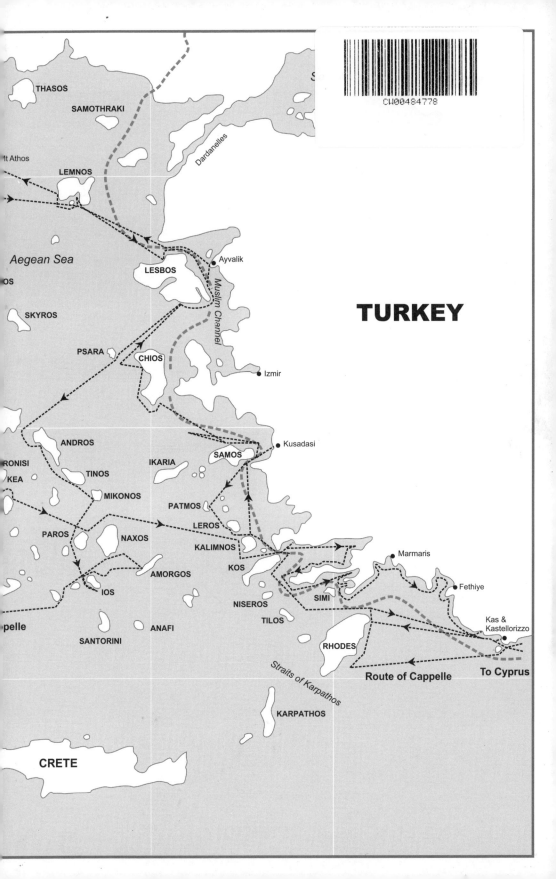

Orchids for Aphrodite

Orchids
for Aphrodite

An Aegean Odyssey

by

Ursula Haselden

Seashell

Copyright © Ursula Haselden 2009
First published in 2009 by Seashell
4 Lockhart Place, St Andrews, Fife, KY16 9XB

Distributed by Gardners Books, 1 Whittle Drive, Eastbourne, East
Sussex, BN23 6QH
Tel: +44(0)1323 521555 | Fax: +44(0)1323 521666

www.amolibros.co.uk

British Library Cataloguing in Publication Data
A catalogue record for this book is available from the British Library.

ISBN 978-0-9556291-0-5

Typeset by Amolibros, Milverton, Somerset
This book production has been managed by Amolibros
Printed and bound by T J International Ltd, Padstow, Cornwall, UK

To the Captain and Ship's Cat
And the wind beneath my wings

Acknowledgements

I am most grateful to my Greek teacher, Mary Hero Lidderdale. What Greek she taught me proved invaluable. I also owe heartfelt thanks to Commander and Mrs Johnny Guard for taking us under their wing on arrival in Turkey and for their generous provision of information. Our live-aboard lives would never have been the same without the many friends we made, including the Asimaki family, Vangelis, Nikos, Mama Zoë and Little Zoë of Lavrion-Sounion; Ceylan Orhun of Torba; the Göndemir family, Yakup, Nermin and Dilara of Istanbul; the Tsimpos family, Stavros, Christina, Christos and Korina of Thessaloniki, and the Gauthier family, Daniel, Mireille and Gaby of Marseilles. My son and daughter, William Haselden and Mel Haselden Kirk gave the project their very welcome support. I owe a special debt of gratitude to the late Lady Helen Louise Bruce Nairn for keeping my letters, and sincere thanks to David Mostyn for permission to reproduce his cartoon of *Cappelle* presented to us by Stephen Kirk. I am also beholden to Richard Unthank for his excellent maps and to Rosie his Schnauzer puppy for not eating them. Tony Denton's lively cover design expresses the spirit of the book to perfection. Terry Smith laboured over the initial proof reading, West Port Printing & Design of St Andrews undertook the scanning of our original prints, and Mail Boxes etc gave every assistance. Finally, without Jane Tatam of Amolibros (not forgetting occasional interference from Dorrit her Siamese cat when Jane was on the telephone) this book would never have been published. Any mistakes should be attributed to a stranger in strange lands.

Photo credits

Mel Haselden for photo of Wacky on Watch (Photo No 14 Colour & Back Cover); Julia Hobday for photo of Wacky streaking back on *Cappelle* after a night out (Photo No 12, black & white). All other photos by the author and Robert Martyn. The Teatowel Incident (Photo No 5 Colour) is reproduced by kind permission of David Mostyn ©1993.

Contents

List of illustrations

Colour illustrations facing page 208

1   *Cappelle at first sight.*

2   *Ursula gets to work with a heat gun.*

3   *Launch of Cappelle, Lavrion.*

4   *Cruising the Southern Peloponnese.*

5   *The Teatowel Incident, Plomari, Lesbos.*

6   *Energetic setting up her winter quarters in the fruit market, Bodrum.*

7   *Cappelle on passage.*

8   *William at the helm.*

9   *Jic accepts a treat, Castle Quay, Bodrum.*

10   *Trianda Carnival, Rhodes.*

11   *Girl talk, Ursula and friend, Kalkan Street.*

12   *Ursula and Wacky: victims of stormy seas.*

13   *Ready for breakfast after a night sail, Chios.*

14   *Wacky on watch.*

15   *Exhausted crew recuperate.*

16   *Film crew for My Grannie's a Cripple in Nashville, Rhodes.*

Front endpaper: General map of Aegean area.

Back endpaper: Map of South Western coast of Turkey showing Gulf of Gököva.

" 'The sailor is better for you,' said Sophie to Sophie.
'Even if he is cold comfort; even if you never see
him or catch his star. Take him for yours,' said
Sophie sternly and Sophie said, 'I will.' "

Rumer Godden
(*Kingfishers Catch Fire*)

One

In the beginning

Boat restoration: Northern Greece

She was on the hard in Lavrion, our new home, blanketed in snow that drifted under the cockpit cover. Anyone foolish enough to think her Mabel Lucy Atwell's:

> "Fairy Boat to take us away
> To the Land where the Mermaids love to play"

had a problem. Lavrion's Olympic Marina, "more like a nuclear bomb-site than a boat-yard", as some wag put it, did nothing to raise the spirits. But the barrier lifted and we jolted in and out of floodwater past joyless yachts. Down by the sea in the bitterest, most wind-blasted spot stood my sugar-coated dream boat, a wooden hull on a botched cradle, its feet in a pond across which skidded chunks of snow. A crazy ladder tied on with string led to the deck. That this scene of arctic desolation was underwritten by an oil drum daubed «Απορρίματα», Greek for "Rubbish", summed things up. But, with the tatters of a red ensign streaming from her shrouds, I knew this thirty-four feet of unhappy ship was ours, for letters two feet high on flapping dodgers proclaimed her name *"CAPPELLE "*.

It was a now-or-never, lifestyle thing. For better or worse, live-aboard was our choice. There had been enough capital to buy an old boat and enough income, barring extravagance, to live on. We made up our minds to throw in our lot together. There is never enough time to tie up all the ends. Best not think about it! I sought no introduction to the art of sailing. If it failed to suit me, so be it! As Matthew Parris wrote, "There is no better way to acquire a skill than urgently and under force of circumstance." Though born and bred in land-locked Derbyshire, suffice that my birth sign was Aquarius, and as a babe-in-arms I held out my arms to the moon.

My shipmate, Bob, who had spent twenty-five years as an RAF officer, was an experienced sailor. He was tall. I was five-foot-two, with a penchant for high heels. I lacked muscle. We had reached a crossroads. Due to the impending recession, the London office in which we both worked closed down. More crucially, we were forced to admit our reluctance to part. My invitation to the Boat Show was kismet. The answer was obvious. Here was my chance to go wide-screen. I had long been widowed. My children and I had brought each other up. Now the nest would be empty. Shortly afterwards, via a yachting magazine, Bob purchased a teak-on-oak Bermudan sloop. She was lying in Greece, a unifying circumstance, since a fascination with Greek script had led me to attend classes in Modern Greek. *Agape* would unite with *Eros* on a boat.

Our plan was to explore the Aegean World.

In Lavrion we expected to be met by one Alan to whom Bob had advanced a substantial sum to start work on restoring the hull. But there was no sign of life. With *Cappelle* an ark in a flood, Bob salvaged a plank across which we wobbled to mount a ladder, lift a corner of a tarpaulin – and collapse into a snow drift. The cabin doors opened to reveal a cavity exuding the stench of engine oil and showing signs of recent squatter occupation. My first impression was of descending into an inspection pit. Stigs of the Dump, we crouched shivering, aware neither of us was prepared to sleep aboard.

When the ladder creaked, bearing weight, my heart missed a beat. Then the doorway was darkened by a bearded giant out of whom antagonism leaked like poison gas, "I want out!" Alan bellyached. "It's your bloody fault I've led this soul-destroying existence! Either you give me a lift back to civilisation or I push off alone! I'm bloody well renegotiating terms!" "Where's my duty-frees?" he added threateningly.

Bob ventured a placatory enquiry as to the nearest taverna. The wind gnawed my cheek bones as we clambered round a barbed-wire entanglement at the edge of the sea where a bitch with hanging teats nuzzled my hand. A rush of moist air and cigarette smoke hit us as we struggled to slam the taverna door. Its windows streamed with condensation. Talk and music pulsated. Five men, office staff from Olympic Marine claiming it too cold to work, stomped to and fro Greek-style, arms across one another's shoulders. Toothless old Mitsos slammed down plates of leathery chops and a jug of home-brew. I had never been anywhere so foreign in my life.

A week or so before, as we shuffled through Dover's midnight snowflakes before boarding the car ferry *Spirit of Free Enterprise*, customs officials vexed Bob by refusing to sign prepared VAT exemption papers on gear for a "yacht in transit". Greece now bore responsibility for reimbursement. Fat chance! In France, a short idyll in the Var failed to compensate for the shadow that hung over our crossing from Ancona to Patras. With the ferry enveloped in a white-out blizzard, on-board television devoted itself to a tragic accident left behind in the English Channel, the capsize at Zeebrugge of the *Spirit's* sister ship, the *Herald of Free Enterprise*, "the worst maritime disaster since the sinking of the *Titanic*". It was not a happy omen for a sailing adventure.

From the port of Patras, our approach to Athens was via the ugly and industrialised Sacred Way alongside which rusting derricks protruded from a gun-metal sea. Piraeus's ice-rutted roads defeated us. From counting dead dogs and cats on the road, as we drove on towards the grubby ore port of Lavrion, I forced myself to concentrate on the undulating Attic corniche. Here we faced the horrors of ribbon development, never-to-be-finished villas sprouting rusty tax-avoidance reinforcing rods, petrol stations and dumps of clapped-out cars interspersed with litter-footed hoardings advertising shampoo and Amanda's Cream Dream.

Back on the road again, Alan cheered up as he steered us towards the social scene in Glyfada. It was Happy Hour. Overhearing we had nowhere to stay, a snow-bound British lorry driver offered his slightly inebriated sponsorship. We were also sure we were better off without

Alan, who now seemed in no hurry to get back to his girl-friend and his boat with wood-burning stove.

Anxious to set up camp nearer our labours, we explored a private driveway advertising "Country Residences" only three switch-back miles from Lavrion. Here we met the Family Asimaki, poetic-looking Vangelis, Nikos, his brother, and black-clad Mama Zöe, who agreed to open up an apartment and provide bottled gas. Proud possessors of two rooms, we celebrated by making a snowman on the doorstep. Milk left out in the kitchen froze solid overnight.

Each evening, exhausted and filthy, we hunched over an ancient radiator like workmen over a brazier awaiting the routine highlight of a meal cooked by the Brothers Asimaki in the vast unheated restaurant. Every night, to Mama Zoe's, «Φωτιά? Φωτιά!?» ("Fire? Fire?") we replied, "Yes, PLEASE!"

It was the signal for her party trick. Piling twigs in the hearth, she lit a blaze with a single match before shuffling about to present culinary delicacies such as spinach pie and milk pudding. Sometimes Vangelis joined us for minuscule cups of sticky sweet black coffee, sighing over his business problems and the short-comings of the Greek government: "It is not Mr Papandreou's money!" he declared. "It is MY money!" So saying, his chin would go up and his mouth turn down like a bucket handle. To bid "Goodnight!" to Mama Zöe, before summoning the energy to scrub dodgers or scrape *Cappelle's* dismantled cooker, became a looked-for courtesy. Taking my hand in hers, she would fold into it a childish treat; mandarins, little cakes or some nuts. Scandalised by the angel-faced ragamuffins of a German neighbour, who played outside in the slush, «Βρώμικο!», she shuddered. ("Dirty!") But, blessed with a raunchy sense of humour, she cackled a lascivious «Έξι παιδιά!» ("Six children!") whenever their mother appeared. An heir and to spare had seen Mama Zoe's duty done.

Yachts stood on the hard, were moored to the quay or anchored off. Once an estuarial swamp, designated the site for a never-built factory during the Junta, the land had been requisitioned as the location for "the most luxurious marina in Europe". This enterprise also came to nothing. Summer desert, winter marsh, it had been taken over by a government-sponsored organisation involved in the manufacture of patrol boats that consistently failed their sea trials. With a quay wall preventing the outflow of water, every morning found *Cappelle* marooned in a swamp. Bob's first task was to dig an outlet channel, which the afternoon to-ing and fro-ing of the travel-lift filled in again.

After ten days Alan, accompanied by Stewart, a hard-working Scot, put in an appearance. This brought a further headache, for the marina operated a closed shop. Owners and skippers were permitted to work on boats, but paid workers might only be recruited from the yard's pool of unemployed miners at grossly inflated wages. Alan surprised us by muttering dramatically about leaving "if the police were called". Within minutes of work starting on *Cappelle*, a German-speaking Greek arrived to cross-examine Bob, who had the presence of mind to assure him that Alan and Stewart were crew members.

The matter was left at that and Alan and Stewart proceeded to fill, prime and paint with the materials we brought with us, just sufficient not to incur customs charges or confiscation at the Greek border. (A German openly importing a van-load of paint lost the lot!) After *Cappelle's* mast was unstepped from its tabernacle, I was promoted from shampooing the bilges to sanding and varnishing the mast. Vesta, Stewart's girl-friend, an emancipated character, was persuaded to join our team. Vesta worked hard when it suited her. At other times, declaring it "not convenient!", she curled up with a book.

The Greek surveyor's opinion of *Cappelle* was the yachting optimist's "All she needs is a lick of paint..." But her deck was another story, Disintegrating fuel tanks also posed a problem until Vesta persuaded a car repair shop to make replicas. Unfortunately, since his free-standing inspection torch had disappeared with Alan's departure, Bob failed to seal a joint when, contorted inside the lazarette, he slotted the new tanks together. This resulted in diesel seeping through *Cappelle's* freshly painted hull.

There were days new lifestyle seekers were unlikely to forget. Our keenness led to a desire to smarten up the four tons of ballast (pig-iron and lead) under the floor boards of what I chose to call my living room. Bob had just enough muscle to heave a single brick out of the bilge cavity and hump it up the companionway steps. When all were cast overboard, we hoisted them onto a rigged platform to scrub and paint with red lead. That was the easy part. The next was the cliff-hanger. With no chance of carrying the bricks up the ladder (so precarious it had the advantage of never being "borrowed"), Bob operated the boom, with the main halyard through a shackle on its end as a pulley. Wedging each brick into an old motor tyre, he posted me on deck for the delicate operation of manoeuvring each gyrating load over the ship's rail. We made it successfully twenty-six times.

General consensus favoured treating the teak with fourteen coats of the Scandinavian saturation oil Deks Olje. On moving enough impedimenta inside to prise open the door to the Baby Blake (as the loo was styled) we found it choked with cigarette ends. Scraping soap scum and matted hair from beneath the duck boards under the shower likewise failed to raise my spirits. This was left to the British Ambassador, who, entering the yard in a car remarkable for its lack of the usual livery of dust. called out with a friendly smile, "I've been admiring your boat all winter! I'm so glad someone's taken her under their wing! Who designed her?" *Cappelle* might have style, but it was plainly something I lacked. The de-haut-en-bas look given me by a jet-setter whose tote bag was emblazoned "Esteé Lauder's Complete Sun Protection Plan" left no doubt as to her opinion.

The marina dogs ranged from a randy pooch, Tou-tou, who raced round the yard on the look-out for totty, to Bonzo who was winched down from his deck in a basket. The Ceremony of Sunset was performed by the two resident dog packs. The Gate Pack, barking a ferocious challenge to the Quay Pack, accompanied the watchman on his bike doing his evening rounds. This was the starting signal. Occasionally the vendetta led to throat-tearing in the swamp. But if a car moved, both packs joined forces to snap at tyres. The cafeteria manager's Alsatian, Rover, spent his days chained. Resenting his superior status, the other dogs goaded him mercilessly. His toys were jetsam, beer cans and worse. Freed of a morning, he would lope upstairs to raid the sanitary bins (open baskets) in the ladies' lavatory, which did double duty as a drinks' store. Here yachtsmen soaked warps in the washbasins or filled them with dirty laundry.

By virtue of the traditional "Easter painting", the situation deteriorated. When Vesta and I found workmen engaged in sloshing paint in the lavatory, one held a door open for me. Paint trickled everywhere adding a harlequin touch to my red-leaded anorak. After the men had slammed out, whistling merrily, Vesta showed me the shower curtains stuck to the wall with paint. "You did not understand what they were saying!" she laughed. "They saved this job till lunchtime because they get paid time and a half!" Worse was to come, when their misappropriation of the "Only for Ladies" sign brought yachtsmen in to use our showers as urinals.

It was springtime and more and more puppies were born. A prematurely aged bitch, matriarch of the Quay Pack, gave birth to seven puppies in the rutted hillocks of the waste ground, their putative father, known affectionately as "Stupid", a slow-on-the-uptake pseudo-Dalmatian from his mother's previous litter. The surviving triplets of the misalliance, an adorable trio, were fed on milk and eggy bread by yachtswoman, Anita, under whose yacht, *Svicat*, the pack sheltered. Whenever we ate together chez Mitso, Anita called for a paper bag, bidding everyone scrape in leftovers from fish-heads to rice-pudding. Long after *Svicat's* launch, Stupid continued to patrol her patch of earth.

When an "Island Sailing" girl fished a hypothermic puppy out of the sea, I fixed him a nest on the back seat of our car. With the pup swaddled in paint rags, Vesta smeared butter inside his ear-flaps to loosen a mass of engorged ticks. We crept away leaving the car door ajar and forgot the patient until excited yapping heralded the emergence of a self-confident little bundle who rolled out of the car and scampered off to join his brothers. From then on he came to see us every day.

Though there were no contractual rights by which a yacht might lay claim to a particular berth, woe betide any boat tying up amongst the flotilla. We witnessed a fight and saw a skipper flung overboard. A further example of marina rage involved a choleric German baron who, apprehending a Greek severing his water hose, grabbed him by the hair and shook him like a rat. (The Greek, it seemed, suspected the baron of employing outside labour, which indeed he was.) An exacerbating problem, with everyone dependent on power tools, became the scarcity of electric points. It was my job to stand guard over *Cappelle's* connections.

Easter in Piraeus

There came the bright spot of an invitation to spend Easter with Vesta and Stewart on Kastella, the acropolis of Piraeus. The weather improved. On three sides of Kastella the damascened Aegean faded into the horizon. Tiny hydrofoils like yellow water beetles trailed snowy wakes. To the north the Parthenon floated thistledown light against its background of Parnassus. Stewart and Vesta occupied the top two-thirds of a mediaeval tenement sporting three balconies and four roof terraces, each facing a different point of the compass. The main roof garden was reached by an iron stairway. Up there a disused bathhouse contained an enormous claw-footed bath filled with kindling. From the courtyard below a door opened onto a marble-floored kitchen where sunshine poured onto a profusion of window plants, amongst which a canary which "flew in one day", sang its heart out. (Monsieur Hulot would have revelled in the ambience!) Down below, at the top of a stone-balustraded staircase, was a living-cum-dining room whose balcony, dominated by a wardrobe refrigerator, gave onto the church on Kastella.

A whopping, smooth-haired Great Dane (or thereabouts) named, for some unaccountable reason, "Tufty" shared the accommodation. (Bob called him "Dafty" on the quiet for, like P G Wodehouse's McIntosh, he was of "low intellect".) The only way to eject him from an armchair was bodily. But at the first sign of my open arms he would leap into them, thrusting an affectionate tongue down my ear. Entered via a mounting block, my low-ceilinged room with its miniaturised furniture made me feel like Alice in Wonderland on Growing Medicine. I was disturbed in the night by the tinkle of bead curtains, and there in the doorway stood Dafty silhouetted in moonlight like some mild-mannered Hound of the Baskervilles.

On Easter Saturday Vesta served μαγειρίτσα, traditional Easter soup made from the entrails of a young lamb cooked with eggs, rice, lemon and herbs. Pancakes stuffed with blue cheese followed. Wine flowed as Stewart regaled us with the history of his total abstinence from the insidious aperitif οὐζο (ouzo). He had been in the habit of taking two glasses as a sundowner when a friend flew in bearing duty-frees. Stewart succumbed to another οὐζο and the guest stayed to dinner. All augured well until he went to fetch the main course, calling in the bathroom on the way. Here a strange thing happened. His mind blanked. Concluding he was about to take a bath, he had undressed and turned on the taps. Vesta found him marinating.

We rose from the table to watch crowds scurrying to the church. Illumination burgeoned as candlelight rippled down the nave. On the stroke of midnight a clamour arose. Flung wide, the church doors revealed that Christ's bier, the Epitaphion, borne through the streets on Good Friday, was empty. Light streamed out as the priest stepped forth to proclaim the Resurrection, «Χριστός ανέστη!» ("Christ is Risen!") We turned to one another with the response, «Αληθώς ανέστη!» ("He is truly risen!") Bells peeled, fire crackers exploded, Dafty hid under the table, and the people issued forth bearing tall candles lit from the priest's own. Their aim was to get these trophies home alight to ensure good luck by drawing a smoke cross on their newly painted front door. (Rules allowed for the relighting of a candle from a friend's, there being a moratorium on the usual neighbourly quarrel.) A night wind blustered and the jiggery-pokery was good natured. Some brought Chinese lanterns as candle protectors, while others struggled into cars and taxis, shrieking as they scattered gobbets of hot wax.

Falling over one other, we raced to the roof. Around us Athens was a flower garden of fireworks. Ships in harbour blared their sirens, "Let Joy be Unconfined for Christ is Risen!" (Which is tantamount to saying "Spring has come! The Festival of Festivals has dawned!" – Easter, Christmas and New Year rolled into one.) Inside again, we played conkers with the traditional red-dyed eggs, leaving one intacta for the Virgin. Or was it an offering to her forbear, Persephone, goddess of spring? The grief of Good Friday is the same grief as that of prehistory for the stricken earth. It was Persephone's resurrection that saved the people from starvation.

Vesta, laying a cloth with Hymettus honey and a τσουρέκι (a plaited loaf with red-dyed egg inside), set Easter Breakfast on a lower terrace. Dafty rested his chin on the table and all I had heard of the Greek sun came true. On the roof it was so sunny and bright we retreated now and again to the lilac-scented shade of the living-room.

It is customary to feast out of doors on Easter Day. On the rooftop discarded building materials lay scattered, with wooden laths and rolls of wire-netting that Stewart said he might get rid of one day (though, this being Greece, never would). Petrol cans held geraniums and culinary herbs. Tickling the dust with a witch's broom, Stewart assembled trestle tables. I stood at the roof margin, looking down on neighbouring roof-gatherers. As the fumes of barbecues rose into the air like the fires of the sacrifices of old, Stewart recounted the Greek tragedy of an English girl who had once occupied the apartment. Recovering from the death of her fiancé, she took a job in Athens where, in the course of time, she gained a new boyfriend. When he, too, died accidentally, she, consumed with grief and lured by the hypnotic view, had leapt to eternity.

A pharaonic Easter banquet was laid on damask cloths spread with runners in the Greek colours of blue and white on which were set artless jugs of wild flowers. Fourteen people sat down to feast, hands reaching out to an ever-replenished array – roast lamb sprinkled with oregano and pierced with slivers of garlic, grilled mussels in puréed tomato with feta cheese, leeks in lemon cream, salvers of tiny coral-coloured spider crabs, παπουτσάκια (little slippers) of stuffed aubergines halved lengthwise, and lambs' intestines with liver and lights. Sloshing wine into glasses, we devoured spit-roasted kid and popped delicacies into our mouths and those of our neighbours. Feasting continued with an amazing Easter cake, a tall confection shaped like a Cardinal's hat. To fill gaps there were bowls of fruit and Easter cookies in starry shapes. When the four dogs at the feast began to snore under the table the more energetic of us got up to dance to Graceland.

On Easter Monday Bob and I set off for the Acropolis. According to Stewart, entry was free on a public holiday. But, as we reached the Propylea, a belligerent ticket-seller barred our way. "You wan' police?" she barked. We paid up. When I leafed through misprinted catalogues in the bookshop, I got my knuckles ruler-rapped. Vesta's comment on this incident was that low-paid civil servants, such as site officials, were a particularly disgruntled section of society.

The seal was set on our Easter weekend with a sea mist so thick a hover-craft ran aground in Piraeus harbour. Back in Lavrion the marina seethed with rumour: Greece and Turkey were on the brink of war over mineral rights, and Greece proposed new restrictions on yacht movement to counteract the departure of yachts for "foreign waters"(i.e. Turkey).

A party of "Sea Cadets", who were to undergo two weeks' training under the auspices of Island Sailing, were expected. Not one of the motley band of teenagers sponsored by children's homes in the north of England, had been on a boat before. In sandals and Sea Island cottons, the girls laboured under the misapprehension of volunteering for some sort of sub-tropical cruise. Kicking out at yacht cradles, the boys resorted to horse play. All attempts to marshal them in front of the flotilla as it tossed in a lively sea failed lamentably. With the weather deteriorating, the party were escorted elsewhere and we did not encounter them again.

Before we could set sail, there was paperwork to complete concerning *Cappelle's* Bill of Purchase. Under Greek maritime law, debts remain with a boat. What concerned us was the annual tax levied on foreign registered craft. When we requested to pay the due amount at Lavrion Tax Office, a woman entered, her jacket swinging from her shoulders, marking her, Bob whispered, as "the boss". However, addressing us as «Αμερικάνοι» (i.e. gullible) she failed to grasp what it was he wished to pay and had never set eyes on a eurocheque. A banner proclaiming "AMERICANS GO HOME!" was stretched across the street, so I was quick to point out we were British. "The boss" then told Bob he must pay whatever it was in cash. But, since it was illegal for him to have imported so large a sum, the money must be obtained from a bank, together with a Pink Slip to prove the exchange took place in Greece. It was obvious that the Pink Slip was more important to her than the money, so our call at the tax office became four hours of crossing and recrossing the street between bank, Port Police and various cramped government departments to obtain an official stamp. Bob's temper wore thin. At last, at the Government Cashier's Office, he was awarded a Pink Slip and we returned to the boss in triumph.

Most days, armed with a Coke bottle for νέφτι (white spirit, sold loose), I drove into the one-hick frontier town to purchase running requirements such as screws, sandpaper, masking tape, drinking water and basic supplies. Once, when it started to rain, having laid newspaper-wrapped eggs on scraps of meat scrounged for the puppies, I made an impromptu omelette in my handbag. Lavrion's παντοπωλείο (Everything Store) was heaped from floor to ceiling with ill-assorted goods. I soon learned that the check-outs were operated by an eye-evading mother and daughter skilled in the art of subterfuge. Bob noted that in every transaction a hundred δραχμές or so over the odds was added, the older woman adding a thousand (£5). There was no print-out. The trick was to cancel the till total so fast the customer had no chance to check.

Vesta explained that cheating was a structure integral to Greek society and so prevalent as to be institutionalised, it being more admirable to practise deceit than be thought a fool. Greeks cheat each other, she said, the best way to prove superiority being to make a fool of someone else. The clever man cheats the stupid (or ignorant) with no quarter given. Lavrion being a flotilla base, tourists were easy meat. (But their pettish whittlings about sell-by dates annoyed me too!) "Never smile when you enter a shop!" warned Vesta. "A smile is a sign of submission that gives encouragement to cheating!" She explained the hidden meaning of certain stock responses: "Of course!" (in English) could mean "No!" rather than "Yes!" while "Αύριο!" (literally "tomorrow") meant "Some other time!" i.e., "Never!" This caused confusion amongst visitors. In delightful contrast, were such courtesies as the wrapping of a single postcard in rose-patterned paper when I said it was to send to my daughter.

Although Bob had set his heart on timing *Cappelle's* launch for his mid-April birthday (an oasis in the live-aboard world), we missed the deadline. To make it up to him, Vesta conjured up a birthday cake with candles, and Anita and Richard, retired publicans from the Elephant & Castle turned yacht carers, took us to view the baron's yacht readied for the arrival of the baroness. *Kalosini*'s interior, in the style of a Bavarian cottage, was not to my taste, but I admired the bubble glass bowl glowing with yellow marsh flowers Anita had placed on the cabin table. There and then, vowing to transform *Cappelle* into a yacht that is "forever travelling but forever home", I crammed jam jars (eyes averted from a spilt sack of chicken carcases) with pink potentilla from the hillside.

The storm

More disturbed weather was poor welcome for the first soft-adventure flotilla parties. Vangelis and Nikos, out chopping and clearing, failed to keep up with the damage. After days of inclement weather came the crescendo of a night of storm. After supper we were obliged to wait for the gibbous moon to light us home over raised walk-ways washed with floodwater. Next day we found the Island Sailing staff fixing extra lines in an effort to stabilise the flotilla. I was uneasy. The keening wind that shook *Cappelle* rose ominously. Glancing through a porthole, I saw people running like ants along the shoreline and then what was attracting their attention. In mid-harbour, where the sea was fogged with spume, a crazed schooner, broken free from a swinging mooring, scudded towards the rocks of the lee shore. As I watched, she broached, keeled over, rose again as if in urgent supplication, suffered a further knockdown and then, flat on the water, masts first, slewed to destruction. I caught a nightmare glimpse of two men on deck waving frantically.

Meanwhile we occupied ourselves on terra firma searching for chocks to shore up *Cappelle*'s cradle. "Hurry! Hurry!" I yelled, a puny Atlas exerting all her strength to support her world. In the cafeteria Island Sailing staff in heavy weather gear huddled in urgent conference. From time to time a gleaming wet figure appeared in the doorway shouting, "THE WARPS ARE GOING!" before dashing off, followed by a stampede, to where the flotilla danced. The loss of the schooner emphasised the seriousness of the situation. Island Sailing decided bare-boat charterers were, if possible, to be evacuated. I overheard one skipper, leaning forward, say, "Remember! Anyone we lose is a goner!" In the event all souls were saved – and one prospective Cabin Boy was revising her ideas about "swanning" in the Med.

In the afternoon our chocks lay back on the ground – a kindly fisherman had deemed our cradle safer less rigid. Now the general mood was one of anger, for, to everyone's astonishment, Olympic Marine staff had locked up and gone home – cutting yachtsmen off from the one and only telephone. Aussie Jack was incensed. When he tried to buy the shipwrecked mariners soup, the cafeteria manager refused service. Then, despite the wind and high seas, we sensed the gale abating.

The following day, the sea streaked greenish-grey like bad meat; the sky troubled, we ventured out along the arm of the bay to view what was left of the schooner. She was an awesome sight. Resembling a ball of wool on giant knitting needles, she lay on her side on the foreshore, her hull stove in, her masts rammed through it by the force of the breakers. High on the rocks above lodged a smashed fishing boat. Debris was widespread. Scavengers, backing off as an occasional heavy sea rolled ashore, had lost no time. Already little of value remained, but Bob salvaged enough veneer for a cockpit repair. (We were learning not to look askance at once ill-considered trifles.)

Live-aloft live-aboards

After farewell coffee and cakes with the Asimakis, the tree-house life of live-aloft live-aboards began. Probably because it made things more awkward, I invariably felt the need to cross the yard to the toilet block in the night. However quietly I descended the ladder, all six dogs beneath it awoke to render me a sort of nocturnal Pied Piper. Outside the cafeteria my Merry Band roused Rover. Although tree-house life was far from convenient, this Mediterranean Swan was admitting to qualms about becoming waterborne. Not for nothing had I shared a cafeteria table with two yachtsmen, each of whom, I noticed with the misgivings of The Boy Who Ran Away To Sea, had an index finger missing – a common injury amongst sailors.

While Bob's concern was whether *Cappelle's* untried 23 hp Volvo engine would let him down in the docking channel, mine related to the puppies. I arranged to hand them over to Thurid, a fourteen-year-old puppy-worshipper, who prepared a rag-lined barrel beneath her family's boat. Suddenly there appeared a newcomer, a fat and fluffy fellow of amiable disposition who set up independent home on the sea front between a lamp-post and a dustbin, trotting importantly about in attendance on departures and arrivals. We called him the "Little Harbourmaster". Sadly, his life was short. He was discovered with his neck broken. It seemed he had tangled with a truck.

Yachtsmen, smiling knowingly over our proposed early launch, said we should not see the travel hoist before tea-time. We were growing wise to the socio-economy of a marina whose work-force spent its days playing backgammon. Stewart confided mysteriously that the men would be "fools" to work and, when I asked why, gave a reason which did not make sense, "Because they are paid wages!" It seemed the efforts of right thinkers were reserved for piece-work and overtime. From seven a.m., when the yard opened, the daytime hours were quiet, while the flurry of activity started at tea-time. This was because from four o'clock on weekdays and all day on Saturdays pay was time and a half. On Sundays it was double time.

On 14th May summer burst upon us and next day we were ready early. The manager then let us know the travel hoist would be with us "around midday". But, as predicted, it failed to appear until tea-time. While *Cappelle* made her howdah-like progression to the launch canal we endeavoured to slap antifoul on the prop spots masked by her cradle. Forming an escort, we jumped aboard when she was lowered into the canal. As Bob feared, the engine spluttered and, like many another yacht, she was towed to the quay. Hailed for the first time as «*Καπετάνιο!*» ("Captain!"), Bob perked up, a crowd of well-wishers gathered, someone produced a Spray Start canister and the engine roared awake.

In dawn's oyster gleam *Cappelle* came alive on a mirror sea. My job specification was Cabin Boy, but, numb with surprise at taking part in a script I endorsed, I took the wheel. As the Captain said, from now on life could only get better.

Two

Water-borne

Poros

My knowledge of the Temple of Poseidon at Cape Sounion was from the watercolours of Hugh "Grecian" Williams, who painted Scottish landscapes in Greek light and classic remains against marbled English skies. To starboard the Real Thing was silhouetted against the blue for which it was intended; stately columns glistening white, "strings of a harp still vibrating". *Cappelle* developed a problem. A broken valve made pumping the loo mandatory. (Boats have sunk for less.) But when the sails were hoisted, I was captivated by the silence that rolled down like a bolt of silk. Sunshine sequined a splintery sea as the island of Kea appeared, with, in the distance, Aegina, island of the pistachio.

The Captain gave orders to steer into wind while he handed the mainsail. With the hauling round of the yacht to face wind and choppy seas, came the uproar of flogging canvas.

Incomprehensibly Bob yelled, "Up! Up! Bring her up!"

"Oh God! Up where?"

Clutching the wheel I burst into tears, sobbing over the death of the Little Harbourmaster. (Bob was heard to remark that, although he had accepted I did not know my Lefts from my Rights, he was seriously concerned on finding I did not know my Ups from my Downs!)

Once order was restored, we motored into Poros Straits, which became the main thoroughfare of a multi-coloured hill settlement. As Henry Miller said, arrival beside the island did have the feel of "sailing on land", the village a tumble of coloured bricks from a toy box on top of which a child had plonked a cut-out campanile. The air smelt of pine woods and fish. In a daze we moored amongst working boats in the orchestra pit of a theatre before a quay that served as the apron of a stage. Piled with onion floats swathed in magenta mantillas, it was backed by geraniums. Beyond came the milling street chorus and a pilastered and pedimented backdrop with fluted roof tiles spaced with ornate antefixes. At ground level were tavernas and *καφενεία* (coffee shops). It was the perfect setting for a musical. I expected the cast to break into song.

Poros had once served as *Cappelle's* home port. When enthusiasm for her by her previous owner, a Toad of Toad Hall, evaporated, she had lain neglected until the nibbling of a potential buyer roused him to devote all of two days to a tarting-up job. *Cappelle* fitted Bob's requirements for a sea-kindly classic, stiff enough to be steady and ripe for restoration. Moreover, she displayed the airy interior, roomy berths, standing headroom and wide doors he sought. He was made much of and a deal was struck.

Our reason for putting into Poros was to collect items missing from the inventory. The dory was presumed "borrowed". The ill-fitting cockpit cushions fell off a lorry. And the spare sails were filthy. Toad's cronies presumed we were there to complain. Life for most live-aboards was serious. Many had a trade and did odd jobs for cash. Competition for yacht delivery was cut-throat, while the rumour of a film company in the vicinity (such as the one presently making *Pascali's Island*) sent yachts scurrying for extras' work. One skipper, whom Bob had previously befriended, was missing, and so was his boat. Enquiries brought enigmatic answers such as, "You're not the only one looking for HIM!" Making off with the jointly owned yacht in his partner's temporary absence, he could not be traced. It was an old story...

I learnt not to prattle about sight-seeing, which put me out of kilter with my peers. "See one ruin and you've seen the lot!" was the nil admirari attitude to cultivate. But I loved threading flights of steps through flower-hung alleys slippery with fruit skin, getting lost and unlost, and lost again. Or watching an old lady at her window let down a plastic bag on a piece of string to dangle in front of the pharmacy door below to be filled with her daily dose of pills. Waterfront life was cheek-by-jowl. "Ooh look! There's a woman in here!" or "Come on! Lean on this one and 'ave Dad tek us picture!"

Knowing we must shortly make room for the full complement of a waterfront flotilla, we worked hard, with the proviso that it was illegal to spread yacht gear onto the quay. One eyesore on *Cappelle* bore witness to a loss of control by Toad who, unable to free a housing inside a cockpit cupboard, had smashed the locker apart with an axe. Bob sought the professional services of a fellow live-aboard, a joiner, who witnessed the assault, to repair the damage. From him we learnt *Cappelle's* history. Toad, a misogynist, had once shared her with a girl known as "The Murderess" for knifing a rapist to death at sea. Arrested, she had subsequently been pardoned in a celebrated court case. She was soon ejected from *Cappelle*. There may have been collusion in the hair-pulling scene that followed – Toad's reputation receiving a boost from the appreciative male audience outside the καφενείο, and the girl, perhaps, wishing to be on her way.

Anita and Richard, arriving from Lavrion in *Svicat,* invited us to share a weekend at an anchorage, when they would pass on the tips learned from eight years' live-aboard experience. Star advice was to acquire a pressure cooker. We learnt that the playing of the "Grenadier Guards" at six a.m. heralded an English translation of the shipping forecast, and that upholstery was best commissioned in Turkey. A shower bag suspended in the rigging was sufficient for personal hygiene, and sea soap was a waste of money. **KEEP LIFE SIMPLE!**" was *Svicat's* watchword. It was a slogan we never forgot.

One of the Bob's first moves was to teach me to enter the dinghy in a seamanlike manner. As I waited to be shown how and when to bring in my second leg, the inflatable shifted and I sat backwards in the sea. Since *Cappelle* lacked a ladder, I was forced to paddle around while Bob worked out how to get me back on board. "While you're in there," he called, never one to miss an opportunity and dropping me a sponge, "you might as well wash the waterline!"

To my surprise Anita had never learned to swim. "You've been in, haven't you?" she said. "We thought we saw you...!" Richard advised us to make taking our car out of Greece a priority. If the vehicle remained in the country more than six months, we would face a substantial fine, plus additional daily charges. "Regulations are forever changing, without warning, at the foreigner's expense! Make sure you keep an eye on them!" he counselled.

Sounion, Mycenae and Epidauros

After a circuitous journey by ferry and bus back to Lavrion to collect the car, we took time on the return journey to explore Sounion. Though Pausanias, second-century Greek geographer, described the promontory, he failed to visit it, for, traditionally the home of Poseidon when not inhabiting his palace of the deep, by Pausanias's time it had become the haunt of pirates. So profoundly did its temple complement the site, it gave the impression of having been there since time began. Dizzily below, shading from a grit-sand beach in bands of celadon to turquoise, cobalt and the ultramarine of deep water, the Aegean Sea eddied over rock shelves.

Eager to appreciate the impact of Homer echoing down from the Dark Ages before the weather got too hot, we were soon bumping away to Mycenae along a track to which potholes added piquancy. Sometimes the track turned back on itself, leading to Bob's despairing comment that "the sun is going down the wrong way!" Such was Mycenae's brutish presence, I half-expected to be ushered through The Lion Gate by a sullen dwarf. As an antidote, we rounded off our tour with a soothing visit to the sounding-bowl of pastoral Epidauros.

Methana and Troizen

It was imperative to find a haven for *Cappelle* while we returned the car to England. Vromolimini ("Dirty Harbour") in nearby Methana offered good shelter, if bad smells. (Its methane gas might even rot sea-cocks.) Here bearded Englishman, Algernon, tied *Cappelle* up next to his own *Fyne 'n Dandy*. One-time winner of a prestigious historical novel prize, his air of authority aroused meekness in the Cabin Boy. I suspected him of having been a school-master. We had hardly sorted our lines before he was rapping orders. Had we dismantled the Baby Blake yet? For two days we were denied a loo, for it stood in pieces in the shade of a spindle tree while all three of us (for Algernon practised what he preached) scrubbed its innards and rammed metal rods down its hose. Had we renewed the Sumlog cable? Bob soon found himself diving into the sulphurous depths – "so good for spots", according to Algernon, Bob muttered he almost wished he had some – armed with pliers to unfasten the log cable from the propeller, and refasten the spare frenziedly threaded by the Cabin Boy before *Cappelle* sank. Later came the matter of the engine's disintegrating inlet-filter. Algernon's instructions, as he made inroads into my Earl Grey tea, was to purchase mosquito netting for repair.

In recognition of his good offices we offered to dine Algernon at a restaurant of his choice. Clearing up from an imposed task made us about twenty minutes late, that is to say, under Greek timing, early. But Algernon shocked us with the reprimand of "keeping him waiting". It was a silent journey along a rutted track in the gloaming to drop down to the hamlet of Vathi ("Deep") at the foot of the volcano, a handful of homesteads grouped round a creek. Lopsided fairy lights shone in the water, ducks were a-waggling and villagers called out, «Καλό Καλοκαίρι!» ("Happy Summer!") One showed off by picking a cat up by its ears. Only after wine had relaxed us did the strained atmosphere thaw. Across the silvery water we made out the olive groves of Ancient Troizen in the green wash of moonlight. "You must go there!" declared Algernon, pointing. Wild bouquet garni scented the night air as we drove back to the sound of the little Scops owl bleeping every three seconds like a mini metronome as it had done since time immemorial.

Methana seafront was disfigured by a sunken yacht. "Insurance problems" was one story, with a hint that her owner had found her so loaded with old debt he could not afford to keep her. Boys, who shouted, «Κυματάκι!» ("Choppy sea!") at undulations and threw jellies when we swam, gave me grins when, richly bedizened and supporting a banner, they paraded on Saint's Day. On wedding days *feux de joie* cracked the skies.

I shopped while the unmade street muddied by housewifely buckets of water smelt of early morning. At one emporium, stocked with cheeses, spices, dried beans, olives, pistachio nuts, pickled fish, tinned sardines and plastic buckets, the proprietor stuck out his hand,

"You Manchester football?"

"For sure!" I gulped.

We pumped hands before he dolloped γαόυρτι σπιτικό (stiff, home-made yoghurt) onto paper with a none-too-clean paw. A certain purchase earned me Brownie points; a socket set whose box was removed from a shop window, blown on, tied with pink ribbon and handed over for a paltry sum, its corresponding rectangle of faded shelf paper left to gather dust forever. I stocked up with fly swats, for ravening flies were affecting the Captain's temper. At night we protected ourselves with Raid, skin-repellent, mosquito coils and grim determination.

Steel yacht *Maraud,* sliced in, trailing her anchor and ploughing up ours. That evening her skipper issued an invitation to drinks. Algernon was cynical over this, telling us there were too many hit-and-run accidents suppressed by the Tourist Board. *Maraud's* skipper said he awaited "friends", which everyone knew to be a euphemism for "charterers" – chartering by foreign nationals was illegal in Greece.

I was detailed to ferry the VHF radio to Athens for service. Algernon also dragooned us into pump repair, oil change and stern gland repack. I assuaged my conscience too with a visit to Troizen. Except for the ruins of the Temple of Aphrodite, there was little left of this city of illicit love where Peeping Phaedra lusted after her stepson as he wrestled naked. To the pleasure of a million butterflies the hills rang with the trill of spring water directed into irrigation channels. Looking down on the silted waters that once formed the harbour, I shuddered as I filled my skirt with lemon fallings. Was that a body down there in the open-cast rubbish dump? No! It was only a discarded rug rolled inside out, a tuft of black nylon hair protruding from one end.

Cappelle's inventory included a rust-holed outboard engine and two scuba diving cylinders. To forestall the theft of underwater artefacts, the use of scuba apparatus, except in strictly controlled areas, was forbidden in Greece. *Cappelle's* gear had been sealed by Customs, one cylinder wired to a berth, putting it out of use, the other, just as inconveniently, wired inside a locker. It was illegal to sell such apparatus, and an indictable offence to tamper with the Customs' seals. The logical solution was to ferry the impedimenta out of Greece. But first we needed its official cancellation from *Cappelle's* transit log. We enlisted Yanni, capitalist, card-carrying Communist, and caretaker of Algernon's yacht. (It was Algernon who supplied Yanni with the duty-free Benson & Hedges that enhanced his reputation in the καφενείο.) For a cash sweetener and the provision of a letter we must write in Greek, a Port Official was persuaded to cancel the offending gear from our transit log under official stamp. Yanni emphasised the importance that the date of the letter and the date of our departure tallied – a gap of more than twenty-four hours and we stood to be accused of illegal diving. On D-day we were still loading the car at midday with Yanni dancing about urging, "GO! GO NOW!"

Arriving back from London with a new pressure cooker and a roll of marine-blue carpet, we could hardly wait to sink into Methana's cooling deeps, described by Pausanias as the haunt of sea monsters. That night a thunderstorm broke over the reed-roofed patio of the restaurant. As the floor flooded, we rushed inside, where a hairy forearm planted a complementary carafe of wine between us. Sometime later we splashed home to find *Cappelle* leaking like a sieve, the heatwave having opened up her seams. Pots and pans filled with water as fast as we could empty them. (So much for "It never rains in August!") In the early hours, crouched under overhangs, sodden towels draped over us, we fell asleep, awaking to find *Cappelle* steaming like a Chinese laundry.

Back in Poros, questioned by an islander as to why we stayed on, I said, "Because it is a happy island!" to which she replied in surprise,

"Of course we are happy. We have WATER!"

It was never easy for live-aboards though. We must recruit Taki the Taverner in his seasonal guise as Purveyor of Drinking Water to lay his hose across the traffic-filled waterfront. I once gave way to a childish tantrum when wrenching dread-locks out of my brine-stiffened hair, but resolved not to be tempted by his "Hot shower for £1" posters. Later I washed my hair under the village pump in the town square, queuing up with those spartan parents who marshalled their youngsters for a sponge down. All of us took buckets to the pump for our daily water supply, not provided by Taki out of season.

The Southern Peloponnese

As soon as the high-season tee-shirts were on sale, "NO WOMEN – NO AIDS!" and "LEGLESS IN GREECE", we were anxious to be off. But the ammeter failed to function. A night sandwiched between the migraine surround-sound of a waterfront disco and the quadraphonic beat of drums from the yacht alongside settled the matter. One Denis, a marine electrician, said to have an out-of-town workshop in Porto Heli, might be able to help. Never far from purple-dark shores, our route to Porto Heli through the Saronic islands was plied by Flying Dolphins, Russian-built hovercraft with a dated look, which converted in a split second from a smudge on the horizon to terrifying blue and yellow hornets aimed amidships.

We planned to tie stern-to in Porto Heli's huge natural harbour, the smart way of doing things. But *Cappelle's* long keel inclined her to crab-walk, while the only instruction I could make out was "MORE CHAIN!" Paying out chain like there was no tomorrow, I brought the yacht up short. We were devising a set of hand signals when a Daz-white policeman appeared with instructions to Bob to take the ship's papers and crew-list to the Port Police to register the payment of harbour dues. A ticking off for failing to inscribe *Cappelle's* name on her stern followed. Concerning the ammeter, Denis the Electrician promised to call, but yachtsmen told us he never visited boats. Why did he not say so? It was not the Greek way.

In Porto Heli it was permissible for us to cut our new carpet on the quayside. I also purchased round-bellied amphoras in Greek blue and key-patterned shepherd's bags to decorate the cabin walls. Our make-over was worth it, for a passer-by, peering in, called to her friend,

"Come and look inside this one! Isn't it *beautiful?*" To hell with ammeter repair! Following a brief visit to the island of Spetsei, after chasing an elusive will-o'-the-wisp south, we made for the anchorage of Drepani ("Hook"). Drepani's sickle-scoop entrance, blended into the surrounding coastline, rendering its "conspic" lighthouse, a ruined stump, indistinguishable from its background. (I was discovering just how much an actual coastline differed from its outline on a chart.) Dropping anchor, Bob took sights on the surrounding hills to warn of drag. Bats squeaked, and on shore I relished the residual warmth of sun-baked earth under bare toes.

"Can I get there by anchor-light?"

Cappelle's hurricane lamp beckoned from the water like a candle in a woodman's window On such a Hecate night, if it went out, we could lose our way home.

Thinking to slip in for a swim, I found the sea infested with a fluther of Cyanea Lamarckii, pantomime jellyfish whose sting is painful. Propelling themselves by heaving uterine contractions, one family clustered in the shade of the dinghy. There was to be no bathe for me. I kept jelly-watch while the Captain abluted.

Genoa poled out, we sailed wing-on-wing to Nauplion past Bourtzi islet, one-time Retirement Home for Executioners. Methana's methane was the scent of Araby compared with the whiff of Nauplion's sewage outfall. Dawn, with the rock in shadow, was the optimum hour to climb the thousand steps to the Palamidi fortress. Here an embrasure afforded a bird's eye cameo of *Cappelle,* solitary plaything in a blue bath.

I was persuaded to lick honey from a spatula in a side street. "Much to America I post!" urged the Greek, beckoning me down a spice-smelling alley before pooling a potful and selling me a trireme dish to stand it on. Shunted from room to room in the Kafka-esque Port Police Station, where each official sat before an array of cardboard boxes stuffed with obsolete paperwork on a desk spread with dirty cups, we completed the necessary business of renewing our sailing permit. Despite prominently displayed notices reading «ΜΗΝ ΚΑΠΝΙΖΕΤΕ» ("NO SMOKING"), the ash-trays overflowed.

Since we were unable to unseize the windlass, in the small port of

Astros Bob hand-flaked a coil of chain on deck to enable me to drop anchor. Beyond a certain depth its weight proved too much. Realising I was about to be yanked overboard, I let the hook rattle to the sea-bed, again jerking *Cappelle* up short. So I sat down, feet braced against the cap rail, which meant I could not see Bob's hand signals while someone ashore called out the added complication of underwater rubble.

After settling Astros's harbour dues (90p for a three-day stay), we floated down the coast of Arcadia on a cornflower sea beside incorporeal mountains rising in shades of plum to the inhospitable Parnons. Flying fish skimmed the air while off Kyparissi dolphins played. Though our Admiralty Chart was dated 1902 nothing had changed. Singing his heart out, Bob perched on a cushion steering sideways with one hand. When I took the helm it was in a more formal fashion as I endeavoured to keep some landmark in sight within the width of two stanchions.

"Where's my cushion?" I demanded.

"What cushion?"

Unheeded by Bob, it had slipped overboard.

With the mountains darkening, we made for Plaka. An offshore breeze as hot as a hair-dryer scorched us as we struggled to hand the mainsail. Though we failed to pinpoint the requisite landmarks, a mill and a white church, on closer approach a thin grey line revealed itself as the harbour mole. When we asked an old man wielding a hose for water, consulting his watch, he locked the hydrant. It was water knocking-off time. At dawn, requested to move stern-to to make room for a Flying Dolphin, we warped *Cappelle* out. Concentrating on rope handling, I dropped anchor after thoughtlessly placing my foot within its circle of chain which proceeded to tighten so fast I was caught off balance. In sudden danger, as I saw it, of amputation, I shrieked my head off. "Now that WAS a silly thing to do!" said the Captain.

That evening an uncomfortable swell entered harbour, hit the inner wall and bounced back to meet its sister surge in the prelude to a night of pitch and wallow. Time to abandon the boat for the beach. Here, among the loveliest pebbles of malachite, alexandrine and rose-pink quartz, tiny fish played hide and seek. A few yards away the sea floor plummeted to depths as blue as the upside-down sky. Playing Sophie-in-the-Sky-with-Sapphires, I turned turtle to find above and below me the same fabulous colour. Pausanias brought history to life when I discovered that 2,000 years ago, on this very stretch of coast, he had gathered the prettiest pebbles he had ever seen.

It was another world next day, the sea grey and Paradise Beach desolate. The wind heading us, we squeezed for the night amongst fishing boats behind the tiny mole of Poulithra. Then we were away again into a sea of veined marble, a treeless, roadless, mountainous landscape to starboard. Goats foraging sea pinks clung like Velcro to the vertical face of a sea-cliff. Wind-blasted bushes, suddenly transformed into grey herons, peeled away. Bob called out,

"You see that headland over there?"

"Yes!" I said brightly.

"Well, point at it!"

Did he think my eyesight defective? I raised my arm and pointed.

"Not your ARM, you fool, the BOAT!"

Monemvasia

Natural features misled, causing us to close the coast prematurely. On the look-out for the Rock of Monemvasia ("Little Gibraltar") we aimed at first for any substantial islet. Confusing national flags on reaching our true destination, Bob called out in German to the skipper of a yacht occupying Monemvasia's short quay for permission to moor alongside. This condemned him in the eyes of a Belgian, who demanded an apology before letting *Cappelle* in, warning us not to get tar on his deck. Before I could yell "Tar balls!" Bob rushed for the beach, creeping back while I drew the Belgian's attention with sweet talk. He soon became Crashing Bore No 1, extolling the life he led with only himself to please until methought he did protest too much. English, he assured me, was the language of trade, which was why no English book was worth reading. "Of course," he bragged, "I don't need people like you. I can cook. I darn my own socks, and my birth sign's Virgo!" Each evening the yachts pitched and clattered in the katabatic wind that died as abruptly as it rose.

Monemvasia ("One-Way", one-way in and one-way out) was a διπλόκαστρο or "double fortress". In times of peace the populace occupied the lower village. In times of strife they moved up onto the Rock, which, with successive invasions, it became expedient to make their permanent home. A tale is told at grandmothers' knees of the Rock's origins. How the Magissa, the Wicked Witch of the North (whose other name is the North Wind), was jealous, for the Rock was too high for her to fly over. When she demanded obeisance the volcano within it erupted, enabling her to winnow the rock's remains into what we see today.

When we entered the city via a Z-shaped chicane, birds were singing (rare in Greece) and strains of *Scheherazade* filtered through a doorway. The settlement was a palimpsest of Byzantine and Venetian underlaid with Roman and overlaid with Greek. In the piazza I leant on ancient gun-slits to gaze beyond the cornelian roof-scape towards the Mirtoan Sea. To the south, the last spurs of the Parnon Mountains reached out to Cape Malea and the end of the world. The longings of a Far Beyonder exerted their grip. I knew that, however far I travelled, another anchorage, another haven, would beckon.

From the sunburnt heights streamed the aromatic scent of toasted thyme. Spanning a path through prickly pear and cactus, a keystoned archway rotted to the texture of an old peach stone bore the eroded outline of a Venetian escutcheon. Beyond it a fig tree pointed the way to the church of Agia Sophia teetering on the edge of a precipice. No need for graveyard or ossuary here, for bodies were consigned to the sea. To the north, the waters glittered a luminous blue and green. To the south, drenched a hypnotic white, they awaited the Enchantress's wand. We paused to swim in a reef-protected channel. On a rock a walnut-brown fisherman in a wide Maniot hat braced his muscles to land dorado, the arc of a silver fish following the curve of his arm.

Back on the quay, the Belgian had disappeared and Swiss yacht *Rêve d'Enfants* vibrated to the wails of Sebastian, a three-year old curly top, who gave new meaning to the phrase "making sail", for he plainly hated it. Returning north, first land in sight was the islet of Spetsopoula (Daughter of Spetsei) where the Niarchos family once tried to establish a hunting park, only for the stag to swim his harem back to the Mother Island.

On 26th September the clocks were put back. "In ten days all people will be gone," a Porto Heli shopkeeper assured me, banging his shutters in satisfaction. But a nucleus of residents remained. An English novelist's wife awaited the exhumation of her husband's bones to take back to England, while in a back street an old crone hobbled towards us. Rubbing Shylock hands she pointed out the letters "O.T.E." ("Telephone Exchange") in amateur script over her doorway. We then met a couple from whom she had demanded a fortune for a local call. Since Porto Heli lacked an official telephone exchange, the Tourist Police told them there was nothing they could do to prevent her.

Hydra

In early October my daughter arrived. The gale that blew in after her officially confined all boats to harbour, the Straits of Hydra no place to be in a strong north easterly. But a few days later Mel was riding *Cappelle's* bows like a figure-head. The blue waters of Hydra, proverbially peopled by admirals and shipbuilders, contrasted sharply with the ebony of its eleven-mile crest. There was an art in timing entry. Too early and the charter yachts had not left for the day. Too late and the harbour was full. Quickly imprisoned by a flotilla, we slotted in. The quayside smelt of fish and donkey, tarred rope and barbecued octopus. A kitten snatched a red mullet from between a donkey's hooves. A ship's dog hurtled after it. We met a team of working donkeys trotting unchaperoned. Chained loosely together, their panniers loaded with marble slabs and bags of cement, they trotted with a baby donkey alongside. Mules, changing resting fore-feet on paving slippery with urine-soaked straw, manure, crushed ice and fish heads, waited patiently, heads hung, beside jewellery stores that radiated gold. Lime-washed or painted laundry bag blue in the coruscating light, salt-white houses, their railings wrought in the shape of enlaced anchors, cast the cubist shadows that inspired the painter Nikos Ghika. At night the harbour took on the solidity of black glass, like an amphitheatre on which to dance for Greek favourite, Fred Astaire, the palazzi behind rising tier on tier like gala boxes. When, shortly after our visit to Hydra, his death was announced, Greek radio devoted three days to his dance music.

Winter in Poros

Swept out in the general exodus next day, we hoisted sail. Berthed alongside in Poros once more, we set up winter quarters. By the time we had discovered our berth was over the sewer outlet, all other slots were filled. Bob got down to boat maintenance. His yearning to respray the engine became a source of amusement to fellow live-aboards, who were not so into aesthetics. Did he think a respray would make it work better?

One afternoon a twenty-four-tonner rammed in, crewed by what to me, fending off with a boat hook, five-foot nothing of primitive womanhood defending her sovereign territory, were disorganised monkeys chattering in foreign tongues. Then a tall figure leaned over. Looking up into twinkling brown eyes, I was chastened. "You've never really sailed until you've sailed with a crew like ours!" whispered the man, telling me his name was David, and adding in mock admiration, "You're very fierce, aren't you!" which caused me to blush. "May we offer you a drink?" he ventured. Such civility acted like balm. *Cassiopeia* had been chartered by a group of Israeli psychiatrists (one of whom knew exactly how to treat female Cabin Boys). Her skipper doubled as an airline pilot. "Remember! NEVER FLY EL AL!" chuckled David, giving me a wink. On the morning of *Cassiopeia's* departure we awoke puzzled to see a pile of cartons stacked in our cockpit. It was our first experience of the cruising tradition of passing on perishables and stores. These were very welcome – even if the cooking instructions were in Hebrew!

If our slot was tough on the nose, it was not good on the waistline either. Across the street a ζαχαροπλαστείο (pastry shop) dispensed chocolate gateaux. Tea-time saw my custom. On 16th October the confectioner had news,

"Better you stay Poros! Is hurricane in England!"

"Oh no! We don't have those!"

But he was right.

The Royal Hellenic Yacht Club Race from Athens to Hydra marked the end of season. After battling against strong winds, several competitors withdrew with sea-sick crews. *Jasona*, a battered twenty-seven-foot marine-ply Armagnac, tied up next to us. Bob was complaining of interference with the cheese we put out overnight, when a mop of brown curls inserted itself through the cabin doors. It was our new neighbour calling to tell us he had to go to Athens for winch repair. If we saw a cat on *Jasona*, we were not to chase her off, for she was his. When George Ghritis returned, we learnt he had just sailed round the world, the first Greek national to do so. (His mother was French). A thirty-six-hour storm in the Sea of Ierapetra had been the catalyst for his voyage – if *Jasona* could survive that, she could survive anything! Autaki, "Little Big Ears", the cheese culprit, presently featured on the cover of his book *Round the World with Jasona*. Given to George to train as a mouser, her master could not find praise enough for Autaki's intelligence. Taking her out in the dinghy, he had taught her to swim, a skill she put to use. Not only did she trace *Jasona* when forced to move berth in her absence in Manila, but, after delaying the yacht's departure by going missing for ten days, turned up half-starved and pregnant on the very day, because of changing weather patterns, the yacht's departure could no longer be put off.

During the "Little Summer of Saint Demetrios"(Indian Summer), Bob put his back out. George recommended the magic fingers of the Wise Old Woman Who Lives in the Woods. With a vague description of a cottage at the end of a track and assurances that "everyone will know Agglaïa", I set out. But other grannies told me she was away to Athens visiting her daughter. Returning to Poros along the coast road, I was irresistibly drawn to the electric-blue flash of a kingfisher. Turning, I followed a path to a cove where, mesmerised by arrow trails of fish bubbles, I perched on a rock. The path, continuing towards Poros, ended beneath an abandoned hotel whose entrance I recalled on the road above. Convinced I should be able to get out, I climbed an inner staircase. Five floors up, a bridge led across a chasm to a padlocked portico. Hurrying down again, my skin prickled at eerie drippings on dank concrete and the echo of my own footsteps. On every landing spooky corridors opened off. Feeling vaguely pursued like a Mary Stewart heroine to whom "nothing ever happens", until it does, I quelled panic but, once outside, took to my heels through black plugholes of shadow. On the main road again I passed the crumbling mansion that had been holiday home to poet George Seferis, and the lodging where a destitute art student, Lucien Freud, set the seal on his future style by working under a bare light bulb to earn his passage home.

I found Bob in the only position he found comfortable, lying on his back on the cabin floor. A Greek-Canadian, Bill Daly of *Daly Express,* came to our rescue, telling us he had a favour to call on after rescuing a yacht belonging to an Athenian orthopaedic surgeon. Later that day we made the painful journey to Athens where, waiving his fee, Dr Andreas Belthekos diagnosed a trapped sciatic nerve. The cure was rest and heat massage. Dr Belthekos also fixed me a dental appointment. The dentist spoke no English but chattered away with, «Γιά να δούμε! Γιά να δούμε!» ("Let's see! Let's see!") Peering into my mouth, he handed me a mirror and together we diagnosed a lost filling. «Να καυτηριάζουμε,» he went on cheerfully. Too late I recognised the root of the word "to burn". My tooth was to be cauterised! My nostrils filled with the smell of singed ivory and the surprisingly painless operation was soon over.

Recognising the kingfisher strand as the one George Millar wrote of in *Isabel and the Sea*, I introduced a holiday-maker to Isabel's Cove. On my fastidious acquaintance confessing to paying more for three showers a day than for the room to which she had escaped after abandoning a well-appointed Nicholson in disgust, I deemed it wise to keep quiet about my newly acquired ability not to overwash. Through mismanagement of the contents of our fifty-gallon water tank, we had become skilled at cleaning teeth, boiling eggs and making coffee in barely enough water to fill a bird-bath. Even swimming palled, for haunting us at Isabel's Cove was a flasher. (Perhaps I had not been so stupid to distrust the empty hotel?) But on Bob's recovery, he and I, stitching footprints in the sand, paid a last visit to Isabel's Cove on a day when the woods were pink-carpeted with a multiplicity of Nikos Gatsos's "two little cyclamen kissing in the dust".

Οχι ("No!") Day commemorates 28th October 1940, the date on which the Greek leader Ioannis Metaxas, gave this monosyllabic, negative response to the Italian government's ultimatum to cede Greece to the Axis powers. A choir fronting the War Memorial sang patriotic songs and a papa in a stove-pipe hat, handing his baby back to his teenage wife, intoned as he whirled a censer fragrant with olibanum. Greek flags fluttered and dignitaries laid beribonned wreaths before haranguing us, fists raised. Grouped nearby were their Athenian consorts in black tailleurs and dominatrix heels. On each side of the daïs ranged a gold-epauletted naval presence. A platoon of white-gloved cadets fired a slightly ragged salute and immaculately groomed school children paraded. Manoeuvred to the front by a grandfatherly figure, my shoulders were pinned. "English good! Good!" he whispered in my ear.

Over dinner with Bill Daly at a waterfront restaurant, we were sampling μεζέδες (hors d'oeuvre) when a malodorous tramp wandered in, foisting on me nuts screwed in a paper napkin in expectation of recompense. Although Samuel Beckett smelt as high as a Billy Goat, I bit a nut out of politeness. Only when the taste of mildew made me spit it out did Bill inform me with a laugh that the old rogue recycled his goodies from garbage bins.

Our winter company was established. As the twice-daily *Flying Dolphin* rocketed through Poros Straits, we live-aboards held onto our crockery.

Three

Maiden Aegean crossing

Life in the Poros community

Knuckling down to the life of troglodytes, we tied boat covers over the coach-roofs. In the darkened cabin our new Tilley lamp, radiating warmth and buttery light, cast theatrical shadows, its gentle purr demonstrating the nautical origin of the word "snug". Live-aboards agitated over gas explosions. Trying out our new pressure cooker led to neighbours banging on the hull fearing its hiss presaged a leak.

"Let us help you!"

When we manhandled gear along the quay, Danish boys from *Talassa* ran to help. *Talassa* was one of a fleet of wooden sailing ships provided by Danish Social Services on the theory that a sea-going environment has positive effects on delinquents. During the time we shared her company her crew's behaviour was impeccable. When Mögens, *Talassa's* captain, and Pier, his bo'sun-cum-social-worker, made a weekend trip to Athens to obtain their favourite tobacco, Bob agreed to be left in charge of *Talassa* to report on any sign of "weakness" in her crew. With routine tasks such as fetching water and airing bedding like the rest of us, the boys enjoyed as relaxed a lifestyle. All was shipshape and Bristol fashion when they lined up spit-smart to greet their Captain.

The scheme was not without its detractors, however. An American who had sold all he possessed to buy a boat was heard to snort that the "seas are teeming with young troublemakers enjoying a luxury lifestyle". Recidivism was high. And, after experiencing life at sea in the company of young fire-raisers and felons, as sometimes happened, Mögens did not intend to renew his contract.

To be baptised in the Greek Orthodox tradition, Greeks take the name of a saint as their given name. While the Greeks celebrated their ονομαςτική εορτή (name day), we live-aboards made our birthdays the excuse for a party. In February *Talassa* dressed overall for Mögens's anniversary. After the Ship's Cook, a street-wise lad, had excelled himself producing smörbröd and trifle, we transferred to a taverna whose keeper, a master of self-expression, had a passion for ladies' hats. Everyday he pedalled the waterfront to show off his latest creation. For Mögens's feast, orchestrating orders with a basting spoon, he attended at table wearing a white apron with the strings tied at the front to embellish his embonpoint. The crew's present to their Captain, a cigar-shaped mystery object, was smuggled in and laid down the centre of the table. Complete with saucy garter, a black-stockinged leg was unveiled with due ceremony. The hosier had showed a certain reluctance to lease out so irreplaceable a window dummy, but cash up front did the trick. We photographed Monica of *Faith* hitching up her skirt behind Mögens as he sat at table, provocative plaster foot on his shoulder, its toe tickling his ear. A splendid cake was borne in. When we banged on the table for coffee Spiro threw up his hands. This was not a καφενείο, and anyway he hadn't enough cups! Nevertheless he cycled home to mother, ringing his bicycle bell on the way back to accompany the rattle of cups.

While volunteering to remove *Cappelle's* sink to unblock an airlock (since Bob, as Mögens put it tactfully, was "office man"), Mögens explained that *Talassa's* dodgy engine obliged them to leave early for Athens. He proposed to hand over to Bob the keys to their landbase, two rooms affording the luxury of a small bath and water-heater.

Since it was against Greek law for the towing of vessels to be undertaken by other than Greek nationals, a moonless night was chosen for motor yacht *Rivka* to tow *Talassa* (now with the awkward addition of a fifteen-year-old girl "beyond parental control" to her ship's complement). Pip, *Rivka's* Alsatian, adored the Danish boys, who spoilt him rotten. If not ambushing a party of Japanese tourists (left reeling in the geraniums), Pip stretched out along *Talassa's* gunwales, nose on paws, ears flicking, eyes rolling, willing the attention of his boys. In pouring rain he accompanied *Talassa* to Athens on escort duty, but once back in Poros without his mates, he succumbed to acute canine depression. Even flipping over tortoises with his nose failed to alleviate the symptoms. Only a rendez-vous d'amour with Bella, a bewitching boxer, effected a cure. All in due season, eleven drowned puppies were fished from the sea.

Minor events put us on our mettle. A television company arrived to film "real life water-gypsies" for a holiday promotion. (Mögens looked particularly good on camera since, on account of a recent eye injury, he had taken to wearing a black eye-patch.) Bill, in hospital after breaking two ribs clambering over *Daly Express's* rail in his socks, returned from Athens bearing the latest version of paraffin heater, which immediately burst into flames. Poor Bill! He also repainted his cabin table. Set out on the quay to dry overnight, it vanished. We boat-wives made marmalade out of the bitter orange fallings from a garden square, but, if I expected Poriots to weed the squares and sweep the streets, I waited in vain. Their only notable winter activity was the demolition of shops to enlarge display space. We watched as a rail of dresses was shoved casually aside so that the ceiling above could be attacked with crow-bars in a cloud of plaster dust.

Of a morning I jogged the village ring road, which earned me a fan-club, but no companions. Goatherds directed their charges by hurling stones, dogs chained to hen-houses barked and καρακάζες (magpies), as the Greeks call them onomatopoeically, hopped up and down. My route took me past clifftop shrines dedicated to some ton-up chancer gone overboard. Each displayed a blank-eyed photo of the deceased along with a Coke bottle of cooking-oil to keep his vigil light burning. Once, as I jogged through the village, I spotted a coffin nestling amongst the cabbages on the vegetable lorry off the Galatas ferry. The butcher delivered a speech, "Old Greek people," he said ponderously, "before time of Χριστός...say...'If body healthy, then healthy head!' Now too much motor bike, too much TV. No walk! No run! Health no good!" Only once did I ask him to dismember me a chicken. Raising a cleaver over his head, he smashed it in splintered quarters. (His regular customers, I then saw, borrowed his knife to slice their own meat.)

When stair-rods of rain fell, I stayed a-bed. One morning villagers with coats over their heads scurried to shift waterfront cars and motor-cycles to higher ground. For fourteen hours the downpour persisted until the sunken road became a dirt-grey river that welled into shops and houses. As *Cappelle* rose with the water level, I had visions of our yachts floating into town like a flotilla of Noah's Arks. Another excitement was to spot a sizeable octopus beside *Cappelle's* hull. Alerted by us, a fisherman hurried over, knotting a fish and a pebble on a length of twine. There was a tug as a tentacle grabbed the prize and the octopus came up captive. Neighbours chided me for giving it away, but we were awarded with a magnificent conger eel from the fisherman's next trip. After suspending it in the prescribed fashion, we found its skin too tough to strip, opting instead to cook the creature as it was, herb-drenched and curled round in wine and brandy.

Sadly there was a British live-aboard faction determined to make us grit our teeth with their constant reminder we were not of their world. Our status was parvenu. Worse, we talked posh. We were expected to find the affected way they pranced up to us hilarious, but it grew tedious, especially with taking the Mickey so strictly one way. Bob's jocular address to South London Arthur as "Arfur" brought forth a flash of animosity. Every day the sea wives draped their booms with washing, whereas I did mine as and when I pleased, scrubbing and scouring in a bucket as they did – but not as if it were my raison d'être. All the boat-wives declared the Greek language "stewpid", especially its "stewpid" writing. It was said that holiday girls marrying Poriots, while picking up phrases orally, strove neither to read nor write. Gossip had it that once honeymoons were over and marriages under mother-in-law's thumb began, each and every foreign bride felt the flat of her husband's hand, be it only in token reminder of just who was boss.

Customs, new to us, preceded Lent. On Smelly Thursday, the first day of the Carnival period, the air was thick with the odour of smoking grills. Cheese and Meat Sundays were celebrated with the appropriate fare. Children decked out in carnival dress paraded. Poor families could be driven into debt to provide the new clothes essential for this sartorial explosion of finery. Clowns and astronauts, eighteenth-century courtiers, shepherdesses and pantalooned ladies with poke bonnets dawdled self-consciously to school. A powder-blue fairy pirouetted in her tutu, one hand holding that of her proud Mama and the other a silver wand. The newsagent's five-year-old appeared as a geisha in a butterfly dress with chop-sticks in her hair. When little live-aboard Rosie begged to dress up, her mother made her a feathered headband and trimmed a cowgirl jacket. But the local children looked down their noses at such a DIY mode. New clothes, not just Easter Bonnets, were essential again at Easter, especially new shoes. To a person wearing something new it was customary to say,

« Με γεία!» ("May you wear it in good health!")

Clean Monday, the public holiday that marks the end of Carnival and the beginning of Lent, inaugurated the rural life. Extended families set off for the Great Outdoors to unload casks of wine, light charcoal fires, fly kites and spread picnic cloths for a seasonal γλέντι (a merrymaking).

During March live-aboards became caught up in serious preparations for departure. British-registered *Daly Express* left in a hurry after a warning from the Port Police that she would incur boat tax if she remained in Greek waters beyond the statutory period. We were surprised to find *Cappelle* exempt from harbour dues. It seemed Poros was still considered her home port. But we planned to depart anyway before 26th March, the date on which our own boat tax would again fall due. Few yachts might leave without inconvenience for the Post Office, guarded by a blackleg, was on strike and we all awaited mail. We were now on good terms with the OTE following a major row in which Bob, with the aid of a Greek dictionary, had torn a strip off the manager for cheating. With counter staff rounding up or doubling charges, we learned to add up our own, slapping the money on the counter Greek-style.

Yachtsman Geoffrey dined us out, notwithstanding the hem of the yacht skirt he lent us rendered ragged by the frenzied bitings of little fish. At a corner table a pretty woman and two students cradled musical instruments. Heads together, they poured over scores. In throaty semitones the woman tried out phrases. Sipping wine, they conferred, composed, crossed out, rewrote and rehearsed. Repeatedly pushing his glasses up his nose, one consulted a file as he scribbled. Then the threesome broke into unselfconscious ρεμπέτικα, songs of the underworld born of the hashish-smoking dens, tunes which trip along blithely to words harsh with bitterness, subjugation, poverty, injustice, exile and the coming of Charon the Ferryman. As if alone in an urban cellar, they sang passionately of unrequited love. Finally the trio relaxed into plangent dance rhythms.

A brawny blacksmith entered, swigging from a carafe. In the most natural way, for his κέφι (his spirit) had risen, Zorba, pushing aside his plate, got up to perform the hypnotic steps of the Ζειμπέκικο. Arms outstretched, head bowed, eyes to the ground, cigarette dangling, he executed the dance of guerrilla Zembekis with rapt absorption, balancing his melancholy and his joy in a release of tension and an expression of individualism. In their separate worlds, the musicians cast not a glance at him nor he at them. It was a breach of etiquette to applaud such dancing, for a dancer dances only for himself. After Geoffrey had settled the bill, the inn-keeper's wife returned to our table wearing a big smile and carrying a tray on which were set three brimming complimentary glasses of Metaxa. It was an open invitation to stay, and three in the morning, the musicians packing their instruments away, when we made our way back to the boats.

The crossing begins

Our first Aegean crossing began on 16th March. Motor bikes and ghetto blasters already disturbed the peace and charter flights were inaugurated. (If Henry Miller should return to "hover as a gentle spirit above the roofs of Poros" he might be shocked at the changes in paradise.) On attempting to raise the mainsail, Bob found the thread of the locking nut on the main halyard winch stripped. To proceed invited trouble, so we returned to the waterfront where our reception was noticeably offhand. It was plain we had chickened out:

"Are you going or aren't you?"

A garage hand in Galatas was prevailed upon to weld on a new locking nut and early next day we slipped east again without a word to anyone. By then the weather had deteriorated and both of us were suffering queasy stomachs.

We planned a passage of forty-nine miles to Loutra on the Cycladic island of Kithnos. After warnings of down-draughts from high-sided St George's Island, we forbore to sail close in. But suddenly a ferocious gust laid *Cappelle* over. Down in the galley I could not think what had happened. By the time I crawled out of the cabin, the yacht had righted herself. But the genoa was split along the leech. With the wind freshening between Kea and Kithnos, we continued on course 090 due east, overshooting Cape Kephalos to give it a good offing before turning south. Though no fetch had built up, we were blasted by gale-force squalls. We had already furled in most of the genoa, but in these conditions it was a mighty task to yank a second reef in the main. Detailed to keep the yacht hove to, I clutched both arms round the wheel, eyes tight shut and head buried, expecting my last moment had come. "GET YOUR HEAD UP!" yelled Bob. Every few minutes I forced myself to glance about, gasping with relief to see him, not swept overboard, but lying on his back on the coach roof struggling with reefing points amid the raging elements.

At last Bob was able to fire the engine to steady the ship. But sailing to windward was impossible. Suddenly the steel furling wire (fitted in Lavrion by the "best rigger in Greece") ripped out of the furling drum and the genoa exploded into the air. To say I was terrified was putting it mildly! We were at the heart of a maelstrom where the roar of the wind joined the whip cracks of the escaped sail shredding itself to pieces. Repeatedly we endeavoured to round Cape Kephalos. Three times I raised my ostrich head only to see to starboard the boiling sea and then, swinging into view as we tacked, the lighthouse on the end of the cape round which we were hell-bent on forcing passage. Sometimes the lighthouse advanced, sometimes it receded. But always it remained unattainable. Catching sight of a storm-tossed seagull, only to identify a scrap of our own sail, I almost despaired. But inch by inch we made headway. Then the wind zapped us once more as we emerged from between the islands. It took us three more exhausting hours to cover the last two nautical miles. Poseidon was on our side, but he had set about our sea trials with a vengeance. Dusk falling, we fought our way into Loutra Bay on Kithnos. It was time to lace tea with Metaxa.

Kithnos

At dawn, sensing we had fallen back a foot or two from fishing nets, we re-anchored. Strands of the ill-fated genoa were twisted round the forestay and knotted about the shrouds like votive rags. It took all morning to refasten the furling wire in its drum, squeezing it through strand by strand. Then we hoisted the spare foresail. Below decks chaos reigned. Lockers had spewed their innards. Charts, books and cushions lay scattered. We restowed, roping the contents of the forepeak.

By evening the wind was abating. "No gale. Wind northerly F5/6. No significant change in the next twenty-four hours," said the shipping forecast. As we nosed *Cappelle* out of her sanctuary under troubled skies, I nervously anticipated the open sea. I should have kept my eyes averted, for my first sight around the southern headland was a broken-backed freighter impaled on the rocks. On we went, making for Paros forty-two miles ahead, sea moderate, sky lowering, and those grey islands, hump-backed stepping stones between Europe and Asia, Siros to the north east and little Serifopoula, with Serifos behind, to the south west, barren, seal-like carbuncles. Studying the depressing scene, I could not help wondering what was supposed to be so attractive about the Greek archipelago.

Crossing the centre of the ancient world, *Cappelle* sailed a reach with a northerly F6 increasing just abaft the beam. Although conditions were near perfect, cowardice kept me hovering near the companionway. We made excellent time. As we drew nearer Paros, the seas grew perceptibly more boisterous – though to comfort the faint-hearted the Captain denied this. At day's end, the Portes Rocks, guardians of Paroikia and as conspicuous as bookends, lay to starboard. (In September 2000 eighty passengers were lost when the ferry *Samina* struck the Portes.) Skirting a contorted arm of rock after rounding Cape Korax, we were embraced by the Bay of Naoussa. Turning my head as I steered into wind to hand sail, I was aghast to see behind us the wilderness of spindrift from which we had escaped.

Hanging onto the mooring line in the outer harbour while climbing over the ship's rail, I leapt for the quay forgetting to twist in mid-air to fend off and allowing *Cappelle* to scrape her bows. The Captain expostulated, as only Captains can. We tied up alongside, put out spring lines, and pumped the bilges. Within the hour a full gale was blowing with waves crashing above the mole. The Aegean Sea remained unchanged since the seventeenth century when George Sandys described it as, "A Sea dangerous and troublesome to sayle through, in so much that a man is proverbially said to sayle in the Aegean Sea, that is encumbered with difficulties".

Paros

We suffered a rough night. In the morning we discovered a snapped warp, a sheared cleat-mounting, and our repaired stanchion re-broken. A fisherman, urging us to put out stern lines, shouted, «*Εννέα! Εννέα μποφόρ!*». "Nine! Severe Gale Force Nine!" Until the gale dropped we could not desert ship to explore, so I curled up on the quay in a nest of fishing nets with a copy of *The Odyssey* by Homer for company. At least Odysseus, though bedevilled by Poseidon, won through in the end. The sun shone, but despite my heavy-weather gear and down-filled squall cap, the wind chill was bitter. Overnight the gale died, just as the fisherman said it would, though the seas slashed with a prismatic gamut of Picasso blues remained very rough to high. Again the sun shone brilliantly, the waves capped as white as Parian marble with what the Greeks call, not sea-horses, but *αρνάκια*, "little lambs".

Naoussa was a revelation in its charm. Corkscrew alleyways, crazy-paved, their seams white lined, twisted through barrel tunnels between cubist houses. No one sat out under the Tree of Idleness, only a cat on a daisy-bright wall paused in its toilet, paw upraised. I hit it off with the owner of the grocery store after asking him to recommend a local wine. "Perhaps you have a house on Paros?" he asked, puzzled about what I was doing on the island at this time of year. When I enquired for a chicken, he sucked his teeth as if the request posed a problem, then, taking me outside, pointed down an alley. I was to visit *Ο Κύριος Πέτρος* the greengrocer, who obliged by setting off at a trot on a circuitous route before diving, me at heel, down basement steps into a cold store where two grizzled ruffians sat swigging *ούζο* out of plastic cups. Passing on my request, Mr Petros left me to it. *Ούζο* was pressed upon me, a wall freezer was opened, and a rock-hard iceberg of boiling fowl was handed over.

By midday, *Cappelle* resting safely, we set out across the island for Paroikia along a road verged with anemones, vetch and everlasting pea flowers. In the Old Quarter a leather boot sprouting a geranium marked a cottage doorway. Above, a fortress entirely constructed from the cotton-reel-sliced columns of a Temple of Delian Apollo crowned the heights.

Left out in the sun, the chicken had defrosted. After supper it was time to turn in, but first Bob sought a weather map. Although we tracked down the only bar open, its television screen was blank, the gale having brought down the antennae. Someone took us on a TV-seeking tour, but none in Naoussa was working. Then the barman volunteered to telephone the Port Police for the latest shipping forecast – in twenty-four hours the wind would increase again to gale force. The Captain made a snap decision. We would set sail immediately. Sleep forgotten, we leapt on board, switched on the navigation lights and cast off into a pitchy night patterned with stars. A fisherman in an unlit rowing boat somewhere beneath our bows called out, «Καλή νύχτα, Καλό ταξίδι!» ("Good night! Good journey!")

Once out of harbour, shining a torch on the binnacle, we steered a precise compass course with intense concentration, calling out the slightest deviation until, at the centre of the exit, we motored ahead, never relaxing until well beyond the boundaries of Paros. Our intention had been to take turns on watch, but in the event we both remained in the cockpit. Ships lit up like Christmas trees crossed our path. A fishing boat circled. A naval patrol boat gave us the once-over. Only after scrupulous identification of the light on Cape Stavros on Naxos (Group Flash (2) 16 seconds) and in the open sea, did we feel confident enough to alter course east, three hours forty-seven minutes after leaving harbour. It was a long night's journey into day before the rim of the original ballon rouge appeared above a band of mist. Rising quickly and rolling towards us, the sun emerged bouncing lightly on the waves like a big red beach ball. I knew then what it was to take the wings of the morning having dwelt in the innermost parts of the sea.

The day was windless and we motored under an egg-shell sky across waters so empty they gave serious meaning to Lewis Carroll's blank Map of the Sea. Neither boat nor bird relieved the monotony, only the sight of the dorsal fin of a shark near the forbidding outcrop of Dhenoussa made me glad to have revised our earlier plan to anchor off this outrigger island. This was the passage that had worried the ancients, the fifty lonely miles between the Cyclades and the Dodecanese. Passing Levitha, I went below to make coffee, leaving Bob head-down in the stern locker staunching a leak round the rudder post. Back on deck I was startled to see the cliffs of this isolated mid-Aegean islet "going the wrong way", and took it, if not for one of Nature's jokes, for some sort of perceptual illusion. But the condition of the sea was strangely altered and *Cappelle's* bows were ploughing.

"Bob! There's something wrong with the sea!"

Straightening up, he grabbed the helm. With neither of us paying attention, the autopilot had ceased to function and the yacht was heading back whence she came. Ingloriously, as he bent to the stern locker, he had nudged it with his behind, impeding its adjustment, which in turn broke the cone. Now, as well as switching on the bilge pump every half hour, we must steer at all times. Throughout the afternoon the void was endless. Then, exactly in accordance with the Captain's calculations, a shadowy scarab, taking a further two hours to reach, solidified on the horizon. This was Kalimnos, our first Dodecanese island. Making out a spit of land and an offshore islet, we joined a troupe of fishing boats heading for the navigable gap in the curve of a cave-ridden coast where birds settled noisily for the night.

Kalimnos

An island of tremendous grandeur, Kalimnos, at one time filled with the shuffle of victims of the bends, had formed the heart of the sponge-diving industry. On the commercial quay, a fisherman approached, I assumed to move us on. Instead he asked,

"You English? English GOOD people! Very nice! «*Καλώς ήρθατε!*» ("Welcome!")

«*Καλώς σας βρήκα!*» ("We have found you well!") we answered in the idiom.

With a further ninety-seven nautical miles on the clock, I was asleep on my feet by the time we finished the bottle of dry red Kavantis.

Kos

When we left for Kos next morning the weather was turning sour. The wind fluctuated across waters that concealed a wartime minefield that had put paid to two British destroyers, the *Hurworth* and the *Adrias*. Abeam Pserimos I spotted the regular dots of floats. For some distance we took fishing-net avoidance action. Then the coastline of Carian Turkey swung into view, sugar-cube housing estates on the slopes of mountains. At tea-time we slipped in alongside in Kos main harbour, where an Englishman skippering a Norwegian charter yacht took our lines, only to inform us in superior tones we had better re-moor stern-to and be quick about it. Instead of ignoring him, as he deserved, we engaged in the palaver of getting in backwards. As I sat in the bows, wellies braced, awaiting orders to drop anchor, he patronisingly suggested we "ought to practise in a bay". I could have throttled him! On asking where we had come from, he was barely able to conceal his shock.

After rejecting a tired loaf from a pavement cabinet, I made enquiries for bread of an old lady carrying a cloth-covered tray,

«*Με συγχωρείτε, Κυρία, υπάρχει φούρνος εδώ κοντά?*» ("Excuse me, Madam, is there a bakery near here?")

«*Ναι! Ελα μαζί μου!*» ("Yes! Come! Come with me!")

She escorted me through the lanes. Was this my first visit to Kos?

It is a beautiful island! "Be happy!" On a street corner she paused to gesture me to a doorway indicating that inside I might select a loaf direct from the ovens.

About to leave Greek waters two days ahead of our tax deadline, we completed the exit formalities and handed in our Greek transit log. A port policeman called us back to show us the latest shipping forecast for the seventeen mile straits between Kos and Turkey – F 5/6 (the yachtsman's gale) γρήγορα (quickly) meaning imminent. Facing a lively sea, I turned *Cappelle* into wind, inexpertly brought her through it and could not hold her head up. Panic! We were being pushed towards the rocks near the Old Fort. Bob dashed across to sort things out. With the sun gleaming through leaping waves, a favourable F6 became F7. But, full of those little buzzes of excitement that herald a new land, I was too busy to notice as we whizzed along at a forty-five degree angle, one reef in the main and half a genoa, while Bob hauled down the Greek flag to hoist the yellow quarantine duster.

Ahead lay the Levant – what we trusted was the sprawl of Ancient Halicarnassus. On spotting the squat towers of its landmark castle, I let out a shout of triumph. (No one had warned me how hard it is to see through wavering binoculars.) Whistling down wind, we made for the islet of Kara Ada before angling for Bodrum's concealed harbour entrance. Since a new breakwater was under construction, the convention described in the Pilot of lining up on the mosque no longer held good. Dropping the mainsail, we steered instead for a red crane. Beyond it, a banner bade us: "WELCOME TO TURKEY."

Allocated a berth and handed a lazy line from the central mooring chain, we were informed that we must purchase a Turkish courtesy flag immediately. (We had been warned not to buy one in Greece where they were not made in accordance with the exacting Turkish standards.) And that a stay of one month would entitle us to a reduction of thirty per cent on a marina contract.

Our path to the Health Department (whose request was for a De-Ratting Certificate) lay through the Farmers' Market, a munificent Garden of Eden heaped with those fruits described by a traveller of 1760 as "not easily eaten with moderation". The stalls were a stupendous sight. While oranges and lemons were cascaded into one shopping bag and boot-black shiny aubergines, celeriac and fat leeks were poured into the other, hands were placed on our shoulders. There, inviting us aboard *Daly Express,* was none other than Bill Daly extolling the value and virtues of everything Turkish from paraffin to haircuts. We already felt at home in Turkey.

That night I glowed. It might only be 215 nautical miles (a nautical mile is slightly longer than a statute mile) but, like all true journeys, for me it had been peppered with a little hardship and salted with a mite of fright. Moreover it had not been undertaken in that insulated travel pod, the aeroplane. The muezzin sounded and all the reward needed was the romantic sight of the Castle of the Knights rising in floodlight against a black Levantine sky.

Four

Welcome to Bodrum

Morning brought an invitation to coffee on Thames gaffer, *Angèle Aline*, a registered Dunkirk Little Ship. We were welcomed with the news that we increased the number of Bodrum's British residents to twelve. From Meriel I was to learn how to bake the fat yellow quinces, the perfumed Golden Apples that Paris gave to Aphrodite.

Next to present themselves were Johnny and Judith, retired British naval attaché and his wife, who were living aboard their yacht, *Amazon*, while setting up home nearby. Johnny was a man of few words,

"Bloody Marys!" he said.

"What?" I asked.

"Turkish vodka – lemons everywhere – place made of tomatoes!"

Judith, exasperated by the facile attitude of the average tourist, quick to criticise while deficient in understanding, had been resident in Turkey long enough to appreciate the native point of view. She cited the case of a certain scrofulous little donkey tourists were forever throwing their hands up about. "They should see the old man that donkey lives with!" she declared. "Those two sleep and eat together in a tumbledown hovel. They are each other's lifeline. In his own way that old man loves his donkey! What do they expect him to do? Keep it in better condition than he can keep himself?" I mentioned a mongrel with a congenitally deformed leg and a broad grin on its face seen lolloping down by the market, saying that back home it would be put down. "Ah!" broke in Johnny, "But have you ever seen a happier dog?"

In the Marina Office Bob bumped into an old friend from his RAF days in Cyprus, another Bill, tall, rangy and a big tease. He and his wife Joyce, had recently embarked on the live-aboard life in their Moody

40, *Energetic,* with the eventual aim of circumnavigation. Though we got on famously, it was from Bill Kerslake that, puffed with nautical success, the Cabin Boy got her biggest put down,

"What's your hull speed?" I asked, full of myself.

"Same as the deck, me dear!" Bill twinkled.

A sudden power cut spared my blushes.

Everyone shared the favours of Felix the Marina Cat. Unimpressed when his owners sold their boat, three times he found his way back to the marina to partner his side-kick, Eric the Gangly Legged, whom Judith said looked like a pony. Supplied with a series of blue velvet collars to show off his Russian beauty, Felix was eventually granted his freedom. *Cappelle* underwent routine inspection. Felix's visits were a compliment to the ship. Unmade beds were his speciality.

We discussed our sail wardrobe with Omar Sharif-look-alike, Yener, over Turkish tea in the converted hamam he made his office. As well as tailoring a new genoa and custom-building a sun canopy, he suggested remaking our old sail from the tatters remaining on its leech. Later I accompanied him to the market to choose towelling for cockpit seat covers. But, faced with overblown pink roses or repeat-pattern Donald Ducks, I voted instead to visit the Museum of Underwater Archaeology. If the 3,000-year-old sea-dredged objets d'art were a joy to behold, the ancient sleeping-stones made me thankful for our more manageable Fisherman's anchor.

Pamukkale

Tasty snacks and a carnival atmosphere were engaging attractions at the bus station. Shoe-shine boyacı hauling ornate brass boxes touted for trade. Young boys bounded onto coaches selling nuts and sweetmeats. When we caught a bus to Pamukkale (Cotton Castle) what we had not bargained for was the hospitality extended to misafir, guests of the country like us. Mehmet, a young soldier, another bus passenger, adopted us, insisting on buying us pide, flat bread filled with piping hot mincemeat, and tea in tulip glasses. At Aydin of camel-wrestling fame, an old couple kept an eye on their cow cropping the motorway verge, while under a tree a camel was tethered, as if awaiting Aunt Dot. When we disembarked at Denizli a child hustled us to a dolmuş mini-van. But the gold-epauletted clerk at Pamukkale's main hotel gave us the brush off. German-run, it discouraged casual visitors, especially ones such as us.

Ejected into the rainy forecourt we were inveigled into a taxi by its scruffy little spider of a driver on the lookout for stray flies. Was there hot water at his pansiyon? "Of course!" said Nazim. (He meant his wife would put a pan on.) His accommodation would have won a Heath Robinson award and given a Health & Safety inspector heart failure. (Perhaps we were lucky not to share it with a Performing Bear and his Keeper, as could happen in lesser known establishments in Anatolia.) The dining-room, the roofed space between two houses, was open to the cold and wet both ends. A ladder led down from the roof trailing Nazim's "central distribution system", frayed electric wiring. Our shower was wall-mounted in a footpad lavatory, the tap over the pint-sized washhand-basin so big the water missed the bowl altogether. When I put my hairbrush on the shelf beneath, the shelf fell off.

Trying not to address him as Frank Spencer, we let Nazim lead us down to the kitchen. Here his barefoot wife and daughter squatted opposite one another, knees spread, hacking up meat on the floor. A startling innovation in tourist facilities was a glass-fronted pharmaceutical cabinet displaying fly-blown medicaments and stomach pills. Dinner will be served shortly, Nazim announced with a courtly bow before ushering us towards his other "foreign guests", young Germans taxi-trapped like us.

Nazim's daughters, dressed in şalvar (baggy Turkish trousers) with colourful overskirts and layers of woolly jumpers, their hair concealed beneath headscarves, trooped past into the family room kicking off their shoes. A German girl explained the day was an important rite-of-passage in the life of the family. After giving birth to five girls, Nazim's wife had presented him with a son only forty days previously. The baby's fortieth day was auspicious, for it meant the infant had survived the period of special danger during which it is exposed to devils and djinns. The men of the village would gather that night to celebrate with songs

52

and dancing. When the mother passed through the dining room carrying the infant, the German girl looked desperately round for a tribute. Seizing a vase of plastic flowers from the table, she presented it with a flourish. Such a charmingly absurd gesture was taken in the spirit in which it was meant. Later we caught a glimpse of the flowers on top of the TV set in the family room. On the baby appearing next morning, wrapped like a burrito, I asked if I might peep. "Maşallah!" ("How wonderful is God's work!") It was not right to praise infants without adding this proviso or the compliment might invoke bad spirits, especially as I possessed the Evil Eye, the blue eye that Ovid called "the eye of the double pupil".

Pamukkale's appeal to the childhood delights of paddling was irresistible. We set off to climb the terraced waterfalls where sky-reflecting pools hung suspended from organ pipes of stalactites. When a storm broke, we huddled amongst tourist booths under a vine arbour, icy rain whipping round our legs. Nonchalantly, Bob wandered into a leather shop. The new season's jackets had just arrived. A stylish jerkin caught his eye. When bargaining, a heady mixture of banter and social occasion, commenced, I kept my eyes downcast. After all, I was economising! But other eyes were on me. Soon the merchant moved aside to hook from the ceiling a poem of a jacket in dove grey lamb's leather with slashed balloon sleeves. "This for you, Madam!"

On visiting Pamukkale in 1939, Archaeologist George Bean had bathed alone in the Sacred Pool among the earthquake-tumbled drums and architraves of Ancient Hieropolis. Now the pool was enclosed within a hotel garden. Blissfully suspended in warm, bubbly water, I waggled my toes while resting my elbows on a sunken capital. A dive beneath floats brought us to the limpid depths of the Sacred Source. Far away across the Vale of the Maeander, the mountains reared snow-capped above wreaths of cloud, while below elliptical pools of calcareous rock brimmed over before cascading down a hillside no longer white but, since the diversion of water for swimming pools and irrigation schemes, the colour of rotting teeth.

Back at the pansiyon the daughters of the house had donned knitted stockings and were carrying firewood into the family room. I sat at the table swathed in blankets. When Nazim saw our departure was inevitable, he accepted Bob's settlement of the bill in Turkish lire with ill-concealed dismay, at which Bob replaced them with a Eurocheque. Then, since Nazim had no idea of the exchange rate, Bob worked it out for him, rounding up the puny sum. Nazim then offered to drive us to the main road, but took us instead the full twelve miles to Denizli, his face growing more crestfallen by the moment. Had he hoped to persuade us to stay? Refusing remuneration for the lift and gulping back tears, he thrust on us a handful of his business cards.

I feared death might any minute overtake one withered crone who was hustled across the motorway between her daughter and son-in-law with her feet off the ground. But, dumped at a roadside table with a plate of çöp şiş ("rubbish kebab" – scraps of herb-marinated lamb skewered on toothpicks) to await the Denizli bus, she came cheerfully to life, champing the meat with toothless gums. A baby with cherry-button eyes, gold earrings and two bottom teeth, whose hulk of a grandfather, bouncing her on his knee, caused laughter by seeking a non-existent lever to widen his seat, was sustained with the universal refresher of a mini-cucumber. On our alighting to change buses, which involved plucking up the courage to cross a roundabout, a whipper-in from the bus company grabbed our bags and produced chairs for us to sit on. Everyone shouted directions to make sure we caught the right bus, where a girl in the seat behind me, stroking my head, whispered in my ear, "Please! Is PAINTED your hair?"

Back on the coast not a drop of rain had fallen. Next day Yener delivered our new genoa appliquéd with his logo, a stylised sea-gull. (For *Amazon*, fitted with something new every season, the proliferation of Jonathan Livingstone Seagulls had made Johnny complain, "Bloody seagulls everywhere!" until Judith put her foot down.) Since Yener had sewn the sacrificial leech – which bore the brunt of the weather when the genoa was wound around the forestay – on the wrong side, back went the sail for modification.

To be scrupulously tidy was essential, for the marina pasha was a martinet who cared much for the appearance of his Paşalik, but not a jot for his bread-and-butter, the yachtsmen. Angry shouts resounded from the marina office when, declaring it "not convenient", he removed the one and only public telephone. Yachtsmen addressed their complaints to Ankara. But to no avail. The pasha was known to kick into the water anything left out on pontoons including baskets of clean laundry. One of his autocratic foibles was to reserve the Yacht Club (to which, technically, we all had membership) for the exclusive use of his family and friends. His staff, though fond of his German wife and pretty children, Daria ("Ocean") and Bora ("North Wind"), were frightened of him. At his appearance in the bakkal (grocery) the young manageress, who was telling me how she was saving up to have a front tooth filled, broke off in the middle of a word.

A rat-a-tat on *Cappelle's* hull brought old neighbours from Poros. We sensed a certain contrition when they said everyone had been worried about us, what with the weather turning nasty. But we played it cool. "Really?" we said. "Well, perhaps the sea had been a bit lumpy and the wind rather strong." Confessing to not liking the sea much, after renewing their visas, they could not wait to return to home ground in Poros. "Remember," was their parting cry, "if you get into trouble in Turkey, don't stop to argue, just cut and run!"

The first of the day's calls to prayer sounded an hour before dawn. I soon fell back to sleep, but the canon blast at 8 p.m. never failed to create a general stir, for during Ramazan strict Moslems neither ate nor drank from pre-dawn call to prayer to the final canon. Judith urged us to listen carefully, for the doddering chief mullah was not known for punctuality. The subordinate mullahs, however, who must wait on him to lead the call that broke the fast, were as hungry as any of their flock. You could hear them, if he were late, impatiently tapping their feet beside their microphones.

Soon the jujube shrubs were decked with flowers, and the stony hills, lathered in cistus blossom spiced with the wine-mauve rosettes of the Judas tree, sprang with grass as fine as baby's hair. Then the Anatolian storms caught up. When the weather cleared we revarnished the cockpit in honour of the arrival of old friend Libby – who was left to lug her baggage, while the Turk deputed to show her the way to *Cappelle* strode unburdened in front. By request she brought Marmite and Nescafé (then £10 per 4 oz tin in Turkey), spares for the Tilley and a new Red Ensign.

Johnny translated for us the Fisherman's Laying up Creed:

"Sleep for the first sixty days
Caulk by the seventieth day
Launch by the eightieth
Rig by the ninetieth
Summer arrives on the 150th day."

The weather in the run-up to 6th May (before which the Ancient Kings of Caria decreed sailing illegal) was warm and sunny. Perversely, on the first day of summer, we awoke to rattling sheets. Not a yacht moved. Investing in a visor embroidered "Welcome to Bodrum – Rest Your Anchor Here", Libby voted to visit the Tomb of Mausolus.

That evening a passing yachtsman recognised *Cappelle* from a blueprint of a North Sea racer-cruiser commissioned from yacht designer Francis Jones by a farmer friend of his father. Built in Maldon, Essex. in the winter of 1959/1960, she was named *Cappelle* after a variety of winter wheat, *Cappelle d'Espoir*, then popular along the Essex coast. This made sense, for a frond of green wheat was appliquéd to her spinnaker.

Cruising north

Wary of Pasha Rock and entranced by the weird vortices of the dromedary landscape, we kept within the lee of Rabbit Island to avoid the submerged mole of Gümüslük (Ancient Myndus) whose defence walls were torn down to build village houses. Whippers-in from a restaurant, much agitated by our stated desire to explore before eating, dragged our dinghy onto their jetty thinking to lose our custom. It was rumoured that the owner of a large harbour-side villa had roped off the harbour's northern arm to restrict it for his personal use. But none of the armed guards the pasha was reputed to employ patrolled the foreshore. And it seemed just as likely the silted area was untenable.

To the pasha's credit was the absence of disco. It was left to the laments of a love-lorn donkey, plus suspect holding, to keep us awake.

Rounding Wreck Rock, we penetrated the wooded creek of Kazikli. Here, mindful of the maxim impressed upon us, "Remember! Always tie yourself to Turkey!" Bob rowed ashore to warp *Cappelle* to a tree. With Turkish anchorages deep and steeply sloping, tying to terra firma serves to dig in the anchor and hold it steady when the wind changes. An avian orchestra serenaded us and wood pigeons cooed. At night the line ashore drew bar tight, the clang of the anchor chain bringing awareness of the song of the nightingale.

In the morning we unhitched *Cappelle* to drift a mile downstream to Johnny's "Paradise Bay". Like many shallow inlets it was difficult to pinpoint, for, from offshore, a coastline gives the illusion of equidistance. But, on identifying a disused lime-kiln, we made to starboard of it and the bay opened up. Here the sun shone through eau-de-nil water to a sandy bottom. We swam ashore. In the woods fork-tailed butterflies hovered over fading orchids. Behind us, all compassed round with pine branches, *Cappelle* rode at anchor picture-book style.

The landmark for Iassus was a monstrous hotel, one of those Janus buildings it is hard to know whether half-built or half-derelict, the answer being probably both because money ran out. Although the ruins of a Byzantine tower rising from the water constricted the navigable channel into Asin Liman, the main hazard was the ancient breakwater extending underwater. Its extremity, according to the Pilot, was "sometimes marked by a stick". (I failed to spot this until we were leaving and then asked, "What's that twig poking out of the water?") To enter the creek, we took a transit of 350 deg true on the minaret at its head where the ruins of the ancient city spread down from an acropolis. Our siesta was interrupted by the clash of chains. Rubbing our eyes, we emerged into a fun-fair of bump boats, their skippers flinging out anchors like tossing bricks. Yet more Moodys careered in. As we stared aghast, still half asleep, our ears were challenged by an aggressive Aussie voice from the larger Moody following in, "You'd best get used to it! We're here every other Friday till October!" Bob's concern was the multiple overlay of *Cappelle's* anchor. The date was Friday 13th. What had joined us was a thirteen-boat holiday flotilla made up of Twelve Ducklings and Mother Duck. "Quick! Let's buy bread or this lot'll snaffle it!" urged Libby. By the time we had crossed to the village Mother Duck already occupied the landing-stage, her crew drinking at a bar leaving the ducklings to fend for themselves.

Dusty Iassus was thrilled to be on the tourist map. Hordes of small boys trailed us, scrabbling to shake hands before dodging through alleyways to reappear and repeat the performance. A brown cur, apparently under the delusion of being invited, heaved itself up from under a cart. It was the usual Pompeii mongrel, dirty, tatterdemalion, half-starved, and in this case malformed, but exuding bonhomie from every matted hair, its crooked jaw and permanently lolling tongue giving its face the queerest expression. Being hit by a truck in puppyhood did not stop it sleeping under one, nor chasing cows, nor getting the most out of life. A five-barred gate led to bucolic ruins where cattle grazed and the flicking shadows of lizards shaved the corner of the eye. Like all such cities, Iassus, brought down by disaster and rebuilt only to be abandoned again, was a palimpsest of Bronze Age, Classical, Hellenistic, Roman and Byzantine. As we set off to climb the acropolis, the custodian called after us that we would touch a flower growing there at our peril: "Bad flower! You die!" he gestured, clutching his throat. It was all good tourist stuff, the purple-black *fleur du mal* for all its evil looks the harmless dragon lily.

Somehow, below, the flotilla had lined up, each Moody tied to Turkey by whatever means, be it boulder or root of tree. *Cappelle* reviewed the fleet, while local youngsters were treated to whizzabouts in a Zodiac. An Aussie from Mother Duck, hands in pockets, loitered on the quayside calling out that windsurfing instruction would be left till the morrow. Knowing the sea-bed to be a net-work of anchor chains, we could not help wishing that more attention had been paid to anchoring instructions today. Bob resolved to leave early. When the flotilla crowd poured into the lokanta waiters fell over themselves in their eagerness to serve. Our table was soon spread with dishes bearing little reference to those ordered. A request for coffee brought a hiatus as a child was sent racing out to fetch cups on a swinging pendulum tray. The bill was so paltry Bob thought it only fair to raise it to something reasonable.

After exercising endless patience extricating our anchor, we were out of Asin Liman well before windsurfing got under way. Sheiro Bay lay down Gulf. Here, Johnny promised, blackbirds sang and a shepherd boy played the pipes. Having matched the profile of the hills with their silhouette on the Admiralty Chart, we made for solid landmass where the arrow indicated. As we closed the coast, part of it transformed itself into an island with, behind it, the navigable entrance to reed-rimmed Sheiro. The bottom was mud, good holding. As Johnny had said, a cuckoo called and blackbirds sang. In the greensward grasshoppers scissored and a spider backed down its funnel. I was about to step on what I thought was a boulder when I saw it was a tortoise. Nearby, in a broken-down bothy sheeted with polythene, a mother and her three small sons awaited the return of the flock that soon streamed down the hill.

Back at *Cappelle*, we were surprised to find ourselves tracked by an escaped duckling, the apologetic English family on board making the excuse of being sure we would know "where to go for a quiet life!" Something woke me before dawn. In the half-light I could discern a child playing a pan pipe. From time to time he lowered it to sing a half-toned auroral song as he led his sheep away. I fancied I saw nubs of horns budding through the thatch of his untidy hair. Later on came disquieting signs of "progress" with the arrival of a jeep and a team of prospectors to survey for a road extension.

The breeze in the Gulf afforded spanking play with the new genoa, which pulled well, though caught the shrouds at the cross-trees when close-hauled. At the primitive port of exit of Gulluk ("Rose Garden") we tied up against cargo-pier boards dark with emery dust (the best mooring already nabbed by Mother Duck playing hooky). Libby's departure presented problems: how to get her to Izmir for her flight to London? And how, on a Sunday evening with the Port Authority closed, to get her taken off *Cappelle's* crew list. If she remained on it, we stood to be accused of harbouring an illegal immigrant – or worse. But scruffy Gulluk was known for its sensible approach. On examination of Libby's air ticket, an official pronounced it in order for her to be removed from our paperwork in absentia. A glance at a bus time-table showed us there was no chance of public transport, but a chat in a shop had someone acting as interpreter running for the village taxi driver. He exhibited a certain hesitation because he would need to fill his petrol tank and we might make a deal elsewhere. However, when Bob suggested paying half the fare in advance, he would have none of it, preferring to shake hands on a gentleman's agreement.

Gulluk's lokanta assigned us two little pages. One stumbled up rolling a chair on his tummy to accommodate our handbags, which prompted Libby to tell of an aunt on honeymoon in Turkey in the 'twenties describing such courtesies. (Other aspects of Turkish life failed to go down so well with the bride, who, abandoning her new husband to a research project, returned home alone.) A jam-jar of roses was popped on our table while we selected raw meat from a display cabinet. On leaving the restaurant it was incumbent on us to shake hands with everyone in sight, including the pages, who lined up like Wimbledon ball boys.

Before midnight a stealthy figure, the taxi driver, reconnoitred the pier. On the hour his engine roared and he held wide the passenger door to whisk Libby off into the night. Next morning he was back in the village. As he turned to wave, smile and bow in one embracing gesture, I knew all had gone well. Months later a letter from Libby, describing him as a "treasure", caught us up. Treating her with old-world courtesy he had stopped twice on the way to Izmir "for her convenience", bought her tea, and insisted on waiting in his cab at the airport to see her safely through the check-in.

News of a yacht in harbour travelled fast. The greengrocer, who handed me a German dictionary, was puzzled when I could not read it. On my enquiry for rose-leaf jam, a man got up from a café table to unlock a shop, while the grocer lined up the basic provisions he reckoned we needed, including two canisters of water. I was to regret not taking both these but, having learnt to count in Turkish, said "bir" (pronounced "beer") meaning "one". The resultant misunderstanding became a big joke as first a can of Tuborg was produced, and changed to Efes when I shook my head. Bob was anxious to be off. He had disappointing news. We had sanctioned Libby washing her hair, but the crew of a cargo vessel told him water was not available for yachts. There was nothing for it but to sail south again for Torba, a newly sophisticated village on the Myndus peninsula.

Torba

The day was Şeker Bayram, the Sugar Feast, the public holiday that ends Ramazan. Of the alarming number of holiday-makers, most were disporting themselves within the harbour confines on rubber ducks, in paddle boats or on surf-boards. No one showed any interest in taking a line. One likely lad flatly refused, thereby ruining Bob's oft-repeated theory that "all boys like boats". The unmade mole having neither rings nor bollards, boats moored on long lines straddled across the mole like trip wires to be secured round rocks at the far side. Rubble extending off made the distance ashore too far to jump. When I dropped anchor it failed to dig in, momentum taking *Cappelle* towards half-submerged rocks. Grabbing the rails of a motor boat to hold us off and detailing me to let out more chain, Bob clambered aboard to secure a line,

"Be quick! Be quick!"

"I can't! The flipping chain's snarled in the well!"

Frantically I yanked at the windlass. Looking up, I was horrified to see myself in no charge at all of a ten-ton missile adrift in a harbour packed with kindergarten watersporters. Bob had searched in vain for a cleat before the playful breeze wrenched the warp from his hands.

Grasping the direness of the situation, I scampered to the blunt end to fire the engine. On seeing no space in which to steer, I compromised by yelling blue murder. Though my whole life failed to pass before me, in swift succession a panorama of fishing trawlers, water-babies in arm bands, wreck rocks and fat ladies in deckchairs did. As I wrenched my juggernaut aside from a much occupied pontoon, Bob, who had by this time done a spectacular racing dive wearing his not-quite waterproof Rolex, reached his ship in a fast crawl. Hauling himself over the transom with superhuman effort, he was just in time to avert disaster. When the anchor was finally laid, I swam ashore with the warp between my teeth (So what! Judith told me she always did this!) to fix stern lines. No damage had been done. And it occurred to us that, far from being the focus of attention, no one had even noticed the fuss. Next day Torba reverted to the quiet village Johnny recommended.

Provisioning was easy, for a dolmuş plied across the neck of the peninsula to Bodrum. Opposite the gates of the holiday gulag of Milita, where package tourists were fenced in by barbed wire and from whence came the rhythmic beat of aerobic classes, was a small convenience store with daily bread deliveries. When carrying shopping along the mole, it was essential to remember to step over trip lines every few feet, before negotiating rocks and the dinghy tied as a causeway to *Cappelle*. An advantage of our slot was that the deep water on the far side of the newly ballasted mole, as yet free of sea urchins, offered perfect swimming on our doorstep. On my first dip I was joined by a doe-eyed beauty in a bikini, who told me what an object of envy *Cappelle* had been as she sailed in.

Over coffee Ceylan told us she had inherited the red-roofed Provençal-style villa on the hillside from her uncle, a Turkish Consul-General, who died of a heart-attack at the wheel of his car. There would be no more houses like hers, she said, for a recently introduced bye-law restricted building to all-white houses of Turkish design. She added that Torba would be ruined if it were ever put on mains water, the hidden amenity of each house being its high terrace concealing a tank for which water was purchased by the ton from inland Milas. In the circumstances we were embarrassed to speak of our own water shortage.

Ceylan invited us to drinks that night. Wrought iron gates swung open onto a hillside undergoing a landscape-gardening transformation. Roses and fruit trees grew. Bougainvillaea screened the house walls and candles glowed in hurricane lanterns on a terrace floored with ceramic tiles into which blue glass Evil Eyes were let at random. Later

Ceylan escorted us to "Titti's", a branch-roofed restaurant packed with the in-crowd. A twice-married-to-each-other couple, who spent the evening flattering each other's egos, were introduced as Turkey's leading classical actors, she a bejewelled Juliette Greco with enormous eyes, he a barrel-chested tragedian with purple lips. Ceylan was glad to have brought friends, she told us, for, much as she liked to socialise, she was "misunderstood" if she ventured out alone. Offering me a lift into Bodrum next day, she dropped me at a downtown fruit and vegetable market, urging me not to miss the honey-sweet white mulberries in their short season, nor the sugary mini-bananas from Southern Turkey so despised by tourists.

An American yacht, *Lengelena III of Honolulu*, joined us, it too short of water. Not only had its crew been refused water by Milita, which had its own supply, but had been told to manage better! Mary, her temper wearing thin, was threatening to break into that "god-dammed" spare canister on deck to take a shower "or else". Brad was reduced to fuming, "Do you realise this country is supposed to be *CIVILISED*!? What on earth can the Third World be like!?" Water-shortage tales abounded. In Bodrum a German skipper had been denied water until he paid the twenty-four-hour short-stay fee.

With both yachts ready to share the cost, I consulted Maria at the store who offered to order a water tanker from Milas. Although promised for the following day, for five days I returned to report its non-appearance. Maria was mortified, saying she has seen the tanker with her own eyes. But it never reached harbour. On the fourth day I met it, and ran joyfully back. It never arrived. Not until the sixth day, bumping along the mole over the mooring lines, did it appear. The explanation was that on previous trips opportunists (probably relatives of the driver!) had prematurely relieved him of his load.

Ephesus

On our long-planned trip to Ephesus the coach was held up outside Milita. This allowed us a grandstand view of a knife fight that erupted among construction workers on the roof of Torba's proposed new shopping mall. One hot-head was disposed to murder. When the foreman intervened, he grabbed a claw-hammer. As our coach left six workmen were roping his legs.

According to the Gospel of St John, after the death of Jesus, John and Mary travelled to Ephesus. Mary's sturdy chapel stood foursquare on a sylvan terrace on Nightingale Mountain. A twisted tree with a knarled bole framed its doorway in a gangly spiral. The air was melodious with bird song and the tinkle of spring water. This pocket of shelter was already seeded with the faiths of Hepat the Hittite, Anatolian Cybele and Artemis/ Diana of the Ephesians when succeeded by Mary (some say by bribery and corruption) as Magna Mater. Metamorphosing from a succession of goddesses stretching back to the Earth Mother of pre-history, Mary cannot be torn from her forbears. By adopting old sites, taking over old dates and transferring old virtues, the Early Christians were careful to render the transition to this new version of the Eternal Feminine as painless as possible.

The sun struck hard when, stumbling into history, we entered Ephesus. A hunchback, a satyr in our midst, was a master of schadenfreude. Concealing himself behind a figure of Nike, he stripped off, a real-life Hellenistic grotesquerie to spring forth, like Magwitch, to terrify. In its hey-day the city had been a bustling sea-port. Every street corner featured the cascades and pools of the most lovely fountains, from the charming Hellenistic to the monumental Roman. Water had once sprouted from the eyes of Eros on a Dolphin. In the brothel a mural showed a servant serving wine to three women, redolent, no doubt, with the perfumes manufactured in the city. At their feet a cat played and a mouse nibbled crumbs.

The tourist who had sobbed over the Virgin's feet at Meryemana now laughed so hysterically in the museum at the figure of an extravagantly erect god balancing a tray of fruit on his member she had to be escorted out. Isolated in glory, the "many-breasted" goddess Diana sculpted in milk-white marble gazed inscrutably into the Beyond, wearing an aura of in-dwelling as if in the knowledge that her fate was to be superseded, as she had superseded her forbears. Like her spirit, her image had metamorphosed. Her necklace of marble dugs was symbolic of the bulls' testicles – themselves displacing the testicles of her priests who in earlier times castrated themselves in her honour – that hung across the chest of the original wooden figure. But her spirit remains constant throughout the ages, the Eternal Feminine, an enigma, virgin and goddess of fertility.

Back on board, after water, next to run out was gas, obliging me to hump the canister to Bodrum for a refill. Dolmuş passengers carried all sorts of impedimenta on their laps, including other passengers. I returned one day cradling a dustbin to use as an anchor bin. By May it was extremely hot and Bodrum swarmed with visitors, many unaware of what to expect. Saddled with my marketing bags, I dreaded the standard question, "Where's beach, luv? It's that hot!" And having to reply there wasn't one. Another regular enquiry was, "Where can we get a decent meal?" (For "decent", read "British".) But Bodrum was catching up fast. We could no longer order Turkish tea at harbourside cafés, for it had been replaced by the more profitable Nescafé. I fell foul of a youth who, grabbing my shopping bag, endeavoured to extract my promise to visit his disco. As I struggled to wrest back the bag (which contained my purse), he attempted to steal a kiss. But his luck did not hold, for out of Gino's Yachting burst its manageress. "I think I save you!" said Suha furiously.

Our starboard neighbour in Torba was company-owned *Bandida*. We became aware she was being serviced when lackadaisical workmen picnicked beside us on the rocks. Just before three o'clock one morning Bob was awakened by a gurgle. What roused me was his shout of *"CHRIST! THE BOAT NEXT DOOR'S SUNK!"* *Bandida* stood on her nose, her mast slewed over us. Enough was visible by torchlight to horrify, for *Cappelle* appeared to be holding *Bandida* up. The slightest movement, or the rise of light airs, could upset the balance. We dressed cautiously, waiting for dawn and the reaction of the outside world. But when it came, it was with camcorders. Bob went off to consult Ceylan. "Who did it?" were her first words, deliberate scuppering not uncommon. Back at the harbour she commandeered a fishing boat, instructing its crew to ease *Cappelle* out. We held our breath. But *Bandida*, her bows wedged between rocks, did not wobble. When a holiday couple reported seeing men on board late at night, Ceylan's advice was to keep their mouths shut or they could find themselves indefinitely delayed.

Torba had a field day. Families brought picnics to watch the comedy salvage operation. *Bandida's* company lawyer arrived first, followed by an insurance assessor, both with entourage. Next came a Big Red Fire Engine, pursued by a second vehicle with pumping gear. A "salvage official" in swim-trunks asked to borrow Bob's snorkel to attach a rope to *Bandida's* pulpit. Arguments broke out. The plan was to pump her out as she was winched up by a fishing trawler. In vain did we caution the uselessness of this, for we knew her portholes were open. With a tearing sound, water jetted into the air as *Bandida*, wrenched from the rocks, sank in deep water. Everyone shouted, shook their fists and went home. A week later a lorry with Istanbul number plates, complete with a professional salvage team, arrived to survey the sunken vessel before attaching flotation bags to bring her to the surface and tow her away. The cause of the foundering was a disconnected inlet pipe and opened seacock. There were rumours of a company wages dispute.

Routine for two little English boys became fishing for cat fish beside *Cappelle* before coming on board for a can of Coke. One posed the burning question. "We've been thinking... What do you DO all day...?" The answer was we found ourselves fully occupied with the basic art of living. On their final evening the family invited us out us to a restaurant. At the end of the meal whisperings in the background hinted at something special. Then two brothers, crouching low, bore in an Arabian Nights extravaganza. Five tiers of plates of diminishing sizes were balanced on wine glasses filled with coloured liquid. Each held prepared fruits: orange and apple slices cut into stars and cog-wheels, sugar plums, cherries in pairs like Spanish earrings, carmine triangles of water melon and sunsets of baby apricots. At the top burned a spirit flare from a tinfoil Aladdin's lamp.

Sunny-tempered Genghis, a fisherman who waited in vain for charterers, asked to borrow kesmeşeker (lump sugar). This, we discovered, was in order to invite us to tea. He later repaid the sugar together with a bucket of fish for good measure. Possessor of the usual "indoor" wife and son, Genghis combined a quick eye for trouble with an Islamic attitude to life's ups and downs. He told us how he had come to spend forty-seven days in prison on what, he claimed, was a trumped-up charge of membership of a paramilitarist group of which he swore never to have heard. To gain his release he had been forced to sign a fabricated confession. With his passport confiscated, he now declared himself "Union man".

One blustery evening, Genghis shouted across that an ill-secured flotilla yacht was about to go on the rocks. Should he go aboard? (We had overheard a teenager call to her father, "Come ON, Daddy, for goodness sake! Just leave the boat! It'll be all right! I'm cold!") Genghis winched the yacht off and was tying it alongside a fishing boat just as an angry punter hurried back, having been informed "some Turk" was on his boat. Bob let him know that if it had not been for Genghis his boat would now be on the rocks. Danger to us all was a large fishing smack breaking loose after what Judith called "typical charterer carelessness" in dredging up its anchor. I struggled to hold the smack off by its davits while Genghis and Bob coped with re-anchoring.

To bid us goodbye before leaving for Cyprus, *Energetic* swooped into Torba Bay. Together with Genghis and his son we spent a Fun Day. Bill played boogie-woogie on the portable organ which rose out of his cockpit locker and we windsurfed on the couple's "expert" board (in our case more off than on). Yorkshire Joyce's plain-spoken exhortation to Bob, *"GO! GO! GO! GO ON IT LIKE A DOG ON A BITCH!"* was born of an event much on her mind. On their previous visit to Torba by dolmuş, having left *Energetic* pulled off the quay in Bodrum with precautionary washboards put in place, Joyce had voiced her concerns about a pregnant bitch she had allowed on board when pursued by a trail of suitors. Now she could not wait to relate the rest of the story. Friends promised to bring back bacon from Kos that day (pork products being unobtainable in Turkey). All was normal when Bill and Joyce returned, except for a note propped on *Energetic's* saloon table, which read:

"BACON IN FRIDGE. CONGRATULATIONS TO MOTHER AND DAD!"

Tip-toe exploration of the forepeak revealed a proud mother suckling seven puppies. How the bitch got aboard remained a mystery but, as Joyce said, "Desperation works wonders!" An attempt was made to keep the Happy Event secret. But news spread. Bill was all for setting off to Cyprus complete with maternity unit until a veterinary nurse on holiday volunteered to administer chloroform. With everyone aware that if the marina pasha got to know of the puppies he would poison them, a hide-away was prepared for the mother, together with one of her offspring. Joyce wept as the rest were taken away, while Bill nursed an undeserved guilty conscience.

(As for us, if I had not wielded *Cappelle's* flagstaff to fend off a herd of goats landed, unchaperoned, on the mole beside us from a flat-bottomed boat, our own encounter with the animal kingdom might well have been closer!)

I was treading water with Ceylan's mother visiting from Istanbul, when she told me her husband, Çanip, had been one of the young Turks recruited by Winston Churchill to train with the Royal Air Force during the war years. Çanip remained inordinately proud of his background. Should she return from shopping in town weary and disgruntled after jostling ("pressing flesh-to-flesh", as the Turks say) with a crowd of tourists, he would put his finger to his lips and say, "Shh! Remember you speak of those I love!"

Çanip sported an air-force blue bomber jacket and cravat, "in tribute to the RAF", as he put it, at Ceylan's farewell party that evening. Before retreating indoors to the blazing fire within (for the evenings were chilly) we picked at chafing dishes on the terrace while a dusky sunset faded from the hills and a "horned moon with one bright star" floated over Torba Bay like a living emblem of Turkey.

Five

Samos to Kusadasi

Samos

Glow-worms lined the grass verges as we made our way back to *Cappelle*.
A few hours later we set off into the whitecaps. The breeze gusting
between the islands soon freed and we sailed a fine reach to find Gulluk
Customs closed for lunch. A villager asked Bob to join him in a game
of backgammon while we waited. Exit formalities involved visits to
three buildings and four offices, the visa rules being reinterpreted to
mean we could stay until the following day. « Yavaş! Yavaş!» ("Slowly!
Slowly!") they said. In any case the wind was too strong! Time enough
to leave at five in the morning!

"No problem!" they said, as we awaited the next official to wield
the next rubber stamp below the next portrait of elfin-featured Ataturk.
Bob, who saw through the window the increasing gyrations of our
mast, grew anxious. From his frowning glances, a clerk thought the
sun was in his eyes and drew the blind. By the time we flung ourselves
aboard, the yacht's position was fast becoming untenable. Shoving off
with boat hooks, we lurched towards Sheiro Bay to be battered by gusts
till dawn.

Out at sea again, a lone sloop approached down-wind When I trained
my binoculars on her, it was to see other binoculars on *Cappelle*.

"It's *Fyne 'n Dandy*!"

"It can't be! We haven't heard of Algernon for a year!"

But a peremptory voice shouting, "Kazikli!" from an anchorage now
some way behind us ordered *Cappelle* to turn and follow.

"No! We are making for Çukurcuk!" we shouted in our new-found independence.

"You're running into wind!" Algernon called forebodingly. Then, his voice fading and his arm indicating the land, came his final diktat, *"GO TO DIDYMA! GET A TAXI!"*

(I knew I had to go there!)

To avoid shoal water off Çukurcuk we moved inshore, thus obscuring the view of Tek Ağaç Burun (Lone Tree Cape) and its "you-can't-miss-it" lighthouse, causing us, cross-patch on developing the feverish cold that swept Torba, to mistake the previous headland for the one sought. In the log Bob wrote, "False idea of proximity of destination engendered by optimism." Three miles further on rose the tall pencil of Lone Tree Lighthouse, marker for the only anchorage between Kazikli and the Greek island of Samos, a cramped, exposed, bite-sized çukurcuk or "cavity" in an otherwise unindented coastline. According to the visa rules, we should exit Turkish waters, but it was common practice for yachts to break passage here. Still well off shore, I was admiring the chrysoprase lights in the sea when their portent dawned on my tired brain and I rushed to switch on the echo-sounder, shouting to Bob I could see bottom. With three fathoms under the transducer, there was no cause for alarm. I was viewing the rock-strewn sand of the sea-bed through the aqueous magnifying lens of a sea area renowned for clarity.

We pinpointed Çukurcuk by the mast of *Ma Biche*, her presence indicating we had missed the one safe spot. As the wind whistled across the bleak Ionian landscape, *Cappelle* swung unhealthily close to shore. Even in the dusk the water's transparency brought the sea-bed all too close. We spent a bad night, bumping bottom twice. After the first heart-stopping touch-down, Bob stayed on deck, adjusting the anchor chain and checking depth. At 3.30 a.m. I joined him. Vowing to adopt the early habit, we aimed departure for five a.m.

The Etesian N/NW wind, traditionally starting around 9th July after a gale, can reach F6/8, making beating in a small boat not only difficult, but impossible. Known in Turkey as the meltem (a corruption of the Italian bel tempo), and in Greece as the "meltemi", it rises, with exceptions to prove the rule, on a daily pattern around 10.00 a.m., blows until dusk and often drops abruptly after building to full strength around mid-afternoon. A strong meltem often follows a humid night, making a hygrometer more useful than a barometer, which in summer may scarcely change for weeks on end.

The crew of *Lengelena* described getting into a "fatigue loop". On the first morning of a cruise they upped anchor at ten a.m. to head into the meltem. At day's end they fell into an exhausted sleep only to be blitzed by the mid-morning sun – and repeat the pattern. If sailing north, it was essential to make sea mileage between five and ten a.m.. The world slept and all was quiet, but by 4.15 a.m. shadowy figures were on the move. We were not about to steal a march.

Puttering along the coast, capillary cat's paws stippling the undulating carpet of the sea, we hauled down the Turkish flag. «Güle! Güle!» – "Go smiling! Go smiling!" they said in Turkey. But I left with a sigh. On the stern stood Ceylan's parting gift, a pot (or rather the traditional old tin can, which she warned me not to substitute) of basil, essential to ensure good fortune and to keep away flies. In a further concession to superstition, Evil Eye amulets now dangled above our berths. Ahead rose the mountains of the Greek island of Samos, a breached headland of the Turkish mainland, while at the foot of hills nestled the long mole of Pythagorio.

It was time to prepare for the assault of a different ambience. We must empty our minds of things Turkish in readiness for the Greek island impact. The Greek's was brittle, frenetic and invigorating. Gone were the honey-coloured gulets and the soft tones of Turkish voices to be replaced by the shrill exchanges of Greek women and the Raoul Dufy colours of caïques. Blurring mists remain with the land mass, while island sunshine has a diamond edge. In an environment so vibrant we must brace ourselves to step ashore.

As we felt our way into Pythagorio looking for the buoyed channel to the inner harbour, entry brought confrontation with cheeky cruise boat *Blue Abacor*. I was wobbling about hanging onto the Fisherman's anchor untied from its position outside the rails, awaiting the Captain's instructions to drop it "NOW!" while Blue Abacor hooted,

"I'm turning *RIGHT!*...I'm turning *LEFT!*...I'm going *BACKWARDS!*... *SIDE-WAYS!*...I'm about to *DANCE THE KALAMATIANO!* What the hell are *YOU* doing?"

"*DON'T PANIC!*" I reminded myself for the umpteenth time.

Butter-fingered when we tied up, three times I dropped the warp that a visitor threw back after looping it round a bollard. The fourth time I caught it but forgot to pass it through the fairlead. "You'd better get it right, or you'll get told off!" hissed the man, who knew his sailing onions. When our warps were equidistantly bowlined, we took stock. We were near the sewer outfall – how those deceiving slots in prime position entice! On the other hand we had successfully avoided the section reserved for fishing boats and, excitingly, taken up residence at the very hub of town. The vista ahead was the rise of the main street.

With *Cappelle* bows-to (now that we were au courant with the proper ways of live-aboards), the coach roof lent privacy to cabin and cockpit. Facing out, also gave us the advantage of an open view of Mount Mycale on the Asiatic spur of Cape Kanapitza. Mount Mycale ascended in lilts, its crescendo so rhythmic in proportion it seemed to sing its way into the sky. Within minutes of tying up, Port Captain Stavros presented us with a Letter of Welcome from the mayor and a town plan, saying that visits to the Port Police and the Harbour Authorities, plus the purchase of a Greek transit log, awaited our convenience. The Customs Officer, obliged to ask us to declare contraband such as leather goods, winked and put his finger to his lips. (It was whispered that the Samian police were not averse to asking yachtsmen to smuggle on their behalf!) The date was significant, for we had put in on the first day of Greece's official entry to the EU. All the same, Bob insisted our passports be stamped to provide formal proof of exit on re-entry to Turkey.

With a wheeze of hydraulic brakes, coaches throbbed to a standstill within feet of *Cappelle*. Aeroplanes roared overhead on descent to the airport behind the town. Frantic barking broke out when a cat high-tailed it past a pair of dogs on a double lead. One of Greece's ubiquitous canaries trilled from its cage under the awning of the postcard shop. My head rang. A French boat pulled in beside us, "Is *STINK!* No?" commented its skipper, grimacing. With Pythagorio water's reputation for hepatitis, I was regretting not importing a bucket of Çukurcuk water. We shopped for brandy, orange juice and tinned meat, all unobtainable in Turkey. A butcher provided local veal, and to "Fill high the cup with Samian wine!" came the light white Samaina, named from a class of ancient warship.

At the Sunday morning march-past, sunshine ricocheted off the instruments of a naval cadet brass band. There was deterioration in cooking standards. My cutlets were so tough I fed them to a woolly puppy. The owner of an arrogant voice heard demanding a "Danish" and a "Blue"(by which he meant a Tuborg lager and a Blue Nun) was presented with a tart's cocktail complete with straw. "Atomic bomb...BOOM!" the waiter demonstrated, flinging up his arms. This was indeed "Danish Dynamite", as ordered. Meanwhile his girl-friend gazed speechless at her very own fireworks display – two purple sparklers (which the waiter ignited with his cigarette lighter) on top of a poison-blue Del Boy concoction. Discovering an up-to-date ladies' toilet, I shot the bolt to find myself locked in with a juicy cockroach so bloated it scraped the floor when I hastened to get out.

The positioning of boats was a democratic free-for-all. Double-decker Italian motor cruisers owned by Arabs and skippered by Egyptians (a lethal combination) tied up next to converted fishing boats and well-worn live-aboard craft. Through the darkened windows of megastar *Margaux Rose* we could discern oil paintings overhung with picture lights. A noisy altercation broke out. Americans, wishing to embark, had missed her departure from Turkey. Sensibly, therefore (so they thought), they had flown on to Samos, her next port of call. But the Greek authorities, hostile to all things Turkish, refused to allow boarding. *Margaux Rose* had arrived without the couple on her crew list and the matter could not now be rectified. Tempers flared. Meanwhile a ragamuffin of a sail boat elbowed between us, all papers correct. And to sighs of admiration *Chardonnay of Wilmington* put in, her uniformed crew leaping ashore to hose down this sixty-foot vision of angel white with liver-coloured sails and all-electric in-mast furling. A spectator highlight was breakfast on the after deck when a black maid poured fruit juice to a family gathering to the nods of the Technicolor parrot perched on her shoulder.

Pythagorio's circular harbour was so congested, the Germans called it Ankersalat ("anchor salad".) Skippers dare not leave their boats unattended. A small Austrian yacht, single-handed overnight from Mykonos, arrived with a torn jib. While its skipper reported to the Port Police, two larger boats overlaid its anchor, dislodging three others. An ad hoc international anchor-aid consortium assembled and the little yacht was held off the quay until its skipper returned. Then a bully leaned over the rail of a floating cocktail cabinet to call to Bob,

"We're sending a diver down to cut your warp. It's fouled our propeller!"

"Like Hell, you do!" followed from *Cappelle*.

Pythagorio baked in a white-hot furnace. The heat was apocalyptic. Shade temperatures shot above blood heat. Radio Athens broadcast heat stroke advice. Only three Aussies cleaning out a charter boat were impervious to the sun. The early hours of the morning, the sea catlicking the pebbles, was the optimum time to bathe. To enter the water was to glide between silk sheets as black as octopus ink, our outstretched arms ghostly with phosphorescence. Cooled by evaporation, we slept in wet swimwear. In Samos, under the white hot skies of the Sea of Icarus, the power of the sun was always paramount. Only after dark did the περιπάτο (evening promenade) bring the town alive. Then shops opened and dogs, cats and the aged emerged. A fiacre, its top-hatted driver holding reins and whip high, did turns under the lamplight. All human life was here. Babies were paraded and small boys armed with fishing rods, crusts of bread and tins of worms, dangled their legs over the quay wall. Some cheeky youngsters trespassed onto yachts, inching forwards to intercept catch before their mates.

We planned passage to Chios. Though the meltemi was setting in, we might make northing if we did not delay. As we made our way up the narrow Straits of Samos, notorious for rip tides, the glint of binoculars from a cliff-top border-post showed *Cappelle* under surveillance. We almost expected pot shots. After passing Bayrak Island we turned into Possidonio Bay to skinny-dip. At the head of the Straits a Turkish gunboat patrolled. When we turned west a coast-following wind came in on the nose. It was a wearying tack in a rolling swell, taking eleven hours instead of the five reckoned. From the pine-clad hillsides the breeze carried the scent of mountain tea. We drank it sweetened with honey while trying to convert the houses of Agios Konstantinos into those of Karlovassi. But the scene lacked the necessary blue basilica. Hours later a dolphin gave a galvanic leap. The first sign of civilisation was a working crane on a breakwater, a tug standing by. Even then there was a built-up area to pass before we reached harbour which, contrary to information, had no room for yachts on its sheltered side. We tied up between yellow wall markings opposite the Customs House. Before dawn a policeman woke us with orders to make way for the inter-island ferry.

To secure *Cappelle* while we undid moorings, Bob slipped a line round the base of a lamp-post, only for a car to park on top, obliging him to explain to its bemused driver that we could not move our boat because his car was on its tether. Not persuaded to depart, for waves were splashing over the mole and a northerly F6 was blowing, we sought another slot, a sympathetic fisherman inviting us to tie to his caïque. When the ferry made its rollicking departure, its place was taken by the tug with platformed crane unable to operate in heavy seas.

A quartet of little boys lined up to stare at us making exhibitions of ourselves as we abluted under the shower bag, obliging me to remember that in Greece it is not rude to stare (although it can be very rude to object to being stared at!). Setting off for the upper town with the empty gas canister, I enquired the shortest route of an old man using a telegraph pole for a back-rest. Smiling angelically, he pointed to his good ear. But bellowing into it failed to produce a flicker of comprehension.

High above harbour, the church of Agia Triada (Holy Trinity) crowned a cave-ridden bluff. Plaster cornices pricked out in sienna and false window insets of clotted cobalt, jade and ruby transformed it into an oversize trinket box knuckled with cabochon gemstones. Breathless in the oppressive heat on our way to watch the sunset, our conversation was drowned out by the discordant yammer of insects. Out of reach of invaders, the Old Village clung to cliffs beyond a tree-filled chasm. Donkeys carrying firewood stepped daintily along marble alleyways.

An old woman, motionless on a kitchen chair beside her cottage door, nodded us on. We cooled our wrists in a water stoop outside the church portico where coins were left beside a bundle of beeswax tapers. Adding to the hoard and sketching the Orthodox backwards cross, head to navel, left to right, thumb of right hand touching the middle finger in the sign of blessing, I planted a wax taper in the sand-ring. It was the beginning of my "keying-in" practice. If I were Prince Vladimir of Russia shopping for a religion, I too would have felt the appeal of the Eastern Orthodox. Watching the eye of the sun sink into a band of lavender mist while an organza train of pink and green rippled towards us, I knew why the Greeks coined the word ηλιοβασιλέυμα or "reigning in splendour" for the alchemy of sunset. At night the illuminated neon cross on the church partnered the moon.

Landbound for six days, my ill-shod feet led me into an embarrassing episode concerning gold fashion sandals awaiting rescue by Cinderella in the dusty confusion of a Karlovassi shop. I was strictly window-gazing when the shop-keeper murmured I should try them on. In a daze I allowed myself to be ushered into the shop. The pair fitted like gloves. How to flee before midnight struck? Deliberately misunderstanding my quandary, the man fetched a second pair of different design in paler gold kid. They too were a perfect fit.

"For your feet only!" he cajoled.

«Δεν έχω λεφτά!» ("I have no money!") confessed Cinders, blushing.

How could vanity have led me into this mess? The man reduced the price. I replied I was sorry to have troubled him. On this occasion the lovely sandals were not for me.

"There is bank!"

It was Saturday. The banks were about to close. On Sunday, we planned to leave early.

«Είναι πολύ δύσκολο!» ("It is very difficult!") I live on a boat. I must go. I apologise!"

"It is not difficult at all!" countered the tempter, eyes twinkling. "Talk me more Greek! Are you English or American?"

«Αγγλίδα είμαι.» ("I am English.")

He was busy swaddling both pairs of sandals in tissue and popping them into my bag.

«Μέ γειά!» ("Wear them in good health!'") Only for you these slippers!"

All Cinders could do was exact a promise that someone would call at the harbour for payment. Tripping over the step as I hurried out of harm's way, I was forced to return to write down the name of the boat. The golden sandals seemed to burn a hole in my leg as they bounced against it.

Of course, no one came near *Cappelle.*

Strong winds continued, rough seas bringing an uncomfortable swell. But at four a.m., we were pitching into a heavy head sea as we forced ourselves offshore, jouncing like flotsam while Bob bled the engine. Though we aimed to be well away from shore before the wind increased, in two hours we made only two miles. Then the coastal swell moderated and a breeze came in allowing us to sail under reefed mainsail and three-quarter genoa, this time making five miles out to sea in two and a half hours. When the breeze died, we still had thirty-eight miles to go to reach an untried coast. Furling the genoa, we motored ahead for an hour until an unprecedented drop in oil pressure was the signal to add fresh oil. The removal of the cockpit floor and companionway steps to aid engine cooling had to be borne constantly in mind, if one was not to step into the whirling alternator.

As abruptly as we entered the doldrums we were out the other side, the freshening wind encouraging us to fly the full main and genoa. This proved too much and we heaved to and took in a reef. At F6 *Cappelle* sailed comfortably with one reef in the main and half a genoa but, with the wind direction at 340M, the best available course was 280M. By midday we had made sixteen miles. A German yacht on course behind us gave up and turned back. The mountains of Samos were fading westwards into the hulk of Ikaria. ("Never go near Ikaria!" Bill Daly had said, his eyes darkening at a memory.) Assuming the meltemi did not strengthen further, we were a good ten hours from Chios, which we stood to reach in darkness seeking an uncharted anchorage. Bob's hand, bruised on the winch, was stiffening, and I was weary of the bullet-headed wind ramming my breath back down my throat. When a bulk-carrier crossed our path we aborted passage, turning with relief onto a broad reach south, sailing now so easy it was difficult to credit how hard the going the other way.

Back in the doldrums, the coast-hugging breeze brought a street gang of dolphins. For half an hour they roistered before vanishing like an illusion. Not tempted to return to Karlovassi, we turned east, surfing wing-on-wing. Bob was kept busy with the genoa while I helmed. Once or twice miscalculation on my part brought the boom crashing across. Fearing me in danger of bringing down the mast, the Captain took over.

Behind us the sunset brocaded the sea with afterglow. Soon we were following the moon's furrow. Trusting to round Cape Prasson into the Straits of Samos before darkness fell, it was pitch dark before we made it. I had not bargained for negotiating the Straits "No Stars to Guide". How I longed for a sensible vehicle with headlights and brakes! Emergent shipping proceeded for Turkey. The wind dropped to a breeze. Standing on the cockpit seat, legs braced, I peered into the wall of darkness pressing on my eyeballs, seeking out the inadequate light, low and recessed, on Cape Gatos. We should never have located Possidonio had it not been for the silhouette of a stranded boulder known as the Rock of Samson etched against the paler sky above. Even then I only located it with the periphery of my eye. We turned in, summoning the last of our energy to avoid illuminated floats and testing holding before folding our wings for the night.

For three days we rested, while across the mouth of Possidonio Straits traffic ploughed to and fro. It was fortunate we did not delay our departure a further day or we would have met the Round-the-Aegean Race head on. As soon as *Cappelle* ventured out, a naval protection vessel swung into view. In Pythagorio's inner harbour race competitors were triple-banked. Quickly we took advantage of a last space against the end of the outer mole. In the early hours the wash from a passing motor launch smacked our line-up against the break-water, skippers leaping ashore to examine their topsides by the light of torches. By then the gusting wind had become the steady drone of a near gale. At 6.30 a.m., the sun shining brilliantly, a typical meltemi combination, the forecast was for "northerly F7 increasing". On consulting Johnny's astronomical/astrological notes we found the date coincided with the Red Plum Gale, and bore his annotation, "This one usually happens."

The breakwater afforded a grandstand view of milling yachts hoisting sail in howling squalls. The Russian contingent, competing for the first time, and the glamorous *Yumura* of the Royal Ocean Racing Club, were attracting attention. The starting gun signalled a fearsomely congested rough-water beat up the Straits. Yachts jockeyed for position. There were shouts and near collisions as yachts vied to take each other's wind. With flights cancelled by reason of strong winds, no aircraft passed overhead. The sudden silence as the tail-enders, shepherded by the naval escort ferrying a wrecked vessel, disappeared round the corner, left me deaf. When we attempted reverse gear, our engine lacked power. Passers-by helped us shove *Cappelle* off the rough-cast mole. As we strained away, I was horrified to see a following trail of oil.

At midday the meltemi cranked up. Next to us *Dowitcher* from the Hague put out two security anchors. When one went, she slewed broadside, cannoning into *Cappelle* and smashing our anchor lamp. Leaping up the companionway steps, I sliced my shin on its brass rim. Bob rowed out to lend a hand to the Dutchman, shouts urging him to hurry before our dinghy was crushed between yachts. On the waterfront that night, a diner remarked,

"Listen! The wind's died!"

"Oh no! The meltemi never dies! It only sleeps!" a waiter interrupted. As if in reply, there was a hiss from the hills and all along the quayside yachts heeled and shuddered. The beast was marking its territory. From that time, as did many sailors, I personified this meteorological phenomenon caused by the seasonal depression in far-away Pakistan. Experience conjured up a mythological monster waiting to pounce: "There be Dragons!"

I longed to wear the golden slippers. Feet were a problem in the heat. We watched a black-clad γιαγιά (grandmother) plump herself down at a café table and demand a glass of iced water. Holding out each boot in turn, she poured water into it before squelching off. Seeing her family disporting themselves in the sea, she marched after them fully dressed until the water was up to her armpits when, cackling with laughter, she billowed and bobbed like a frilled cork. The problem was never Getting Granny In, but Getting Granny Out. After the others had left the water, a determined daughter took charge and led her mother up the beach, still bubbling with merriment. Screened with a blanket, she changed into dry garments identical to her swimming togs. Old wives knew how to cope with the heat. A favourite ploy was to arrange the outer leaves of a cabbage beneath the headshawl.

August arrived. The quay was crowded with the negligent. I stepped barefoot on a fuse carelessly tossed on deck, obliging me to hop, blood streaming from the ball of my foot, for Bob to tweezer out splinters of glass. Many yachtsmen, disliking both the high heat and the intensity of the meltemi, were laying up in Turkey and flying home. We attempted to leave, but must attend on our neighbour loosening his anchor chain. Dinghy work with loops of rope eventually raised our hook. After firing with a deafening clatter, the engine settled down, though the oil pressure remained abnormally low. Once through the Straits, I set course on 035 degrees on the tail of a distant yacht. When a dolphin, rocketing into the world of air, broke the surface of the clingfilm sea, it seemed an improbable idea tearing the membrane between dreams and reality.

Kuşadası Marina, Turkey

Soon we spied the fortress on Bird Island just off Kuşadası. Then we were becalmed. Firing the engine gave rise to an alarming bang and smoke signals. Kuşadası Marina responded to our radio call by sending out a fishing boat, which slid *Cappelle* with eggshell deftness to within six inches of a breakdown quay where a dude in knife-creased ducks broke off chatting on his cell phone to take charge. Requesting to service our passports, he sped off in a white jeep.

The kiln of summer on the shadeless mainland where heat pulsated from a brassy sky, put an edge on what Hilaire Belloc termed "arrival inertia", low spirits brought on by the loss of adrenalin when a passage is over. All the same Bob, like all good sailors, insisted we make shipshape before R & R. This involved adjusting the warps, fastening on the sail cover, erecting both sun awning and wind chute, tidying up and washing the deck. On average, working at our appointed tasks, it took us an hour and a quarter, though longer on such a stultifying afternoon. The Dude was soon back to enquire what else was needed, so Bob explained about the engine trouble and the Dude promised to notify the Volvo agent in Söke. After this Bob went to the office to pay for the tow and to take out a marina contract. There were no problems, he was told, except that fresh water was severely restricted. Volvo would be notified concerning the engine. The manager added a caution that the marina was endeavouring to stamp out pirate operators. Should he be approached, he was to repulse such infiltrators. It had never occurred to either of us that the duty officer who welcomed *Cappelle* was not on the marina pay-roll! To be entrapped by him was easy. To shake him off was not.

A multi-branched signpost pointed the direction of the haven's many amenities. I turned on forked taps above a washbasin. Suddenly it sagged away from the wall on rusted brackets to crash at my feet. Further exploration brought an up-to-the-minute launderette. But a notice pinned to the door, "Customers not allowed to use service themself. No dry. No iron. This service not responsible for the shrink or the fade," failed to inspire confidence. Armed with smalls, I sought out a washroom with well-anchored basins. Rubbing away, I smiled when a head-scarfed Mrs Mop entered. To my surprise she went berserk, threatening me with her mop. "Verboten! Verboten! Be off!" she raved. It was easy to gather that it was vandals like me (rather than a combination of brackish water, cheap alloys, shoddy workmanship and lack of maintenance) that destroyed fittings.

With the cockpit opened up and the floorboards removed, the cabin doubled as an inspection pit. Sweating profusely, the Volvo engineer made a thorough assessment while I stood by to administer apple tea. A complete engine overhaul was necessary. Bob was given a list of spares to obtain in London. Then the Dude popped up again bearing a pirated copy of the same list. He must have a mole somewhere!

Assuming charge of operations without by your leave, he saw fit to ignore the work in hand as we laboured at warping *Cappelle* stern-to for the back-breaking task of uplifting the engine. (While Bill Kerslake's eyes lit up at the very thought of re-bedding his engine, it had never been Bob's cup of tea!)

We decided to treat ourselves to dinner at the Marina Hotel that night. Its waterfront entrances, except for the one past the swimming pool's unattended pay desk, were chained off. Arranging poolside loungers, staff took no notice when we mounted a dimly lit staircase leading to the hotel's rear entrance. Here our way was barred by tall padlocked gates. But to reach the front entrance meant finding our way through town to an upper road parallel to the coast road. So I hitched up my Posh Frock, tied the golden slippers round my neck, and we climbed the gates.

Service was by Red Jackets, the music wall-to-wall and the cuisine bland. A microphone crackled and the resident belly dancer was announced. Dressed in tulle and sequins, a scarlet bow on each hip, she gyrated belly-close, her hands weaving patterns in the air, her wrist-watch facing inwards for time check. That her manner betrayed Luton Airport rather than the Levant was confirmed when she invited punters to join a belly-dancing teach-in. When tired of watching the Generation Game in the one-time retreat of the Brothers Barbarossa, we escaped over the gates and stumbled home giggling. There was just time to snatch forty winks before the last-minute jobs of closing the sea cocks, lacing on the boat covers and heading to the airport.

Back in London, Bob arranged for the speedy air-freight of the engine parts. On arriving back in Istanbul after a two-week break, we were informed that a further four days' work would be required to complete the engine installation.

Fate thus provided us with a golden opportunity to explore Istanbul.

Six

Istanbul and the Dodecanese

"Morning in the bowl of night
Has flung the stone that puts the stars to flight:
The hunter of the East has caught
The Sultan's turret in a noose of light."

Edward Fitzgerald

Istanbul

The city was everything I dreamed. The awesome interior of Ayasofya belittled us, while the jewels and jacinths of the Treasury of Topkapı and the labyrinthine palace-within-a-palace of the Harem enthralled me. We bathed in harlequin reflections within the Blue Mosque, quartered the costly avenues of the Grand Bazaar, and were taken aback by the vulgarities of the Palace of Dolmabaçe (Sweet Garden). The magical arena of watery darkness, the Yerebatan Saray, an immense and splendid cistern, afforded a cool resting place. Pocketing my sandals (for blisters were killing me) I could not wait to lose myself barefoot in The Street of the Chicken That Could Not Fly.

Our reward for resting on the steps of the Bosphorus was an invitation to share the picnic of a young Turkish couple and their toddler daughter, Dilara. Afterwards, the family drove us across the Bosphorus Bridge to Çamlica (Pines of the Hot Springs) where wedding parties paraded, to look down on starlit Istanbul.

Months later, a miniature carpet on a loom, our names woven into its pattern, tracked us down. The accompanying card read, "May All the Most Beautiful Things on This Earth Happen to You – from Yakup, Nermin and Dilara."

It had taken us four nights to solve the puzzles set by the hotel suite. Finally everything functioned, even the television showing mud-wrestling and the popular *Yes, Minister* dubbed in Turkish! While we had endeavoured to comply with House Rule No 6 urging us to "avoid dirting and doing rumours", and even succeeded in prising a window open for air, I awoke sick on the day we were to leave for Kuşadası.

In addition to the luggage, therefore, the Captain had a groggy cabin boy to cope with on the journey back. On arrival he was not through the wood for there was disappointment to face in *Cappelle's* condition. A tourist who hailed from her birthplace in Essex had published an article in his local newspaper describing her as "bleached white by the Aegean sun". But we were more concerned about saturation oil extruded by the sun disfiguring her in glutinous lumps. When I rubbed down the cap rail, the calloused hand of a fisherman, eager to demonstrate how best to wield a sandpaper block, closed on mine. I kept up supplies of paint and varnish by trips into town while Bob undertook remedial work. Once I fell over an old woman squatting amongst rotting vegetables. Holding out a bird's claw hand, she turned a leprous face, her nose a cavity. In the back streets I recognised death in small animals by the interest of flies or spatter of vomit.

Didyma, Miletus and Priene

The day came to skive. At Didyma the Head of Apollo that once dominated the giant Manifestation Doorway, flanked by columns as thick as the trunks of sequoias, now scowled from tumbled masonry. The formerly clamorous harbours of Miletus and Priene were long silted, while the fate of sea-girt Priene was to be stranded on the inland slopes of Mount Mycale. But a magical quality remained. Beyond the theatre stretched a breath-taking view across the Vale of Maeander. In the soft reflective light conjured up by the sea mist once scanned by look-outs, my ears caught the clangour of the ships that Apollo the Dolphin God failed to save.

It was dark when I got home to help scoop away the eddying body of a kitten and stow the spare sails on deck to free the forepeak for occupation, for we expected night visitors. At three a.m. suppressed laughter and hoarse whispers heralded the arrival of Mel and her brother.

Once *Cappelle's* official sea trials were over, we faced exit formalities. These included an exorbitant charge in US dollars for customs duty on imported engine parts and for translation of the associated Power of Attorney notarised in Turkey. Finally, who should reappear but the Dude waving a bill for "assistance with engine repair". Bob politely but firmly refused to have anything to do with this, but settled with him for servicing the passports. Taking defeat on the chin, the Dude then presented each of us with a leather key ring as a mark of his undying esteem, and hoped to see us again soon. (Not if we see you first!)

Mesmerised by the Russian cruise ships manoeuvring in Kuşadası Bay, we churned off in an uncomfortable swell. It was the first cloudy day of autumn. Once the sails were hoisted, the motion improved. Soon, well heeled on a beam reach, we were speeding for Greek waters. With cries of, "She's going like a train!" William, at the helm, was enjoying himself hugely. Once inside the Straits of Samos he pointed *Cappelle*, smoking along bathed in golden light, as close to the wind as he dared. Taking the tide rips round Bayrak island to starboard, he gasped as a curling wave caught him in the back of the neck. Mel, foolhardily engaged in sunbathing on the stern deck, had her laughter choked out of her by the next curler. Soon we were rattling down the Turkish courtesy flag and lining up on the ruins of the Monastery of Metamorphosis to sweep into Pythagorio, where Port Captain Stavros greeted Bob like a long lost brother. Then came a surprise encounter with *Energetic*, about to exit Greece.

Patmos

After exploring one of the Seven Wonders of the Ancient World, a spooky mile-long burrow hewn to transport water through the Hill of Astypalaea, we set off to cruise the Dodecanese. A moderate sea rolled with a nice breeze astern. Some way behind us three yachts pulled out of Pythagorio. The third was lost sight of. Free to play with binoculars, I remarked on its reappearance. We all whooped, for *Energetic* was on our tail and gaining fast. "Now through friendly seas they softly run..." She stayed a while to starboard, as trim as a James Elroy Flecker ship, goose-winging in sunshine, but suddenly picked up her skirts and shot off we knew not where followed by our hurled insults. *Cappelle's* own landmark was the Monastery of St John Theologian on the saddle of Patmos. With Port Skala already well established as a pirates' lair its abbot had wisely encouraged a policy of laissez-faire (or something warmer) when the monastery was founded in 1088. In the seventeenth century the French traveller, Thévenot, recorded the port as still favoured by corsairs for refitting and laying up. But by 1988 piracy had merged into a flourishing trade in duty-free liquor.

Whom should we see awaiting us on the quay but Bill Kerslake? He explained that the introduction of an illegal levy in Samos on any yacht leaving for "foreign waters" had prompted him to revise a previous decision and exit Greece from Patmos instead. Over bean stew in the harbour hostelry our κέφι grew high, mesmerising the children of the taverna presided over by a formidable dowager, a fat girl of twelve-going-on-forty-five. They were sipping Coco Cola from wine glasses and dining on potato chips while exchanging the latest gossip: «Τι λές!» ("You don't say! Well I never!") the young hostess exclaimed, rolling her eyes and wagging a matronly finger.

We clung to our seats next day as the asthmatic village bus wound up into the blue to deposit us (except for Bill who stayed home to smoke his pipe and Keep an Eye on Things) at the foot of the monastery curtain wall where, in defiance of a notice in Byzantine script reading *"NO SHORT"*, *"NO BAD DRESSERS"*, the breeze blew my skirt over my head. In the inner court we gained an impression of flower-filled amphoras, stairways leading to galleried walks, white-washed slopes, the whisk of a cat's tail and the glimpse of a monk's habit. In the chapel Byzantine saints mesmerised us with basilisk eyes. When we climbed to the triple belfry, the sun smote. On all sides stretched the tortoise-shaped brown island set in a sea of laundry-bag blue and cinched by the opposing bays of Merika and Skala. Misty distances hinted at the presence of other islands. From up here the world was washed forever clean in Aegean light. Below, in the crepuscular shade of the Treasury we peered at the fifth-century Codex Porphyrius and objets d'art gifted by the Russian Imperial Family.

Outside again, we were soon lost in the maze of the χώρα (main village). Mel and Joyce encountered William who, eschewing religiosity, had taken himself off to explore. He claimed to have met a cat dragging a rat as big as itself. In our absence a British yacht had moved in next to us. Samantha was busily polishing a fender and explaining to William how live-aboards "must do their housework", while her young sister was heard to refer to *Cappelle* as "the little one in the middle". Cruise-liner passengers made bee-lines for the liquor stores and even faster bee-lines back to their ships.

Bill and Joyce were showing little immediate inclination to abandon *Cappelle*. Moreover, contrary to the information given in the Pilot, Patmos was NOT a Port of Exit. The Port Authorities suggested we make for Leros instead. When we left Port Scala, *Energetic* was in no hurry, Joyce's nose was in a book, and Bill, stretching back, hands cupped behind his head, mumbled a relaxed, "All in good time!" as he puffed at his pipe. But the moment we were out of harbour, *Energetic* materialised going like the clappers. (I swear that yacht could cock a snook!) Creaming past *Cappelle*, she raced though the skerries. Four hours later we watched her turn broadside ahead and vanish through the cliffs of Leros.

Leros

It was not easy to spot the light structure on the steep-to headlands that marked the gateway to Port Lakki. Inside lay the vast natural harbour of the fortress island over which the Aegean War was so hard fought. In one of many clandestine wartime missions writer Ernle Bradford spoke of navigating a blacked-out British escort destroyer into the bay by dead reckoning in order to put ashore a crack band of the Greek Sacred Brigade.

Avoiding the restricted naval area, we made for the inlet's head. "What kept you?" shouted Joyce from *Energetic's* position alongside, gesturing us away. On warping to a wobbly iron rod running the length of a derelict landing stage, we found she was not being churlish, but saving us from mooring over the sewer outlet, plus triple dues to lie alongside. Joyce was far from happy. The Harbour Master, who offered her the use of his telephone, had demanded four times the cost of the call. And, without explanation, though we made arrangements to eat there, the taverna bolted its doors. (I recalled reading that a yachtsman might winter on Leros only if he fished and shot for the pot.)

Bill wore a long face. He had been misinformed in Patmos; Leros was not, after all, a Port of Exit. An officer at the Port Authority, covering his eyes like a wise monkey, volunteered "not to have seen" us, saying we should make straight for Turkey. But this plan had its drawbacks, for infringements had a habit of rebounding. They could mean delays and fines (at worst the sequestration of a yacht). If we hung on to our Greek transit logs, the dates would fail to tally with those on our passports showing Turkish entry stamps. And when we purchased new logs on re-entry to Greece our failure to surrender the old ones might be revealed. All in all, jiggery-pokery could land us in trouble.

Finding the jet of the Tilley jammed, we talked the situation through by candlelight over a scratch supper. With the wind forecast to rise from the north, the most convenient Port of Exit was now Kos. But this was complicated by the fact that the island was lately rumoured to have become notoriously uncooperative to those wishing to travel to "foreign country", i.e. Turkey. Bill's vote was to set off immediately on a night sail. The rest of us, yawning, took the optimistic view that, if we left at first light, trusting to a fair wind and sympathetic treatment, we would make it to Bodrum in time for William and Mel to catch their flight home from Izmir. Before turning in, William came face-to-face with an even bigger rat, this time on the pontoon, not good news, as neither of our boats was equipped with rat preventers.

When *Cappelle* slipped away at cockcrow, all was silent on *Energetic*. Dawn encompassed all the Homeric clichés, "rosy-fingered", "wine dark sea" and "bright-eyed goddess". However, outside the gateposts of Port Lakki, Poseidon had his thunderbolt waiting. *Cappelle* had just turned under the beetling cliffs when the sea god's bolt was shot in the form of a fearsome down-draught that stuck us amidships. It was as if Poseidon had filled his cheeks and puffed with all his might at this impudent little stranger. Here we were, under full sail, seeking an early breeze, when *Cappelle* was flattened. "Up into wind, William!" yelled Bob from the cockpit floor. But William's legs were in the air, the helm wrenched from his hands. In the cabin I crashed backwards with a strangled cry and the contents on the opposite berth on top of me. Mel could not afterwards recall what happened to her. But, with no one remotely in charge, *Cappelle,* shaking herself like a wet dog, came up into wind, copy-book style, like the well-designed ship she was. Although we congratulated ourselves on being first off the starting block, our discomfiture was witnessed, for *Energetic's* sleep had been feigned, her crew lying in wait to slip out like a porpoise on our tail. *Cappelle's* sudden knock-down alerted them to rattle down their own canvas double quick.

Both yachts then proceeded soberly, the crews on the look-out for the black palls of squall. None appeared, not even as we passed Glaronisia, the Seagull Islets. Mel, who sensed Leros's presiding daemon, remarked with a shudder she found the island sinister. Its age-old reputation for evil-living is thought to have derived from an ancient cult of Artemis practised here long after its demise on other islands. Latterly, Leros had become a woefully inadequate dumping ground for psychiatric patients.

Kos

We wallowed in cross seas, encountering a seemingly unmanned gulet, a ghost ship fated to lurch forever on the same unhappy course. This was no way to reach Kos. The barren screes of Kalimnos loomed and then, clear on the horizon, the mountains of Caria, rocks like Pashas' turbans and hills topped with creamy whorls and blobs, from a distance unsolidified as if newly squeezed from a celestial nozzle. With a wind increase, *Energetic* forged so far ahead we could no longer set our course by her, so missed the boat-load of sheep that transferred to her their cloud of stinging flies. When the sea paled to the celadon of shallows, Mel called out she could see bottom; our approach to Kos was too close to Kum Point. The surrounding seas teemed with surf-boarders, paddle-boaters and water-skiers, while parascenders swooshed onto rafts. Beach sports were in progress against a hoarding of a bow-tied Playboy rabbit.

No sooner had we tied up than Bob was on the run for the Port Authority with the ship's papers. Mel and I, taking our life in our hands, braved the waterfront to re-visit the bakehouse where the baker, wrapping a μισό κιλό (half-kilo) of oven-warm bread in brown paper, tucked in a free cookie for each of us. We hurried back neck and neck with Bob, who was given fast-track treatment. "Nothing to pay!" said the Port Police. Without loss of momentum, we cast off. Bill, idling on the quay, took a nonchalant hand out of his pocket to wave goodbye. We knew that he, too, had been quick to attend to *Energetic's* papers. But, "See you sometime!" he called, adding that Joyce has gone off on her bike (which was odd, for I thought I glimpsed her through a port hole). Hardly had we turned our backs when *Energetic* whistled past, Joyce working at the winch with demon energy.

In a favourable F5/6, *Cappelle* too, made excellent time. The only casualty was William's box of Turkish Delight left to swill in a sea locker. Over Gumbet way, the acrylic butterflies of a dinghy regatta dipped and chased.

Back in Bodrum *Energetic* rode at anchor as if she had never moved. (William was not to see her again for two years, when he joined her to crew on her maiden Atlantic crossing.) Red flags barred the entrance to the marina, already full to capacity, but willing hands pulled *Cappelle* onto the outer wall.

Bodrum Marina

With booming expansion in the yachting world, the occupancy of Turkish marinas had increased by forty-two per cent in less than two years. The season was now too far advanced for us to sail farther. Moreover, should we wish to go home for Christmas, we had no choice other than to assign *Cappelle* to a government-controlled marina (or "machine for the manufacture of foreign currency", as yachtsmen called them). Under Turkish regulations, unless thus assigned, a yacht remained in her Captain's passport. Without her official cancellation from it, he could not exit the country without her.

For a few days there was no news of *Energetic*. Then came an invitation to meet a new member of crew. It seemed that, while lunching at a beach restaurant in Bitez, the attention of Bill, still upset over the stowaway litter, had been drawn to a tiny bundle of despair wandering by the sea. Here was a way to salve his conscience, for the bundle was a black puppy. Enquiries proved fruitless. It was obvious the pup had been abandoned. On Bill picking him up, he buried his nose under Bill's armpit. At this Bill took the pipe out of his mouth just long enough to say to Joyce, "You've got a Ship's Dog!" Taking surrogate fatherhood seriously, he pedalled off with the waif in his bicycle basket to be wormed, inoculated, and given an official Bodrum Corporation Identity Tag to distinguish him from any stray that might get involved in a round-up. A sleepy fellow, he was named *Lethargic* (*Jic* for short). He liked to curl up in his blanket-padded box under the shower hood. One thing was certain, Jic worshipped Bill.

After gaining official permission to squeeze into a shared berth inside the marina, we purchased a flimsy bar-fire to keep us warm of an evening. Though the solar water heating system was switched off out-of-season, our position afforded us the advantage of mains electricity. Bill and Joyce, on the other hand, chose to spend their "marina money" on a generator (though Joyce grumbled its light was too poor for her to work her tapestry). By remaining on board over Christmas, the Kerslakes were free to tie up on the Town Quay where mooring was cheap. But competition was fierce. Since several yachts awaited their chance of a slot, Bill arranged with friends to radio the anonymous instruction *"MOVE!"* at the first hint of a space. When word came *Energetic's* reaction was characteristically fast and she tied up in the shadow of the castle.

On Thursdays and Fridays, the Town Quay was the venue for the Farmers' Market. Rewarded by the heaping of provender on *Energetic's* deck, Joyce was soon making tea for the marketeers who set up pitch beside her. Bill learned to his chagrin there was little prestige in yacht ownership. His pride was soon tempered by the discovery that these peasant farmers felt only pity for foreign outcasts so destitute as to be condemned to winter on boats.

Some days purple clouds built up over Kara Ada before hail stones as big as pigeons' eggs hurtled down. Amongst the winds most to be feared was the "Southwinder" or Lodos, the most prevalent of the winter gales. Known as the "Scourer of the Seas", legend has it it was the revealer of the Spoonmaker's Diamond that winked so seductively from a black velvet cushion in Topkapı. Long-lasting (sometimes with a break in the middle), the Lodos is brought about by a depression passing to the north and can be dangerous. Lows often hover outside the Aegean for a considerable time before advancing rapidly with little warning. In the fine early and late summer spells it was best to be wary of the gathering or lingering of cumulus cloud in the south west. Often the worst part of a gale comes violently and without warning from the south east and persists for some time. Usually this stage is followed by a short period of calm, a build-up of stratus cloud, a sharp veer to the south west, and then rain, which can be torrential and marked by squalls of extreme violence. Until the recent extension of the harbour arm, severe damage had sometimes occurred, with boats driven ashore. Even the most experienced sailors were capable of underestimating the forces of nature. During one Lodos a fishing boat edged out towards the boat-yard, thinking to stay within the lee of Kara Ada. Its skipper had only saved his ship by hurling grappling hooks onto rocks at the harbour entrance.

Our first experience of a Southwinder began on 21st November when a south easterly began to build. On the 25th and 26th the winds in the marina reached Severe Gale Force 9. Although the central mooring chain held, awnings left up by the foolhardy were torn to shreds. As soon as the wind dropped, we were served with an official order to replace our gale-torn Turkish ensign. Then the heavens opened. Soon it was blowing Storm Force 10, rendering the manhandling of a new gas canister on board impossible. This was the weather that persuaded George not to abandon *Angèle Aline* over Christmas. On *Cappelle* we settled for doubling up on lines and, on Johnny's advice, on commissioning a retired Turkish naval officer to keep an eye on things. As the festive season drew near, one enterprising Bodrum printer produced a yachtsman's Greetings Card showing Santa Claus expressing a wish for the "Goodness Winds" to be with us always. (Turks love Santa Claus, for he is their very own Noël Baba, Bishop Nicholas of Myra, who, famously, is said to have lobbed a bag of gold down a cottage chimney to serve as a dowry for three impoverished daughters – the origin of the Christmas stocking.)

With the intention of purchasing suitable fabric in London I invited Yener-the-Sails to measure for new curtains and covers. We also dropped a line to Talat the Carpet in Istanbul's Street of the Bushy Beard, with whom we had bargained for carpets. He promised free delivery. One day there was a knock on the hull and there stood Talat. Convinced that buying a carpet should be like falling in love, he insisted we unstring the brown paper parcel Bob had put his name on, and again ask ourselves the question, "Does my heart stop?" It still did. Talat was anxious to be off, for the delivery was an excuse to extend his buying area. If he could make enough money, he said, he would buy himself out of National Service and stay "business man".

Istanbul in winter

On our return from London after Christmas Istanbul was a cement-coloured city under a cement-coloured sky – think Los Angeles on a bad day – the air sleet-filled. An hotel's solution to our request for a quiet room was to put us on the fifth floor. Out in search of supper, we had not crossed the street before being accosted with "Are you looking for restaurant, sir?" from the usual over-eager young man.

"Are you English?"

"I like English girls!"

"Why your country not let me in? They send me home!"

"I like your tie!"

"So do I!" said Bob.

They would sell us carpets, they would clean our boots. Though we did not venture far in the bitter streets of shuttered shops, loiterers and corner boys, determined to palm off fake designer perfume or "expensive" shoes, popped out of the pavement. One youth clung like a limpet, hell-bent on off-loading multi-packs of cotton socks:

"We don't want socks! We give you nothing!"

"How much! How much!"

"NO SOCKS! GO AWAY!"

It made no difference until I recalled the strongest negative in Europe "YOK!" at which, grown weary, he melted away. Turning back, we came across the only lokanta open. I was the sole female customer inside and nothing but water was available to drink. But the kebabs served with a lid of pitta bread to keep them hot were delicious.

While we were experimenting with the wall lights in our room, all the lights blacked out. Trying not to dwell on the recent devastating earthquake in Armenia, and the fact that we had no hope of locating a staircase in the dark, I felt my way to the paler square of window in the paper-thin walls. A power cut had swept the whole district. We were fast asleep at 2.30 a.m. when the lights blazed.

Though our aeroplane rose into a leaden sky, somewhere along the way the clouds parted. From Izmir our taxi sped through the wildly beautiful gorge of Cine Çay, the Ancient River Marsyas, tinkling with flute music. Here and there the rich blood of crown anemones (the biblical "lilies of the field") spread cloaks of crimson and Tyrian purple across the puritan grey of the hillsides. Bafa Golu, a vast freshwater lake, was all that remained of the Latmian Gulf. On the slopes of Mount Latmus, Selene the Moon lay with Endymion the Shepherd Boy whom Christianity re-evaluated as a saint, and bore him fifty daughters.

Winter in Bodrum

Back in Bodrum a feeble sun shone and the air struck chill. A further Lodos had resulted in a written request to us to purchase yet another replacement flag. The excitement in our absence had been an earthquake measuring 4.5 on the Richter scale. After mild tremors the police had toured the town ordering the citizens out of their houses. Everyone felt the Big One, one skipper convinced someone fired his engine. Bundling into the street with their bedding, the townsfolk rolled out their barrels and settled down to a street party. George described the event as "the nearest you get in Turkey to a drunken orgy". Indeed everyone had been rather sorry when the emergency ended.

The town choked in clouds of dust as the opportunity was seized to rebuild. I marketed with a handkerchief pressed to my face as buildings were flattened with JCBs or walloped with pickaxes. Shops were extended to run from one street to another to catch trade both ends. Genetically nomadic, the citizens felt none of the sentimental attachment of the Englishman for his castle. Cement, gravel and sand arrived by camel train. Reinforcement rods and packing-cases were dirt cheap, and labour could be kept within a family whenever the itch was felt to bulldoze the house and put it up again somewhere else or, failing that, in the same place in another shape or with an additional floor. Even the older generation revelled in these seasonal upheavals. But one night we heard fire engines careering to a disaster. A whole family had perished in a house explosion. Gas bottles moved to the basement blew its roof off.

Without warning, the town's arterial road was dug up for the laying of drainage pipes. A lorry loaded with sacks of cement, attempting to force a way through, toppled into a trench, wheels spinning. We joined a crowd cheering on the efforts to rock it out. Meanwhile a shepherd drove his sheep through from the other direction, and the lorry stayed put. Confronted by chaos, traders moved elsewhere. I came across my butcher in a back alley. "You find me!" he said gladly, placing a chair. Assisted by a boy he then put on a theatrical display of prime cuts. "I chef too!" he assured me proudly. My leg of lamb was expertly filleted off the bone in medaillons. Rosettes of kidney were added and the lamb, pressed with a flat iron, was arranged in layers between sheets of corrugated paper. I was urged to carry my parcel home flat. We never did locate the coppersmiths to repair the Tilley lamp and sorely missed its warm puddle of light.

Feeling like Bodrum's first cuckoo of spring, I received a warm welcome back from the fabled Western Festival of Christmas. Someone shouted, "Not for twenty days we see you!" Baba Halin, airily rounding down prices, pointed out the cheaper varieties of the new season's produce. But I became aware of disquieting undercurrents. One morning, sensing unease, I turned to see an armed guard boxing in a phalanx of ruffians handcuffed together in threes. "Problem people!" whispered Baba Halin. Eyes averted, shoppers pretended not to notice.

We could no longer afford to treat ourselves to a two-day-old British newspaper and the cost of bread and postage stamps rose daily. At the post office a customer shoved me roughly aside, only to be jerked out of the queue by a member of staff. Waiting for him by the door, the official proceeded to kick him down the steps. Though resort to fisticuffs was never far off (nor, according to Judith, bloody murder at election time), banter was never far away either. I was asked where I got my hat of Dedham reeds,

"It's an English hat!"

"That is not possible! In England you make only umbrellas!"

When my tooth ached, Judith recommended a professor of dentistry back in Bodrum to look after her sick father. I arrived at her surgery over a garage to find her ushering out a small crowd, it being the habit of patients to be supported by their extended families. Embarrassed to see me, she sighed over her equipment's inadequacies, saying of my tooth, "I not touch. I have not the instrument. You must go to your own country." Came the tramp of footsteps on the stairs, and the garage mechanic in his grimy overalls entered to collect a pile of disposable syringes. "It is arrangement we have," she told me. "He use my old syringe. It is best not waste."

Across the road was a butcher who specialised in kıyma (minced meat). This fortuitous discovery came about when Bob asked the garage mechanic to fashion a stainless steel insert for our broken stanchion. Turks were masters at precision copying, no job too small. As Johnny said, "A Turk will fix you up, no matter what!" Crossing the road to consult the English-speaking butcher, elbows on the counter, the mechanic spilt cigarette ash as Bob's blueprint was deliberated. The butcher, a wet cheroot dangling, continued to push spelched lumps of flesh into the mincing machine as he talked, pausing like some mediaeval scullion to smear gory messes along his work surface with a dish-cloth. From time to time carters dumped sacks of opaque-eyed sheep's heads behind the door.

Cappelle's stanchion infill, calibrated to millimetres, was ready within the day.

Every week Chicken Pilaff with Pine Nuts featured on our menu. I would have preferred not to see cages of live pick-your-owns outside the poulterer's, but thought of Freya Stark's remark when cruising in *Elfin* in the 1950s that "one can easily starve" on the coast of Caria. (Reluctantly, she had been obliged to accede to the cook's request for a crate of live hens to be roped on deck.)

My fitness routine was to jog out of the marina gates nodding «Günaydın!» ("Good Morning!") to the gateman, coins jangling in my track-suit pocket for a loaf sprinkled with Love-in-the-Mist seeds to spread with delicious Tam Tad jam purchased from the boy at the bakkal we called "Not-at-all" from his routine politesse. Turning left past the Army Camp above the old Phoenician boatyard, I took the long haul up to the windmills. One morning, a local youth, asking if I was "training for football", joined me, suggesting we run backwards. On the heights I took in the view while the early sun trammelled through mist. On one side lay the village of Gumbet, now little more than a collection point for building materials. Across the water, sunshine winked on the windows of Kos, while beyond the mouth of the Gulf of Gököva the silver sea stretched ad finitum. Standing on this pleasant lea, I heard old Triton blow his wreathéd horn.

On the downward run my regular rendezvous was with two matronly peasants driving their cows to pasture. One was soon chiding me if I was late on parade. While I elbowed through her charges, pointing at the skies she delivered a weather report – not a word of which I understood. But it allowed me to practise my few Turkish phrases, «Çok güzel!» ("Very nice!") the most useful. Then there was the granny who shared a tumbledown cottage with her beast. With her back fixed at right angles by osteoporosis, she moved her head from side to side to see about. As she shuffled up hill on escort duty she raised her walking stick to shake encouragement to Claribelle. One Market Day I met her struggling with loaded bags. Unclasping her fingers I indicated I would carry them for her. Hobbling faster, she chattered away, smacking toothless gums and muttering, «Mandalina!» Accepting her spinal affliction gracefully as the "Will of Allah", she considered no effort too great to treat herself to juicy tangerines.

Seven

Springtime in the Garden of Eden

Farmers' Market

The Farmers' Market transformed Bodrum Town Quay, bordered on one side by boats and on the other by castle and mosque, into a polychromatic boulevard where porphyry and white aubergines, cabbages, beetroots, tomatoes, oranges, apples and quinces lay piled in colour blocks. Stacked alongside them were neat bundles of wild greens – chickweed, mallow, nettle and dandelion, all with culinary use. Responding to the cry of «Beş yüz! Beş yüz!» ("Five hundred! Five hundred!") I clutched a bunch of 500 TL notes (each worth about 20p). Market families slept in their vans. Small boys learned their trade from their fathers. Eyes averted from bundles of ducks and hens with their legs tied, I was served with aplomb by a four-year-old, who bowed before casting surreptitious glances at his father for help in reaching the scales.

«Teşekkür ederim!» ("Thank you very much!")
«Güle! Güle!» ("Go smiling! Go smiling!")
«Allahaısmarladık!» ("And God stay with you!")

At the rear of the market, together with live sheep, pirated cassettes, cheeses and pickles, bring-your-own-jar honey was sold for a few pence a kilo. I bought spices, dried morello cherries, pine nuts, curry powder and saffron, reminded that 2,000 years ago Cleopatra had sat to admire these hillsides mauve-misted with the saffron crocus so sought after by Anthony's men.

At midday we perched on the harbour wall to watch the world go by, each holding a pide, half a loaf sliced lengthwise and flattened with a hot iron before being doused with olive oil and lashed with lettuce, chopped onion and broad-leaf parsley. Layered with sizzling mincemeat and cheese, they were finished off with black pepper, coarse salt and my favourite seasoning, crimson powdered sumac.

It was difficult not to end up saddled with too much provender, especially on a Friday when the stallholders were packing up. When I asked for a kilo of tangerines, a trugload was tipped into one of my shopping bags. Then, after I had paid, the farmer's wife ran after me to fill the other bag with another trugload. The market was not only a source of income, but the glue of social unity. The womenfolk, like ships in sail in their multi-coloured layers, floral şalvar, check jackets and headkerchiefs folded individual ways, made any excuse to attend. Panniers of dandelions were strapped to the backs of self-aware gipsy girls, remarkable for the sequinned brilliance of their tiered skirts. Chanting market cries they chinked gold bangles and coined headbands. (When the bandit hero of Yaşar Kemal's novel *Mehmet My Hawk* asked for essential supplies to set up camp in a cave, they included a mirror for his girl-wife.) A mother from the East showed off her two small sons dressed to the nines in şalvar banded below the knee, hand-knitted leg-warmers in bird-of-paradise colours with tasselled hats to match, and low-slung cummerbunds into which, from their swagger, I knew they longed to thrust yatağans (curved daggers). A granny, who put in a regular appearance, sat cross-legged on a blanket with her treasure-of-the-week laid out before her. Once it was a few sprigs of pennyroyal she freshened with water, and once a dead pole cat.

I developed a passion for flowers. Traders pushed hand-carts of anemones. Soon bluebells followed and the tiny butter-coloured narcissus tazetta whose scent dominated the market for an all-too-short spell. As spring wore on, villagers grubbed up the violet-red orchis laxiflora from the boggy hillsides, boiling their pestelled tubers for salep. (Tasting like boiled vanilla custard, the beverage was sprinkled with sugar and cinnamon and served hot at bus stations.) The flowers provided table displays. Later came country bunches in which bee orchids nestled among the ubiquitous ox-eye daisy of the Turkish postage stamp. I was soon handing over 500 TL to have my arms filled with flowers. While clutching a sheaf of purple stock, I met Yener-the-Sails, who rebuked me for not gathering my own flowers on the asphodel slopes of the acropolis where George gathered mushrooms. In the shady dells, starred with wild lupin and the bruise-blue signal flags of dwarf iris, the lilies-of-the-field were not yet faded.

Yat Lift

Keeping up with maintenance had ensured *Cappelle* was in good nick above deck. But she was due out for antifouling. In partnership with *Energetic*, therefore, we arranged a package deal at Yat Lift to include take out, relaunch, high-pressure hose-down and two weeks' stay on the hard. Lifting, by whatever method, was traumatic. Johnny warned that a boatyard was unlikely to be insured. After submitting photographs of *Cappelle's* underwater profile, we motored into the narrow entrance canal for girthing by the yard boys well before the wind got up. Then the travel lift set both yachts up end to end on the splayed skirts of timber props in a clearing amongst pine trees. What this country park lacked in creature comforts, it made up for in rustic beauty. Both decks were soon carpeted with resinous yellow catkins.

Ideally our task was to rub down the hull and apply two coats of antifoul. For the top sides we must prime bare patches, fill cracks and rub down (twice) before applying a double coat of gloss paint. But the pressure hose revealed damage to the leading edge and foot of the oak rudder, with some delamination along its trailing edge, the worst impairment opposite the propeller. Opinions were offered by all and sundry. One yachtsman diagnosed gribble worm. The yard could not supply boat-builders, but a message was passed to a Frenchman who might help. Our situation now ruled out the simple rub-down. *Cappelle's* hull must be taken back to the wood. With no time to waste, Bob borrowed a disc grinder to tackle the iron keelsome. A gas-powered blow-lamp, also borrowed, was the answer to stripping antifoul. Crouched opposite one another wearing face-masks, Bob with a blow-lamp and me with a scraper, our foreheads braced, we were soon dubbed

"The Gnomes". Some further damage to the oak frame of the bows was disclosed, but the teak hull remained in prime condition. Yachtsmen suggested varnishing to show it off.

Our boats were close enough for the crews to shake hands, while the reverberating thump of Jic's tail on *Energetic's* bows was our morning greeting. At midday we knocked off to buy pide from a fly-infested shack propped up with crates of empty Coke bottles. We then laboured again until dusk. Anyone in the yard obsessed with hygiene would have had cardiac arrest. Knuckling down to the life of a guttersnipe, dust-larking with dogs, I thought it a brave thing to stick my head, woad-blue with antifoul, under the brackish water of the boatyard tap.

Jic was still puppy enough to appreciate his morning descent of *Energetic's* boat ladder slung over Bill's shoulder. He was quick to learn. The growing number of commands he had mastered already reached twenty. Whilst perched on planks over lunch, we put him through his paces before a fascinated audience of Turkish workmen. At the command "Sit!" he slapped down his rear end; at "Speak!" he barked; at "Paw!" (trembling with anticipation for reward was near) he offered his right paw. Then came the moment to throw pide with the command "Stay!" at which he froze. At "Fetch!" he dashed to retrieve the prize and drop it at the thrower's feet. At "Eat!" the pide disappeared in one gulp. It was a riveting performance, its star ever eager for encore.

Our Easter egg, sporting a red bandanna, arrived in the form of raffish Frenchman, Christian Manacci, on his rusty bike. Rapport was instant. Christian, descended from Corsican brigands, was a perfectionist who never let life get him down. Irrepressibly good to have around, his craggy, suntanned face with its warm brown eyes was good to look at too. Propping his bike against a tree and taking charge of our gouvernail (rudder), he proceeded to give us the devoted support of a mentor and friend. In other circumstances it might have been simpler to build a new rudder. But here quality hardwood was unobtainable. Somewhere, by fair means or foul, Christian acquired enough mahogany for a patch, plus a block of seasoned eucalyptus.

Having commandeered pickaxes, Bob and Christian set to work to hew a pit in the iron-hard ground deep enough to lower the rudder off its shank. Clearly visible on its lower edge were the pencil-thick cylindrical holes of that sinister marine mollusc, the teredo. It was a grievous discovery! Nonetheless, Bill, like the joker he was, forced polystyrene bubbles down the largest funnel-shaped hole while Bob's back was turned. Wearing a grave expression, he then clapped him on the shoulder saying sympathetically, "Look, old chap! They've laid eggs!" Completely taken in, we fetched cameras to record this biological horror story! When Bill could contain his mirth no longer, I gave chase.

Meanwhile Christian settled Romany-style cross-legged in the grass jointing a deep leading edge. Yachtsmen, gathering round, assured us that, whether the smaller gribble or the larger teredo, no worm had ever been known to survive more than a week out of water. Suffice to say, twelve days after *Cappelle* was lifted, Christian shouted out he had found a live one! The hammer-headed mini-monster was four inches long. (In warmer seas they can grow to a metre.) I intended to preserve it for posterity, but, with everyone larking about endeavouring to plant it on *Energetic* in Bill's absence, it breathed its last.

Down by the sea a Lodos began to scream. Yat Lift's launching programme was cancelled and in the next yard a gulet was blown off its cradle. That night the rain turned the catkins to pulp. One of the Cabin Boy's jobs was to trek the five miles to Bodrum for chandlery and provisions. Under rainwashed skies I glimpsed the castle ramparts through a screen of mimosa flowers as fluffy as little yellow chicks. To return was easy, for there was a taxi rank outside the marina gates, but to get to Bodrum was not. Once I wimpishly went back to the yard with the excuse I could not find transport, only to be sent off again by Joyce with a flea in my ear and instructions to "keep walking". "Sooner or later you'll be offered a lift! It doesn't matter who from! *JUST TAKE IT!*" I consequently climbed into a van containing four disreputable-looking blackguards who, saying they hoped to see me again soon, dropped me exactly where I asked. One day I was obliged to visit town twice, once to buy paint, and then to return it when it proved old stock. I was lucky to get a lift the second time in Yener-the-Sails's jeep to whose dashboard I clung as, cornering like Schumacher in a temper, he swerved round potholes. Always there were the results of accidents to negotiate, where vehicles had fallen foul of a ditch or rolled into a stack of drainpipes.

After the peace of the country park, Bodrum's urban chaos was disorientating. A paradise garden on split levels with a pool had materialised as part of an improvement scheme. But cows still sifted rubbish from overturned bins in the dust-choked town centre. My attention was caught by a crocodile of British youngsters with learning difficulties. None too politely, the officious nurse-in-charge set about the purchase of a fluorescent tower of lime-green base-ball caps. Well-hatted, but uncomfortable with their surroundings, she led them stumbling off hand-in-hand. I also watched a British zimmer party attempting to cross a pot-holed road and not looking pleased with their lot. A puzzled stall-holder whispered,

"Why these people?"

"Because it's a cheap package and sunshine's good for them!"

Inadvertently, I handed him too much money, whereupon he spread my palm to count into it denominations of lire, explaining the difference, "You must be careful or you will be robbed!" he said. A limousine swished past, the newly elected councillor inside clutching a bouquet. Torn posters flapped on walls while the pavements were littered with discarded election literature from the previous Sunday when the fate of Turgut Ozal's Motherland Party was at stake. Though the Aegean coast remained traditionally liberal-minded, polling had been marred by fundamentalist demonstrations.

With the traditional return of the gulets from the boatyard on the 1st of April, an upheaval was about to commence on the Town Quay. An impressive number of gulets was to be launched. (Anyone commissioning a gulet was entitled to a government grant.) Although their construction of unseasoned pine meant an average life of only six years, investors, many of them farmers, hoped to make a fortune out of the burgeoning tourist trade. Beamy and spacious, with Captain Hook windows in frigate sterns, jutting bowsprits and gingerbread scroll-work, their appeal was pirate-ship. But, although they retained the twin masts tradition demanded, their boom-covers rarely concealed a sail bulge. The modern gulet was equipped with powerful twin engines.

March ended with one of those lambent days without refraction that give the visual impression the air has drained away. The mountains, two-dimensional and sharp-edged, scintillated like cut-glass. The nights were cold, the stars spoked with ice-flower radiance. To me, Orion's Belt formed the diamond-studded cross-trees of a heeling yacht. A day dawned when the temperature rose to seventy degrees. Hearing the sportive shouts of a flotilla crew, I embarked on my first bathe of the season. Entering the water was one thing, but getting out over urchin-infested rocks was another. I did not linger, but enjoyed whistling up the yard twirling a wet towel.

When our renovated gouvernail, an intricate dovetail of oak, mahogany and eucalyptus, lay clamped on bricks in the lee of the hull, Christian set about patching the oak frame of *Cappelle's* bows. Cutting a wedge deep enough to encompass the worm holes, he shaped, screwed and glued. Though work on *Energetic* was finished, blocked by *Cappelle*, she was unable to move off until we moved away. Sadly, we could not, of course, take our rudder hole with us and Bob and Christian were obliged to excavate another.

Since the yard lacked drinking water, our enforced work extension put severe restrictions on our water supply. Soon Bob was talking in terms of "never-ending nightmare". Being the smallest, it fell to me to wriggle supine amongst partying cockroaches as big as horses to paint red lead beneath the keel. When I crawled zombie-like into the köfte-seller's shack, he kicked me the rattan chair he slept in.

Christian, meanwhile, took away the rudder shaft to build up with stainless steel and reinforce with copper sheeting. With copper rivets unobtainable, he utilised steel bolts with the heads sheared as fasteners. His plan was to treat the hull in the traditional Turkish manner as for a gulet by first applying the undercoat Kvik as a key for the filler. After he left, yachtsmen gathered round, insisting Christian was working in the wrong sequence. "The application of antifoul on top of Polymarin is not chemically viable! A sure-fire disaster method!" they warned. Bob reported to Christian, who stuck to his guns. We never had cause to regret our trust in him. Three coats of rubber-based Tekne Astarı ("Hull Primer) laid on with a spatula were rubbed down, with extra

Kvik between coats. With the application to her topsides of International Yacht Paint, *Cappelle's* good looks were restored.

We had hoped to economise by using Turkish antifoul but, with the consistency of melted chocolate, it spread reluctantly and cost more money and effort than Micron 25. An article in a yachting magazine circulating the yard advised the addition of tetracycline to antifoul for extra protection and I was despatched to a pharmacist for one of the fast-selling bubble-packs. My final errand, at Christian's insistence, was to purchase an artist's brush for him to touch up *Cappelle's* name incised in her teak, a task he, proprietorial about her now, undertook with his tongue between his teeth, while we stood behind in case he should step backwards off the trestle in his absent-minded devotion to duty.

There was one further undertaking before relaunch. Since it was three months since we re-entered Turkey, our visas were again about to expire. With Yat Lift also under government sponsorship, we signed *Cappelle* over for the inside of a day in order to board the ferry to Kos. The purchase of a new Tilley, a copy of the *Telegraph* for the Kerslakes, plus a box of Bonio for Jic, still left me time to view the giant plane tree under the likes of which Hippocrates lectured his students.

Launch Day dawned blustery and wet. Those on shore jumped up and down waving their paint rags, and, to Bob's surprise, the yard manager presented him with a farewell bottle of champagne. The breeze was favourable and the sun came out. Christian, self-appointed major domo, slung his bike on board. There is nothing quite like the feel of a boat coming alive. Once out of the canal, cracking open the champagne, we burst into song. I thought of Siegfried Sassoon:

> "Everyone suddenly burst out singing
> And we are filled with such delight
> As prisoned birds must find in freedom
> Winging wildly across the white...
> ...on, on and out of sight."

Just to be at sea was a joy! Those hellish four weeks...every miserable minute...worth it! Nothing beats the joy of the Do-It-Yourself Sailor!

It was strange to pass *Angèle Aline* on her way back to the yard. She should have been gone long since to the Charter Parade in Marmaris. The salutes of George and Meriel lacked spirit. Too heavy for a travel hoist, she had been hauled out by the traditional skid method in which a boat is lined up opposite the slip with lines ashore from bow and stern, The skid, which is in two halves lashed together, is then positioned beneath her. Somehow, its halves split and *Angèle Aline* was dropped, only eighteen inches, but enough to spring her planks. Back at the marina, Christian showed no signs of leaving us. Curled up on a cockpit seat he was soon fashioning a new Sumlog propeller fin from a plastic spoon to replace that snapped off by the yard lads when they carelessly kicked away a prop.

We were eager to start cruising, especially since a neighbouring CB radio interfered with our electrics, but we still awaited Yener's delivery of new curtains and covers in the fabric I had bought back from London (an amount generously in excess of the yardage he quoted). Against my better instincts, and for the sake of immediate comfort, Bob had decreed the refurbishment of the back-rests must await "a second stage". On being reminded of this, Yener's face blanched. He had used up all the material! A further problem was our life-raft. Put in for service locally, it had been forwarded unbeknownst to us to Istanbul by bus and had not so far been returned.

In the marina a reverberating row erupted. Flotilla crews knuckling down to yacht preparation were behaving as if they owned the place. But House Rules were not to be flouted. Catching a flotilla girl emptying a bowl of detergent into the yacht basin, the marina pasha gave her due warning. When, in defiance, she did it again, he ordered the yacht's expulsion. The flotilla company referred the case to the State Governor – who, imposing an additional fine, upheld the pasha's decision.

Signs of summer increased. A cherished memory was of a Clint Eastwood type in a leather hat striding to the end of the pontoon to the tumpetty tump of Bodrum's Junior School Percussion Band relentlessly practising for Çocuk Bayram (the Children's Festival). Bracing himself for embarkation, Dirty Harry, his parrot, spread his legs to get a better grip on his master's shoulder.

In town the dust settled. "New York! New York!" blared from loudspeakers and a MISS GLOBAL UNIVERSE banner straddled Tourist Alley. I was sickened to see a market granny menaced with cameras. A tourist in a bra-top and shorts, trilling, "Are you all right, dear?" poked her in the ribs as if she were a circus act. I had gone right off Theme Parks. Too many visitors, looking upon their air fare as entry fee, persisted in seeing unfamiliar customs as put on for their entertainment. Pizza and chips had replaced traditional Turkish cooking, while competition burned fierce among gulet skippers. Among standard customer enticements, such as "Free Beer", "Free Wine" and "Shiny Sea", a star attraction was "Dirty Water Tank", referring to a holding tank. (Tourists could be fussy about effluent pumped into the water in which they were about to bathe.) The crudest exchange I overheard was between two yobs in Union Jack shorts:

"Well, I'll tell yer one thing, mate. I'm that disappointed! I 'aven't 'ad me f*****' leg over once!"

"Tough s***, lad! 'Av 'ad three int' last fortneet!"

"It wer me own fault reely! A wer joost too f*****' droonk to do aht ab'aht it!"

Away from the tourist trail, life remained pleasantly normal. On hearing a faint sound when purchasing curry powder from a pokey little shop in an alleyway I peered over the counter. Behind it a contented baby made sucking noises from inside a cardboard box. He was lifted up to be admired by his adoring fifteen-year-old mother. She told me her husband, who was seventeen, was a fisherman. She hoped for more babies soon. I thought of what the British tabloids would make of "CARDBOARD BOX BABY UNDER COUNTER IN DARK ALLEY". The use of the curry was not merely culinary, but also aesthetic. We were repainting the deck. With non-slip paint unobtainable, we had created our own brand, adding sand from a building site, plus curry powder to perfect that special shade of duck-egg blue. One skipper, teasing me about the "missing factor" in his own deck paint, never failed to sniff the air on boarding *Cappelle*. Similarly, Nescafé powder proved a useful addition to epoxy when rendering a cap-rail repair invisible.

Turkbükü

Johnny and Judith were engaged in setting up the wattle-roofed house that graced a hillside in Turkbükü as a permanent home for their retirement. Johnny maintained a presence since the foreman took to drink if left unsupervised. Their plan was to add another storey and put in electricity. Things were now progressing well. A camel train (complete with baby camel) had lately delivered a load of sand. A terrace to hold a water tank was also under construction, after the original plan of sinking a well had foundered with accusations from a local factor of trying to tap into his master's spring. (Ominously though, planning permission had lately been granted for the building of eleven holiday villas on an adjoining plot.)

Occupied by a workforce from Eastern Turkey, who lived on site, Camp Turkbükü, put together from materials not yet in use, was even more fascinating than the main house. From the spreading branches of the tree that formed its roof, cooking utensils dangled. A central fireplace of bricks had been improvised, together with a table made of brick piles with a door laid across. Bedsteads had been commandeered and a porcelain soup tureen (tactfully replaced by Judith with something more suitable in aluminium) raided from the cache of family dinner service. The workmen, small, thin and berry-brown itinerants, wore woollen pillbox hats and baggy, tight-banded nether garments that drooped between the legs. Unpopular with the Aegean Turks, they were reminders of the East of bride-price, polygamy and blood feuds.

Invited to lunch with Johnny and Judith, a taxi took us to Myndus Bay, where *Amazon's* launch awaited us. After lunch, refreshed with water from a Gilbey's gin bottle in a Colonial-style holster, we swam in a secluded creek amongst bright orange fish until Judith brought out the Book Swap Bag beloved of yachtsmen. Since acquiring a paperback stamped "HM Prison Wormwood Scrubs", I was interested in book plates almost as much as books!

Our cruising preparations gained momentum. Bob called on the local barber and I visited the hamam on Ladies' Afternoon. In *Portrait of a Turkish Family* Irfan Orga wrote of accompanying his grandmother as a young boy when, every two weeks, marshalling her servants to prepare an elaborate picnic, she devoted a whole day to the hamam. Grandmama was so particular about food that, if any dish were not up to scratch, it would be cast aside with cries of, "Fit only for Christians!" Accordingly to Irfan, it was far from true that a young blade knew nothing of the charms of the girls within his circle, for the hussies were in the habit of parading naked in front of the mothers of the boys they fancied in the certainty their vital statistics would be passed on.

Cubicles opened from a reception area. Each contained a day bed, a pair of wooden clogs, a mirror, clothes hooks and a towelling robe. When, suitably attired, I pulled open an inner door, the blast of jungle heat knocked me back. On summoning up the courage to try again, I found myself in the steamy circular chamber of the hararet. Booths around the perimeter were furnished with a marble bench, a plugless sink, a tin bowl and a pair of ferociously high-pressure hot and cold taps. Water gushed everywhere. I was washing in a restrained boarding-school manner when in strode the hamam attendant who, pressing me down onto the bench, threw water over my head and chucked more up the walls to demonstrate that now was the time to cast aside my inhibitions. Being too much of a novelty to leave to my own devices, she then gave me and my hair a boisterous spring-clean. Feeling I had already completed a ninety-minute cycle in a washing machine, she tugged me to a central slab where I was laid out and re-soaped. The vigorous loofah scrub that followed caused dirt to roll off me like the rubbings from an eraser. Next, back in the cubicle, came a mind-bending massage, followed by a lively triple rinse. Here I entered into the spirit of the thing and, best mates by now, we flung water at each other. Finally, she unpinned her long hair, indicating it was my turn to wash hers with my shampoo. I was not permitted to escape until I had rested in an anteroom where women flipped through damp periodicals. When I did venture outside, the air struck chill. Had I really thought the day hot? As I scrambled over slit trenches, I resented the dust that gathered on my skin. Such a definitive ablution should guarantee immunity.

Cappadoccia

Faced with further delay over the freeing of an injector, we seized the chance to take the night coach to Cappadoccia in Central Anatolia, the fairy land in the geographical heart of the steppe,

> "Magic casements, opening on the foam
> Of perilous seas, in faery lands forlorn."

"Have a biscuit!"

The coach driver swivelled round to offer me a chocolate digestive. He followed up by spraying my hands with lavender water. As the bus powered along, I thought of Père Guillaume de Jerphanion, the Jesuit scholar, who, coming by chance on Cappadoccia on a journey by horseback in the summer of 1907, wrote, "Our eyes were astounded: I remember those valleys in the searingly brilliant light running through the most fantastic of all landscapes." A Salvador Dalian panorama with a higgledy-piggledy skyline of tufa dwellings and fairy chimneys greeted us. In such a fertile paradise, stranger than fiction, at the heart of barren lands, an exiled prince in seven-league boots might seek strawberries in December.

Marvelling at the rupestrian architecture of Göreme, and at the play of light on the eroded tufa of the red-coned village of Zelve, we discovered a Secret Valley; descended into an Underground City and explored once-upon-a-time Mustafapaşa whose air of melancholy made me feel as ephemeral as that sad city. Returning home through the brutal vastness of the steppe, we broke our journey at Konya to enter the monastery of the Whirling Dervishes, not without trepidation since Konya had recently been involved in murderous fundamentalist demonstrations. But its citizens treated us with a courtesy far beyond the call of duty, a stranger ordering the laying of exquisite carpets on the dirty pavement so that we might sit and take tea during Ramazan.

Eight

The Gulf of Gököva

South West Turkey

At noon on a dull mid-May day we made haste to escape the womb of Bodrum marina to sail the southern quarter of the western Turkish seaboard. To test stowage, we set out north to Bitez where rose-alabaster flamingos paddling in the shallows were reflected "uppity down down", as my son used to say, their attenuated legs vanishing into their inverted images. After a slight bump, hands grabbed the cap-rail and the sweet face of an English girl popped up: "Oops! Ever so sorry! You wouldn't think I was a sailing instructor, would you?" This was our introduction to the Bitez Dinghy Sailing School. "Not to worry! But I've told my class to use you as a race marker. Bye!" and she was off. Class of mid-May '89 followed in short order, some cannoning into *Cappelle*, some not.

When all had departed for the last time, I slid into the water, clear over a reed bottom, not good holding. Our stowage had been so efficient, it took us twenty minutes to find pudding packed in an egg-carton. I awoke late and lay watching the watery reflections on the cabin ceiling and sunshine balloons on the walls. *Cappelle* at anchor, nosing into the citrus-scented breeze as it changed from offshore to on, revolved silently, the scene panning by, the cabin full of gentle glugging sounds. The floor shifted, lacking gravitational pull. Suspended in a bubble supported by opposing energies, I felt secret and secure. Though wide-awake, I felt feather-light and disassociated, a sensation that on land is the privilege of the dreamer.

1 Above: Death of the schooner, Lavrion.

2 Puppy love, Lavrion.

3 Cappelle *and the Rock of Monemvasia.*

4 Special occasion table setting.

5 Forty winks at dawn for Ursula.

6 Ursula paints red lead beneath the keel.

7 Above: Bob varnishes the
mast.

8 Bob investigates a little
problem with the engine.

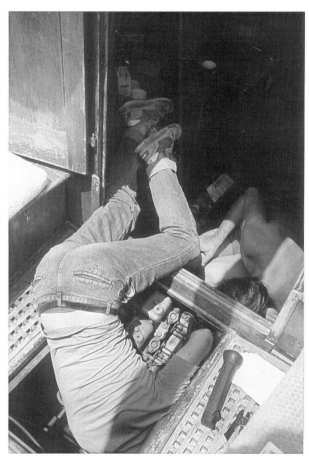

9 Mother and baby camel in festive dress, Cappadoccia.

10 Live-aboards hold their Christmas party in a land base.

11 Wacky graduates to Ship's Cat.

12 Below: Wacky comes home after a night out.

13 *William and Melanie, brother and sister.*

14 *Oops!* Cappelle's *neighbour founders in the night, Torba.*

15 Ursula nurses the
damage.

16 Below: Wacky
catches his own tea.

Gulf of Gököva

From Bitez we turned south and set course southeast for the Gulf of Gököva, a jagged forty-mile gash in the western Turkish seaboard, one of the world's most unspoilt cruising grounds. Such hamlets as there were communicated by sea, as did the ancient cities, and in winter not at all. Anthony and Cleopatra cavorted here in their salad days. On its northern side a 3,000 mountain wall rose steep-to, while the southern shore was as remote and wild. It is said that to explore Gököva takes a week, a month, or a lifetime. It is essential to provision well.

Around the coast of Western Turkey the Etesian winds blow in an arc, almost due north in the north, while gradually westering towards the south to surge up the main gulfs, making them easier to get into than out of as the winds are constantly drawn towards the land mass. Though they lose strength towards the spade-shaped estuarial marsh at the head of the gulf, they can gust over the mountain wall with gale-force ferocity. Johnny had furnished us with the Coptic List of Gales taken from the Turkish Naval Hydrographic Office calendar. Based on a mixture of astronomical and astrological phenomena, many yachtsmen logged it to check for accuracy, the general consensus being that gales did tend to occur as listed, some more regularly than others with a margin of error either side of a day or so. The names of the more reliable gales reveal their ancient origins.

We first crossed the Aegean at the time of the Swallow Gale, a sign of spring, preceded by the Old Wives' Gale of mid-March and followed by the Gossips' Gale of the second week of April. The Last Rain Gale, due on 13th May, had passed. The next, the Red Plum Gale, was not due until the end of July. In September comes the Quail Gale and, at the beginning of October, the gale known as "When the Rams Go to the Ewes". During the third week of the month, a southerly, the Meryemana Fırtınası (the Virgin Mary Gale), possibly with a break in the middle, is a certainty. (Johnny annotated it as a bad one.) A gale on 7th November marks the onset of winter, and on 9th December the Falling (Oak) Leaves' Gale confirms it. The year is brought to a close by the Black Winter Gale of 12th December. It is also to be remembered that gales can occur at any time and that strong winds in the Aegean may be very localised, especially in summer, yachts not far apart individually experiencing near gale and no wind at all.

By tea-time we were within the mouth of the Gulf. The Pilot described Karcicik Bay as deserted. But, though the season had scarce begun, it was already occupied by two gulets and a catamaran. On shore amid signs of boat-building, a donkey wheezed and a goatherd, roughly clad as in a nineteenth century drawing, shinned up and down the rocks with an unruly kindergarten of thirty-six kids. Dutifully tying ourselves to Turkey, a tree trunk, we prepared to settle for the night, dismantling the sun-awning when it gave too much windage.

We awoke to the sound of goat bells and Daniel Defoe leading his herd back to the hills. At breakfast something fluttered before my eyes. A pretty linnet, presumably mistaking the cabin doors as entry to a shady spot beneath trees, had flown in. Paralysed with fright, it came to rest on my plate, eyes tight shut, willing this terrifying new world to go away. Wriggling out of my shirt to lay over it, I carried it to the aft hatch. The bird never moved as I disentangled its claws. Around us lay forest, but the newcomer stayed, bending to the sway of the boat. An hour later it hopped onto a coil of rope to preen. But the moment Bob untied the dinghy, it flew off.

We made for Çökertme (pronounced "Chuck-ert-mie", but known as "Cocoa Time" by British yachtsmen). Although I searched the waterline for Çökertme's dark curdle of trees on a plateau, it was a flotilla on the move that led us in. Since we aimed to dine ashore, we devoted two hours to making sure the anchor was dug in. Free transport was a tradition. Kapitani Ibrahim, owner of the shore-side restaurant, was at pains to suit his launch's flag to each visiting yacht, a nicety which assured him the patronage of her crew. A portly figure with a waterfall moustache and boot-blacked coiffure, he affected the knee-booted garb of a Barbary Corsair: şalvar worn with belted over-tunic, embroidered waistcoat and a sash stuck with pistols which he fired to let off steam while dancing. His soirées were a family affair, Mrs Ibrahim keeping both her spouse and her customers well fuelled with rakı. Daughterly talent lay in carpet-weaving. A loom displayed a half-finished work. Completed articles were flung to the ground to dance on or to purchase (preferably both). Under trees hung with fairy lights a nargile (bubble pipe) was handed round. Ibrahim, in the knowledge that he was in charge of transport, let his clients set the pace.

The fiddlers upped tempo as the evening wore on. For a cabaret turn Ibrahim cavorted with a brown-legged girl in gipsy skirts whose eyes were familiar. Who should she be but Christian's sister, Aysha, come from Marseilles with her children to spend the summer? French-speaking children crowded round: "My Mummy's thirty-three. How old are you? Have you got television? Have you got CB radio?" Receiving negative answers to the important questions, they soon lost interest. Two more children belonging to Christian's cousin, Claudine, were also aestivating chez Manacci. These, together with his own boy and girl, meant that Christian was entertaining a litter of eight youngsters on board his chalutier *Corail of Caen*. He himself was away to Izmir to collect Grandmère. With her arrival, the family would be en fête. It appeared he had "bought a house" in Çökertme. When we saw it, we thought it purchased with the money earned from *Cappelle* – leaving plenty to spare, for it was a ruined sheepfold.

While Bob repaired a fault in the echo sounder, I sank into the sea to be out of the way of the insects that plagued us. At night we kept a can of Raid handy and I was up before dawn to light a second mosquito coil. Echo sounder fixed, we hauled ourselves ashore by means of the long line tying us to Turkey to follow donkey pats along flat rocks across the neck of the headland. Claudine swung towards us in a kirtled skirt, a wicker laundry basket on her hip. Dark-eyed, with Titian ringlets bouncing on her shoulders, she looked as if she had emerged from the gipsy encampment in *Carmen*. "L'eau douce!" she announced blithely, on her way to a Nereid spring issuing from the recesses of a cave. Singing as she rubbed, she spread washing out to dry on a thorn bush. In the village we met Aysha in heliotrope şalvar. Waif-like, with rings under her eyes, she seemed, as Bob said, too fragile to be the mother of four children, the youngest a hyperactive half-African boy. When we asked Christian her story, he shook his head distressfully, saying only that it was "very sad".

Below Ancient Ceremos the chimney of a coal-fired power station was a rare excrescence to blight the Gulf. From then on the wall of mountains dropped sheer all the way up the northern coast, with only one possible, though unsafe, anchorage. We crossed towards Değirmen Bükü, a large bay indented with coves, seeking a land-locked cleft whose dark waters were known as "English Harbour". Surrounded by rolling hills, with glimpses of distant mountains reminiscent of Scotland, it had an exciting history as a refuge for British submarines who were given a nod and a wink by Turkey during the Aegean War. That evening two hunting dogs playing hooky poached along the sedge. Guilt comically written all over their faces when apprehended, they ran off with their tails between their legs. Then we were alone in the light of a tarnished moon.

I swam out to admire our new blue curtains next day before we made our way to the jetty of a back-water restaurant in the bay. Here the scenery changed to Windermere. Shade-giving trees flanked a strand backed by hollyhocks and roses. White clouds puffed in the blue sky. But there was a difference. At siesta time veiled women curled up in the grass and a granny sat on a wall drawing sheep's wool onto a distaff. A visitor, anxious to sketch her, gave her a bar of Cadbury's chocolate, with an indication that it should be kept out of the sun. But Granny was so proud of her trophy she kept it beside her where we watched it melt.

Pursuing pine-needled trails that, often as not, petered out, we set off to ramble in the magnificent forest. A track led to salt marshes and a valley where, between corn and maize fields, a brackish channel struggled towards the bay. Terrapins sunning themselves made popping noises as they plashed into pools at our approach. Between the Byzantine fronds of young bracken comatose tortoises crouched like big brown cowrie shells. Many were dead. Nearer shore, dragonflies darted and mating butterflies danced like the petals of periwinkles before settling momentarily, letting their wings fall apart like an open book. Deep inside, the brooding forest was airless. Despite etching arrows in the dust of the main track, we missed the trail. In order to orientate ourselves, we forced our way upwards through virgin terrain over rocks, tree roots, dead timber and around bushes with enormous spines, ducking spider webs, whose owners I, for one, had no wish to meet, until we were able to glissade over the watershed on tinder-dry pine needles. When I put out my hands to save myself, I was stabbed by thorns, so settled for bruises. Soon we were choosing our own line, Bob progressing so far ahead that communication was by bird call. By the time heavy globules of thunder-rain were falling, we recognised a tethered pony and found ourselves on home ground in the grasslands of the lakeside. Caught in a shaft of sunlight against a blueberry sky, *Cappelle* stood out in relief.

Our mission had been to seek out the Perfume of Mohammed in the form of a strand of fragrant amber trees "at the head of the bay". But we were learning that vagueness in the Pilot meant its author had failed personally to check his information. *Cappelle*, shaded by the stupendous trees of the genus Boswellia was, in fact, moored right beside one of the few places in the Eastern Mediterranean where frankincense grows.

All afternoon it teemed with rain, the storm centred across Gulf. Treading water in an early lull, I looked down **Değirmen Bükü**, on one side tree-covered hills, on the other side scrub. Forested until recent years, it marked the site of wildfires (said by some to have been caused by the cigarettes of yachtsmen). A drop in temperature left us shivering and the wind rose. Soon official gale warnings were out.

The restaurant allowed us fresh water from a stand-pipe and sold day-old bread. That night we dined under the frankincense trees on clay-baked kid. Cooked in an open pit, it "came off the bone like the petals of a rose". For a small fee, the restaurateur, who farmed in the valley, agreed to give me a lift when he drove up Gulf to **Soğut** (Place of Willows) to top up on provisions. We crossed the mountain ridge in a four-by-four by forestry track, impassable in winter, he told me. Except for eggs and yoghurt, there was little to buy. I had not the heart to ask for one of the domestic duck which quacked in the stream. And the balık (fish) in a pool were "Hotel Only". Back in **Değirmen Bükü**, a friendly German bartered a bottle of wine for a scrawny chicken.

Since a charter yacht had sailed off with one of its legs, the jetty was in danger of collapse when more shelter-seekers arrived. A gulet forced itself in beside us. To make amends, the jolly Kapitani hauled us through the window of his wheelhouse to meet fellow countrymen, a Sunmed party from Huddersfield. Pale bodies crashed into the water, leading Bob to muse on what it was that made showing off part and parcel of the male tourist's psyche. He was button-holed by Ginger-nob with sunburned feet whose stock phrase, referring to anything and everything, was "...and I don't mind paying". Bob, cross-questioned as to the value of each yacht – *Cappelle* not counting – caused delighted exclamations of, "Cor! 'Ow 'bout that then! A quarter of a million! 'Arf a million! Cor!" On our other side was a Love Boat chartered by Izmiri business men for the entertainment of leggy model girls – a sort of short-break floating harem. In the daylight hours bikini-clad lovelies showered, jived and did aerobics on the pontoon. Around midnight, reverberating to pop music and squeals, the Love Boat removed itself to anchor less publicly.

Moving up gulf, we found it difficult to separate Castle Island from Snake Island at Şehir Adaları (City Islands), site of Ancient Cederae, while keeping a close eye out for the half-submerged, razor-backed hazard known as "Duck Rock" which had spelt doom to many a yacht. A letter from Libby, describing the sacrilege lately committed in the siting of a holiday village at Taş Bükü (Stone Bay), once Cederae's necropolis, gave us our bearings. After failed attempts to drop anchor onto a sovereign patch of golden sand where it would dig in, we negotiated shoal water and the remains of an antique mole, to anchor off in congested East Bay. Here, watching boats disgorging day-trippers at the landing stage, we bided our time. In late afternoon the traffic dried up. One by one, gulets and yachts left for safe anchorage. To stay courted trouble, but, having achieved this fantastic location all to ourselves, we crept inshore and tied to a tree, dropping anchor with only a foot to spare between keel and sea-bed. Keeping watch, for *Cappelle* yawed and the breeze died late, we dozed uneasily, aware of the graunch and shift of the anchor chain.

After Caesar's murder in 44 BC, Anthony, his most brilliant general, and Cleopatra, Queen of Egypt, pursued their pleasures in the Roman province of Asia Minor. Cleopatra was smitten, so it is said, with the beauties of Cederae. All it lacked was the perfect beach. With queenly extravagance, so the legend goes (for a monarch who rinses her sails in rose water is not to be put off by logistics), she commanded galleys to bring sand from the Sahara to furnish its bewitching cove. At five a.m. we scampered across the isthmus. Sheeting the sloping sea-bed, the aquamarine water deepened to green and blue until, forsaking the cove, it joined the ultramarine of the Gulf in a ruler straight line. Stretched on the surface, I looked down three fathoms, still seeing the pristine ramp on which not a weed grew. Only the tumble of rocks on the eastern shore marred the water's flawlessness by casting black shadows that shortened as the sun rose.

For the idyll not to be spoilt, we must be away before midnight struck (or rather eight a.m.). But, anxious to explore the amphitheatre before the day-boats plied their trade with the bucket-and-spade brigade and the serried rows of litter bins filled, we delayed until the last moment to chase across the saddle of land. It was wise to proceed with caution, for an ill-judged step meant to plunge through a curtain of Old Man's Beard into the foundations of a Temple of Apollo. I sat on a fallen log feeling the first person in the world ever to notice the half-buried capital at my feet, before raising my eyes from a treasure-in-the-grass (commonplace amid so much history) to look down the empty Gulf sparkling with sea sapphires. A snake did a lightning squirm. And when the tinkle of a bell made us start it was only a goat in a bramble bush. At the heart of the bois dormant lay the amphitheatre. Olive trees, so ancient as to seem part of the archaeology, corkscrewed through the antique rubble that covered the proscenium. A mile and a half away across the water the mountains, lilac pink in the early light, formed its backdrop.

Fleeing at last like fugitives from reality, we hoisted sail into the roller-coaster seas of the Gulf. West of Windy Island lay Honey Water Bay. Since there was an apparent choice of mooring, we circled, to the exasperation of a woman on shore. Snatching off her white headscarf (commerce counting for more than culture), she circled it round her head while hallooing us, to Bob's annoyance, to tie up in an awkward position on the end of Restaurant Çardak's jetty. Rival restaurants were vying for trade. The other's whipper-in was absent, so it paid the price.

Çardak might translate as "Shack on Stilts" but its garden, thanks to the purity of the local spring water, was a true paradise. On top of a mudbank Melek, our whipper-in, had created a petrol-can parterre of arum lilies, geraniums and giant flame-coloured dahlias. The breeze shook flower petals down like confetti and ducks swam across, followed immediately by a Sahil Güvenlik (Coastal Protection Vessel) to check our papers. (At this time the BBC World Service was reporting a diplomatic row. Turkey, a member of NATO, was refusing the examination of an advanced combat plane landed in Turkey by a Russian defector.)

Dining that night under the pergola, the first I knew of Melek's approach was when she twisted her fist in my hair and buried her nose in it before pulling up a chair and asking how many children we had. The answer did not matter, for the information she wished to impart was that she and her bey, Yusef, had three strapping sons, one "diplomat", one at the University of Istanbul, and the third (I suspected the cleverest) stayed home. Built like an Amazon, Melek was strong-featured, youthful and fierce, so much the equal of any man that I thought the blood of the Yoruks, the Turcomen nomads who lived in such insecurity that both sexes were brought up as leaders, must flow in her veins.(Yusef, I suspected, took a back seat.)

Beyond the football pitch I came upon the sort of petunia-bordered pavements that would have graced a suburban housing estate. When I crossed the stream by its nursery-rhyme bridge, terrapins belly-flopped into pools. But as I drew level with a row of Toy Town lych gates leading to cuckoo-clock chalets with weather-eaves and looped lace curtains, I found the unfortunate brook choked with cardboard boxes and household detritus. These were the discards of the Marmarian matrons who overflowed the basket chairs set out on their dinky holiday-home verandas.

A solar-heated shower serviced by a tank on the restaurant roof was a feature of Melek's garden. Tripping forth in my bikini, I soaped myself in front of a blank-eyed party of men sipping coffee under the pergola. Heated water was a luxury (in Alexander the Great's time only granted to women post partum). But it was not my day, for, with a sneeze and a cough, the nozzle spluttered dry. As I stared in disbelief, Melek's son heaved himself up to make an inspection indoors. The roof tank was empty. He had barely suggested hosing me down straight from the spring before he was treating me to a prolonged blast of pressurised snow-water.

In the evening we filled up with Soğut's honey water for sparing use. The night was noisy. After capturing a German yacht, *Sommerwind*, Melek saw to it that the crew caroused until dawn when we slipped away, weighing anchor for the seventeen-mile run down the Gulf taking a bearing on Cape Balisu light for Yedı Adaları (Seven Islands). Though, under such conditions, there was little to worry about, we could see why the pilot urged caution by day and forbade all approach to the southern shore by night. The prevailing north westerlies could howl here, setting up considerable seas in waters bristling with razor-edged reefs, rock needles and too many concealed obstacles to bear thinking about. Paying strict attention to all sources of information: the Admiralty Chart, the Turkish Waters Pilot and the Turkish Chart, we attempted to coordinate the most hazardous features of each, while remembering that the scales varied from fathoms to metres and feet (the undoing of many a yacht).

Crossing unscathed through the Seven Islands, we penetrated a fiord leading to Saklı Liman (Hidden Harbour). Pulling forward the echo sounder, I crouched in the cockpit, excited when the fathom count failed to register and panicking when it changed to feet. Where were the three clear metres the pilot promised? Before hysteria overcame me, we were inside the lagoon and back in ten to fifteen feet of water. Here we found bilge-keel *Islay Mist* in situ. *Cappelle* was playing gooseberry, for her pony-tailed captain and a Close Friend were disporting themselves in their birthday suits engaged in the foreplay of caressing each others' tresses. Ruining an idyll or not, we were not willing to chance our arm going straight out again. Lonely Saklı was described as a bird sanctuary, haunt of all manner of feathered vertebrates. But in the three days we lingered, we saw not a bird. A fisherman's camp had also vanished.

The sandbar took possession of Bob's dreams. Plagued with nightmares, he shouted, "We're locked in! We can't get out!" Shallow-draught *Islay Mist* retreated, and I idled in an eyeshade and suntan lotion while Bob struck out on a long-haul swim to reconnoitre the sandbar. In the evening we rowed back for a more detailed survey. It was clear *Cappelle* had crossed the bar more by luck than judgement. There could be no margin of error if we were to exit the fiord in safety. Keeping the tip of the northern entrance at a precise angle of ninety degrees with the extremity of the southern shore, we stuck rigidly to a line. A nervous passage through Vlad impalers brought us the freedom of the Gulf once more. Ghosting south, we cleared Mortuary Point.

A banner on poles beside a padlocked caff on the far shore of Amazon Creek announced "CAMP AMAZON". Though praising the creek's marvels, the pilot was oddly vague, a sure sign, we now knew, that its author had failed to verify what he was talking about. The clarity of the water revealed how quickly the sea-bed shelved. In anything stronger than the light breeze that funnelled through its high-sided entrance, the anchorage would be untenable. We had difficulty in identifying any sort of passage to the much praised "inner creek" which, the pilot assured us, even gulets might penetrate "with care".

On shore I followed "YACHT SERVICE" arrows on trees. There were signs of the abandonment of a large-scale complex. Posters showed crocodiles with big teeth, and I met two Safari Trucks driven by guys in tee-shirts proclaiming them "Jungle Wardens". The trail ended at Base Camp, consisting of a set of toilets palisaded with breeze block, a deserted kiddies' roundabout and an empty paddling pool. In a deckchair beside a caravan, a crinkle-permed British grandmother, lips pursed, ankles crossed, sat knitting a cardy with the air of one intent on kidding herself she was back on her own doorstep. The bars were devoid of customers. Yacht Service did not mean provisions available on site, but, if furnished with a List of Requirements, a Great White Hunter would be despatched to Marmaris to buy what was required (or, more likely, its poor substitute). When I asked for a loaf of the advertised "village bread", a search produced a pan containing something black and unleavened best put to use as a door-stop.

To be sure of missing nothing of the Amazon Experience, I crossed a rustic footbridge to skirt a perimeter wire and hail Bob from the other side of the lagoon. When I told him the inner creek was less than four feet wide and, I suspected, not more than two feet deep, ending in a dried up ditch, he plainly did not believe me! It was too late in the day to leave. Moreover I had a point to prove. We spent a precarious night before manning the dinghy. (I had omitted to tell him I witnessed a rowing boat ground itself.) Though we kept within a stick-marked channel, we poled off bottom. Within the inner creek had once been a basin, but so long ago that mature trees grew on two-thirds of it. When we sounded the stagnant brook which ran round the eastern edge its depth averaged eighteen inches. So much for berthing gulets! At my smug insistence Bob pulled manfully until in sight of the footbridge. Here ended Expedition Amazon.

Büyük ("Big") Çatı was a pleasure to come. As soon as we realised that the pilot, muddling his "Bigs" and "Littles" had given sailing instructions for the unnavigable Küçuk ("Little") Çatı, we knew it was up to us to sort ourselves out. Then a small island, which refused to separate from the land behind until we changed tack, slid aside like a secret panel enabling us to nose our way through the hillside into a kidney-shaped lagoon. From the rim of its crater I looked down on the widening waters of the Gulf. A brown bear had lately foraged Büyük Çatı's sylvan shoreline until its mate was killed on the newly constructed road beyond where the sun struck beams off a bottle mountain. Fishing boats were drawn up on a pebbled strand. In the orchid light of evening the fishermen's camp fire became a focal point. *Cappelle*, hitched to a silver birch, did not budge an inch. At dawn, the visibility brilliant, the sky magnesium blue, every shimmering leaf etched and every pebble clear on the sea-bed, I became aware of the sound of a truck engine. A child shouted and a woman sang a song of glee. The cause was explained when a refrigerated container lorry, to be met by a party of fishermen hammocking a sand shark, backed under the trees. We rowed over, hoping for smaller fry, but the truck had taken the whole catch. Balık was «Yok!». The fishermen offered to fish for us later.

The anticipated south easterly failing to materialise, we motored twenty-three miles down Gulf to Kormen, the conditions saving us from turning beam on to confused seas that piled up garbage and tar. Scruffy Kormen was at best a useful staging post. There was little to do but fish and swat flies. A child sent to meet the car ferry was ignored as passengers embarked on a bus to cross the peninsula to Datça. Feeling sorry for her, I told her we would eat at her father's lean-to on the hillside, where I spent the meal flipping over miniature flying armadillos that hit the bug-zipper before falling supine.

That night a pair of donkeys rasped like rusty saws as *Cappelle* swayed in the rising wind. We awoke to a sky streaked with mares' tails. Then the wind veered into the Lodos position before mounting to a steady roar. The psychological affect of the southerlies was dispiriting. Unlike the invigorating meltem, however hard they blew their taste was lifeless. Next day came a blessed north westerly and viridian seas. A flotilla boat on free-sailing put in. Its skipper, airing his woes, showed us the inadequate diagram of Kormen (described as "always safe and comfortable") with which he had been furnished. Forty knot winds had come as a shock, and without log, proper chart, echo sounder or binoculars, the coastline had presented problems.

A taxi took us to Datça for provisions and lunch in a pide salonu. Its proprietor, whose cast of feature was recognisable from many a Byzantine painting, his eyes as dark as a peat lochan, kept half an eye on his child outside in a pedal car. Given his father's ignition keys, the little boy, whenever he felt the need for security, trotted in calling, «Baba! Babaçi!» ("Dad! Daddy!"), gravely hanging the keys on a hook before removing them again and running back outside. None were so popular as us in the supermarket where the size of our order brought the compliment of a tray of tea and sent boys scampering up ladders to deal with requests for anything useful we could see. Bowed out, we were assured all would be delivered to our taxi.

The sea was soon breaking over Kormen mole. We were not in sole occupation of the harbour long, however, for gulet *Öguz* put in, charging over our stern line at full throttle. It took all our strength to hold her off while Bob yelled at the deck hand to put out fenders (though sitting on a pile of them the lad did not seem to know what they were for), and shouted at the Captain to "For God's sake get a line on!" whereupon he tied the leeward warp first and *Oğuz* swung down on us, the scene ridiculous for the harbour was empty. Tales abounded of the new breed of farmer gulet-owner taking out charter parties on the strength of a tractor licence. We suspected Captain Öguz, the first gulet driver seen wearing a cap decorated with scrambled egg, fell into this category. His gulet had been hired by a party of Turks. From the way they addressed him, we realised he was even less in their favour than ours. With picture hats clutched in the driving wind, the women posed coyly for camcorders. Then the group's mood changed big time and they wrenched off their baggage in a glorious, gesticulating row-to-end-rows. They would hire a better gulet in Datça!

A poignant silence fell, the despondency so total I almost felt sorry for Laurel and Hardy. The deck hand set about cleaning the ship, hosing down carpets until dye ran in rivulets. When his bucket was blown into harbour, he thought it a joke. We thought him not right in the head. Diesel as a cleaning agent was new to me. The sea was soon pustuled with oily rainbows, putting paid to any hope of cooking potatoes in sea water to stretch Soğut's Special Brew. Though the Baby Blake flushed diesel, instinct told us complaints would only make matters worse and, more significantly, we were involved in fitting a new Sum Log coil. This required ingenuity, delicate finger movements, accuracy of measurement and my red toe-nail varnish for a marker, plus, considering the state of the water, more determination than usual on Bob's part. While I crouched in the engine cavity, one arm thrust to the armpit in coils of piping in imitation of the Dutch Boy and the Dyke, Bob, clutching a pair of pliers, submerged himself to remove the old coil from the impeller and fasten the new one. Threading was my job. The moment I dreaded most was when the old coil popped out leaving a hole in bottom of the boat. Calling desperately upon the spirit of Algernon, I plugged the outlet with nervous fingers before dragging Bob out of the water and towelling him down.

That evening the wind backed from NE to SW: Full Gale. We awoke to a rattle of chains that levitated Bob into the cockpit. *Öguz* was leaving and might well take us with her. First she turned stern on, her gangplank missing our rigging by a hair's breadth. Then the deck hand, of two minds what to do, with reckless abandon leapt into our arms to save himself. Meanwhile, Captain Öguz, unaware his crew was missing, charged off in a series of zig-zags to avoid a sheltering ferry and the rocks at the harbour mouth, all of which held magnetic attraction for his blunderbuss. At the same time he attempted to raise anchor (suspected by Bob to be entangled with ours) from within the wheelhouse. We were shocked to speechlessness knowing our warps would go and we would be dragged along behind Crazy Horse. Mercifully, our anchor ripped free and we joined in with the shouts of the lad, who, in immediate danger of falling off, was balanced on *Cappelle's* rail flailing his arms. Alerted by his cries, me batting my hands and wailing childishly, "Go AWAY! Go AWAY!" Captain Öguz slammed his waterborne HGV into reverse. Somehow the deck-hand grabbed *Öguz's* gangplank and swung himself up as, with thundering reverberations, the gulet careered out of harbour and our lives.

Because of a depression over the Eastern Mediterranean, together with high pressure over the Cyclades, the wind then picked up from the WSW. Two bareboat charter yachts, each holding a complement of eight Finns, entered to rousing cheers. "Come!" cried Flaxen Locks, waving a bottle, "You are Breetish? It is the gin-and-tonics? Yes?" They were in a jubilant mood, for the sea was very rough indeed. This was the Baltic they loved, only warmer! Tomorrow they would race round the end of the peninsula. I talked to Platinum Hair, who told me it was a family holiday. The women and children, all seasick, were to be left behind to cross to Datça by road to await pick-up. We retired to the shrieking of a SW Force 8.

That night the gale died.

Knidos

Force 4 was blowing from the west as we stood out to sea to work our way clear of Tekkir Point, notorious in bad weather for heavy seas and severe gusts, on the end of the Dorian Peninsula. Topped by its gleaming lighthouse, the Cape, like a gigantic slab wave turned to stone, was a spectacular sight. Behind it lay Ancient Knidos. Cautionary tales from yachts dislodged by the sudden onslaught of strong winds made for misgivings. "Go by all means! But DON'T be tempted to stay the night!" had been the universal advice. There was nothing to fear, however, as we trickled round Cape Krio.

The view from the part-submerged moles was the same as that seen by antique trading vessels. With ships forced to shelter from the meltem in the lee of the Cape, it was brilliant strategy on behalf of the Knidians to move their city from halfway up the Dorian peninsula to its end. By constructing a causeway to the mighty offshore rock, a catchment harbour bound to foster economic prospects was created. Some twenty boats lay within.

Hard would he be of heart who could resist the ruins of Knidos as they turned liquid gold in the sunset. Narcotically cradled, there was no question of *Cappelle* leaving. A crescent moon hung in the water. A dog barked, a goat bleated and from somewhere came the faint beat of a finger drum and the familiar metronome of the Scops owl. Bob was up at three a.m. to fix the anchor light when the moon set. At cock-crow I slid into water as green as glass and cold as a mountain stream to glide among our sleeping neighbours: *Bernadette, Jessana, Varinia, Solar Flare, Amarena, Cavalier, Song* – today's pleasure fleet harnessing Aegean winds.

Pulling myself ashore in the dinghy, I explored the ruins growing up the slopes of the opposing hillsides. A goat track led to the remains of temples and agora, defined enough to rebuild with the mind's eye. Below the crest of the acropolis, an amphitheatre enjoyed the whole splendour of the scene. How the hearts of the Knidos's 70,000 citizens must have swelled with civic pride! Numbered amongst her celebrated sons were Eudoxus the Navigator, Sostratus, architect of the Pharos of Alexandria, and "a certain Artemidorus" who warned Caesar of the Ides of March. Hot sunshine drew forth the resinous smells of thyme and rosemary, sage, rue and hyssop. In the dry grasses speckled with candytuft the westerly breeze whispered. I captured its evocative rustle on my pocket tape-recorder. Before taking refuge in immobility, a lizard sunning itself on a half-buried stele swivelled its head to regard me with an unblinking eye of Pan-like wisdom. I could see the pulse palpitating in its throat.

Notwithstanding her famous men, Knidos was best known for its statue of Aphrodite which immortalised Phryne, the Athenian hetaira, letting slip her vestment before stepping into her bath. Commissioned by the city, this first example in art of the naked female form caused a sensation. She was said by Pliny to surpass "not only all the works of Praxiteles, but those of all the world". The passions she engendered revealed themselves in the sour sniff of Pausanias, who commented that it was obvious the sculptor was her lover! When King Nicomedes of Bythiny offered to pay off Knidos's not inconsiderable debts in exchange for Aphrodite, his generosity was turned down. (One could imagine the heated discussion that went on in the Bouleterion over this!) But the Knidians were right, even in practical terms, for her appeal was universal, bringing recognition and early tourism to the city. Soon security was necessary. Pliny reported that fences arose half the height of her temple. A story is told of how one love-sick Adonis, playing knuckle bones all day in the precinct, one night bribed the elderly custodian to unlock the doors. Thenceforth there was a dark stain on Aphrodite's inner thigh.

As a seafarer, I had particular reason to pay homage to Aphrodite of Knidos, for she was Aphrodite Euploia, Goddess of Fair Sailing. Sitting on the steps of the circular plinth, all that remains of her colonnade, I poured a libation (wine from a vial in my pocket) into a myrtle bush. (Experienced sailors, even the most practical, assert that it is as well to pay attention to the Old Gods.) That night the stars sparkled from the water like spoon diamonds. Half-seen, the ruined city was magically remote. It was easy to imagine Aphrodite at home once more.

Not tempting fate with a third night, we weighed anchor to round Aslan Burun, the Lion Cape, from the ruins of whose mausoleum Charles Newton in 1859 removed an eleven-ton lion. As soon as the naval party cast off, the peasantry tore the tumbled masonry apart in a search for the missing gold, convinced the stone lion could be but a consolation prize for strangers who put up camp at the mercy of bear, wolf and jackal in such a godforsaken spot.

Somewhere in that moonstone sea must live a memory of the coloured temples on the slopes and the ships of old. Wondering how I would feel, months later, when I visited the British Museum to pay my respects to the Lion of Knidos in his adopted home, I experienced only relief that, sightless now, his eyes once filled with coloured glass, but revered by all the world and in most honourable retirement, Aslan was safe from element and vandal. As the custodian said, "He's a real Lion King!"

Nine

The Dorian Peninsula

Advice to yachtsmen was to keep their nerve when entering Palamut on the southern side of the Dorian Peninsula. Aiming straight for the beach to enter harbour, within a whisker of disaster, they must take a sharp turn to port behind a low mole. The village headman, who asked a paltry sum "for a stay of a few days" to include fresh water, bade us welcome. When two boys held a whispered conversation as to how to end our first meal, one ran outside to pluck a branch of wild pears to lay along a platter for desert.

Pelagaea followed in. In Knidos the Swedish yacht had distanced herself beneath an overhang, a bronzed and bearded figure stepping ashore to stroll the headland holding the ankles of the blonde child perched on his shoulders. After diving to dig in *Pelagaea's* anchor, Joran told us that if he ever deserted the little yacht she got into trouble. A gulet mistimed entry. Then another hooked our line. In the early hours both our boats were side-swiped by a hit-and-run speed merchant. Afterwards Bob lay awake devising a riding weight to sink the stern anchor warp. The shackling on of a canvas bucket of stones became an extra chore to add to arrivals and departures.

Backed by a row of single-storey cottages held together with morning glory, the breeze-block wall along the sea-front was redeemed by strawberry-milkshake emulsion. A girl-mother spent her days in a stone shell with an excuse for a roof, no door and boarded up window spaces, her children running to say, "Hello!" before shyness overcame them. Knotting my towel pareo-style, I wandered barefoot along the shore trailed by a retinue of pi dogs. Nearby an old man shooed his grandchildren away from the rocks, the habitat of the fearsome Moray eel. Ahead, a woman lugged a horned ram down the beach in an attempt to force it into the sea. As I drew near, the creature reared, threatening to knock her backwards. Dropping my towel, I ran to grab one of its horns, while its booted and headscarved keeper clung to the other. After one ovine eruption that nearly had us both under, Aries succumbed to a dunking. I was shown how to scratch deep into his shag pile with my finger nails, paying particular attention to ears and scut. There never was a more subjugated, spring-cleaned and deinfested beast. «Tamam!» ("All right!" "That's enough!") said the shepherdess patting my arm and displaying blackened stumps of teeth as she smiled. It then occurred to me that the men lolling outside the coffee shop had failed to stir a muscle. Ram-dipping was women's work.

Of an evening Joran's wife, Grethe, mother of the blonde Nataja, carried her to the public shower, where, on occasion, a local exhibitionist, rolling his eyes as the water jetted in, held his shorts away from his stomach to ablute. One evening, letting down the back (a Briton once spent twenty-four hours in a Turkish jail for less) he mooned with a wiggle at an oncoming yachtsman who, quick to act stooge, staggered about as if struck blind. Grethe's northern reserve thawed. Slim as a willow in her leopard-spot bikini, she wore her pale hair coiled, braided in Heidi plaits or let fall in a Godiva cloak. To Joran's disapproval, especially since she had progressed to purchasing them by the carton though promising to "give up when I get home", she had taken up cigarette-smoking to "calm her nerves". Joran's looks matched his charisma. I could not help feeling he had just stepped off stage from *Jesus Christ Superstar*. Chubby and enchanting, blue-eyed Nataja was vociferous in pain – as when she tumbled down the companionway steps – but, for the most part, as sunny as the days were long.

Unseen by us, *Pelagaea* had toured the Gulf behind us. After enjoying a night on Cederae, the family were tempted to risk a second night. But the storm blew up and, despite rafting up with another yacht, running two engines and putting out four anchors, *Pelagaea's* situation became desperate. Worse was to come at Amazon Creek. Hoping to exit before dawn while Grethe and Nataja slept, Joran had nosed *Pelagaea* out of the creek only to have her propeller fouled in a fishing net. Being entangled below water in pitch darkness as he struggled to free her, he described as one of the most frightening experiences of his life.

Most fishing on this part of the coast was undertaken by small two- or-three man boats laying ground nets that floated about a metre above the sea-bed on long lines of baited hooks. At each end a recovery line was supported by a float (commonly a plastic bottle or lump of styrofoam – either of which might easily be mistaken for flotsam). Nets were streamed over the stern and pulled in over the bows. Though these lines should be no problem for a yacht, it was best to go round and, of course, avoid the end floats. The technique of seining was also practised. With one end of a net secured to shore, the fishing boat performed a wide arc before tying itself to another part of the coast to haul in. The fishing vessel could be difficult to see against the land. Moreover, the floats at the net's extremities were often poorly marked. Although there was probably sufficient depth of water for a yacht to pass over a ground net, the practice was not recommended, and would not be popular with fishermen. Advice was to circumnavigate the area, which might be some distance, the onus being on the lotus eater to give way to the bread earner.

A more awkward type of net, a very long surface variety supported by floats (usually plastic beach balls) at ten-metre intervals, with a lump of styrofoam or plastic canister at each end, had recently been introduced. These nets were truly graceless, very close to the surface and exceptionally long, usually starting near shore to extend invisibly across the entrance to an inlet, embaying a yacht and making anchorages unsafe. To try to cross in a fin and skeg was a surefire disaster method, though a long-keeled boat like *Cappelle* might, stopping her propeller, get away with it if crossing at right angles between floats, i.e. at the maximum point of natural sag. Nevertheless, to cross at all was risky. Such nets were illegal during the tourist season. The fishermen at Amazon Creek had hoped to get away with a haul of fish undetected.

A branch-roofed clearing formed the Harbour Restaurant. A voice called, inviting us to a get-together on an adjoining roof. Here, together with the waiter, the kitchen-boy and the fisherman-cook accompanied by his small daughter, we sipped mulberry rakı and nibbled hazelnuts.

Bob played the spoons on his knee, the kitchen boy strummed a lute, the cook fingered a hand-drum and the waiter a tambourine. Berrak ("Clear Water") and I clapped hands and we all sang. When it was time to go down to the restaurant, the waiter set a ghetto blaster on a rickety chair in the middle of the beaten earth floor, attaching it to speakers in the branches of the greenwood tree.

The crew of *Pelagaea* joined us for dinner. Nataja clad in pink dungarees and blue sandals, her hair tied in bunches, one ribbon pink, one blue, was soon stomping away in a trance. "I wonder what she's thinking?" whispered Grethe. But, with her Teddy Bear stuffed down her bib, she was absorbed in the simple joys of being, living within each pleasured moment in the way of small children. Berrak dragged me to my feet. Skinny as a monkey, she pranced up and down waving stick-like arms and rolling her thin belly. Two other village children brandished paper napkins in a handkerchief dance. Plucking flowers from the flower pots, they stuffed them behind their ears and twined them around our wrists. A five-year-old with belladonna eyes paused to push daisies into his fly before capering solo. Everyone danced the night away. Though Nataja wilted like a flower, her feet continued to drum and her lips to repeat, "Want to come tomorrow!" We left the staff attending to a late night fishing party who handed their catch of snout-faced schweinfisch to the German couple on *Terrathree*, Moslems refusing to eat a fish called "pig".

We awoke to find *Pelagaea* gone. Her disappearance left behind that wholly disproportionate sense of loss, akin to the sickness of abandonment, that only a boat's disappearance can inflict. Empty water gleams, too clear for secrets, as if a floating home and its family have ceased to exist. Later in the day Berrak brought flowers. Looking for something to give in return, I found a purse. Perched on the quay she was soon absorbed in opening and closing its fastener. When we dined that night with the crew of *Terrathree* conversation turned to the Berlin Wall. In their opinion it would not fall for a long time, "God willing!" After forty years, the East Germans were strangers, "not civilised now", said the Berliners. None of us had an inkling the Fall of the Wall lay only months ahead.

We left Palamut cautiously in fog. As it lifted, we lurched through swell towards Kalaboşi Headland. When the sun broke through, the clouds boiled upwards trailing handspan shadows to reveal flowerheads of surf bursting on tortured steep-to cliffs, an aspect strictly the seafarer's prerogative. We lolloped around Ince Burun (Slender Cape), a steady blow easing our search for Ata (Old Man) Island and Kuru Burun (Dry Cape), which hid Datça. My heart leapt as our sights picked up the familiar figure of Grethe curled like Copenhagen's Little Mermaid on the end of Datça mole. We had made no arrangement to rendezvous, but Joran, striding the hills with Nataja on his shoulders, spotted us on our way.

Datça

Misinterpreting Grethe's signal to join *Pelagaea* on the fishing quay, we moored on the town quay. This was our first mistake. The second was when I accepted the offer of a hose to top up our water tank, only to be warned – too late – that Datça water was undrinkable. Rude awakening to the first mistake came at tea-time when it became clear we had tied up in an area traditionally reserved for gulets and large yachts. Nemesis arrived in the guise of Captain Joe's *Lady Zoë* which, though hollered at, plied inexorably on until her propeller tangled with *Cappelle's* anchor warp. Only then, his drunken passengers glassy-eyed, did the equally inebriated Captain Joe realise there was no room for *Lady Zoë*. All set to wrench off our pulpit, he slammed into reverse.

At this point Bob lost control. The forget-me-not blue of the sky could not compete with the blue of his language. In a series of verbal fireballs, Captain Joe and his antecedents were roundly cursed. I wept. On-the-spot assistance was rendered by the crew of a gulet who hung onto *Cappelle* while Bob frantically knotted on an extension warp. Someone dived to free us. We re-anchored grimly. It was impossible to get out, for our stern was clasped each side by bigger yachts like a bung in a bottle. At this point the Cabin-Boy-Behaving-Badly jumped ship with the housekeeping purse to seek retail solace in the form of the bougainvillaea skirt last seen in a shop window on our previous visit to Datça. (To salve her conscience she also treated the Captain to half a kilo of his favourite Morello cherries.) But her absence went unnoticed, for, back at the harbour, a further traumatic event took precedence. To general astonishment, Captain Joe had re-aimed his war machine further along the quay, the noisy result of which divers were once again sorting out. Someone summoned the Harbour Master and *Lady Zoë* was officially banned from harbour.

If we thought Bob's outburst forgotten, we were wrong. That evening Madam Crimpelene of Chigwell, waddling past, looked him straight in the eye to remark tartly, "Well! I never expected *THAT* from a *TITCHY LITTLE BOAT LIKE YOURS!*" Joran, seizing this delicate moment to come to the rescue, insisted *Cappelle* join *Pelagaea* on the fishing quay just as soon as we could get away. Grethe had a tale to tell. A local youth had swum up to her asking if she "would like a love story?" When she demurred, he had persisted hopefully, "Well...how about a love-story tomorrow then?"

Since putting my hand in the pocket of my shorts had ripped away the whole side of the garment, it was high time to replace our sea-rotted wardrobe. Chairs were produced and we were invited to sit and explain the slump in tourism. To us this was far from noticeable. But bookings were down forty per cent. Forbearing to mention the lurid publicity in the British tabloids with headings such as *"GOAT SLAUGHTER HOLIDAY HORROR"*, *"COSTA ANYWHERE"* and *"TURKEY WITHOUT THE DELIGHTS"*, we cited the recession. Motivated by profit, some Turkish resorts, notoriously over-optimistic over the completion of building projects, were offering "chicken shack accommodation". And, as far as marinas were concerned, custom was being lost through shoddy or non-existent promised amenities, while charges in hard foreign currency outstripped inflation.

Buying supper direct from the fishing fleet, we were assured of "Strong body! No bad stomach!" And a visit to the fruit and vegetable market on the outskirts of Datça brought the harbourmaster hurrying up to shake hands. From then on *Cappelle* was accorded the "Friends of the Harbourmaster" status already granted *Pelagaea*. We did not fully appreciate the significance of this until we found ourselves regularly bypassed by the Harbour Dues Collector. But we were disturbed by nightly brawling. One morning we noticed the plate-glass window of a waterfront carpet shop cracked from side to side. The rowdies had moved in. The weekend brought an end to peace, with the fishing quay adopted as flotilla overflow.

From then on we slipped easily into the routine of spending our days beyond the boundaries of the tourist circuit. At the back of South Beach a thermal lake gushed over a mill-dam before fanning across the pebbled foreshore. Wearing arm-bands, Nataja dog-paddled in the chilly sea, where steps disappeared to the ruins of Old Knidos, before flinging herself off the mill-dam into the arms of any water-treading Turk who held them out to her. At the end of the day we took turns to sit beneath the tail-race letting the mill-pond's warm load pound our shoulders. Strange tales abounded of the lake at night when lights were reflected in the red eyes of aquatic creatures. Snorkel investigation of the reed beds by Joran and Bob revealed eels and terrapins half-buried in lava mud.

While idly nibbling sesame bread rings from the "Hoş simit!" boy, who did the rounds with a tray of simits on his head, we surveyed the movement of boats. Sight of the Greek island of Simi gave rise to a craving for tinned meat and Nescafé. One yacht had brought off a successful run, changing flags in mid-channel, but the peacock-banded waters were patrolled by gun boats on the look-out for yachts doing just that. Joran was weighing up the idea of a quick solo to provision for *Pelagaea's* cruise south. But, getting caught was a serious matter, meaning Grethe and Nataja would face time alone and homeless. One morning Joran called to tell us of their discovery of a shop selling tinned chicken. Hastening out to buy a supply I met him running back to report that a sample opening had revealed a tin packed solid with potato beneath a layer of chicken skin.

Sundowners were taken on either *Pelagaea* or *Cappelle* before we sauntered into town, Rapunzel-haired Grethe in silver-thread şalvar with baroque silver bangles and Joran magnificent in black leather Moroccans. Not to be outdone, Nataja's dungarees were embroidered with love-birds and a paper napkin fluttered from her top-knot, a fashion adopted ever since the Palamut experience. I paired the bougainvillaea skirt with an organza halter-top sprinkled with multi-coloured hundreds-and-thousands (the trouble with these they fell off in the soup), while Bob wore his best white shirt and peppermint ducks. Holding out her arms for strangers to lift her up, Nataja, a great favourite in Datça, delighted in puzzling out the letters of the alphabet on sign boards. One night we caught sight of a Swiss couple arguing in a carpet shop. Grethe, who suffered a recurrent nightmare in which Nataja was drowned, was appalled to discover that they regularly abandoned Simone, their three-year-old daughter, anchored off alone at sea at night, when they went ashore to fix carpet deals.

Doomsday loomed, the date our Turkish visa expired. Since Nataja had made friends with the little boy of the pedal car, *Pelagaea* decided to stay on in Datça. *Cappelle* surged forward, a virile wind giving us first a close reach and then a superb beam reach under full sail. The breeze sang in the shrouds and, just as we would have stayed in Datça forever, we would have sailed on forever. But the fiddler must be paid: "Life's a reach and then you gybe." The breeze veered astern for a run that petered out. Chastened, we gybed in confusion before trickling into Kuruca Bay. Not a ripple disturbed the water as I swam ashore into the spokes of the early sun. On my way back, I got the shock of my life to see below and behind me a frog-like monster as big as myself! I was gasping with fright before I recognised my own shadow on the sea-bed.

Koruca enjoyed a miracle reputation as a restorer of youth. History relates that seven worn-out donkeys were once left to end their days in this isolated spot. Years later a construction company prospecting for a holiday village, was astonished to discover a thriving community of twenty-eight donkeys! Naturally, the new village specialised in the rejuvenation of the elderly.

In Bencik, "The Place Where the Fish Jump Across", the narrowest point of the Dorian Peninsula, anchoring was awkward. Moreover, the creek had a reputation, fostered by warm water emissions from a meteorological research station, for maxi-mosquitoes and sand sharks. We were content with a peep behind the saw-toothed rock that guarded the entrance. Bencik figured prominently in the history of Old Knidos. The oracle at Delphi, its priests no doubt in league with the Persians, had warned against the digging of a canal to turn the end of the Dorian promontory into an island. Thus the Persian armies encountered no resistance.

Gulf of Hisarönü

In the narrows of the Gulf of Hisarönü white floats were barely distinguishable from breaking wavelets. But on Bob raising his binoculars, he spotted identical floats at regular intervals. Realising a fishing net stretched from side to side, we turned at right angles seeking an end float, only to find ourselves boxed in by more floats in a system of parallel netting that had all the complexity of a minefield. Turning back, we proceeded tensely towards the southern shore until we identified the end float, which freed us to coast-hug up Gulf.

Keci Bükü (Goat Horn Creek) announced itself by the noisy quayful of flotilla yachts in the outer bay. Beetling cliffs pressed in as we penetrated beyond an ancient fort crowning a central islet. A narrow passage past a sandbar brought us into the curl of the goat's horns which formed an oleander-rimmed anchorage. The beached whale of a half-sunken motor vessel reared from the water by the jetty, while on the other side a turn-of-the-century schooner lay canted over, her masts appealing for help. Torn polythene sheeting showed someone once planned salvage.

As evening drew on, a small shepherdess positioned herself on the hillside against a recumbent sheep to keep an eye on *Cappelle*. Whenever our eyes met, we waved. Then a boy rowed over in a boat marked "SEA TAXI" to present an impressive folder of Yacht Service provisions. Divided into columns translated into three languages, it listed 150 items from varieties of olive oil to types of sugar. Aspirins and clothes pegs figured, but nothing remotely suggesting a square meal except, perhaps, "Meat Pieces" (not available).

On shore two little girls popped out of a ditch, the elder holding up minute tomatoes taken from their mother's garden. «Güzel! Güzel!»

("Nice! Nice!") she said. When I asked how much, she answered brightly, «Iki bin!» ("Two thousand!") I was used to paying a quarter of that for two kilos! When I walked on, the smaller girl ran after me, so I offered her a coin. Snatching it, she rushed back to her big sister. Then two little termagants chased me, shouting, «Iki Bin! Iki Bin!» the little one battering me furiously with her fists and scrabbling in my bag to get at my purse. When a villager appeared they dived for cover. It seemed local youngsters had grown accustomed to getting their way with flotilla crews.

Back at base, Bob was producing our ship's documents at the request of a Coastal Protection Vessel. After it departed *Banana Bliss*, *Cool Breeze* and *Mint Royale*, pastel-coloured speed boats registered in Southampton, hurtled in. Seeing *Cappelle* as a decoy, they swerved towards us slinging their hooks. At this Bob leapt up, knocking over his pot of stripper. When *Banana Bliss* upped anchor again to trawl it across our stern, Bob called out she should anchor further away, otherwise we would collide when the on-shore breeze got up. In quelling tones Hyacinth Bucket retorted, "Don't worry! My husband knows what he's doing!" Satisfied with his position (though we were not), Hyacinth's nattily dressed consort then stepped into his dinghy to bring in the outboard engine. On taking its weight he overbalanced and – in true sitcom style – executed a perfect header. Not long after that the Tootie Fruities' minder arrived to lead them somewhere secluded. Last incomer was a yacht flying the Irish flag. Again it made a bee-line for *Cappelle*. A woman, dumping her anchor and chain beside us, asked to share our tree. Again there were explanations to make. Our last memory was of three Irish children belly-dancing on deck in the dark.

The book-end mountain of Eren Dağ was two-dimensional against the citrus gleam of dawn when we pulled out of Keci Bükü. Two herons, fishing for breakfast, rose ponderously. Taking care to give Atabol Kayası (barely visible rocks with a magnetic attraction for yachts before slicing a hole in their bottoms and sinking them in deep water) a good offing, we sailed smartly round Cape Apostoli. Beyond it the Hisarönü and Loryma peninsulas formed the voracious jaws of the Gulf of Sömbeki. Here the wind died. (Pausanias in his testy way once remarked that it was as impossible for a boat always to find a prosperous wind as it is for a man to avoid trouble in life). Once through the narrow freeway of the Bozburun Channel *Cappelle* took wing towards a village with a sky blue minaret. But we were nearing civilisation. Only fifteen miles from Marmaris, Bozburun girded itself for tourism. The harbour attendant, cautioning us that disposal of dirty water was "verboten", demanded 10,000 TL for a night's stay.

As we mused idly on the doings of *Pelagaea,* to our astonishment the family materialised before us! "We've come to find you!" they said. When Nataja, now a Koruca-practised dog-paddler who hummed a water-baby tune as she swam, got down from a restaurant table to draw letters in the dust, Joran related the reason for their sudden departure from Datça. Datça harbour, whose surface resembled debris-strewn brown gravy, had girdled both our yachts with such a tinkling array of bottles and tins afloat in the scum that Joran was wont to make, "How's the orchestra?" his daily salutation. With Grethe out shopping one morning, he had been washing his hair when a young policeman, seeing bubbles, hailed him, asking to inspect his ship's documents. On enquiring the nature of the bubbles and being told they were shampoo, he informed Joran that he was guilty of "serious crime". Too late, Joran realised he should have held onto his papers, for the policeman refused to give them back, saying Joran must attend the Port Police. Here he was told his fine was fixed at half a million lire (£500). Until this was paid, his papers would not be restored. Refusing to pay, and producing a shampoo bottle marked "biodegradable", Joran said there was no case to answer, particularly as no notice against the use of shampoo was posted outside the Port Authority.

Purporting not to understand, the sergeant ordered him to return the following day, when an interpreter would be present. Again meeting with intransigence and with his family hostage (for it was illegal for *Pelagaea* to leave Datça without her papers) Joran, not surprisingly, lost his temper. His expostulation of "This is BLOODY RIDICULOUS!" was swiftly interpreted to mean him to have sworn at a police officer. Claiming to have been telephoning Ankara, which Joran did not believe, the sergeant then slammed down the receiver with the words, "I hereby sentence you to twenty days in prison!" Needless to say, Joran blew his top, telling them his wife worked for Amnesty International, and vowing to headline the family's predicament all over the international press with disastrous results for Turkish tourism and Datça police in particular. Summoned to report again next day, he was greeted with smiles, handshakes and the return of his papers. At which he had not hesitated to raise anchor and leave.

In Bozburun the gas ran out, the radio batteries faded and the strut of the sun-canopy snapped. While the woodyard fashioned a new strut for a few pence, I explored. Beyond the waterfront chaos was endemic. Bindweed spread a picturesque disguise over sagging bothies made from packing cases, old tyres and fish boxes, while petrol cans of Canna lilies and hibiscus served as eye-candy beside open-fronted lean-tos shared by goats, chickens and families. Any roof strong enough formed the base for a dung heap. Women, grasping handfuls of twigs, swept circles in the beaten earth, while handsome children played hopscotch.

On the last night of June two flotillas put in. It was the end of their charter period and party time. A fight broke out to the sound of hysterical sobbing, and at four a.m. a drunk, chased by a New Zealand skipper bellowing, "F****** WELL STOP IT!" roared round the harbour in a purloined Zodiac. At six a.m., *Pelagaea's* slot already empty, we slipped away, rounding Kızıl Burun (the Red Cape) to sail the lower jaw of the Gulf of Sömbeki. "Whatever's that?" says Bob, pointing a piece of toast at something off our bows. I choked, for the two black pyramids poking out of the water bore an uncanny resemblance to the humps of the Lesser Loch Ness Monster. Close inspection identified them as the sponsons of a vertically floating dinghy. Our erratic movements, as we attempted its unsuccessful recovery, alerted a gulet to organise salvage from its davits.

Loryma

Karaburun (The Black Cape) marked the Aegean Sea's boundary with the Mediterranean. At Loryma round the corner, Bozuk Bükü (Ruin Point) was topped by an ancient fortification wall. A flash blinded us and a light bubble danced across our sails as Joran mirror-signalled us to wheel in. (The only "naval duty" required from Freya Stark at this spot, I recalled, as I flaked chain, was to ensure *Elfin's* dinghy painter was not fouled.) Suddenly a Turk swung aboard and grabbed our stern warp. Dropping back, he rowed for dear life. The warp snagged, but not before the rower had yanked *Cappelle* sideways against a rock, only to abandon her in favour of a more lucrative prize, a guletful of tourists who bombed themselves over its side with cries of, "Ow! Ooh! Cripes! It's bloody cold!" and shrieks about sharks. In the late afternoon we toiled up scrubland to the carriage-wide wall enclosing the fortress. Dizzily we stood beside the towers, the sea on three sides. Here in 305 BC its garrison had given protection to the fleet assembled below to launch attack on Rhodes.

A Seller of Wares circled. To get rid of him I accepted his offer of transport that evening to the "simple restaurant" at the head of the bay. Vitreous water shone spectrally over the limestone sea-bed. Moonbeams pierced mini-headlands where the stirrings of bleached seaweeds revealed pebbled paths to mysterious doorways. I peered into the undersea world, the lagoon half-confessing secrets but withholding more. Beyond balloon moorings where yachts swayed in unison like a corps de ballet, we were handed on shore by a virtual reality family, the women in gipsy skirts, knee boots and head-kerchiefs, one with Jolly Baby on Hip. On the hillside other "family members" were grouped. It was all very stagey. Seated at a wobbly trestle under a pergola I regarded our fellow diners, a South African family and a party of Germans. Ali, the father figure, asked Bob to accompany him to a cave where, surprisingly, he kept a freezer. His reply to Bob's enquiries as to fish prices all met with a routine, "No problem, sir!"

During the very ordinary meal, Uncle Ahmed, assuming a Thespian pose while keeping his eye on his watch, played the flute. At this, three well-rehearsed nieces transformed themselves into belly-rolling provocatives to sidle between tables. Uncle Ahmed was soon replaced by Auntie Ahmed who circulated with a basket of head-bands. Tying bandeaux round the foreheads of the Germans, she pulled out scarves to match the women's dresses, an unusual nicety in Turkey. I watched the South African argue hotly after signalling for his bill. Ignoring Grandmother hawking honey, he then marched his family angrily off. On presentation of our own bill, Bob, adding we were not the average charterers but "old Turkey hands", accused Ali (vainly protesting "waiter service") of avarice. We learnt later that the erstwhile "simple restaurant" had become a rip-off run by Turks from Marmaris in cahoots with German businessmen.

Fog adhered to our eyeballs next morning. Somewhere within its blanket islands lay in wait for the unwary. Unable to pierce the monochrome with blind eyes, we strained our ears as we crept towards neighbouring Serçe, a boomerang-shaped lagoon that in the 1940s acted as a Forward Operating Base for British MTBs (motor torpedo boats). The passengers of a Thompson gulet cheered as *Cappelle* rocked violently in its wash as it forced its way past. Shielded by the sun-awning from the blistering light thrown back from limestone cliffs, Bob prepared to freshen varnish. Soon, first-time-out flotilla crews arrived to compete in tugs-of-war with anchor chains. Determined to be out of the mêlée at first light, Bob dived repeatedly to ensure our freedom.

We stood off the coast. When the suggestion of a sun burned through bringing the world back into focus, it hung suspended in the sky like a pale disc of communion bread. Sailing wing-on-wing over the clucking sea with the breeze abaft, I was all eyes for the scenery until semi-garrotted by the preventer when trying to take a bearing on Aspro Mittas as we rounded Cape Marmaris. The true entrance to Marmaris Bay lay not via False Bay but via Goat Island, past which we sped, still under canvas, into Pendulum Passage, while converging yachts handed their sails. We soon found out why! In the fairway the wind changed direction, keeping us occupied winching in the genoa with no chance to raise our eyes to the land-locked waters of Marmaris Bay, which had served both as Süleyman the Magnificent's base in 1522 for the conquest of Rhodes, and as Nelson's fleet anchorage in 1798 when chasing Boney.

Marmaris

From the forest of masts beside the Old Town, we pinpointed the marina. Here we were treated to an extravagant welcome by the resident manager Lt Cdr Adrian Brady: "Allow me to bring you in, sir! I will put a man on board!" Wow! We were scarce able to credit our good fortune. Then a passer-by from Taiwanese ketch *China Belle,* seeing *Cappelle,* cried out, "Great little ship! Nearly bought her in '77 when she was lying next to *Gypsy Moth II* in Knox-Johnston's yard!" inviting us to a party.

The barely completed marina with a capacity for 676 boats, was three-quarters empty. Although the launderette was not yet operational, and there was no shop (let alone the advertised shopping mall), the mirror-walled marble halls of a spacious ablution block beckoned. The marina boded to become, if not "the jewel of the Eastern Mediterranean" the handout vaunted, at least the "turquoise delight" it promised. Even when we studied the small print advising, "Please note this brochure is for guidance only," we forgave exaggeration, content that our four-way connector post should provide drinking water and power (though not yet the projected telephone connection and satellite TV).

It was dark when we set off for a meal along an unguarded backwater. Finding the Bailey Bridge illustrated in the brochure not yet erected, we returned for torches, and, by means of the bus station and a main road, reached town to find it thudding with jack hammers. Along one side of the waterfront gulets and ferries rubbed shoulders, while along the other stretched hotels and gin-palaces. There was a hot-fat-and-sewers smell of a Margate-in-August Costa.

"I like your shoes!"

"I like your hat!"

"Can I help you spend your money, sir?"

"I want to tell you about me!" ("I know about you! You're lovely!" said Bob.)

One gambit had already been tried in Datça. "Sir! I KNOW you!" Asked where the meeting took place, the answer was always, "Marmaris, sir!" It was a good bet that all tourists hailed from Marmaris.

The seas were swept by gales and the temperature rose. From dawn onwards the air thickened. The harbour water grew sluggish and everyone talked about the year when metal burnt to the touch and no yacht ventured out. With the marina no stranger to power cuts, we were glad not to possess a refrigerator to plug into the mains. But, like everyone else, we were affected by the increasing scarcity of water.

We sighted *Pelagaea* anchored off. With Grethe fazed by the fog, the family had sailed straight for civilisation. In Marmaris Nataja made a traditionally dressed little friend named Bahar ("Springtime"), who awakened her desire for şalvar. We could not pass a shop window of an evening without Nataja stopping to admire her şalvar's reflection.

It seemed a good plan, since Marmaris doubled as a yacht pound, to renew our visas via a quick trip to London. This way we could bring back spares, more charts, plus a big jar of Swarfega. With tourists pouring in from nearby Dalaman, we were confident of picking up cheap return flights. However, the airline agencies were less than interested in us, the reps positively rude as they barred us from flights out of Dalaman.

"Where did you enter the country?"

"By boat in April…"

"I didn't say 'on what?' or 'when?' I said, 'WHERE?' "

Since there had been no putdown in Dalaman, there could be no uplift, however empty the aeroplanes. The girls retired behind their periodicals. However, a Turkish agency was happy to render assistance. It was true our only way to London was via Istanbul. But, if we took the fourteen-hour Marmaris-Istanbul night coach, we should arrive in Istanbul in the nick of time to board the newly inaugurated Turkish Toros Airlines flight to Heathrow.

On Bob's checking the procedure for leaving a yacht in bond, Brady informed him, surprisingly, that there was a fee for customs' inspection. To Bob this smacked of extortion. The complicitous attitude of the customs officers as they sat in the cockpit, pointedly flicking through a bundle of bank notes while ticking off items on our transit log, confirmed his suspicion. We were short of time, however. There was no more to be done but pack up and place *Cappelle's* keys in the care of the marina, an obligation listed as contractual under the Terms and Conditions of Bonding. In Brady's absence, Bob deposited the keys with his assistant, an off-hand English girl with an assortment of local boyfriends. Retorting she was too busy to put the keys away there and then, she said she would do so when she had time. Our taxi was waiting and we did not delay.

It was the eve of Kurban Bayram when every Moslem family decorates a sheep or goat for sacrifice, purchasing a bright new knife. The half-built marina complex was requisitioned as a herd assembly point. As our taxi swerved through the doomed animals, Bob remarked prophetically, "Keys are only as safe as the person you leave them with!"

Ten

A nasty surprise

A shock awaits

As we alighted a week later from the Izmir coach into the white heat of the Marmaris afternoon, a bus passenger bidding me, "Welcome to Turkey!" unscrewed a bottle of Attar of Roses to stroke my arm with its stopper. Brady, hospitality itself, offered tea and despatched a boy to hose off the "Gaddaffi dust" that had gathered on *Cappelle* framed in his office window.

As we opened the boat up, Bob noted with surprise he forgot to shoot home the top inner bolts of the cabin doors. Thinking to try out a new cassette while we unpacked, he unwrapped our cassette radio, stowed in blankets behind pillows in his trotter box. His blanket roll was as he left it – but contained no radio. We thought we must have stashed it elsewhere, until my eyes lit on the Sea Voice. On top of it was Bob's spare wallet, normally kept hidden at the bottom of his document case at the back of the wall locker behind the map chest. It was clear – *Cappelle* had been done over! Bob strode off to see Brady, who telephoned the police. My "secret" locker was empty, my tape recorder was missing, and the sea lockers were bare.

Bob returned to say the police were sending a car for us. The Assistant Marina Manager, a Turk, would accompany us to the police station to act as interpreter. In a rush of adrenalin we smartened up. *Cappelle* was still held out on long lines, and it was not until in mid leap for the pontoon I knew my skirt too tight for the stretch and measured my length. The Assistant Manager seemed sympathetic enough. Asked at the police station to make a statement, Bob was careful to emphasise how he had surrendered his keys according to contractual obligation. All this our escort translated verbatim, so he assured us, to a policeman manning an ancient typewriter. Before signing his statement, Bob again questioned our interpreter as to its content and accuracy, again being assured the translation was verbatim and in full. He was refused a copy. When the police inspected *Cappelle* they made drawings, took measurements and noted the lack of forced entry. Having sorted through the yacht, the thieves had apparently left, as would charterers at the end of a holiday, taking with them our spare suitcases stuffed with all the loot they could push into them, including the special occasion clothes we left behind. They had used our keys to enter and only neglected to fasten the top bolts to the cabin doors on leaving.

Brady's attitude then underwent a sea-change. It became a question of "not on my patch". He prevaricated, saying it was doubtful if the marina bore any responsibility whatsoever for the felony. Bob's point of view differed, for he had taken out a prepaid contract to cover his absence, leaving his custom-bonded yacht in the marina's safe-keeping after handing over her keys according to his legal requirements. Who then was responsible?

At first Brady argued Bob had surrendered the keys "purely of his own volition". On Bob's showing him the relevant small print, he murmured weakly he "did not know about this". He then declared it "quite impossible" for the keys to have left his safe. Bob pointed out he had not witnessed them put in. Brady categorically refused any questioning of his staff, and his final insult was to chide Bob for tying on the yacht cover under screen of which the burglary took place. "Let's put it this way, sir! It's like your London Club! Hang your hat on the hat-stand and you'll find a notice underneath saying, 'The Management does not accept responsibility for items left on the premises'." So, according to Brady, a bonded yacht in safe-keeping was no more secure than any item left on the premises.

In a double irony, when we returned to the marina after a meal that night, an armed soldier prevented Bob boarding *Cappelle* without first checking proof of ownership – though we could see he could not read when he examined the ship's papers upside down! We spent the following night at home with a bottle of wine, but could not open it, since our Screwpull bottle opener was among the many missing items.

When I began to feel ill, I told myself the sickness was psychosomatic. It was no use crying over spilt milk. We had not lost any vital marine equipment. We shopped in a desultory way to make up for our losses, but failed to find a suitable cassette radio. One morning I slumped groggily under an umbrella in the Bazaar taking a sip of Bob's iced beer. An old herb seller, making his rounds, stopped beside me, head cocked, regarding my flushed face with concern. Raising his cap in reassurance, he then ever so gently removed my hat to fan my face with it before placing it on the chair beside me. His solicitude allowed my eyes to focus on a signpost reading *"TO THE BRITISH CONSUL"*.

Bob, determined the marina's insurance should bear our loss, pestered the marina office. Brady, with equal determination, refused all approach to his insurance company until Bob made a deliberate nuisance of himself in front of German clients. Meanwhile the Assistant Manager was at pains to avoid us. When I waited for him on the concourse, he deliberately turned at heel. To Brady's fury, Bob took to camping out beside the office telex machine. When the reply to the insurance query came, it was as Bob expected: Brady's question had been non-specific.

In the Marble Halls, the lavish water supply was drying up. Soon water was rationed, buckets of water stood outside lavatory doors and yachtsmen made sure their tanks were topped up. Muttering, "No water!" crews complained vociferously. I overheard a disquieting conversation:

"They say the water table's at its lowest!"

"And the sewage is at overflow!"

"So we'll all end up with cholera!"

Soon no buckets, and the marble halls were middens.

We were getting nowhere with our theft. Moreover, the marina was itching to be rid of us. Early one morning I made up my mind to struggle to the Consulate. Here a young Turkish lawyer, Dilek Doğan, introduced herself as the Honorary British Consul. At my story's end, she asked, "I don't suppose the police let you have a copy of your statement? They are giving us a lot of trouble this year. Until 1988 there was virtually no crime in Turkey but since last year it has doubled. The reaction of the authorities has been to deny crime's existence because crime reports are 'bad for Turkey'." She had the power to obtain a copy of Bob's statement via diplomatic channels. But this would be a lengthy process.

On our return to the Consulate with our passport details, Dilek advised Bob that onus for restitution rested with the marina. *"YOU MUST BE STRONG!"* she said. He was to go back to the police station and lodge a complaint against the marina for failing to safeguard his keys. While there, he was again to demand a copy of his statement – even though it was unlikely the police would accede to this request. "I tell you what will happen!" she said. "The police will make token enquiries in the market and, in a couple of weeks, when you are safely home (for *ALL* visitors are on package tours, whatever they claim), they will drop your case." What made Dilek hit the roof was my happening to mention Grant's initial demand for a fee for Customs Inspection, with a hint that failure to pay would delay the release of our ship's papers. Exclaiming, "But this is *SCANDALOUS!* Inspections are the Customs Department's JOB!" Dilek vowed to report to the State Governor. "We do not countenance rackets like this!" she said. *"And you can tell Brady from me he is to steer clear of corruption!"*

Back at the police station, in the senior officer's temporary absence, two bulging files of current crime reports were produced. When his own report could not be found, Bob took charge, retrieving the relevant document and slapping it on the table with Eastern Mediterranean bravura. Two policemen poured over it and a discussion took place. One was recruited to fetch a shopkeeper to act as interpreter. Having studied the statement, the man came over to Bob, "I very sorry!" he said, "There is problem! In statement you do not mention keys you say you leave with marina. Police want receipt." So that was it! Our case had been undermined from the outset! The reason the Assistant Manager was sent to accompany us was clear. His task had been to suppress any information that might cast a bad light on the marina. Bob's declaration that he had handed over his yacht keys had been intentionally omitted from the Turkish transcription – and, sadly, he had failed to obtain a receipt when he handed them over to the dismissive girl in the marina office.

Bob continued to demand a copy of the statement, and was about to be given one, when in walked a senior officer, who delivered a diatribe to his men while casting angry glances at us. Bob tumbled to the gist of it, which was that we were "foreign criminals" who had staged our own robbery in order to put in a false insurance claim. Towering over the Turk, Bob retaliated, using his former more senior rank. I have never seen a policeman deflate so fast. Bob was not only handed a copy of his statement, but saluted as well.

If you want to put the boot in, choose your audience. We accosted Brady when he was surrounded by an angry deputation of French. On Bob telling him in a loud voice that he now held a copy of his statement, a flicker of alarm crossed Brady's face. Bob then informed him he was to be reported to the State Governor. To add insult to injury, we stayed to give ear to the Gallic grievance. It seemed the French yacht had put into Bodrum only to be told water was reserved for long-stay visitors. They had then sailed six days for Marmaris only to be again told water was unavailable.

"I have ladies on board and I *MUST* have water!" thundered the French skipper.

"Maybe we can help out with buckets!" said Brady.

"And do you intend to carry *TWO TONS* of water bucket-by-bucket?"

"Well, I trust you will buy your ladies champagne!"

It was not Brady's day.

Despite the arrival of Mel with a trail of pi-dogs and most welcome reunions with old friends George Ghritis and Christian Manacci, I was forced to take to my bed of sickness. From George we learned that victims of the lurgy were keeling over like flies. The cure was simple: rest, starvation and copious draughts of bottled water. Collecting our papers without further problem, Bob brought news that Brady was under police interview.

Skopea Liman

Once out at sea, my recovery was swift. Beyond the reed-plumed channels of Ancient Caunus, habitat of the sky-blue crab and the Loggerhead Turtle, our passage around Kurdoğlü Burun (The Headland of the Gate) demonstrated my reflex actions were back in trim. Here a freshening westerly caught us unawares: I had thrown myself prostrate almost before the warning cry that heralded a swing of the boom. Dolphin-shaped Kurdoğlü Burun cradled the island-dotted lagoon of Skopea Liman. Handing sail in strong gusts, the textured chiselling of cicadas competing with the strumming of the breeze in the rigging, we pressed on into a lagoon where the prevailing south westerlies of summer provided exhilarating sailing in protected waters. Ahead darted a dinghy. Drawing close we saw the craft was custom-built for a six-year-old whose blonde tresses fanned out in the water as she ducked on the gybe. The frolic involved three, for a pair of dolphins vied with the Fairy Boat. A coach and cameraman stood off in a Zodiac directing the act through a megaphone. In Ruin Cove, we passed

> "A tiny house
> With a silver smile"

perched on an islet, such a one as in Yaşar Mirac's poem (or would have been, had its roof not been torn apart).

Skopea Liman's shoreline was slashed with ravines that divided wooded slopes sheltering a number of anchorages. We tied up in Wall Bay under eagle-haunted crags. At the breathless hour of dawn the world inchoate hesitated in painted stillness while the scene lightened from indigo to the grisaille of a Japanese print. Ashen hills solidified like a woodcut above the pearly sheen of water that reflected perfect double images. Ebony branches hung motionless, and somewhere out of sight I imagined pagodas. To bathe was to tear grey silk. Care was necessary when stepping back on deck barefoot to avoid the dew-sipping wasps that gathered there.

Mel encountered a Turk who showed her his "storm damaged"

restaurant built on painstakingly constructed retaining terraces. With the area lately designated a National Park, it had been destroyed "By Order...because without permit". The owner of neighbouring Red Roofs, the Turk explained, rich enough to buy special consideration, had been able to restrict his own damage to token wrecking – windows smashed and walls bludgeoned, but the roof left on to protect his generators for later removal. Such establishments were listed in the Pilot. If yachtsmen had failed to provision for Skopea Liman, it was just too bad.

A week later we dropped anchor in a cove on Tersane (Boatyard) Island whose air of abandonment stemmed from the loss of its boat-building past. Tall palms added a North African air. Broken doors banged in the wind and a hircine smell seeped from a farmyard. I found myself adopted as goatherd until the herd transferred its allegiance to a girl who came out of a farmyard tying on her head-scarf. Smilingly she offered me a raffia-bound bunch of sage tea, indicating its efficacy for heat-stroke and headache. Emptying the coins in my pocket, I buried my face in the fragrant nosegay. Her name was Tula and she was fifteen. Her baby son was asleep. How many sons did I have? Pointing out the way back, she stood to wave, "Go smiling! Go smiling!"

That evening an elderly Californian rowed over from an East Coast cutter to ask if we knew what had happened to the restaurants. Sipping Malibu and peach juice on the deck of *Bonnie Doone* (sic), while keeping an eye on the goats sniffing at her warps, we wondered how long it would be before the raggle-taggle mob chewed through them. "Do go away, sweethearts!" coaxed Corky, Andy's tubby spouse, flapping her hands mildly. Andy was maddened by flies, and we soon discovered that the cloud of goat pests actually preferred human blood.

Across the liman in Taşkaya (Tomb Bay, Pliny's Crya-of-the-Fugitives) we manoeuvred in and out of gear, to avoid shallows, before tucking into shore within a cove and tying to rocks beneath trees. From high above, the empty eyes of pigeon-hole tombs stared down. That night Bob jerked out of an anchor-slipping dream to see a fishing boat laying its nets across our entrance.

In the morning I pursued a headland path to discover yet another eating place minus its roof, chairs cast about and refrigerator and deep-freeze clobbered. In the adjoining bay, rough justice had been inflicted on the popularly named Restaurant Robinson, an elaborate complex with quay, fish ponds and a wall sign reading, *"HOT CHIPS AND TURKISH PIZZA"*. Here wanton destruction had reached a crescendo. I immediately recognised the site described in a letter from Joran, *Pelagaea* having borne witness to the attack. The air still twanged with the currents of the violence that so upset Nataja. Traditionally, the myrmidon Başi Bazouks left nothing undestroyed. A boulder was white-washed with the catch-phrase *"I LOVE ROBINSON"*. Clearly there were those who did not. Fairylights and a sound system lay in smithereens. The barbecue and outdoor ovens were stove in with crow-bars. The shell of the restaurant smoked in the midst of this battle field. Sacks of onions and potatoes had been tipped into the sea, stacks of plates smashed against a wall, and wine jars emptied. Customers had fled in the middle of a meal. A pegged-out tent against the skyline was evidence, perhaps, of Robinson reverting to life as a castaway.

On the forest track I met a Turk in swimming trunks who passed me by on his way towards his family, a party of veiled women and children picnicking under an awning slung from a fishing boat to a tree. Returning towards me, he was carefully bearing a superb bunch of grapes across his outstretched hands. He thought we might be hungry! Grateful for the gift, I asked him to point out the çeşme, Skopea Liman's not-to-be-missed spring of sweet water.

By afternoon the erratic angle at which *Cappelle* swung told us our anchor had indeed slipped. We were quick to escape up-lagoon to the çeşme marked by the Balıkı Taş, a Byzantine fish carving. Beside it were the cleared sites of two more illegal cafés. From the distance I had spied a small temple tomb, now hidden by a bluff. It was further away than I remembered. Scrambling higher I could not judge whether it was above me or below until I saw eroded steps cut into the rock face and recognised a bleached log I had noticed from water level. The tomb was exquisite, its frieze and pediment near perfect. Only the capital of the central column was eaten away. Grasping tufts of grass, I pulled myself up. From the absence of litter, no human being had lately passed this way. The burial chamber, adopted by a pair of lizards with apple-green tails, was as peaceful as a sunlit loggia. Its ambience acted as a sedative. In my time-proofed world I dallied until recollecting a promise to hurry. As soon as I renegotiated the bluff, I saw Bob beckoning. The sea-bed was unsafe. A puff of wind could have us on the rocks.

Fethiye

After passing the russet-winged moth of a windjammer in the Bay of Fethiye, a boy perched on the jack-crosstrees of her topgallant mast, we tacked round Pacariz (Pair of Trousers) Point, to enter Fethiye (Ancient Telmessos). Tucked into its mountain embrace, Fethiye was sited with its back to the sun, which rendered its great rock-carved temple tomb, the Tomb of Amyntas, an unreliable landmark since it was almost always lost in shadow.

I purchased the entire stock of a nearby food store useful to us – six jars of apricot jam, two packs of toast, one tin of sardines and a packet of banana pudding. In the main Post Office an American caused mild consternation with his "Shurrup and gimme ma letters!" in reply to the clerk's polite greeting. Then a half-naked German woman waddled in, pink flesh bulging round her G-string. While she engaged in a telephone call, the queue of veiled women stared impassively at her jelly-wobble buttocks. She was joined by her ape-chested partner, jock-strap below paunch, the pair as alien in the Post Office as the Gadarene swine.

Back on the quay tensions had built. The skipper of a Beneteau was attempting to sort out an entanglement of yachts, while the bikini-clad bimbo on his sun-deck never looked up from tweezering out leg hairs one by one. *China Belle* (last seen in Marmaris) had moved in. Striding about in gleaming ducks telling tall stories, Hugh, whose charter business had dried up, was keeping his hand in by taking over the stranded passengers of a broken-down gulet.

Lycia

Once we were off the Lycian shore, space again became our element. Now that the flow of time was uninterrupted, there came an uncanny sense that yesterday might yet be reactivated, today being of no more significance than that it happens to be where the light focuses. In Lycia I had the sensation that historic times were never quite past. The air zinged with their energy. On a wooden boat, harnessing the locomotive power of the wind, in a setting whose features remain constant, the present ceases to dominate. Only inadequacy of perception holds back the past. No longer a prisoner of my own time, I might pick any bead I choose in history's necklace.

An anvil-shaped headland gave us our course for Gemiler, Isle of Ships. Standing off to avoid underwater reefs extending from Karacoren Island, we followed day boats into the narrows behind Gemiler. Dropping anchor awkwardly in sixty feet, we tied to the ruined walling sprawling down the slopes to the water's edge where steps and arches descended to anchor-trapping shelves. Strong currents forcing *Cappelle* to lie at an angle, Bob spent an exhausting afternoon trying to straighten her out, losing patience with the Cabin Boy's incompetence. Mutinying, after trapping her finger in the winch, she told him to "Shut up!"

At tea-time we moved across to the mainland to wallow in swell. That evening a çöp boat approached to collect refuse and escort us – our return denied until "after belly-dancing" – to a less ill-fated restaurant than Robinson in Skopea Liman. A sultry beauty, reportedly on a belly-dancer's circuit, who bore a jewelled sun-burst in her belly-button and banknotes in her Madonna bra, was delivered by taxi. Her minder was a comic-opera policeman. Placing a coin on the floor behind her, he encouraged her to retrieve it with her teeth from a backbend to the sound of snapping castanets. Rolling her belly in the tsifteteli, she sprang lightly onto our table, never losing her rhythm as she ogled Bob. Leaping down, she tugged at my hands, goading me to gyrate with her.

East of Gemiler, the limestone peak of Baba Dağ, whose feet plunged steep-to into the sea, demanded a Claude Monet to record its aspects in the light play — plumed with an Everest cloud by day;

spellbinding pink in the sunset; spectral in moonlight, and at sunrise all but lost in mist, before recreation out of nothing by the discovering sun. At dawn, Baba Dağ two-dimensional, came a tap on the hull. It was the comic-opera policeman, alias the village baker, rowing over to offer us a fresh loaf. Thus roused, we made haste to the pirate stronghold. On its crest, among tangled brambles screening dusty mosaics framing the Byzantine blue of the sea, reared the triple arches of a ruined basilica. Leading down to the water were the remains of a covered way built to provide, legend has it, shade for a Queen with photo-sensitive skin. Not until we were untying our dinghy did the first day boats pile in.

Down-coast, behind a sickle-shaped sandbar, lay the landlocked waters of Ölü Deniz (The Dead Sea) lately prohibited to yachts by reasons of pollution. *Pelagaea* with Nataja on board had received special dispensation to enter, but blasts from Jandarma (local police) whistles directed us to the unlucky dip of an outside anchorage where parascenders hovered, water skiers cut corners and paddle-boats churned, while charter yachts jockeyed for space, their skippers bad-mouthing. At night a myriad midges descended from the trees until in the grey of dawn, the sea rainwater clear, we extricated ourselves from fluke-trapping rocks to lie off the sandspit. As soon as the sun rose the film-set sandbar glistened with well oiled beer-bottle-brown bodies.

That night we isolated ourselves in a situation we believed ideal – until *Cappelle* buck jumped, not the one-off result of a cruise-liner passing out at sea, as we first thought, for the pitch and toss increased. Held beam on to a vicious cross-swell, *Cappelle* fought her anchor. With sleep impossible, I staggered about seeing to stowage while Bob kept anchor-watch. As soon as a pale glow suffused the east, we were away, heading nine miles south for Yedi Burunlar, the Turkish Cape Horn, from Kotu Burun (The Bad Cape) to Zeytin Burun (Cape of the Olive Grove) bold, remote and refugeless. After the seven miles of the Seven Capes, came the seven miles of the Sands of Patara where Esen Cayası, the Ancient River Xanthos, disgorged its alluvial mud. Heeding nautical advice, we stood three miles out.

Joran had suggested we avoid Kalkan, an exclusive Turkish St Tropez whose harbour was under restoration, because of its high dues. But we convinced ourselves that, now the season was ending, prices would have dropped. However, with Levantine logic, they had doubled! We were aghast when the Harbourmaster told us the fees. He was at pains to explain that we might see reason. "Of course!" he said throwing wide his hands. "Now September, many less boat! No less cost repair harbour! Therefore less boat pay more money!" It was incontrovertible, and all a question of balancing the books. However, knowing his Turkish ropes, Bob appealed to the man's better nature, saying, just as reasonably, that, in this case, we could not stay, and the village would lose our custom: "You must inform your Mayor that we are poor people who cannot afford these dues!" he said. The Harbourmaster retired for a telephone consultation and came back beaming:

"No problem, sir! You pay one night! You stay two night!"

We were now at the heart of the area of the tragic exchange of populations described by Louis de Bernières in *Birds Without Wings*. Kalkan remained very Greek, though not officially so since 1922. Its gentrification was restrained. Flowers watered by underground springs cascaded. Stepped streets gave on to alleys where the display of carpets was discreet. No one importuned. I bought some lily-patterned şalvar in olive and petunia from a white-veiled dress-maker with a green-eyed cat. In a pastry shop near the Turkish minaret where Greek Orthodox plaques decorated the walls, French coffee was served with a sherry glass of goat's milk beside each cup. After washing my hair in spring water and donning the new şalvar, my crowning moment came with a visit to the bank, where the teller, clutching my passport to his chest, asked,

"You United Kingdom?"

"Yes!"

"You very pretty!"

To someone who has not enjoyed the pagan luxury of a bath since goodness knows when, such words were manna!

In Xanthos, whose citizens committed mass suicide rather than subjugate themselves, we were brought to a halt by the immediacy of a decorative stone daisy as sharply incised as if a long-ago sculptor had just laid down his chisel. Spread below, the great River Xanthos divided the plain, while to the north east reared Ak Dağ, the White Mountain, over 10,000 ft high, its sun-scorched slopes the colour of wolves' pelts. In Xanthos there was a pervading feeling that "that which hath been is now". Where had that erstwhile present gone? Moments dropped into the same silence. Was it beyond reason to wonder if landscape had a memory, and to feel the earth warm with the home fires of a people who twice chose death rather than displacement? Magic was surprisingly easy to attract in a Xanthian setting. To flow with as little interference as possible, all it required was a stilling of the body and mind in concentration outside the self. Then, as the senses slipped into receptivity, edges blurred and sights and sounds on the periphery of experience moved in and out of consciousness. The places in the world where magic may be attracted grow fewer, but the Lycian shore still numbers amongst them.

The Letoön lies beneath the water-table. Legend has it that, after the birth of her twins, Apollo and Artemis, Leto, exhausted and parched, halted here on her flight from Hero, Zeus's jealous wife. When the peasants fouled the sweet water, Leto, in her anger and despair, turned them into the frog ancestors of those that croak today in the half-submerged garden. Truncated columns and a Roman nymphaeum emerged from mirror-water in a way that was fitting, as if Leto herself had decreed that her sanctuary should rise from the Thirst-slaker. Ducks paddled the ruins and cattle grazing beneath the trees stooped to drink their own reflections. Intent on choosing our own line between contingents of besmocked French archaeologists in Impressionist hats, who did not look up from scrubbing shards, we strode from ruined wall to ruined wall. Only on turning my head as we left the arena, did I read too late, "Chantier Interdit!" ("Work Site – Entry Forbidden!")

Patara, principal port of Lycia where thrice-shipwrecked St Paul changed ships, had long been abandoned. The sands of time blown back across the seas we lately sailed veiled it to a considerable depth. Its fine blonde grains sealed the cavea of the theatre, creamed around the ruins of the lighthouse and filled our shoes. When we held out to sea again, *Cappelle* pirouetted in a pushy breeze.

The entrance to Kaş whose light structure had collapsed, was guarded by a Lycian sarcophagus. An underwater rock and beam seas all made for cautious approach to this oasis at the foot of a mountain wall ornamented at night by the fireflies of spot-lit Lycian tombs. Wooden balconies overhung the sweep of the main street as it rose to a miniature Arc de Triomphe, an elaborate house tomb with Gothic lid, a living example of the Lycian ghost that lies within Palladian architecture. A seafaring nation, the Lycians copied the ogee of their roofs from the shape of the upturned hulls of their boats (themselves copied from the natural twist of tree-boughs). At first the ends of the wooden beams (laid beneath the ogee like upside-down decking) protruded beyond the gable to support a top dressing of turf and animal skins (plus, in the more imposing houses, the heads of lions). Later these beams were squared off under the pediment. With the development of stone roofing, masons simply copied the ends of the obsolete wooden beams for the sake of tradition, which continues today in the dentil of classic architecture.

Eleven

An uncomfortable crossing

Kekova

With lozenge-shaped Kekova Island our next destination, we sailed past Ulu Burun, where in 1982 a sponge diver reported seeing objects like "biscuits with ears" (bronze ingots) leading to the discovery of a Bronze Age treasure ship. Having taken a line on a light structure, we were alone, so we thought, in this bewitching roadstead. But a speed boat intercepted us, its driver hailing us with glad cries as he brandished a tee-shirt emblazoned "Hard Rock".

"You know this 'Hard Rock'?"

"No! No! We don't want a tee-shirt!"

Escaping his attentions, we penetrated Üçaiz (Three Mouths) Liman, which cut at an angle into the mainland. On the island skyline opposite jutted the curtain wall of the machicolated Genoese fortress that surmounted the village of Kale Köy. Here in the late 1950s women brought Freya Stark all they had to offer – muddy water in a goatskin, and one egg. We had avoided the harbour, a maze of sunken ruins, for it was tenable only in calm weather, and even then not to be trusted. But at dawn, underestimating the distance, Bob set out to row round the headland between quarried islets where flights of steps left the upper air to descend to drowned Simena. He pulled into an inlet where domestic ducks circled a water-logged house-tomb. Here a girl helped us tie up before springing ahead in bunched skirts, taking goat trails that scribbled through ochreous clay between tumbledown houses, a basket of scarves on her hip. Hens scratched in the dust at the boles of trees as old as Methuselah, while Nuray ("Light of the Moon") chatted away, plucking sage and oregano to fill our pockets. Throwing stones at a carob tree until the twisted "goat's horns" pattered down, she snapped a handful in two for us to chew. They tasted of honeyed fig.

Everything in Kale Köy was scaled down. Carved into rock on the small height were the seven tiers of the prettiest amphitheatre in the Ancient World, only fifty feet in diameter, seating at most 300 citizens elbow to elbow, chewing carobs in season, no doubt, and chucking the husks at actors. Nuray sat on a rock busy with handiwork: "I make you present!" she said. Soon she was tying a tatting bracelet knotted with pearl drops round my wrist. Then, cupping my pale morning face in her hands, she scrutinised it, remarking, "You have face like child!" As we leaned over the winged battlements she pointed out the new school house, a converted byre, saying she was training to be a teacher in nearby Demre. Across the stretch-marked sea motor boats buzzed like angry water-beetles, trailing pennants of wake. Nuray was eager to show us house tombs. But we knew we must be on our way, for the breeze was rising. Promising to return next day, when I would purchase scarves for Christmas presents, we pointed out *Cappelle* from the rear of the castle.

The dinghy swirled in the breeze as the pyramid of houses surmounted by a flag-flying fortress receded. With the wind on the nose, Bob tried to keep within the lee of the land but, by the time we reached the headland, he was exhausted. Another speed-boat swerved up:

"You English? I take you to your ship!" Never was a tow more welcome.

Üçaiz (Ancient Teimuissa), a ramshackle hamlet "where everything but stone has passed away" was sited within a necropolis, its sarcophagi providing goalposts for the local lads. It felt fitting that such a village was not freeze-dried in its "vanished day". That night cats and stock wandered in and out of the steadings-cum-restaurant where a fat cook with a long-handled pan sweated before a bee-hive oven. But, with the building of an inland link road, the Hard Rock brigade had taken over.

We ordered fish just as a flotilla put in, its crews demanding chicken. A boy-girl foursome plonked itself down at the next table, the blonde crying expansively,

"Order everything! Red wine AND white!"

"So the skipper said, 'Don't you EVER do that again!' and I said, 'Look here! I can do what I like! I'm on holiday, I am, so PISS OFF!'" grumbled the brunette.

It was their first experience of cruising. On the whole they found it rollicking fun, especially when old so-and-so drove into the quay wall at seven knots. Among such Big Spenders our order was forgotten. When Bob remonstrated, he was met with, "Not possible cook fish yet!" It seemed there was not enough chicken to go round either. At last a dish containing two small mullet was put down in front of him causing him to ask in surprise,

"Where's the lady's dinner?"

"No for lady!" said the waiter firmly.

Rowing towards the rear of the castle next morning, we ventured, so we thought, upon an easier route of ascent. But reaching the ridge over chunks of sharp volcanic rock protruding through thorn bush, was more daunting than anticipated. With the cyclops eyes of pigeon tombs staring at us from the most unlikely places, we made a snakes-and-ladder progress, frequently finding ourselves waist-high in holly oak. We were becoming disorientated when, after several detours, we emerged onto an overgrown castle approach. Here, seeing large paw-prints in the soft earth, Bob voiced the hope we were not about to meet a bear! After bridging a collapsed thornbrake, we tumbled, much scratched, onto the footpath beneath the fortress.

Nuray, who had witnessed our progress from the battlements, ran to meet us. Skipping ahead, she conducted us on a tour of the necropolis. Singly, in pairs, or grouped with a social air, many house-tombs stood upright. But centuries of arboreal growth had choked the certainties of ancestor-worship by forcing others, no match for the dogged resolve of any obdurate olive seeding beside it, to lie at crazy angles or with their lids levitated into the forks of trees. Nearer the village, the tombs took on practical use as wood sheds. Looking down from the castle we worked out a better line of descent along a dry stream bed. Before the light faded we were away down roadstead to Gökkaya, a group of islets only navigable by day. (One skerry stood proud, since it offered a convenient garbage-dumping point for gulets.) There was to be none of the skinny-dipping Nataja recommended (with illustrations), for Gökkaya played host to a gulet convention.

Since, at 29 degs 54' East, we were approaching *Cappelle's* insurance limit of 30 degs East, we had reached our sailing horizon. With leaden-winged herons flapping across the foredeck, and a memory of gulets silhouetted against a crocus sunrise seductive enough to turn the head of many a Far Beyonder, we raised anchor. Taking the shallow channel via Sicak Yarmadası (the Hot Peninsula), we were soon back in Kaş. But Bob was unwilling to undertake a lengthy passage until the oil strainer was freed. So we made the circuitous inland journey to Fethiye by bus where the Volvo agent handed over his personal socket with extension arm against neither deposit nor references, but Bob's promise to return it via the bus driver. While Bob laboured, I spent the last of our Turkish lire. At the butcher's, motionless beside the till to which it was loosely tethered with a piece of twine, sat a magnificent hawk, its hooded yellow eyes scanning the skies.

Kastellorizzo

Though required to enter "Rhodes" as our destination on our exit papers, we planned to make Kastellorizzo our first port of call. Here on Kaş's doorstep lay the farthest flung Greek island – so far flung it was off most Aegean maps. Everyday an old woman hoisted the Greek flag over the Red Castle. But, should the population (once 20,000 but now only 200) fall below forty, Kastellorizzo is destined to revert to the traditional enemy in whose shadow it lies. So low was the quay, *Cappelle* bade fair to sail onto land.

We were careful to exchange our Turkish flag for Greek, but the Harbour Master, presenting Bob with a complimentary bottle of οὐζο smiled, "Don't worry, sir! Here you are nowhere!" When we outlined our plan to leave next afternoon in order to negotiate the surrounding skerries in daylight before setting overnight course for Rhodes, he cautioned against departure until the strong winds currently blowing abated. If we must leave, our best chance of finding a "window" lay in leaving between two and three o'clock in the morning. But Kastellorizzo, an island we were not prepared to navigate by night, was waterless. And we were short of it, having been too lazy to remoor nearer a water source in Kaş. Persuading ourselves we knew best, for it was already September and the meltem was due to subside, we planned to get well away during daylight, sail all night, and be in sight of Rhodes by morning.

In the event, a disgruntled *Mood Indigo* left precipitately, her skipper yanking up our anchor. This set the scene for confusion for, to save relaying, Bob cast off while I was still prancing about half-naked repacking stores. The jumble of mooring lines and anchor warp, plus the shortness of my arms and my inability to be in two places at once, lead to my being bawled out for letting go the remaining mooring line. We were not a happy ship. Departure on passage, an act of trust in boat, crew, weather and sea, is always tense. At least the preparations should be satisfactorily concluded, so that one faces the future all senses alert. Ill-prepared and in a bad temper was no way to tackle the rapids beneath the castle wall. Out at sea, I looked doubtfully back at the ominous anvil-shape of a huge cumulonimbus cloud filling out above the mountains of the Chelidonian peninsula, home of the Chimaera, that mythical beast part lion, part goat, part snake, whose fiery breath (Jack O'Lantern's ignis fatuus) might yet be seen in the night sky.

We beat into Force 5, pointing as closely as we might. The sea roughened. Time dragged gruellingly. Weary of *Cappelle's* head-butting, I longed for the wind to go down with the sun. At 17.40 hrs Bob vomited and I lurched into the cabin to pull on oil-skins. From baying like a pack of hounds, the wind, developing an edge, began to hone the nerves like a razor. The night, shading black at the edges, collected itself. When the moon rose we hove to. Bob failed abysmally to convince me we could return whence we came, for we both knew this would be foolhardy in darkness. Neither was I persuaded we had travelled further than we had, for I could see the lights of Kalkan and, too close for comfort, the twin humps of the Çatal Isles of ill-repute. Only fifteen miles from our starting point after all these hours, we were in the shallow seas off the Sands of Patara, a notoriously unhealthy spot where sandbanks shift and fuse for hundreds of metres out to sea. Ahead lay the Seven Angry Capes. Bob took sights, reading the compass by torchlight. He had to admit that *Cappelle* was drifting inexorably inch-by-inch towards a lee shore, the current forcing her backwards towards the Çatal Islands. It was essential to undertake the fraught operation of changing tack in heavy seas.

With the moon a cruel headlamp, I was detailed to crawl on all fours along the cockpit bench to take the helm, while Bob assumed control of the sails. The time was 20.30 hrs. "Listen to me!" yelled Bob above the eldritch shriek. "The moon is on the stern! OK? Bring the boat round until it is on the starboard beam!...Do it... *NOW!*" Gritting my teeth, I wrenched the helm over, slipping and sliding on the streaming deck to brace my feet the other way. The boom crashed across. Motoring into wind, we lashed the wheel, more satisfied with our situation, for the capes and islands kept their distance.

Life was lived from moment to moment, wave to wave. From my angle, wedged on the cockpit floor, sea water sloshing round me before self-draining, the waves were towering. But, like Fear itself, they were better faced. Periodically Bob threw up. Although my teeth chattered and ague swept me, I was not sick. Under the hard and blazing moon riding high and white in the sky, some disembodied banshee was challenging the villainous night with a never-ending scream. ("Force 9 is a scream; Force 10 is a shriek; Force 11 is a moan... after that you don't want to know.") Irritatingly, for the umpteenth time I faltered, "Is that the wind?" for the decibels were too insane. "What the blazes do you think it is?" snapped Bob.

A criss-cross of pointed water mountains topped with spindrift that gave the wave crests a fragile, furry texture, menaced us from all angles. It was our first experience of pyramid seas, and a relief to feel *Cappelle's* competent rise as she compressed each hissing monster beneath her before letting it surge on to dump more sand on Patara and punishment on the Seven Capes. Hitting shore, the muscular waters deflected to repeat their assault in reverse. What I dreaded most was a simultaneous hoisting by opposing seas. Experiencing what sailors call "uncomfortable" conditions, I recognised that the sea, beyond holding the secret of adventure, its solitude, its precariousness and its constant surprise, was a Pandora's box whose lid might blow at any moment: "Only consider how far *DOWN* the beautiful islands go…" wrote the poet Seferis. Right now it was better not to. Life assumed perfect simplicity, for it consisted strictly of the present, each wave on its own merits.

As the gale tore past our ears, *Cappelle*, maintaining her balance like a spirit level, adapted to the onslaught like a professional. The way to cope was to shorten focus. Seeking a positive thought to hold onto, I found the phrase, "I am not cold!" for I had on heavy-weather gear and the September seas were warm. Letting the phrase run in my head like a mantra, I repeated to myself, "I am not cold! I am not cold!" After two hours, conditions marginally improved, Bob made up his mind to crack off on a course he had been working on between bouts of nausea. And get the hell out of it! Tactics must be based on where the weather would allow us to go. Reefed right down, with the engine on to steady the ship and a storm jib hoisted, we ploughed off on 260 deg, south of west, in F 7/8, lee rail under, state of sea high and confused.

I had prepared a thermos. Together with a packet of UHT milk and canister of sugar, it was wedged in the sink. Lurching into the galley I poured coffee in the caesura between waves, but the sugar canister flew out of my hand sending sticky drifts over cushions and carpet. Worse came with a trip to the loo. With *Cappelle* heeled to port I sat on the throne with my feet dangling and nothing to hold onto but the wall-mounted wash-basin. Then came the dreaded combination of circumstances, the collision of opposing waves beneath the hull. The impact catapulted me headfirst into the wet wardrobe. My face caught its edge full tilt. Splintered wood and a loosened nail from the split fascia gashed my eyebone. When I hauled myself back into the cockpit I was blinded by blood running into my eye and down my numbed cheek.

Wedged tightly in the cockpit we churned on, sipping coffee and nibbling the biscuits I had pushed into my pocket. Fat stars bounced up and down. Rhodes was the Never Never Land. When it was the Lost Boy's turn to take the helm and keep straight on till morning, I steered by the second star on the right. Unlike my namesake, Horsel (a later guise of Aphrodite), whom Teutonic poets saw sailing the heavens in a silver moon boat, the stars in her wake her 11,000 virgins, I lacked the divine gift of celestial navigation. But any bright heavenly body held constant between the shrouds relieved the necessity for compass check. First light revealed a right eye like a cluster of blackberries.

By the time the morning sun struck rainbows in the spray, dead reckoning showed our position as between fifteen and twenty miles off the southern quarter of Rhodes. Pushed south, we were in the dangerous Sea of Karpathos and nearer than is desirable to its Straits of Evil Repute. We therefore went about onto a northerly heading, which to me in practical terms meant changing the position of the sun from port quarter to starboard beam. As the state of the sea improved, we sailed a series of tacks; at 09.30 hrs on a westerly heading; at 10.30 hrs on a northerly; at 11.15 hrs on a westerly again (after involuntarily going about twice), at 11.45 hrs on a northerly once more, and at 12.45 hrs on a westerly, a course held until first sighting the acropolis of Lindos, which gave us our position.

By 14.30 hrs, seas decreasing, Bob fired the engine and we motored slightly off wind at 320 degrees, making better than five knots and reckoning thirty miles to go to Mandraki, the yacht harbour of Rhodes. I bathed dried blood from my gummed eyelid and spread the cushions, trying to scrape up wet sugar with the bread knife. Bob combed his hair and, in a mood of over-optimism (possibly engendered by hoisting the quarantine flag), put on his clean shorts and shirt carefully preserved in polythene, ready for officialdom at Port of Entry. When we closed Rhodes, the wind, following the coastline, headed us again.

Our aim became to reach harbour before dark, though more sensible sailors might have settled for another night at sea. (Miles Smeeton, archetypical prudent skipper, once abandoned an attempt to anchor

Tzu Hang off a remote island in the middle of a 4,000 mile passage.) Swallowing paracetamol for my head, which throbbed like a bad tooth, I snoozed upright while *Cappelle* roared into short, steep seas. Having opened the boat up to dry, if we were not wet before, we were very wet then. Periodically, apart from the bilge water flung up the insides of the hull, a chute of sea water jetted down the anchor's navel pipe to the chain locker. Then Bob fielded facefuls of sea across the coachroof. Every few minutes, too weak to react positively, though my position was worse than nesting under a garden sprinkler, I was half aroused by water gushing down my neck. A glance told me that Bob's clean shorts and shirt lay in a puddle on the duckboards and that he was back in his discarded oilies.

Darkness descended. At 19.00 hrs on the second day, Bob roused me to look at what he believed were the lights of Rhodes town, but were, in fact, those of Faliraki (Capital of the One-Night Stand) further south. We presumed we were abeam the eastern end of Rhodes. In reality this curved away, its extremity a yet considerable distance ahead. Even after we had rounded the next cape, the peninsula remained cut off to view, did we but know it. Closing land, we sailed off the coast for another three and a half hours, until doubling a final cape at 22.00 hrs into the dazzle of coastal illuminations, including airport lead-in lights. If navigation beacons were among the concussions of light, they were indistinguishable. But I had recovered a little and we handed sail.

Unlike the Captain, who had been consigning harbour diagrams to memory, my mind was unencumbered by preconception. After thirty-six hours of physical and mental stress, Bob's exhaustion, on the other hand, rendered him susceptible to perceptual illusion. This, coupled with an over-whelming desire to make harbour, sowed the seeds that can transform the pattern of what a sailor sees into what he wants to see, a supposition that can develop into a dangerous idée fixe. Thus the floodlit funnel of a cruise liner inside the main harbour of Akandia, seen over the top of the mole, became a light-house. Likewise three cylindrical storage tanks (though I pointed out there was something odd about them, for even in darkness they had a strangely industrial aspect) became the sought-after landmark of three windmills.

All the while Mandraki lay still out of sight. When Bob swore he could see a ship moving above the darkling band of the mole, this was the old moving platform and stationary train syndrome. Unconvinced, I urged him to keep going. Then we passed a bastion surmounted by a red light. "This is it! It *HAS* to be Mandraki! We're going in!" shouted Bob, seeing it as a navigation light. There are many shades of black and this supposed entrance loomed at us in the darkest of nights the deadest of lamp blacks, a depthless black. As we motored forward I knew without a doubt that something was very wrong indeed. That was the clue! *THE BLACKNESS WAS DEPTHLESS!* It had to be a wall! I started to scream, *"NO! NO! DON'T...GO!...YOU MUSTN'T!"* We were aiming for a concrete mole. Just in time, Bob wrenched the helm to starboard. Breathing heavily, we trickled on.

Only after we had passed the entrance to Akandia, which faced east, not south, and beyond Emborikos the commercial harbour, did we positively identify the landmarks sought, the silhouette of three ancient windmills and the roof of Restaurant Kontiki triangulated in fairy lights. Further ahead, from behind the bulky newel post of the Fort of St Nicholas, came the intermittent red and green flash of the navigation beacons which replaced the fiery cresset held aloft by the Colossus of Rhodes, who once bestrode the Great Gateway. Keeping centre fairway, we turned to port into a cramped outer harbour where I called out warnings of rocky outcrops dimly distinguishable by their liquid edgings of white lace, to turn to port again into Mandraki. Bob, eyes staring, fingers in rigor mortis on the helm, was thankful at least to be under no obligation to unstep the mast, as had been the custom when entering between the spread legs of the Sun God. Inside, yachts were triple-banked. Though it was the early hours of the morning, I failed to prevent him, after circling twice, banging on a hull to request permission to tie up.

Next morning, after dealing with the Port Authorities, Bob approached Georgios on his bike to unlock the water hydrant, and we borrowed extra hoses to reach out to *Cappelle*. Damage was relatively minor – mirror on loo door cracked, fascia (with blood on it) of wet wardrobe shattered, one cleat lost, main halyard winch not working, bilge pump pulled apart, dinghy painter snapped (though dinghy saved by the life lines), wet bedding, wet upholstery and fourteen feet of wet books. "What sort of passage did you have?" yachtsmen asked, giving my black eye a funny look and reminding me that my presentation left much to be desired. "So, so..." we replied nonchalantly, "A bit wet though!" A French couple, Daniel and Mireille, were quick to bag us the slot next to theirs on the North Quay. Pegging out our belongings, we spread enough books on the coachroof to start rumours of a book sale.

We were disappointed to find Rhodes's Nea Agora, located beyond the noise barrier of its fascist-style waterfront, rubbish-strewn, the crowds within intent on chips and candy floss. With a choice between Summernights Bar and Smileburger Fastfood beside racks of day-glow tee-shirts claiming Rhodes "Capital of Europe", we settled for chicken on a spit. Sourly I recalled the words of Alan Bennet: "The crowd has found the door to the secret garden. Now they will tear up the flowers by the roots, strip the borders and strew them with paper and broken bottles."

Twelve

We gain a new crew member

Our life is changed

The timing of our landfall on Rhodes was momentous. Our lives were never the same again. Our adventure acquired a new dimension. *Cappelle's* arrival at a particular place at a particular time was under the influence of Artemis, Creator of the Cat.

When my teeth were set on edge by a grating noise that bore token to a hungry seagull, a human baby, or, more likely, a neighbour using a power tool, I stuck my fingers in my ears and turned the radio up. But, once off *Cappelle*, I investigated, for the sound was now so compelling I knew I was nearer its source and that it was not mechanical. Crossing to the outer harbour, I convinced myself that to rescue whatever it was I must climb the base of the Fort. Then, between the sea-shuffled boulders at my feet, in the approximate position of the Colossus's right foot, the bedraggled head of a black and white kitten appeared, its body rocked by wavelets. If, as the Poet Laureate Robert Southey said, "A kitten is to the animal kingdom what a rosebud is to a garden," this one was the exception. "You're not very pretty, are you!" I told it, as I grabbed it by its scruff and dropped it in my shopping bag. Filthy and tar-streaked, it screeched louder. Puzzled tourists regarded me accusingly. "I've got a kitten – but it's all right, *I DON'T WANT TO KEEP IT!*" I called to Bob. My plan was to clean the sorry little thing up and let it go to the clowder of cats in the rocks, for nothing qualified so unsightly a mite for adoption.

Never were words less prophetic. The decision was not mine to make,

172

for the kitten intended to keep *Cappelle.* Its mechanism was so wound up that, once in the cabin, it continued to bawl its head off as if unable to stop until the clockwork had run down. Smearing Marmite on the end of its nose to take its mind off its troubles, I rubbed it down with a towel. Its coat came out in tufts. Its bleary eyes were a myopic grey, one of its bat-wing ears was congenitally crooked, and it had great big spoon feet. I judged it to be four to five weeks old, in which case, according to cat astrology, it had been born under the sign of Leo – a lucky star sign! When I attempted to feed it bread and milk, it crawled into the darkest, most insalubrious corner it could find – under the outlet pipe behind the loo. Here, crying convulsively, it stayed all day. By evening it was spewing sea water and retching so piteously I spread a towel for it at the foot of my berth. But it refused to settle, preferring to stagger up me waving a small stiff tail to push its face round the back of my neck, convinced that somewhere about my person was a teat full of warm mother's milk. Failing to discover this, it stuffed its nose down my ear, sucking and kneading with oversized paws. When it fell asleep it was to be woken by hunger pangs and start the cycle over. We spent a bad night.

Since we intended to sail on as soon as the weather improved, Bob and I agreed we should seize the opportunity to explore Rhodes. After ensuring the kitten's every convenience (such as a baking tin filled with beach gravel for a dirt tray), leaving the exhausted orphan asleep in my warm patch, we caught the early bus to Lindos. By nine o'clock the village was crammed with day-trippers. After an elbow-to-elbow toil up flights of steps to the acropolis and a quick look at the scaffolding-shrouded Temple of Athena, we joined the endless Indian file hustled back down the inside of the steps to allow a steady stream of newcomers to mount four abreast on the outside. Women touting table linen spread on the hillside like washing out to dry clutched at our ankles. Down in the village, we sought peace in the black and white pebble-patterned courtyards of the grand old sea captains' houses. Lighting a candle in the church of the Virgin of Lindos, I prayed that her spirit was not troubled by the insensitivity of the crowds outside. By eleven o'clock we caught the bus home.

In the cabin silence reigned. The kitten was nowhere to be seen. I could not believe he had escaped. On the carpet were patches of spittle. Then a hissing noise alerted me to the recesses of the damp hole under the draining board out of which I pulled a pitiable little object foaming at the mouth and trying to defend itself by spitting and scratching. In less than twenty minutes, although he retched, the frantic heart beats slowed and he cheered up. Soon he was ready to try drinking. By the third day he was nibbling scraps, squeezing behind the spare water tank in the forepeak and experimenting with his tray. He also developed a penchant for chewing bare toes and suckling on skin. The only action that drove him crazy was any attempt to take him out of the cabin. As far as he was concerned, he had come home and was determined to stay put. As Mireille said, "Il a senti le beau bateau!" Having sensed the beautiful boat, he had cried and cried until taken aboard.

On cleaning his ears and nostrils with cotton buds, I saw fleas running through his fur, so, brushing up on vocabulary, set off for the pharmacy. In my crumpled wardrobe that had suffered a sea change, I was far from prepossessing. But, since my eye ceased to pain me, I forgot it. It was a question of "My face I don't mind it, for I am behind it". By day I tipped my Dedham straw at a rakish angle. But in the evening, dissolutely hatless, "The people in front got the jar!" When I launched into an explanation about "my little pussy" and the need for flea powder, the white-coated pharmacist's assistant backed off. Looking disapprovingly down her nose, she took out a puff-pack decorated with many-legged varieties of flea, handing it over at arm's length. I asked if I should rub it in. «Ακριβώς!» ("Exactly!") she sniffed, advancing my change with a ruler. I left wondering why my pathetic story had been received with quite such distaste. Then, blushing in the dark, I was brought to a halt under a street lamp as I examined the carton of Pubex. The penny dropped. It was ME she believed bug-ridden!

There were two sides to the coin: from certain quarters, particularly amongst Greek women accustomed to the flat of their nearest and dearest's hand, my eye earned me sympathy. It was fundamental amongst Greeks, brought up for a thousand years in the Eastern Orthodox tradition of the authority of the scriptures, to equate men and women with Adam and Eve. Woman is Eve, flawed by nature, no matter her position. The sexes may be equally necessary to the survival of the human race, but Man is born superior, for he stands on the right hand of God, while Woman stands on the left, nearer the Devil. Whatever her character or prestige, her nature is such that it is the duty of Man to control her illogicality, unreliability and excess. Who tempted Adam with the apple? It was Eve, of course. All the same, Greeks were not accustomed to encountering a Western woman who had felt her consort's fist. Even the mini-marketeer was puzzled. After sizing Bob up, he ventured to enquire how I came by my injury. On being told, he slapped his sides in relief.

A volatile character, the mini-marketeer wooed our custom with mini-packets of fruit juice, sweets or a pear. I was in his pokey shop one day when a tourist couple brought things to a halt by dallying over duty-frees. Suddenly the dam of his patience broke. Chucking empty packing cases after their scurrying heels, he threw them out. "GO! GO!" he shouted, arms waving, eyes blazing. "Such people! Problem people! My price the best! Always the best!" I was fortunate to have been taught the courteous way to ask for things, not couched as a demand but as a suggestion. «Μήπως έχετε?» ("Perhaps you have…?") made all the difference. Historically, the retail trade's association in Greece is with barter. Sometimes, especially among older people, barter nudged close. A market woman, taking a shine to Bob, bowed before placing the strawberries he wished to buy down in front of him, indicating that he was to place his money in front of her. In this way the transaction became the exchange of gifts between friends rather than the payment of filthy lucre.

The mini-market's stock was limited. But even after I had discovered a basement supermarket selling tinned cat food, I was careful to retain our benefactor's goodwill, for we enjoyed his fresh-baked bread of a morning. Since I could not enter his shop without him diving into my shopping bag, unpacking everything without by-your-leave, brandishing tins under my nose and muttering as he checked prices, I practised open subterfuge. Sometimes I repacked my bag so that it revealed only fresh produce from the Nea Agora or butcher's meat. At other times

I made a detour along the sea wall behind his shop. Although I patronised other suppliers, as well he knew, as long as I was mannerly enough not to be blatant about it, it was all right by him, and we remained friends.

Each evening the sprawling fourteenth-century Castle of the Knights Hospitallers advanced in floodlight. Its *Son et Lumière* told the story of the castle's last stand against the encroachment of Islam. Beguiled by cypress trees jade-lit against the afterglow, the recorded voice whispered, "See! The cypresses are thinking!" Then the light focussed on the tall palms, "And the palm trees are dreaming of their Nubian past!" Heavy with night scents, the garden recalled a Greek haiku,

> "Whether it's dusk
> Or dawn's first light
> The jasmine stays
> Always white"

"Now smell the jasmine!" urged Mystery Voice.

These were our halcyon days. Dawn brought Bluebirds of Happiness. Kingfishers were our joy. We awoke to their piercing whistles. Low, swift and direct in flight, in our world but not of it, they populated the harbour more numerously than boats. Compact, short-necked and rapier-beaked, oblivious of human presence, they preened on cap rails pin-pointing the water until a sudden dart for fish. Catching fire in sapphire, green and ruby-gold, as scintillatingly solid as Fabergé eggs, they delighted in swinging on anchor chains. If, as the saying goes, only the righteous can see a kingfisher, then we were all heaven-bound. One morning when we had been shopping neighbours came to meet us, fingers to lips, "Mind you go aboard *QUIETLY!* Your kitten and a kingfisher are sharing your stern deck!"

The Ugly Kitling, bare in patches and scabby-nosed, soon gained the confidence to explore the anchor locker. Among his favourite toys were a cardboard loo-roll with a crackly foil bottle-top sellotaped inside and a float on a piece of string fastened to a locker handle. Bob described the cabin as a nursery. Summoning courage, I approached another pharmacy for worm powders, this time using measured BBC World Service English. "Spik English!" snapped the assistant. "I not understand. You English or what? Why you no spik good?"

On 26th October "The Little Summer of St Demetrios" dawned gloriously. Since the kitten no longer resented being left, we took the bus to Kallithea, one-time Graeco-Romano watering hole to which the Italians added a colonnaded Art Deco approach, plus an Indo-Turkish dome fenestrated with pastry-cutter pentagrams. Benign Greek neglect further enhanced the little spa.

By reason of the itchy scarlet lesions that were bubbling on my chest and arms, I took to swimming in a long-sleeved shirt. The trouble spread rapidly. At yet another pharmacy (keeping mum this time) I presented my arm. «Γιατρό!» ("Doctor!") blurted the chemist. I was horrified! Though concerned for myself, I could not bear the idea – certain he must be the cause – of turning the kitten out. On consulting the Yellow Pages for a skin specialist (all Greek doctors specialise), I found a Dr Koutalianos. Clutching a map, I twice missed the way to his surgery in dread of arrival. Then, faced with a sign reading "Venereologist and Dermatolgist", I prayed no one saw me go in. Dr Koutalianos smiled when I showed him my sores. "You have a cat!" he said in kindly tones. "This happens all the time. In your country you call it 'ring-worm'. Don't worry! It is not a problem!" As if reading my thoughts, he continued sympathetically, "And would you like me to treat your cat as well? I think you wish to keep him. It is best I treat you both together." I left the surgery with prescriptions for us both – and a glowing impression of Greek doctors.

We recovered fast. The kitten's fur grew thick and lustrous. He was as clever as chop-sticks. His eyes registered everything, even when I changed the colour of my head-band. If I put on a hat to go out, he took to his bed. His favourite game was to be netted in a cat's cradle of string tied with enough toys to render him a feline German band. From this he extricated himself with the speed of Houdini and stood waiting to be tied up again. Bob taught him to perform back somersaults off his knee, which became his party trick whenever he was hungry.

If this failed, he posed Greuse-eyed beside his blue bowl on the step beneath the cooker.

He did, however, remain a Cat-with-No-Name. In the morning, executing a witchetty dance along the boom, tail fluffed, back arched, ears flat, he was the Sorcerer's Apprentice. For his ambipawtrous dexterity with a ping-pong ball he was Georgie Best; dancing he was Nureyev, and swinging on the table-cloth he was Tigger. Sometimes Bob addressed him as "Ratbag", and sometimes I called him "Scruffy" after Paul Gallico's Gibraltarian ape. Whatever his guise, we loved the little rascal. It was time for serious bonding. After his discovery in the proximity of the Sun God's right foot, he had a legitimate claim to the name "Colossus". It fitted his big paws too. But the name that stuck ("for a cat needs a name that's particular") was put forward by our new friend, Julia of *Golden Prospect*, whom he reminded of Pyewacket, the witch's cat in *Bell, Book and Candle*. Indeed Mireille referred to his bent lug as "sa marque" ("his sign"), seeing it as evidence of his falling off a broomstick while undergoing tuition in pillion riding (or possibly Quidditch). Of further cabalistic significance were his eyes now turning yellowy-green for spice. From Pyewacket, born of Mandraki, he became "Wacky", which suited his bent luggit and extrovert personality.

A Ship's Kit in earnest, Wacky eschewed all attempts to entice him down his custom-built gang-plank. With him, terra firma was strictly non grata. Cutting a red leather puppy collar down to size, I hung on it a miniature Evil Eye as a protective φυλαχτό (amulet). Thus presented in all his glory, he was a charming sight, reducing French boatwife, Denise, who had never recovered from the loss of her own Ship's Cat, Zéus ("si beau, si gracieux") to tears.

Winter in Rhodes

The seas continued rough. Yachts in transit stayed put. Bob smoothed filler on abrasions on *Cappelle's* bows, while on *Baraka*, Daniel, stylish in cut-off denims and matelot vest, was surrounded by pots of paint. Occasionally, expostulating "Merde!" he dropped his hammer on deck from the cross-trees. The French yacht's name, meaning "Blessing" in

Arabic, held a portent of the future, for she was under preparation for passage to France. To Daniel and Mireille's joy, they expected a second child.

The initial warning of an approaching southerly came in the build-up of suffocating cumulonimbus clouds as tall as obelisks and louring as a stage-set for *King Lear*. These were followed by marching squall lines flicked with lightning. After violent thunderstorms had cracked the skies and metallic-smelling rain fell, sou'westerlies scarified the sea. Blown onto the quay, we pulled off on the stern anchor. Then *Baraka's* boom landed with a crash in our cockpit. That night the gale swung north, forcing us off-quay again. Scarce able to breathe, Bob crawled ashore via a neighbouring gang plank to fix extra lines. With the sea a tumultuous malachite, the weather bulletin reported seas κατακυματώδης to τρικυμιά (very rough to high) with winds Rodos/ Samos area Storm Force 10. The harbour filled with fishing boats. For fifty miles down coast the Turkish mountains were brought forward as if in a zoom lens. Two sail-training yachts from the Armed Forces Heavy Weather Sailing School rollicked out of harbour, spinning close to reefs as they raised storm jibs. Still the expert wind-surfers took air, rocketing like mad butterflies. The bad weather persisted. Living in the teeth of the wind had a strangely debilitating affect, chipping away at reserves of well-being. One morning a yachtswoman ran back, excitedly waving a newspaper after making a routine telephone call to her mother in England. The international press reported Rhodes struck by hurricane-force winds that had caused three deaths. This was the first we heard about it!

Guy Fawkes Day was shared with the Greek Elections. I celebrated calm seas with a swim off the shingle beach Lawrence Durrell listed as the finest in the world. In summer the annealed pebbles were plastered with bodies. But in November only residual litter and regiments of concrete umbrella stands remained. We walked the cannon-ball scattered moat encircling the Old City and the carriage-wide wall above it, and visited my favourite artefact the "Marine Venus", the lucent, sea-smoothed, satin-textured Aphrodite of Rhodes. A small white marble figure, she kneels smiling, holding out the wet bunches of her hair. That night, huddled around a bonfire in the rocks with fellow live-aboards and bottles of wine, we kept out of earshot of the amplified electioneering.

The miraculous visibility climaxed in a fourteen-hour carwash performance that overlaid the harbour with bouncing raindrops. But, except for cabins transformed into sounding drums, we boat-people were best off. The rainstorm developed into a veritable $\Delta \varepsilon v \tau \acute{\varepsilon} \rho a$ $\Pi a \rho o v \sigma \acute{\iota} a$ ("Second Coming"), as the Greeks say, the worst deluge in living memory. Twice Bob bailed out the dinghy before it sank with weight of water. Villages were inundated, apartments ruined and deaths by landslide occurred in the Ataviros region. In the Old City mediaeval walling collapsed, and in the New Town the supermarket basement, where cat food was stored, was flooded. For the rest of that week a sticky south easterly dominated. Then, after two more days of heavy rain, the gale force winds veered north west, forcing us off quay once more. With northerlies from the Balkans alternating with southerlies from Africa, temperatures fluctuated wildly.

On St Andrews Day the saint "sported his white beard" – snow. All thought of moving on was then dismissed by the live-aboard contingent. Daniel, abandoning his plan of sailing for France, booked Mireille's confinement in Rhodes hospital. Gaby fretted as his mother's time drew near. Hearing him weeping on return from play to a deserted *Baraka* one lunch-time (his parents only late back from shopping, but Gaby fearing the worst), we fetched him onto *Cappelle*. Mireille, cheerfully rocking back on her heels as she swung onto *Baraka,* was soon rushed to hospital to be delivered of lusty son Simon. Mother and Baby were back on Baraka almost before we had time to miss them, Mireille telling the tale of how she had found Greek obstetrics "barbare" and about a pretty tsigane whose presence in the labour ward had scandalised the bourgeois mothers.

On 3rd December the Bush-Gorbachev Summit (to become known as the "Sea-sick Summit") scheduled to take place off Malta on the *Maxim Gorki,* was restricted to Valetta Harbour on account of foul weather. This proved a point, for there were those at home still accusing us of "swanning in the Med". We busied ourselves with odd jobs. When

Bob took a taxi to the out-of-town gas factory to exchange the gas canister, it was not until arrival at the factory gates that the driver informed him that since, under Greek law (unlike Turkish) it was illegal to transport filled gas canisters in taxis, he would be unable to take him home again! We were forced to ration our emergency supply until the local dealer returned from holiday. We also devoted a day to servicing the Baby Blake (another job not normally undertaken by "swans") flushing it with a mixture of hydrochloric acid and cooking oil.

Boomerang, a large motor-sailer, with the circumnavigation of Australia under her keel (Skipper Digger's finger missing to prove it), moved in next to us. Wacky, while still rejecting terra firma, could not resist leaping across to "Buckingham Palace", where he cheekily availed himself of Siamese Sam's dirt tray and committed other light-hearted indiscretions. Digger, who had sold a canning factory to sail (as he so often reminded everyone, it became a standing joke), indulged in grown-up toys, buying a Suzuki motor-cycle and recruiting Bob to hoist it aboard.

Three lost cities

We celebrated Digger's birthday as a foursome by hiring a car to tour Rhodes's three Lost Cities: Ialyssos, Kamiros and Lindos, named from the three sons of Helios the Sun God. Legend had it that the cities were abandoned on account of a plague of house flies, the citizens then cooperating in the founding of the city of Rhodes. We failed to locate Ialyssos until a passer-by told us it was signposted "Phileremos", and that the modern village was called "Trianda" anyway. But Kamiros, framed by ilex and cypress, lay white-boned within a limestone knuckle, the peculiar three-dimensional quality of the soft winter sunshine making shadows surreal. From the bluff, the main street lead to the hard blue line of the sea backed by the distant cliffs of Loryma on the Turkish mainland.

High in the mountains telegraph poles lay scattered across the river beds like match-sticks. Debris from flash floods hung in the trees. Skipping ahead on Lindos headland, Mavis called, "Come on!" before reappearing on a further promontory. The goat track she took petered out in a Bad Step scarcely a foot wide, sloping seawards and halfway down a 600 ft precipice. The cliff face above leaned outwards, while that below fell sheer to a cauldron of rocks and white water. I am a devout coward when it comes to heights. It needed all Bob's cajoling – "Come on now! Don't look down!"– to persuade me to sidle forwards and grab his fingers. Then, dizzily aware of the ignominy of sliding to destruction below the Temple of Lindian Athena on a landslide of New Age drink cans, it was a hands and knees scramble over unstable rock and rubbish-strewn screes. Meanwhile the others gambolled ahead through pastures starred with autumn crocus, a potent flower said to have spawned on the slopes of Mount Ida from the heat of the passion of Zeus and Hera. We looked down into St Paul's Harbour, its rock-fringed waters ink blue in a pot of tarnished silver. Perhaps St Paul's sleep had been disturbed, for a heavy swell siphoned in.

When the winds howled remorselessly, everyone was out of sorts. Digger, taking advantage of a gap on the main quay, handed over Wacky (up to his juvenile tricks on *Boomerang* as usual), before recruiting Bob to assist him with re-berthing. But before I could say "Whiskas!" Wacky popped out of a porthole and leapt back onto *Boomerang*. Too late, he saw the widening strip of water between himself and his ship. With a panic-struck yowl, he raced frantically up and down trying to judge his return jump. Bundled in disgrace into a blanket, he was later reunited with *Cappelle,* thanks to another yachtsman (also recruited by Digger) wearing leather gauntlets. While sleeping off the melodrama, Wacky opened his eyes wide at intervals to make certain he was home.

With plans to spend Christmas in England, we inspected the boatyard, whose mole had been extended to forestall a repeat of a tragedy of recent years when gales brought parked lorries crashing off the quay onto yachts below. Bob made a provisional booking at the boatyard. But we both felt uneasy, especially, after a warning to strip *Cappelle* of her contents since theft was rife. Our other problem was Wacky, who, for quarantine reasons, could not be taken to England. Neighbours offered to feed him if we left *Cappelle* in the water, but his expectations were far higher. Again I consulted the Yellow Pages for a vet to recommend a cattery. But Dr Limberopoulos told us there were no catteries on Rhodes, "for cats run away". If we still had the kitten at six months old (which he doubted), he would neuter him. The solution to Christmas stared us in the face. I would stay behind.

Over-wintering yachts came under Harbourmaster's orders to line up on the main quay between two ferries laid up for winter. With anchors in Mandraki frequently fouled by underwater debris left over from Aegean war bombing raids, we were fortunate to gain a place on the central mooring chain. After Bob's departure for London armed with a list of spares (including several at Digger's request), a derelict fishing tramp containing German tinker brothers, a woman with two small boys, and a Steptoe collection of any old iron, moved in beside us. Wacky's tour of inspection of the new arrival was brought up short by an encounter with its resident Alsatian. Neighbours advised me to lock myself in at night.

While stuffing foam-rubber off-cuts in the gaps behind the bookshelves that swallowed odds and ends before dumping them in the bilges, my attention was drawn to an Enid Blyton *Famous Five* adventure. Of all the live-aboard parents, Daniel and Mireille were the most concerned with their son's education. Daniel coached Gaby in maths and science, while Mireille followed suit with history and geography. I therefore proposed, subject to Gaby's approval, he join *Cappelle* for English lessons to consist of reading *Five Go to Demon's Rocks*.

At ten o'clock next morning Gaby climbed across for a chat over coffee and peanuts. Having coached me in the proper pronunciation of cacahuètes (peanuts), he played hide and seek with Wacky, while somewhere in between we got through the first page of the book. It was an instant hit. Lessons out afforded Gaby promotion and Mireille more time. Thus it was that six days a week, come rain or shine, only excepting Christmas Day (for he was back on Boxing Day), Gaby, armed with his exercise book, spent the next three months from ten a.m. till noon on *Cappelle*. Urged by his father (who suspected his son was taking up too much of my time), I once suggested he need not come on Saturdays, only to be put firmly in my place. "Leçons," Gaby insisted, were for every day except "dimanche" (Sunday). Before we had finished

Demon's Rocks, he was asking where we were to get our next adventure book, so together we composed a letter to Mel requesting a follow-up from England.

Four-year-old Alessandro of *Ernani* lacked the instinctive boat sense most youngsters quickly developed. His mother, a Ghanaian Mission girl, was upset when playmates tired of him, but his lack of coordination spoilt their games. According to his parents, Alessandro spoke Ghanaian, Italian, Arabic and English. But the word he was known for in Ramsay Street was "Caramella!" whined with a begging hand outstretched. Alessandro's obsession, with no sense of the danger involved in the inevitable back swing, was pulling on mooring ropes. There came a day of crisis. Alessandro was discovered floating face-down in harbour. Yachtsmen had revived him with the kiss of life before anyone succeeded in locating either of his parents. Told it was imperative their son wear a life-jacket at all times, they did nothing until a jacket outgrown by another child was provided. Even then, neglecting to wear it, he was soon tugging on lines, eyes unfocussed, his mother gone fishing or out on the town in her African robes, his father nowhere to be found.

Christmas in Rhodes

On Christmas Eve, after tightening the Baby Blake's pump washer with its Brobdignagian spanner, a daily chore, I bought stick-on silver stars for the cabin walls. There were beggars in the streets. A fisher-lad with an amputated forearm hung out by the bank and a pretty gipsy girl sat in a garden square wheedling coins for her baby. Nearby, a veiled widow, her husband recently killed in a car crash, accompanied by a daughter on crutches, was made much of as she shyly attempted to hawk felt-tip pens. A car was airily parked on a zebra crossing, the lead of the poodle plonked in the driving seat looped round its steering wheel.

The Town Council's concession to the festive season might be a single blow-up Father Christmas hooked onto a lamp-post, but Ramsay Street pulled out all the stops. One yacht dressed overall with fairy lights. Even the tinkers suspended a Yuletide Bough (a pine branch on a piece of twine) from the boom. As Christmas Eve drew to a close, I twisted tinsel in my hair and round Wacky's collar. Cormorants dived, kingfishers darted and a heron winged in silhouette across a buttercup sky that deepened to crimson, staining the sea before paling again around the Evening Star shining on *Cappelle* as it had once shone on the *Great Carrack of Rhodes*, flagship of the Knights Hospitallers.

Our Christmas Party, hosted by Hong Kong Chinese Patti and her Dutch boyfriend, in Rhodes to reclaim her yacht (minus its effects) stolen out of Poros, took place in a borrowed apartment in the Old City. Double oak doors opened onto a stone-flagged chamber laid with Turkish carpets, and a ladder led to a sleeping gallery from which the kitchen was spied through gaps between the ancient floorboards. After the children were carried to bed, we played old-fashioned games until it was time to sing "Holy Night" in our several languages.

An untoward note was struck by Maureen, who sat in the kitchen chain-smoking. "You see," she said, biting her nails, obsessed with the trauma she suffered earlier, "it was me that found the cats!" In winter the feral colonies existed as best they might, licking the fly-infested paper of food parcels left by tourists. Every day the Ramsay Street children fed the "Mandraki Harlequins". Unlike some cat colonies, these cats were fit and healthy, though it was a puzzle how they survived the winter storms. No one paid any attention when a Council van toured Ramsay Street on Christmas Eve. But its lethal mission was to deliver the poisoned chalice in the form of doctored fish. All the Mandraki Harlequins were now dead or dying.

In the first hours of Christmas morning we stumbled back to the boats, imagining the days when link men held flares above the heads of becloaked Knights as they strode home from an errand of mercy or a clandestine meeting. I was aroused from a nightmare of slaughtered kittens by the biting of mosquitoes. After spraying the cabin, I snoozed again to wake to a downpour. Dragging on oil-skins, I yanked the cover over the coachroof. Then, with a pot of tea and a saucer of milk, Wacky and I relaxed to the Gregorian chant that replaced the weather report. As I struggled ashore with the garbage to telephone Christmas greetings home from a bedraggled swan, I let my umbrella fall into the water.

Consensus among Ramsay Street parents was that each child should be restricted to one Christmas present only. (With living space at a premium, some children were expected to give away a plaything before acquiring a new one.) Gaby's gift from his parents was a second-hand bike secretly renovated by his father. The tinker boys got hand-whittled whistles. Balloons, crisps and fizzy pop made up for deficiencies. Children were never happier! Wacky and I were both invited to Christmas dinner (tinned turkey) prepared by Mavis on *Boomerang*. Digger waxed eloquent about his canning factory while we sipped Buck's Fizz made with Greek champagne. By constant repetition of a prawn barbie tape from his son, interspersed with snatches of "Waltzing Matilda", Digger brought tears to his own eyes as he refilled his glass while ignoring other people's. The pelter of rain on the coach-roof soon drowned out the cross-harbour reiteration of the Town Council's sole festive cassette, a Greek rendition of "White Christmas".

On Boxing Day, Gaby and I, raising our voices against the patter of hail, cleared up the poisoned fish and cosseted the four feral cats left alive. Gaby had been instructed to invite his "professeur d'anglais" to dinner after making sure she ate rabbit (rumour having it the English believed rabbit was cat in disguise.) On *Baraka*, a miracle of domesticity where strings of onions dangled against mellow wooden walls and Baby Simon slept in a home-made sky cot, we washed down rabbit à la provençale with Rhodes-bottled French champagne. The availability of this was a good excuse, according to Daniel, for any Frenchman to winter on the island. A sleep-inducing tisane of lime flowers replaced coffee. On my way home, I thought I detected an ominous persistence in the build-up of the wind as it rattled the riggings of Ramsay Street. The rocking of the hull woke me at six a.m. "Storm Force 10 Rodos/ Samos area, state of sea high" replaced "No gale". Here in Mandraki it added a frisson of excitement to lolling in bed listening to the decade blow itself out. I knew it my duty to check the warps. But that could wait.

That night it was my turn to entertain. I had prepared a casserole with the leeks that were habitually seen poking out of my shopping bag. The greengrocer, noticing my predilection, had taught me to say,

«Το *αγαπημένο μου φαγητό είναι τα πράσα.*» ("My favourite food is leeks.") A dinner party on *Cappelle* was a tight fit. When the table was laid, the bunch of flowers rescued from a dustbin re-arranged, and the candles lit, anyone needing the loo must crawl under the table to reach the Baby Blake in the forepeak, or go on deck. Digger's conversation opener was his usual, "Did I tell you we were in the canning business?" Much-taxed Mavis, married thirty-five years (who once confided it thirty-five too many), revealed the catch phrase with which she counselled herself on waking to yet another day of drudgery on her hyper-active husband's behalf. "May, I say, be aimable today, May!" Spoken in open-vowelled Aussie it sounded terrific.

What none of us had bargained for was the town closing down after Christmas for an eight-day holiday period. Even bread became unobtainable. More serious was the sinking of the "owner abroad" yacht on the exposed North Quay, the local man employed to keep an eye on it bucking his duties for the holiday period.

Thirteen

Sailing into the 'nineties

Here's to next year!

Ramsay Streeters gathered in the Old City for a Turn-of-the-Decade party. No twigs burned in the hearth on this bitter New Year's Eve. The children batted balloons, Baby Simon slept in his pram, Mireille had lost nothing of her dancing skills and Ghanaian Mary – with rumours of another baby on the way – gyrated sexily to an African beat. It was clear the tinkers and a straggle-bearded carpenter (who sought lucrative employment in vain, for the state of his boat put would-be clients off) were unused to company. It was not long before Kiwi Mark, a solitary live-aboard, was goosing the children. Daniel chalked "PÉDÉ" on his back and he was thrown out by a fiery Irish boatwife, who later initiated a drunken punch-up. But by this time, after lighting up the lemon tree with ship's flares and singing "Auld Lang Syne", many of us had left.

«Και του χρόνου!» ("Here's to next year!")

On New Year's Day I noted that contentment was "a duvet, a cat, a hot-water bottle, a good book and melted Mars Bar eaten with a spoon". Maybe the New Year kisses did it, but flu spread. I sipped hot lemon and Metaxa spiced with ginger while across the water Asia Minor lay under snow. With covers lashed over our coach-roofs, each boat became a womb in which to curl like a foetus awaiting spring rebirth. Storm-force winds emphasised the cosiness of the cabin where I wallowed in sluttishness. When the wind engaged high gear it could drive to distraction, as could a frapping halyard. Every day I adjusted the lengths of hose threaded on the mooring warps to counteract friction and used cloths to muffle squeaks, which, when the wind changed, started up elsewhere.

According to tradition, had we occupied a house during the Twelve Days of Christmas, it would have been essential to keep a fire burning in the hearth, for during this period the Καλλικάντζαροι are abroad. These maleficent hobgoblins, red-eyed and as hairy as monkeys, come out of the earth on the first day of Christmas to enter houses via the chimney and plague householders with their pranks. It is they who sour the milk, tangle hair, crack mirrors, frighten the livestock and steal umbrellas. (It was impossible not to recall our festivities in the Cottage-With-An-Empty-Grate where a tinker child swung a kick at Mireille and Mark was "possessed".) This period of torment is brought to a close on Twelfth Night when the Bishop's Blessing of the Waters drives the Καλλικάντζαροι underground once more. Crowds lined the sea wall to watch the local youths dive for the Holy Cross tossed into harbour by the Bishop. (It was not unknown for a lad to secrete a knife in his bathing trunks to foil a rival!)

At *Baraka's* Epiphany party, for which Mireille prepared a Galette des Rois stuffed with cherries and kirsch, my turn of luck was confirmed when a champagne cork bounced off my head. Oddly enough, on return to *Cappelle*, I found that Tony of *Chaton*, diving on routine maintenance, had fished up my umbrella.

The January sunsets were Valkyrian. With high pressure in the Balkans and lows in Crete and Libya, the barometer rose eight points in as many hours. When the Emergency Channel broadcast warnings of F10/11 (Storm Force/Violent Storm Force) imminent, we battened down. With Rhodes the centre of three depressions, the Harbourmaster stayed on all-night watch. Though the tinkers' trawler dragged its anchor, we hoped in vain she might re-moor elsewhere. One evening, after the barometer had fallen twenty-three points in twenty-four hours (latterly more than a millibar per hour), the town and harbour lights dimmed to a lurid red preceding the big southerly which brought total blackout. As ever, we Boat People, with our generators and oil lamps, were best off.

Though set apart by background and blood, we were a close-knit community, not least because our security demanded it. We accepted the role of social outcasts. To the Greek psyche yachts were for the summer pleasures of the rich. Those wintering aboard were necessarily beyond the pale. We were also the products of an alien culture. Boat wives organised jumble sales, whilst no Greek would be seen dead wearing cast-offs. Often our past was a closed book. Many of us carried mental baggage. And some of us lacked probity. Benny set up his own risk business, letting it be known he was available to steal to order from the boat yard. (It was rumoured that one of our own circle availed himself of Benny's services.) With Benny "one of us", no one shopped him. The maritime custom of first names only was jealously guarded. You took as you found. We cut across class from a peer of the realm (who kept his nose clean on the Town Quay) to Boat-moll Helga, forever changing boat allegiance progressively down-market, all her worldly goods in one shoddy basket.

One thing we Ramsay Streeters had in common was our devotion to the animal kingdom. Perhaps our alienation and vulnerability made us identify with lives on the fringe. When an asthmatic bitch gave birth to four puppies, we constructed a packing-case pen against the sea wall to help rear her litter. The puppies thrived, growing to the stage of the fearless swagger. One morning Gaby arrived for his lesson waving his arms in a dramatic bilingual version of earlier events of the day. It seemed Mireille, up at dawn to feed Baby Simon, had spotted the interest of rooks in mid-harbour flotsam. Sizing the situation up in a trice, the dauntless Grace Darling at once launched the dinghy and rowed out to find one of the puppies at its last gasp. Given the kiss of life, it made a full recovery. When the litter was eight weeks old we chalked *"PUPPIES TO GIVE AWAY TO GOOD HOMES"* on the sea wall. Soon three were spoken for, and the one rejected for piddling inappropriately re-housed. Hero-of-the hour, Richard rowed out to rescue a dog dangling overboard half-strangled when left tied by leash on the deck of a yacht. Another boatwife leapt into harbour in her nightie to grab a cat thrown in by an ill-tempered New Zealander who had apprehended it in his galley.

On the day Digger serviced his gang plank, Sam, strolling off *Boomerang* in his usual high-minded manner, did a double-take and plummeted into the harbour. "But I *TOLD* Sam I'd taken it away!" expostulated Digger. This was our signal to acquire a stout fishing net in case Wacky should need rescue. But his instinct for self-preservation was acute. His morning routine was to scamper across the quay, up the sea wall, and over to the cat caves to play with the few extermination survivors. He only acted injudiciously once when, panicked by a dog, he misjudged his jump back, though saved himself by clutching *River Rat's* fender. Pretty and precocious, the question of his ever leaving *Cappelle* was not an option. If we paid a social call of an evening, he homed in on our voices, two bright eyes peering through some Ramsay Street sky-light. As Mireille said of his kind, "Ils s'attachent!" Discipline was strict. If Bob caught him snagging the furled genoa with his claws, he got his ears boxed. Despatch from *Boomerang,* after making Sam a "come-out-to-play" call in the early hours, also earned him a rocket.

The birthday party season

By the time of Bob's return, the birthday party season was in full swing. First to arrive at the Hamam in the Old City for the afternoon session, I was directed to a high-windowed chamber in which a stone basin was centred by an ornate fountain sprouting as many arms as Shiva. Opening all the doors (except for one down cellar steps that appeared locked) revealed only store rooms and broom cupboards. Where was the water? The answer had to lie in the fountain, which sprang to life when I wrenched on a big brass tap. Leaving my clothes in a dressing cabinet, I stepped daintily into the basin and pranced about like a Maenad. But did not linger, for the water showed no signs of warming up. Corybantic dancing was a poor substitute. I was back in the cubicle when my attention was drawn to the vehement complaints of Mrs Char the Hamam Daily concerning splashed water. When the angry rattle of buckets reached my ears, I made my escape while her back was turned. (The Hamam proper lay behind the lower door, which was weighted. I had turned on a rarely used ornamental fountain.)

What's a party without a yacht – even one as lacking in glamour as *Cappelle*? For my own birthday, we crammed aboard fourteen people (including Julia and Gary, just back from cycling down Egypt as far as the Aswan Dam) for mulled wine and titbits. Daniel celebrated his birthday with French champagne. Swiftly replacing the word "rabbit" (bringer of ill-luck to sailors) with ears made with his fingers, he told shaggy rabbit stories while we gobbled popcorn as fast as Mireille could shake the pan. Afterwards the couple demonstrated the Rastafarian puppets they had made and sold under licence on a street corner in Mykonos to earn pocket money. While Daniel manned a ghetto-blaster, Mireille had danced, her life-like paper doll cavorting beside her, its invisible threads wound through the railings behind to run up the back of her skirt.

When Digger forgot Mavis's birthday (though she reminded him often enough), we rallied round, dressing *Boomerang* overall with Skippy the Kangaroo flags and raiding the delicatessen. Among the party-goers was pale-faced Fabrizio of *Sirena,* without his girl-friend Tizziana, who had just given birth to their son, Lucca, in Rhodes hospital. Suspicions were voiced that Fabrizio, who disappeared frequently on trips abroad, was dealing in drugs. Tizziana was a woefully neglectful mother, while Fabrizio's return heralded a succession of nocturnal visits by shadowy bikers. During the course of the party, Digger surprised us by proposing we join *Boomerang* at Easter to sail to Israel. He said he was loath to sail alone since the course lay close to the Lebanon, and, as a counter-terrorist measure, the seas were patrolled by gun boats "full of trigger-happy Israelis". Aware that Bob had once worked as a Russian interpreter in Berlin, Digger further extended the carrot. If Bob, on his behalf, would write in Russian to a certain sea captain with whom Digger had once scraped an acquaintance, it might secure *Boomerang* an invitation to Odessa. *Cappelle* would, of course, be included in the trip.

After his own birthday celebration, East Ender Vernon in his "Saturday Night Fever" suit, out to impress mates from Peckham, escorted a group of us to a restaurant in the Old City. Tables laid with crystal and silverware gave due warning that the Restaurant Dinoris was out of our league. But we sat down in front of a two-tier log fire, aware we could barely afford one course, let alone a meal. Patti saved the day. Summoning the manager, she begged his forgiveness, saying we must leave, for we had made a silly mistake and could not afford to dine in so beautiful an establishment. We hoped he would not take offence. Charm met charm. Giving us time to discuss how much we might spend, the manager said he would be honoured to arrange a three-course meal within our budget, "But," he added, eyes twinkling, "go easy on the wine!"

Wacky surrenders his manhood

Wacky's operation fell due. In the vet's waiting room the Kilkenny cats belonging to an old lady illustrated a popular joke, for her cats were on the pill (το χάπι – pronounced "happy" in Greek). The vet's surgery was lined with the teddy bears of his nursery days. The walls were decorated with Greek icons and animal cut-outs. A battered refrigerator stood in a corner, while a desk, an operating table spread with old newspapers and two armchairs with the stuffing spilling out completed the furnishings. The atmosphere was that of a jolly Junior Common Room. A builder's mate strolled in covered in plaster dust, his hand dripping blood, to deposit advance payment of two cartons of cigarettes on the vet's desk. Accompanying him was his Alsatian, not the patient, for that was the dog's master, who had had an argument with an adze, so he told us with a wink, adding, "Always I come to Adrianos! Hospital is for aspirin!" Ears pricked, Rastus rested his chin on the operating table where I was holding Wacky after his pre-med.

Everyone gathered round to witness Wacky's operation, for which the vet prepared his instruments in a chipped enamel bowl. "Not too much! Same as baby! Otherwise might die!" he said as he administered anaesthetic. Then, making a precise incision, with the words, "One penis!" he tweezered out a tiny testicle and popped it into the bowl, before, declaring "Two penis!" he extracted the other before stitching up the wound with gut.

As soon as Wacky's heart beats regularised, we laid him in his holdall. He was to remain in a darkened cabin, there were to be no loud noises and he was to be given nothing by mouth. Later on sweetened tea was to be administered and his wound sprayed with antiseptic powder. Gaby brought him yeast treats, which he called "antibiotiques". Spatially disorientated on regaining consciousness, Wacky had to be restrained from leaping imaginary gaps.

By special request, since Digger wished to play him a Billabong song about Bill the Cat and his master "Who, to Bill's regret, left Bill's balls with the family vet", we dined on *Boomerang*. The following day the patient escaped to the rocks where he bumped along on his bottom to rid himself of his embroidery while a concerned couple from a Dormobile endeavoured to find out what was the matter. Twelve days later his drawn-thread work was snipped out.

Carnival time

Carnival Sunday brought picnic-time again. Vanessa and her baby son, Alexander, flew out from England to join his father, Richard. Up on Phileremos, Bob and Richard slung Alexander's push-cart between them, while the rest of us larked about waving sticks and bursting into song. To Vanessa we walked into the pages of *My Family and Other Animals*. In antique times Rhodians worshipped the Great God Pan. Up there on Phileremos one understood why. The sun shone, the birds sang and the grass sprang with a myriad spring flowers and yellow pom-pommed fennel.

Below the acropolis a natural balcony afforded stupendous views over the chiselled, china-blue sea. Here we opened Alexander's sunshade and spread the picnic. When we lay back chewing blades of grass, the sun pricked our winter-soft skins. Above us four sea eagles as big as pterodactyls cartwheeled in the vault of sky. Alexander slept, bloated, legs wide, a sunhat over his nose. Meanwhile, Damian, the eight-year-old son of Vernon and Maureen, not to be outdone by the local kids in fancy dress, roistered about in a quasi-Batman outfit complete with high boots and an eye patch. All too soon, it was time to winkle him out of a war-time dug-out and meander down six kilometres of hairpin bends bordered with cyclamen persicum. Seething balls of caterpillars dangled from the trees under which Batman glissaded the slopes.

Arriving as the curtain was about to rise, it seemed we were the only merrymakers unaware of the fame of Trianda Carnival. Infants in prams sucked dummies through painted lips. A toddler, whose mother and grandmother were swathed in widow's black, was tricked out as a strawberry in a spotted frock with a strawberry-leaf collar and a hat like an inverted fruit. Real horses trotted alongside paper dragons pulling floats packed with sober-suited politicians in look-alike masks. Bands paraded so close their music formed a cacophony. Troupes, dressed as anything from Coke cans ranged rank on rank, to lollipops and dominoes, threw sweets to the crowd. Favourites were a clown on stilts and a fire-breathing monster. A wedding party processed. The bridegroom, a bewhiskered octogenarian in a tail coat, hobbled along on crutches beside his bride, a ginger-wigged farmer all of six feet tall, whose mud-caked gum boots peeped from beneath his bridal gown.

The following day was Καθαρά Δευτέρα (Clean Monday), the day of the Great Outdoors. This time our destination was Rodini Park where a river as greeny-grey as the Limpopo ran through a gorge crossed by Japanese bridges. Peacocks and pelicans scratched in the dust while hardened yacht skippers, feet tucked up, flung themselves at the Maypole. At Rodini's heart lay the ancient stadium, a circle of beaten earth surrounded by eroded Ptolemaic tombs. Cars and motorbikes swerved, barbecues belched acrid smoke, while children, their carnival gear bedraggled, flew kites, chased, kicked footballs and fought.

After a session of French bowls on the green sward, we crossed cave-ridden hillocks to a sunlit hillside in search of a picnic spot. Here a puppy trailed rickety legs. Maureen fed him a ham roll and we fetched him water in a tinfoil dish. Since no one was in any position to adopt, we discussed taking him back to the harbour. But all too soon we would go our separate ways and he could not be left. Bemoaning the cruelty of nature, Maureen asked if one of the men would put him out of his misery. None volunteered. Perhaps he had been born in the bushes and his mother was about? It seemed more likely he was abandoned. He licked our hands and we played with him, putting daisy chains round his neck, a carefree pup enjoying a few hours of affection. In the end, placing more food and water beside him, we left him in the sunshine beside the public track in the forlorn hope that a family on its way home would take pity. From far away we turned to see him waiting expectantly. That night I dreamed of a puppy in a daisy chain gambolling in the Elysian Fields.

As if Spring had never burst upon us, the most extended gale yet roared in. A deputation of Ramsay Street skippers approached the Port Police to report a fire at sea. But they were indifferent, as the Port Police in Poros had been indifferent to the theft of Patti's yacht. Johnny and Judith, who were visiting Rhodes, were marooned by the gale when the return ferry was cancelled. We joined them for a day's exploration in a hire car.

In the cloisters of Phileremos we found shelter from the wind. But there the pock-patterned wall of an inner court (evidence of an execution by firing squad) and the peppering of bullet holes on the revivalist plaques along Monks' Walk, were distressing reminders of the German vengeance wreaked on the occupying Italians in the Aegean war. Butterfly Valley, where the Jersey Tiger Moth aestivates, a rushy mountain glen whose limpid pools are fed by a never-failing spring, also offered some respite. From here we made our descent from the hill tops to the village of Psinthos where we were served σουβλάκια (kebabs) on bicycle spokes. On reaching the great hollow oak tree at Seven Springs, we mounted the steps of the Basilica of St Nectarios. As we entered, the double door opposite creaked and a tiny figure straight from Grimm's Fairy Tales limped in. Garbed in sweeping black, her wrinkled face lit by Mother Theresa eyes, she thrust forward a papery hand to support herself on a gnarled stick as she laid a sprig of Japanese medlar on the lectern. The surprise was mutual. "Ingliz?" she enquired, hopping forwards eagerly to tug me towards oleographs of St Nectarios, a handsome gentleman in his prime, «Γιατρό! Γιατρό!» ("Doctor! Doctor!") she exclaimed, crying, "Tank dew! Tank dew!" in gratitude when we slipped coins into the offertory box. Our καλή νεράιδα (fairy godmother) refused to let us go until she had fetched a parting gift — two mandarins.

With yachts now under serious preparation for departure, Ramsay Street hummed with activity. News came of missing correspondence. Letters had awaited us in Bodrum since November. And the Hippy Chippy brought mail addressed to both *Cappelle* and *Golden Prospect* (ripped open and with the stamps torn off) accidentally discovered in the waste bin at the Port Authority. Surplus tackle marked "FOR SALE" piled up, and the flurry of scraping, varnishing and painting increased. Tempers frayed and everyone moaned over some piece of equipment or other.

Boomerang, booked into the yard at Keci Bükü in Turkey for further maintenance, was to leave Mandraki before us. Digger promised to keep in touch via yacht brokers Camper & Nicholson.

Ramsay Street had passed a reasonably harmonious winter, only two disputes serious. One concerned a refrigerator engineer who refused to reimburse the payment he had received for a repair that proved faulty, and the other the shameless undercutting of a charter fee. But universal harmony was shattered when Aussies strode up the quay shouting, "Raus! Raus!" It seemed we were on their flotilla pitch. Under brutal orders to shift our arses or face the Port Police, it was no contest, for the flotilla took out regular contracts with the Harbour Authority. Tying up elsewhere between *Golden Prospect* and *River Rat,* we were careful to advise Wacky of our change of position. Tossing a defiant little head, however, he raced across to the cat caves. That evening Denise called to report, "Your leetle cat – 'e look the water!" We found him staring in dismay at the empty slot where lately floated all he held most dear. Bob made him follow at heel to our new berth and he did not mess up again.

Corroded tracks restricted the adjustment of our genoa. Penetrating oil and a muffled hammer failing to solve the problem, Richard and Gary helped cut away part of the track. In Ramsay Street assistance was mutual, but Digger, though comical and hail-fellow-well-met, soon gained the reputation of failing to reciprocate the demands he made on others. I no longer expected a lift on his scooter when it skidded to a halt beside me, Digger saying with a grin, "I'd give you a lift, if I wasn't going the other way!" He never was going my way.

Good-looking Vernon of *Star Turn,* a gas fitter who had purchased a boat with his redundancy money, was a celeb manqué. Maureen, his doting wife, who had chain-smoked ever since setting eyes on him at the age of fifteen, bore the brunt of the chip on his shoulder, but, since Vernon took against people for exercise, the rest of us got a taste. Acting as star and director, he proposed making a video of Tommy Cooper sketches. Afternoons out at Vernon's expense had universal appeal and a Ramsay Street cast was easily recruited to support his ego trip. I fluffed my audition by failing to give the right answer to "What is the most frequently used word in the English language?" Vernon found my efforts hilarious. According to him, it was the f-word. Bob, a very reluctant participant, was eventually persuaded to take on a silent role, but, to his chagrin, found himself backed by a wall motto packed with obscenities. This set the tone.

Piling into a camper van one afternoon, we drove to the hill of Monte Smith to film the country-and-western *My Granny's a Cripple from Nashville.* Vernon, accompanying himself on the guitar, warbled Granny's ditty country and western style, while a trio of Ramsay Streeters (none of whom could sing for toffee) acted as his backing group. Since nerves made Vernon dry, I was detailed to stand off-camera holding up prompting boards. When a guitar string snapped, Vernon's temper snapped with it. Fashioned by Maureen, a splendidly realistic Granny with a long nose, dark glasses and a tartan rug over her knees, was wheeled past in a perambulator pulled out of a rubbish tip. The site chosen for the runaway wheelchair to topple over a sea-cliff was a drop of about four feet onto a concealed ledge piled with mattresses. Filmed from behind, Granny's demise was heart-stopping. The tragedy did not end there, for, with the cliff crumbling at her funeral, the entire congregation, brought up by Parson Bob (collar back to front), who had just given his blessing, followed her into the wide blue yonder. The funniest moment came when Julia paused thoughtfully on the edge of the cliff to select a comfortable bit of mattress to land on before launching herself off with a dainty hop. This had the rest of us helpless. Other sketches followed. Gary gunned down in a spoof White House assassination pre-empted the puncture of the bag of tomato sauce in his shirt, which made the scene side-splitting to all but Vernon. And the failure of Richard, in the guise of a media interviewer, to come up with the required F-words on stepping backwards into harbour, instinctively substituting the "Bloody Hells!" that came more naturally, did not please the director.

Stringent editing was the unanimous plea of the cast. But Vernon would have none of it. At the "premmier" (sic) the credits, littered with redundant apostrophes, rolled a mile long. From the way his eyes flicked over to me, I knew I had it coming. After irrelevant references to "Jew's" and "Iti's" (sic) came the final credit:

"URSULA – WOMAN THAT WONT (sic) SAY FXXX".

Rhodes' annual celebration of the 7th March commemorated the date in 1947 when the Allies handed Rhodes back to its islanders after the Aegean War. Ships sounded their hooters. Jet planes screeched overhead. Along the waterfront dancers led phalanxes of school children and teams of athletes. The Brits were represented by a stave-carrying Baden-Powell scout troup in flapping khaki shorts, lanyards and broad-brimmed hats. Flags fluttered and white-gloved policemen snatched up toddlers who strayed under the ropes. Alexander, perched on Richard's shoulders, looked cool with an Egyptian prayer hat pulled over one eye. After the procession, the unscrupulous refrigeration engineer, now on commission to a mustard company, threw a frankfurter barbecue to win back friends and influence people. Alexander, this time sporting an Icelandic titfer with ear flaps, attended the quayside party curled up in his buggy like a cashew nut.

Remembrance day continued with a double birthday party. Shadowing us onto Vernon's boat, a gate-crasher, as roses-and-cream as a Watteau demoiselle, plumped down behind us on the companionway steps. Alarm bells sounded when we discovered that her other half, a brooding Jean Marais look-alike with a knife strapped to his leathers, had already assumed command of a banquette inside. Leaning forward and demanding a light, the porcelain blonde, appropriating a carton of Vernon's cigarettes, challenged, "Me boyfriend's says your wife's got a lovely bum!" Sensibly, Vernon bit his tongue. Raising her voice, she related a long story about accepting a lift, "Me in me 'igh 'eels and mini" from a "suit" in Athens who "Took his Willy Out and Waved It All About!" The more we attempted to disabuse ourselves of the pair without upsetting Baby Alexander, the more they stuck. They'd come to gamble, they said. Muttering, "MY boat! MY drink! MY cigarettes!" Vernon resorted to a Blackadder video. At last Easy Rider heaved himself up, a purloined six-pack under his arm, and lurched off, his side-kick following clutching the carton of cigarettes. Turning at the top of the steps, as if to bid us a fond farewell, she sneered, "Piss off, you f****** lot!" adding with a mocking simper, "...And don't you speak to me like that again!"

Discussion turned to cruising. Vanessa declared the right proportion to be half a day's sailing to three days' recuperation. All the skippers admitted to situations that stretched them. Naively, I asked exactly what constituted a "bad experience". Maureen summed it up, "It's when you think you're going to die!" It was the reason, I was told, *Terrathree* was holed up in Palamut; the athletic German blonde refused to move on. I recollected that Richard, on first meeting, had worn the look of one acquainted with a dark star. It transpired he had been single-handing in the build-up to the hurricane. For some a bad experience meant triumph over a new level of fear. The adrenalin surge could make it addictive. But for the most part bad experiences were taboo. It was as if the mind blanked off the trauma, leaving emptiness.

As the first charter flights were inaugurated, shutters were taken down and last year's unsold garments were wheeled out. Tee-shirts bearing the slogans *"DON'T DRINK THE WATER. FISH F*** IN IT!"* *"PUT SOMETHING EXCITING BETWEEN YOUR LEGS –* (small print) Buy a motorbike!" or *"LET'S FORGET THE LOVE AND PASSION– GIVE IT TO HER DOGGY FASHION!"* were hooked onto awnings and tabloid newspapers appeared on stands. On street corners the καμάκια ("harpoons", Greek equivalent of the Turkish avcι) flexed their muscles.

Such garbled messages as were received from Digger via Camper & Nicholson mainly urged the sale of *Boomerang's* gear left on the quay. We understood *Cappelle* was to delay her departure for Cyprus because of *Boomerang*'s need to recaulk. Deciding, nonetheless, to stick to our original arrangement of reaching Cyprus during the first week of April, we extended our insurance cover and purchased a second-hand Walker Log. After we had scraped dead men's fingers off the dinghy and checked the shrouds and stay fittings, we were assisted in repairing the wind vane and revarnishing the top spreaders. Finally, with a visit to the vet for the rabies and feline leukaemia injections that entitled him to a WHO passport, Wacky was officially promoted to Ship's Cat (or, as Bob put it, *"Cappelle's* cutting edge of technology").

Daniel, meanwhile, negotiated a land base with the intention of opening a voilerie (sail loft), *Baraka* to remain in harbour as the family's second home. The Gauthiers' parting gift to *Cappelle* was a drum of Turkish honey, plus twenty litres of wine, with a special jar of tadpoles from Gaby.

Like all British yachts, *Cappelle* sailed off to a barracking of "What have you done with my dinghy then?" and "What about that money you owe me?" which German yachtsmen were at a loss to understand. (English-speaking was never English-joking.) Off on the next leg of our odyssey, we raised the mainsail in gathering darkness to nose out on course 110 degrees, south of east, for Cyprus.

Fourteen

Cyprus

Passage to Cyprus

About to experience his first exile, Wacky let out a prolonged howl at finding himself, like Piglet, entirely surrounded by water. Expressing the conviction we had failed to notice that disaster had befallen us, he crawled inside my Puffa.

We followed the shipping lanes until dolphins surfaced in the sunrise. As we altered course towards the barely discernible coast of Turkey, discovering a photographic memory of that distant shore, I disagreed with our charted position. According to the Captain's plotted course we were south of the Seven Capes, while I was sure they still lay ahead. When he tried to bring me to heel, I confidently described salient landmarks soon to appear. Time proved the Cabin Boy right!

The spring sun burned. On a perfect midday, the surrounding seas a keyboard of lime-green to royal-blue, we tied up again in Kastellorizzo beside the Estiatorio Thalassina, now sporting a splendid new dining extension beneath a triple-arched roof. Floodlighting was under assembly. Wacky, who had despaired of ever seeing land again, quivered with anticipation, paws on the cap rail, making sure the natives were friendly. After leaping ashore he returned chirruping. He was further impressed when bickering swallows pegged out on the shrouds.

At the turn of the century Kastellorizzo was home port to hundreds of sailing ships. Now it played host to *Cappelle* alone. From the heights above the harbour, a prohibited zone, the Greek military kept an eye on Turkey, the Enemy over the Water. Sokrati, owner of the Thalassina, came to enquire why we remained on board when he had such good οὔζο to offer? Bob was concerned with our slow progress. With the dinghy stowed, which should have achieved an extra half knot, we had averaged only 3.7 knots. Although red-eyed and hoarse with the infective laryngitis that had spread through Ramsay Street, he dived to clean off the hull and propeller, remaining immersed for twenty minutes, with another forty-minute session to follow. When he emerged livid with cold, he lay shivering, Wacky cradled in the crook of his arm.

That evening Thalassina's swordfish steaks melted in the mouth. From each of two side windows in the restaurant, Sokrati had removed a pane of glass to give swallows freedom of access. Like miniature parsons' pulpits their nests hung in the angle of the inside wall. Ignoring the thump of the juke box into which fisher lads pressed coins, the parent birds shared hatching duties, taking turns to rest on a Campari bottle behind the bar. According to Sokrati they "made babies three times" before leaving for Africa at the end of season. Only even numbers of fledglings were tolerated. The weakest of an odd number was mobbed to death. He had witnessed this, he said.

The fishing boats stayed in port. In the morning little girls stopped by to play with the bloody carcasses of three goats landed on the quay from a rowing boat, their throats slit. We were about to be on our way when Sokrati advised against it, saying "bad winds" were forecast. Was this because he wanted us to eat at Thalassina again? We were not sure. But what did a day more or less matter? Black clouds gathered over the mountains of the mainland and hailstones rattled. At tea-time, thunder rumbling, we abandoned all idea of departure. Though the night was calm and the morning clear, F 8/9 gale warnings were out. Since accuracy of forecast varied by twenty-four hours either way, we thought reference might be to the storms of the previous day. Taking binoculars, we followed a path round the base of the Kastello Rosso to the south-eastern tip of the island. As far as the eye could see, the scrolled Aegean stretched placid as a dream. Around us early poppies, black lilies and lascivious gladioli flourished in the grass. Kastellorizzo was the island of Sabrina Fair, who lay somewhere in a limpid pool,

"under the glassie, cool, translucent wave
in twisted braids of Lillies knitting
the loose train of her amber-dropping hair."

Remaining puzzled as to why the Kalymniot fishing boats did not depart, we enquired of a fisher-lad, who consulted his uncle. His answer was Delphic: if we wanted to lose our sails, we should leave. To add to our confusion, Sokrati waylaid us with the offer of free coffee, saying the weather was "very good now", and we could go. But why not lunch at Thalassina first? He would cook wild vetch omelettes. He soon ran back in some agitation with the news that the fishing fleet's powerful shortwave radio transmitters (purchased with EEC grants) were picking up the Italian weather bulletin. According to this, Kastellorizzo lay directly in the path of an Atlantic depression that, after deepening in the weather kitchen of the Gulf of Genoa, was tracking our way fast. In mid-afternoon the harbour water went into convulsions. Three fishing boats moved to anchor off. But rather than be bothered to unstow our dinghy, necessary if we were to go ashore, we settled for pulling *Cappelle* off the quay later on long lines.

Restaurant trade was brisk that night. Sokrati aired his views on politics, for elections were pending. Athens he declared dirty and provincial. As for Papandreou, "from here (he placed his hand on the top of his head), to here (he pointed to his feet), Andreas is *MAFIA*! They are all the same, these politicians, ability to squeeze money out of the *EEC* all that matters!" Three children, who came banging on the door, were allowed in out of the rising wind, and there was laughter when each child, given a free can of Coco Cola wrapped in an election leaflet, was told to take it home. With a twinkle Sokrati explained the joke, "Their mother is Socialist! Those leaflets, you see, are for Democrats!"

The early bulletin was for F 7/8 in sea areas East Karpathio (in which we lay), and for areas Taurus, Delta and Crusade in the path ahead. Although the riding weight steadied us, I was dimly aware of breaking seas at the harbour entrance. Glassy-eyed and feverish, Bob lay prone clutching a hot-water bottle. At breakfast the wind gathered strength.

My instructions were to stay on deck and keep an eye on the warps, for gusts across the hillsides against the west-flowing current in the channel were causing difficult in-harbour conditions. He did not respond to my shout that white water was advancing into harbour, except to tell me to get the engine started and hold the boat off. By this time she was buck-jumping on her long lines. With the gear lever jammed in reverse with my knee, I endeavoured to do as I was bid, but was soon task-saturated. I could not release the gear lever (which jumped out if not held) or *Cappelle* would ram the quay. Even if I were able to let go, I could not raise the anchor, as, combined with the riding weight, it was too heavy. Likewise I stood no chance of reaching the bows to cast off. In any case, if I leaned back over the stern and slashed the warp, it might foul the propeller. Negative thoughts raced through my head. I was dimly aware that the fishing boats had moved off. The sea went into a paroxysm, and fishermen yelled, «Οχτό Μποφόρ στο λιμάνι!» ("Full gale in harbour!") Then the starboard bow warp snapped and *Cappelle* slewed crosswise.

At this moment two things happened; the fishermen ran to line up on the short stone pier in case *Cappelle* broke free and hit beam on. And Bob emerged ghost-like. Something made me glance behind me. All I remember is a wall of fog hurtling down at the speed of light before spume enveloped the world and we bounced down under a tsunami. The quay's low elevation was our salvation, for the rogue surge did not pause to backlash, but swept on unimpeded over the low quay wall to smash Thalassina's new extension to smithereens. For a split second, I was transfixed as I caught sight of sturdy brick columns crashing down, heavy-duty metal supports buckling like straws and all-weather roofing ripping to shreds. *Cappelle* was abandoned as the fishermen rushed to Thalassina. But there was nothing they could do. It was all over in seconds. On the ground lay tumbled brickwork, twisted metal, smashed floodlights and flogging strips of PVC in and out of which the sea swirled. Meanwhile *Cappelle*, bows digging, pitched like a bronco on a six to eight feet swing. Catching the momentum in a superhuman effort, Bob heaved in the anchor, riding weight and all. By this time the fishermen were back to hold us off, and Sokrati, abandoning his wreckage, ran forward to throw off our remaining bow warp. At full throttle Bob reversed, swinging the stern to port. As he wrenched the bows round, we roared into a turn, missing the stone pier by a hair's breadth.

This wave proved the climax of the sea's operatic performance. In fifteen minutes the squall swept on. The fishing boats moved back and the crews devoted their afternoon to clearing up operations. *Cappelle* was miraculously unscathed. To say I suffered qualms over the Ship's Cat was untrue, for during the crisis he never entered my mind. Not surprisingly he emerged subdued from behind the water tank after his Big Dipper ride, but was quick to recover his spirits. That night we commiserated with Sokrati. Yes! He had spent all last year's profits on this year's extension! No! He was not insured! But, «Τι κάνετε?» — "What can one do?"

Bob telephoned Larnaca Marina to book a berth. "Impossible!" said the manager, suggesting he contact Limassol instead. A lengthy interrogation ensued with the Sheraton Marina in Limassol on our movements in relation to Turkey and Northern Cyprus. Finally, *Cappelle* was assigned a slot. "Why not stay here?" asked Sokrati. We explained we had a rendezvous to keep.

At tea-time next day, in conditions as serene as those that preceded the squall, the fishing fleet trooped out. *Cappelle* brought up the rear. Behind us Sokrati organised the removal of the wreckage of his restaurant. Once we were under way, Wacky resigned himself to his fate. At midnight, wearing safety harness and armed with a torch and thermos, I stood my first solo night watch. I was to check our course, engine revolutions and oil pressure every fifteen minutes, and on the hour lean (strictly clipped on) over the stern to read the mileage to enter in the Log. When the Walker Log failed to register, it was because a polythene bag was caught in its spinner. At all times an eye was to be kept on shipping,

"If to starboard red appear, 'tis your duty to keep clear.
Green to green and red to red, perfect safety, go ahead!"

ran the couplet. But it is never as simple as that. The navigation lights on illuminated ferries are not readily distinguishable, and it takes time to estimate a ship's course. Moreover, while the eyes are glued on one ship, another might appear over a different sector of the horizon. With collision averaging a mere twenty minutes from the emergence of an obstacle, there was no time for inattention. The simplest way to judge an encroaching vessel's speed and direction was to sight the stranger between stanchions. Should she remain in the same position, both navigation lights growing brighter, she was on a collision course. This was the moment to "starboard wheel and show your red". Whatever may be said about steam giving way to sail, it was never safe to rely (like Michael O'Day "who died maintaining the right of way") on avoidance by the other party. A large vessel could not readily change course, Greek boats rarely bothered, and too much shipping forged about on autopilot with no one on watch.

At 03.30 hrs a crescent moon like a segment of orange balanced by its tip on the surface of the sea before being slowly sucked in. At 06.40 hrs, after a false dawn as cold as steel, the rim of the new day appeared. We were sailing at barely half a knot faster than before. It seemed optimism had led us to over-compensate for the under-reading of the Sumlog. Away from the shipping lanes, there was nothing but "water, water, everywhere". It was as if *Cappelle*, carrying with her the disc of the horizon and without terms of reference to prove she moved, was the motionless centrepiece of a circular blue disc. Being at this centrifugal point gave a sensation of omnipotence, as if the world, our oyster, existed in a perpetual present created for our convenience.

The next 02.00 to 04.00 hrs night watch was chilly. Although Wacky was keen to share my watches, he was a constant anxiety, since, clipped on, my range of movement was limited. Suddenly, taking it for a searchlight, I was startled by the Morning Star "flaming in the forehead of the morning sky". At 05.00 hrs Bob woke me, needing confirmation of the distant coast of "Black Cyprus". Cheerfully we hoisted the Cypriot flag. But it was afternoon before we gained the coastal ribbon of Paphos.

Cyprus

The entrance to Paphos harbour lay between floats marking the submerged half of the ancient mole. With no space available on the quay, we picked up a mooring buoy and gobbled a sandwich apiece before rowing ashore. The Harbourmaster frowned. Of the three new arrivals that day only *Cappelle* had been dilatory over reporting to the Port Authorities. Since Customs closed officially at two p.m., we would be charged extra for out-of-hours service. We were also ordered, despite our argument that we were merely passing through, to surrender our passports. The Captain would be permitted to collect them immediately prior to his yacht's departure and not before. Business complete and his authority established, the Harbour Master, all smiles, offered us glasses of delicious Cypriot lemon juice with ice. Later we shopped for Bovril, marmalade and Schweppes tonic water in streets crowded with British pensioners. On waking from a nap we found copies of the *Daily Mail* and the *Daily Express* dropped on deck.

At 22.30 hrs Bob rowed ashore to retrieve our passports for the sixty-mile night sail to Limassol. With the floats marking the harbour mouth unlit, great caution had to be exercised in exiting Paphos by night. At 03.30 hrs Cape Aspro gleamed white without benefit of moonlight. On rounding Cape Akrotiri in the grey light of dawn, the air was compressed as the Red Arrows trailing red, white and blue streamers, took off with a beehive roar from the Sovereign Air Base to execute their glorious classic trademark, the Diamond Nine. It was an unforgettable moment for a small British yacht that almost made up for our cracked exhaust repaired "with initiative", as Algernon would have said (i.e. a split Coke can and fuse wire).

Rusting commercial hulks welded to the metal sheet of the sea cluttered the roadstead outside the industrial sprawl of Limassol. East of the town stood the rectangular block of the Sheraton Hotel. Behind it a storm brewed over the Troodos mountains. Rain pitted the whale-grey water as we made our approach. When we radioed the marina for entry instructions, the operator told us to "come in on the left", when she meant her left, with a consequent nasty moment when we

1 Cappelle *at first sight.*

2 Below: Ursula gets to work with a heat gun.

3 *Launch of* Cappelle, *Lavrion.*

4 *Cruising the Southern Peloponnese.*

5 *The Teatowel Incident,*
Plomari, Lesbos.

6 *Below:* Energetic
setting up her winter
quarters in the fruit
market, Bodrum.

7 Above: Cappelle on passage.

8 William at the helm.

9 Jic accepts a treat, Castle Quay, Bodrum.

10 Trianda Carnival, Rhodes.

11 *Girl talk, Ursula and friend, Kalkan Street.*

12 *Ursula and Wacky: victims of stormy seas.*

13 Above: Ready for breakfast after a night sail, Chios.

14 Wacky on watch.

15 Exhausted crew recuperate.

16 Film crew for My Grannie's a Cripple in Nashville, *Rhodes.*

attempted to sail round the dead end of the mole. We tied up on the Welcome Quay, in smart company, our neighbour the motor cruiser Aristotle Onassis gave his daughter Christina for her seventeenth birthday.

Bob returned puzzled and drawn from putting out a call to Larnaca on the offchance *Boomerang* might have arrived. His first words were "We are not welcome!" It seemed *Boomerang's* departure from Turkey had not been delayed after all. Taken aback at the sound of Bob's voice, Digger had been unable to conceal his dismay. Fed up with sailing, he had intended to avoid *Cappelle* and, suddenly, here she was two days before he had arranged to fly to Sydney for a holiday! Gathering himself together, his best defence attack, "You're late!" he challenged. (Wrong.) "The trip's off!" With Bob's breath taken away, Digger launched into muddled excuses, the principal one being "wrong time of year". Suddenly, as if recollecting himself, but with his habitual eye on the main chance, he suggested Bob "use his influence" to fix *Boomerang* a berth at the Sheraton when we "could discuss things".

In a daze, Bob approached the Sheraton to be told all berths were booked, but that his friends might be given special dispensation to double in a reserved slot. When *Boomerang* arrived, Digger retreated behind the victim philosophy. They had had a "terrible time" and "nearly lost the boat". (Not true, though *Boomerang* had been battered by squalls.) Far from being assigned a berth on arrival in Larnaca, as Digger anticipated, after being granted the customary twenty-four-hour emergency stay, *Boomerang* had been summarily turned out, strong winds not withstanding, forcing her to raft up with another yacht fated to contain, of all people, erstwhile Australian friends who refused to speak to him.

Digger so far talked himself round to the right of the situation as to remark condescendingly that he thought it "very courageous" of "people like us" to come to Cyprus for a holiday! "Who'd ever have thought you'd make it?" To say the least, we were deeply shocked. I was unable to contain myself from asking what had happened to our oft-discussed plans to celebrate Easter Sunday in Jerusalem. Digger, saying – what do you know? – he'd "forgotten all about it", then set about trying to persuade Bob to fix him a cheap telephone call to Sydney via the Sheraton. But Bob had had enough.

As we parted, on our side in stunned silence, Digger, as if it were an afterthought, threw back, "By the way, did I mention we're off to Russia this summer? We've got an invitation to Odessa Yacht Club. It's just been finalised at the Embassy!" So that was it! Bob had been dangled only until *Boomerang's* trip to Odessa was confirmed and his possible support no longer required. We never saw the couple again. The story of old friends from Australia no longer on speaking terms with Digger was revealing. It seemed that some sort of mutually beneficial meeting in the Maldives had been fixed for the sail out. Needless to say, Digger conveniently "forgot" to honour his side of the arrangement. It had been sheer bad luck that the couples met again in Larnaca when in need of mutual security.

The wind metaphorically taken out of our sails, we made up our minds to air-brush *Boomerang* out of our lives and make the most of Cyprus, to which end we took out a marina contract at the Sheraton. Perhaps because of my exertions, coupled with disappointment, I found myself obliged to make a conscious effort to put one foot before the other. On the other hand, the Ship's Cat was in splendid form. According to the rules, domestic pets were "to be retained on board at all times". In practice the marina was a menagerie. Wacky's engaging little figure flew up and down the pontoon with wings on its feet. To starboard lived Bessie, an enormous Pyrenean doormat, rescued, like most pets, as a stray. We were warned to watch out for Lord Byron, a tom-cat who would "have your pretty kitty for breakfast". Apparently under the delusion of owning the marina, Lord Byron was presently away cruising, but was due back. We caught him stalking the oblivious Wacky just in time to jump to the rescue. Later I apprehended His Lordship boarding *Cappelle* with nefarious intent. But, after spitting his disgust at my boat hook in a most unaristocratic manner, he kept his distance. Bessie and a yappy Sealyham on a Beirut yacht also served as loyal Wacky minders by breaking into furious barking whenever the lordly tyrant showed his whiskers. As for Wacky, his new game was to pop through the porthole bearing sunbaked small fry (hand-line discards) to crunch on the carpet.

We become aware the Pleasure Harbour was a sort of blandly international No Man's Land in which Israeli and Lebanese yachts flew no identifying flags, an anti-terrorist precaution introduced since the notorious murders in broad daylight in Larnaca Marina. A close observer might note that the guards in desert uniform strolling the concourse or manning the barrier of the Sheraton's single approach track carried Armalite rifles.

We remained thankful not to have burdened ourselves with a fridge, for a fire caused by a deck-mounted refrigerator had gutted a neighbouring yacht. But we set ourselves up with a French pressure cooker and, on the theory of work first, play later, succeeded, after long hours of toil, in removing our cracked exhaust. The Volvo agent's suggestion, since the design was no longer available, was to get the pipe copied at a car workshop. This led us, bearing the pipe wrapped in newspaper, to traipse around Limassol's hinterland until we found a garage prepared to fashion a replica in stainless steel, a long overdue up-grade. The boss, explaining how he had kept down the cost of the flexible section by using material of less high quality, but which, he assured us, would be more than adequate to resist all possible marine stresses and strains, delivered the pipe himself and helped fit it.

I invested in a packet of Easter egg dye and Bob embarked on repainting the deck. When International Light Blue proved too brash, he was not satisfied without a final coat of our special designer paint, the tasteful "curry blue". Feverish again, I took to my bed, but resurfaced in time for lunch on Easter Sunday at the Continental Hotel where in 1974, according to Bob, in his earlier incarnation in the RAF, the chef served a mean coq au vin. The first brandy sour made me forget sore throats and the second put paid to the earache as well. Coq au vin still featured on Continental's menu and our plates were borne forth in triumph – each topped with a dollop of soggy chips! Scraping the fries away, we left the chef to discover he had met the first Brits to fail to appreciate their national dish.

Nearby was the Crusader Castle where Richard the Lionheart married Berengaria of Navarre, crowning her Queen of England. In stark contrast, far less than royal, a primitive headstone in an adjacent burial plot displayed the symbol of a pregnant woman, her stomach a crude circle, a matchstick child within. At Ancient Kourion, our next expedition, Bob had once attended a nativity play in the amphitheatre, which had opened with Mary on a donkey. Silhouetted against the sunset, she was led into the proscenium along the crest of the opposing hillside. Now propaganda sheets displayed a weeping child, a shrouded woman and the outline of Cyprus dripping blood.

But "AND YOU... BE JOYFUL!" in Roman script flanked the entrance to the Roman Villa in Paphos. If I were a barefoot maiden stepping on mosaic floors, my feet would have drawn back from the snarling jaws of lions and tigers to tread amongst rabbits and peacocks within chain borders of leaves, each link framing a song-bird, a daisy, a rose or a pair of apples. That the scenes were set in Cyprus was self-evident, for the strong shadows contrived in mosaic attested to the sun's brilliance. On the coastal flat, from whose springy turf our feet bruised the aroma of camomile and thyme, we slithered into the Tombs of the Kings, a sea-girt burial ground of Ptolomaic catacombs, chambers of shadow into which the midday sun beamed down from a square of blue sky. But, on discovering the waters of Aphrodite's birthplace swirling with sea wrack, my desire to bathe there disappeared.

The keys to our hire car were handed over by the garage owner's mother-in-law with much friendly advice. We should carry sufficient petrol, for garages were closed on Sundays, she told us, failing to add they closed early on Saturdays, which was nearly our undoing. Should we visit the Troodos mountains we must be sure to eat at the Caledonian Restaurant in Platres. Here the floury potatoes served on hot plates were worth waiting for. (In Greece plates are not warmed, for, to a Greek, hot food is bad for the system.) Our visit to Mount Olympus with its hurdy-gurdies and chips-with-everything was brief. The sun caught red wounds in the barks of trees, and we gazed in disappointment at a half-hearted fork of water known as the Caledonian Falls. Too much was dying in the ring-fenced forest.

Beyond Larnaca a track whiplashed to Stavrovouni, the Mountain of Cross. Before reaching the monastery we were confronted with the sign "NO WOMEN". On the road again, a posse of policemen flagged us down to hand over a letter. Beginning "Dear Visitor" and ending "Friends of Tourists", it warned us to ignore all requests for lifts, however pitiful. (It seemed the police were trying to stamp out a lace-selling racket at the village of Lefkara.) But in a curl of the River Maroni all was tranquil among the remains of the ancient round-houses scattered on the hillside. As long ago as 6,000 years, the village of Khirokitia had prospered, for its community expanded. We looked down into a canyon once used for stock-breeding. Like the expanse of the sea, the expanse of time might lack terms of reference, but when I sat at the ravine's edge I found a time-peg in the cone of Stavrovouni marking the vanishing point to which the canyon's spurs led. The monastery had been established some forty generations after the birth of Christ, an age ago to me. Yet a woman of Khirokitia, wearing a cornelian necklace, perhaps, and wielding a pestle and mortar of green river stones who sat, as I did, beside a patch of convolvulus in the westering sun, must see into the future a period of over 200 lives laid head to foot to witness the raising of its foundation stone.

Goodbyes are never easy. Explanations to the islanders that we must leave to pick up my daughter in Samos met with requests that I persuade her to visit Cyprus instead. But on 27th April we obtained as accurate a forecast as was available from the weather station in Crete, SW F4/5, fine and calm. (All the same, I remembered a Coptic gale fell due on 29th April.) Darkness showed the masthead light not functioning. At 23.00 hrs Bob was still finalising our course. While he did so, I read a book on mountaineering whose Ten Commandments translated to sailing:

"Thou shalt prepare thoroughly before starting.
Thou shalt set out early.
Thou shalt set out properly equipped.
Thou shalt chose thy company with care.
Thou shalt destroy nothing which is thy neighbour's.
Thou shalt oft keep silence to hear the sirens sing.
Thou shalt leave no sign of thy passing.

Thou shalt remember others in their strength or weakness.
Thou shalt bend to the weather and be strong."

I would add an Eleventh Commandment:

"Thou shalt sail humbly before the gods",

for no one may lay ultimate claim to control of the sea.

We were up at 04.30 hrs to collect our passports. Under a pall of mist the greasy sea smoothed by weight of atmosphere, was as dull as the spongy sky. *Cappelle* seemed to sail beneath a dove's wing or into the hammered pewter of a mussel shell. Wacky was restless. Dolphins gambolled, a cloud of flying fish glided by and the body of a dead hawk idled on the water. Fifteen miles out from Limassol a finch rested on the jib sheet before winging away towards land. With a sportive cat on board, I was not sorry to see it go.

We made good progress in a movement so steady as to allow us to eat on the cabin table.

But my ear ached again. We were out of sight of land before the cherryade sun sank into a band of mist. At 00.20 hrs, eighty-five nm off Paphos, I was fast asleep when enough favourable wind came in for Bob to cut the engine. At half-past midnight Bob shook me awake to assist with reefing. More energy had entered the system. With the waves cranking up, we beat into a strengthening north westerly. Before I could slam Wacky unceremoniously into the forepeak, the decks were awash and the Captain was yelling for his sea boots. Stupid with sleep, I scrambled about distractedly, forgetting they were stowed behind the paraffin canister in the wet wardrobe.

"BOOTS!"

"I'll give you boots!"

Tugging at the offending footwear, I spilt paraffin. By the time I fell up the steps, it was too late for boots. *Cappelle*, over-canvassed, was pounding into a wet lunar landscape cratered, gouged and deformed by wind. Winch fodder or not, I made a mental note to murder the Captain when this little lot was over! (I might even stage my own "Οχι!" Day)

As *Cappelle* lurched from crest to trough, it took more than two hours to get a double slab reef in the mainsail. I thought I must explode with the effort needed to pull on the down-hauls, while the beleaguered Captain made Herculean efforts to tie reefing strings in pitching darkness. As I hung onto the helm as we heaved to, the rhythmless slap of the bows burst open the forepeak doors and Wacky staggered out, much agitated. There was nothing for it but to shove him in again with a murderous yell and lash the handles.

At intervals Bob vomited. "What am I DOING here!" I heard him groan as he lay supine on the coach-roof smothered in canvas. Dimly we saw a confused pattern of crenellations erupting in pyramids, white-capped Alpine peaks, evil-genii which, acting in synergy with their wind shadows, took the power from the sails to force a yacht out of control. Between them gaped black holes.

When the vital double reef was at last in place, we attempted to head off towards Southern Turkey, but this afforded no relief. It was hard going to pick up a westerly course again. Heaving to twice more, by 04.20 hrs *Cappelle* made eight nautical miles before the Captain was persuaded to go below. Off course in the raging dawn, both of us on deck, we saw we had torn a reefing point. Sucking in air and running out of fuel, the engine coughed discouragingly, obliging us to cut it. With seas this spiteful, refuelling, a balancing act at the best of times, was out of the question. At 09.00 hrs came a small windshift in our favour. From then until 13.20 hrs we continued to sail north west at tolerable speed, plunging, jouncing, taking water across the deck and ploughing through water cavities. For twenty minutes we concentrated on picking up a better course, but were consistently forced off it. Not until 15.00 hrs could we resume proper direction and sail on.

When it was my turn to knock off, Wacky clutched to my chest, we were both aware of chaotic seas powering along the side deck close to our ears. As the waves died down Bob increased sail, boosting our speed to 4.5 kts. That night I took the 22.00 hrs till midnight watch. Bob rose at 23.00 hrs, so that together we could wobble about on the stern, manipulating canisters, funnel and torch to refuel. After this I went below to make coffee. The seas might have slackened, but it remained essential to corral the kettle. Wedged in the galley, I realised how exhausted I was when spilt coffee reduced me to tears. As that veteran sailor Eric Hiscock said, "No yacht is comfortable at sea, though some are less uncomfortable than others." Be thankful for the strength of *Cappelle's* hull.

When I took the 02.00 to 04.00 hrs watch, we were on course and sailing at 3.8 kts. Awaking groggily at 06.00 hrs, I hauled myself on deck. The yacht was under autohelm, the wind had dropped and the sea had settled to a flaccid swell. As we exchanged watches, Bob urged me to keep a look out for the potential hazard of an oil drum lost sight of. From time to time, retching over the side, I shook with ague. Dawn found me not clipped on (a life-threatening idiocy in the circumstances), draped over the rails, hot and cold by turns, throwing up stomach juices in time with the heave of the sea, while the part of me in mental suspension muttered about oil drums and was aware of a smug sun bellying out of a jacaranda sea.

With no land in sight, I turned in. At 10.30 hrs Bob woke me to identify a coastline. Seen from the shore the sea is fluid, while from the water, advancing and receding, shifting and changing, portions of it sliding in and out like shutters, as mutable as a stage set on rollers, it is the land that is a liquefaction. Nothing exists of itself. Mountains wander about. Deceiving islands appear and cease to appear. Bob wanted to know if I could make out Kastellorizzo. What I could discern was a low-lying cigar shape that had to be Kekova Island. Kastellorizzo, though from *Cappelle's* angle it blended in with the island of Strongili in an altogether new identity, must lie to its north west. A ray of morning sun, like the whitened finger bone with which the Wicked Witch beckoned Hansel and Gretel, suddenly illuminated a headland I recognised as Ulu Burun, wrecker of the ancient treasure ship. The sight came as a revelation of just how this laser-pointed promontory had lured exhausted oarsmen, desperate for landfall, to raise their stroke and pull for disaster.

Bob broke into my reverie with, "You'll have to buck up and help us in!" adding sternly, "You've GOT to!" when I failed to react. So I manned the wheel between skerries floating in the lime-lit shallows of speedwell blue water while Bob directed operations from the bows. "Port!" he shouted, holding out his left arm at the approaches to Kastellorizzo. Claiming better recollection of the navigable passage into the island's mini-archipelago, to which most entrances were false, and where mini-headlands that shimmered as if sprinkled with a million mirrors concealed underwater reefs, I argued. So we changed places, the Cabin Boy assuming responsibility for inshore navigation.

The mini-headlands were persuaded to let us pass. Once in harbour, where Sokrati waited to tie us up, we exerted ourselves to put out fenders as we circled a dredger. At my last ebb, I stretched out a shaky hand to fend off *Ciccellino*, finding my fingers grasped as a motherly voice said, "You look TERRIBLE, dear!" as she guided *Cappelle* to the quay, where Bob wolfed down a whole packet of Cypriot chocolate digestive biscuits. My head had been kicked by a horse. Clutching a bottle of water, I lay down. Hang spring-cleaning! Tidying up could wait...

It was May Day. That morning children dressed the fishing fleet with garlands before setting off "to bring back the May". Strangely enough, stress had contracted time. The inaccuracy of the figure failed to register when I heard Bob tell *Ciccellino's* skipper we had taken thirty hours (a day, a night and half a day) to sail from Limassol at which he looked impressed. In fact it was fifty-five hours, fifteen minutes, or *two* days, *two* nights and half a day, a more realistic time-span in which to sail 220 nm by small boat. The worst of the conflicting seas lasted thirteen hours. As for Wacky, he was ecstatic to be back on familiar territory. After scoffing a slap-up meal he danced off to explore paradise regained, returning in the early hours to check on the Old Folks before scooting off again. When at last he settled, it was as the dawn chorus was breaking, and the twittering of swallows had him back on parade.

Sokrati promised swordfish that night. While I put the cabin to rights, Bob changed the reefing from slab to roller to cover a tear in the main sail. Pulling away from the wall, the chart table had deposited the teapot in the cat tray. And – there was no doubt about it – *Cappelle* stank. I attributed one odour, wrongly, to Wacky. But, with a personality all its own, it was suppurating rabbit stew. (I should have remembered rabbit is unlucky on a boat!) The loo pullulated because *Cappelle* was so heeled on the port tack that the water inlet pipe sucked in only air. However, the most pervading reek was paraffin, for, with my failure to right the canister, it had leaked into the bilge water, which in heavy weather sloshed through the lower lockers. Our precious Cypriot back bacon was ruined.

Before we left Kastellorizzo two days later, I donated our spare books to the tiny island library endowed by "Cassies" who had emigrated to Australia «γιά το καλό» (to seek their fortune). (One islander became Mayor of Perth in Western Australia.) Although concerned that once having "fallen to the sea", as the Greeks have it, sea-sickness might become a habit, I was anxious to get on with the passage. When other yachts turned into Yali Liman to await the prescribed hour of 04.00 hrs to tackle the Seven Capes, we headed out to sea. Off the Çatal Islands, beating into F6, we just held our own, while to starboard batallions of white horses galloped in dazzling sunshine towards the Sands of Patara. Above the exhilarating roar, I yelled to Bob to buckle his safety harness – "And that's an order!" – a moment before, drenched by an overspill, he missed his footing. Zipping up my Snowgoose as we forced forward progress by clawing off Patara in long tacks, my heart sank when, after each extreme effort to beat away from shore, the next tack forced us almost back onto our original position.

The scenery, when I had a moment to look, was sensational. Beside the Capes, the brittle light fell blue. Baba Dağ, wearing another Monet enveloppe, rose from a Corryvreckan glittering in sunshine. "Come on! Let's shout!" Bob mouthed above the tumult. From just such turbulence the beautiful witch Olympias was wont to rear, demanding news of her son, Alexander the Great. (How else, but by giving the desired reply, did the fisherman out of Lesbos reach safety?) «Ο Μεγαλέζανδρος ζεί και βασιλεύει!» we hurled in unison to the wild waves. ("Alexander the Great...lives...and...reigns!") The stirring syllables, echoing to the Seven Capes, bounced back. If it was no longer a spell to calm the raging waters, at least it was great to shout.

On the stern, the anchor bin, bungees at breaking point, slithered crazily. When the cords burst, the contents spilt. The last thing *Cappelle*

218

needed was a sea anchor. Somehow we dragged the hook out of the water. Cheered on its way, the bin took air, somersaulting into the sky. At the sharp angle at which we were heeled, sea water, siphoning back through the sink outlet, flooded the galley. Sailing lee under never made for fast passage, so we heaved-to to change tack and adjust sail. As we did so, a chute of ice water clobbered me in the back of the neck, making me wish I had released my hood snarled in the safety harness. This time it was I who regretted not wearing sea boots, for water flowed so fast in the cockpit it had no time to self-drain and my feet froze in soggy deck shoes. But as veils of iridescent spray took off from the crests of waves, I revelled in a tiny taste of ocean.

As always at the most trying times – our new Cypriot door hinges already buckled and sprung – the Ship's Cat emerged. Grabbed by his scruff as he lurched onto the coach roof, the state of his coat, spikey with sea water, reminded me we forgot to put a bung in the navel pipe to the chain locker. From the look in his eyes it was clear there were times when Wacky would have given anything not to have signed on for a sailor. After all, there were more enviable careers for a Likely Lad, apprenticeship to a fishmonger perhaps, or appointment as Chief Mouser in a bake house?

On her final surfing zig-zag *Cappelle* forged parallel with the Bad Cape, last of the Seven. Reducing sail again, we tore ourselves away into a maple-leaf sunset that stained the cabin walls Phoenician red. Our incantation had worked, for out there the indigo sea, ridden no more by white horses, subsided. As if exhausted, *Cappelle* floundered, going about.

Though we could not take out the final reef, since the roll of sail covered the tear, Bob settled us on course for Rhodes. With Wacky confined, I took the midnight watch, The yacht's balance was delicate, the breeze fluctuating. It was the clearest of nights and I steered by an arbitrary star. Knowing it was important to stay on red alert, I pulled on a fleece-lined jacket, a parody running through my head,

> "The seas are lonely, dark and deep
> But I have promises to keep
> And miles to go before I sleep…"

Bob was in a mood of uncertainty. On checking the engine, he had been aghast to find our invincible new exhaust already cracked! It was Friday and the workshops in Rhodes would close for the weekend at midday, so it was essential to reach our destination without delay. A lilac sunrise suffusing the lacquered sea, Rhodes prominent on the horizon, there was nothing for it but to fire the engine. At this the new exhaust fell seriously apart. Soon we were enveloped in oily smoke. But not before, in broad daylight this time, we had confirmation that it was impossible to see the three "conspic" windmills described in the pilot until after we had passed Emborikos.

Almost invisible inside a black cloud, *Cappelle* re-entered Mandraki.

Fifteen

A necklace of islands

Stopover in Rhodes

We tied up hastily. Bob raced to the tasks ahead. The faces around were those of strangers, but from the mini-marketeer I received a hug before rushing Wacky to the vet for his feline influenza booster. In the surgery all activity ceased, for Adrianos, having stitched a puppy's ear, sat me down, kitten in arms, to share a bag of pumpkin seeds and talk of cabbages and kings. Bob returned all smiles. Daniel had agreed to urgent sail repair over the weekend. Moreover, Camper & Nicholson were arranging for a hyper-quality flexible steel exhaust section to be flown in from Athens on the morrow.

Daniel, accompanied by Gaby bearing a bunch of "Welcome Back!" roses, brought an invitation to dine chez Gauthier. Our landfall was well timed, for a sleep-disturbing NW blustered that night, while across the channel fresh snow topped the Turkish mountains. The latest new exhaust pipe section was soon fitted. But not before, finding it hard to get my land legs, I had twisted my ankle in the engine cavity.

We took a taxi along the arteries of the Old City until its conduits narrowed into capillaries. Here Gaby waited to guide us along a donkey walk opening onto a passage leading to the walled pleasure garden-cum-potager of La Voilerie Gauthier complete with goldfish pond and medlar tree. On the terrace logs blazed in an iron cradle. The living quarters comprised a lean-to kitchen giving entry to two reception rooms, the most architecturally interesting of which was a circular cistern entered down steps. In a bedroom Baby Simon, whom a local girl was employed to nurse, was asleep. The adjoining barn, converted to sail loft, housed Mireille's treadle sewing machine.

Ούζο was dispensed in the moonlit garden by Belle-mère visiting from Marseilles. Clutching her wrap, she said how she adored the Greek islands, but that springtime in them made her teeth chatter. After barbecuing brochettes strung with marinated lamb and onion rings, we tossed a coin as to whether to eat à la belle étoile or indoors. To Mother-in-law's relief, indoors won. Bowls of salad and herb-drenched potatoes were carried into the cistern where we perched on ill-assorted chairs around a table where a cracked jug held wild flowers. Quaffing wine from mugs, matching only in the sense of being chipped, and enfeebled with fatigue, we were soon mellow.

Between the first and second round of brochettes Daniel led us on a tour of the premises. A local carpenter or "vrai bricoleur" ("botcher") had been employed to remedy its more glaring defects. Again Monsieur Hulot would be at home. The first time Mireille flushed the loo its tank emptied itself on her head, whilst opening the doors of an armoire brought the entire piece of furniture, only supported by two bent nails through knot holes, tottering into her arms. Frayed wiring was bunched in swags and sockets dangled out of wall cavities like bell pulls. The bricoleur, to put it mildly no skilled worker, had twice set about glazing the eighteen-inch gap above the kitchen door. But every time the door banged in the wind the glass broke. Window frames were not his speciality either. On Daniel pointing out that one of them was made from a (badly) chopped-up broom handle, we clutched one another giggling. Superior household effects were a kitchen cabinet and a washing machine salvaged from a rubbish dump.

On return to the table we found straight-backed Belle-mère fussing over her inability to provide matching dinner napkins. This notion contrasted so sharply with the look of me perched on a beach chair, my elbows round my ears, the scene was too much for Mireille whose cheeks ran with tears of laughter. Soon, sloshing wine into broken mugs, we were in paroxysms. Pudding of mandarins sliced in rum, with more strong drink straight from the bottle, did nothing to sober us and neither did the cognac to follow. Baby Simon never woke up to share the joke.

Gaidharos

A gangplank waving beside us like a battering ram was our signal to up anchor. With the forecast of a smooth barometric field covering the Central Aegean and Eastern Mediterranean, we set off to meet our commitment 120 miles north. Two cruise liners, four tankers and a car ferry later, we were motoring off the barren coast of Simi. All day long the sea remained a glassy stasis. Evening found us abeam Cape Krio, its lighthouse aglow in the sun's last rays. Raising my sundowner, I poured a libation to Aphrodite Euploia for safe passage through the night.

Before we reached the far side of the Gulf of Gököva, the sky darkened. It was essential to avoid the shallows in the narrows off Kos. But it was one thing to study colour-coded light systems on a chart and quite another to distinguish them in practice. Bob, already tense, took as many bearings as he could. The joy of day dissipated and the air struck chill. We held our breath as a brightly lit ferry shaved us. Noting to port the profounder darkness of the bulk of Pserimos, the periphery of my eye picked up lamp-black patches to starboard that dissolved on scrutiny. I called out warnings of the Loch Ness Monster humps of unlit islets. Such waters were no place for a small boat on such a Hecate night.

When the coast of Kalimnos loomed, its attendant light structure some way off, we altered course by fifteen degrees, sensing a connecting reef. With the passage ahead theoretically clear, I went off watch. After we had passed the island of Pharmokonis at 04.15 hrs, Bob woke me. With the yacht on autohelm, all that was required of the Cabin Boy was to remain alert, complete engine and navigation checks and be on the look out for Gaidharos light, due to appear to starboard in about an hour. At 05.30 hrs, peering into the darkness, I could see nothing. Twenty minutes later, I jerked awake in spreading daylight with an alarm cry loud enough to jack-in-a-box Bob out of the cabin to slam the helm hard over. *Cappelle*, already in the shallows with a following breeze, was heading straight for a beach. Only his prompt action averted disaster. (The autopilot, correctly set to pass to the west of Gaidharos and not given to misbehaving, had apparently suffered some sort of magnetic anomaly, altering our course eastwards and into danger. There was no note in the Pilot, but we discovered that others had encountered compass problems in this area.)

Paralysed with shock, having fallen asleep on my feet with no recollection of even blinking, this was a never-to-be-forgotten experience. Ever after, Bob's murmur of "Remember Gaidharos!"("Remember Belgium!" World War I style) restored my concentration. What had alerted me? Probably subtle changes in sound and rhythm as *Cappelle* made for shore. But I liked to think Aphrodite Euploia had whispered in my ear.

Samos

In Pythagorio an unexpected welcome awaited us. Both *Golden Prospect* and *River Rat* were on the quay. So excited was I at this reunion that, tardy with tying up, I laid myself open to a public reprimand from Port Captain Stavros who, picking up his megaphone and reddening my ears, called, "Look after boat first, please! Talk to friends later!" All were agog to learn how we had fared in Israel. We made light of events. But Vanessa brought the subject up again, asking if we remembered that she and Richard were present when Digger formally presented Bob with his Russian proposition? "It was a con trick," she said hotly, "just to get *Boomerang* an invitation to Odessa! Be warned!"

Much merchandise in the main street was familiar. (I even recognised the position of embalmed bluebottles in display cabinets.) New features on the waterfront included a mains electricity box and a contemporary sculpture of Pythagoras. Baby Alexander, growing up fast, had invented a noddy head game, his bright morning face popping up over *River Rat's* cap rail to challenge Bob to the early bout. Wacky, out most nights bringing home very dead cockroaches, had grown so much, Big Tease Richard suggested fattening him up for a fender. We made the most of our time together, for, after Vanessa and Alexander had flown home, Richard was to sail to Sardinia for the Football World Cup.

Soon the old routine of tea on *Golden Prospect* and brandy sours on *Cappelle* fell into place. The blue and gold polka dot glasses I purchased to dispense the sours had lain in the dust of the shop window for "many, many years", the old lady handing them over at a pre-war price assured me with pride. There were the usual fiascos. Vanessa's decanting of Sintetik Tiner into a plastic Coke bottle for us caused it to dissolve and thinner to flood the paint locker.

With high season under way the air buzzed with the succession of aeroplanes on airport approach. Within minutes of waving to the early flight from Athens, Mel, accompanied by her boyfriend, Stephen, stepped aboard. Eagerly, they accepted invitations from Julia and Gary to windsurf after breakfast...by which time Mel was fast asleep in the cockpit.

On the day cruising was to begin, Problem No 1 arrived in the form of lack of ignition. The breeze died as we entered the Straits of Samos where Problem No 2 occurred, a shortfall of oil pressure. Harnessing every puff of air, Mel and Steve took turns to helm. *Cappelle* inched north, *Golden Prospect* followed tack for tack. Entering Possidonio, we anchored under sail. Inspection revealed a corroded connector-head on which Bob and Gary worked until brandy sour time, when a cloud cap laced with lightning built up over Ionia. Storm light intensified the carmine of Julia's shirt, the emerald green of the hillsides and the peak of Mount Mycale lifting above a feather boa of cloud.

Chios

Next day *Golden Prospect* elected to partner *Cappelle* on her second attempt on Chios. Over a chart conference we reckoned that if we set sail on the right side of midnight we should reach its untried shores, a passage of some seventy miles, in daylight. At 23.30 hrs, gingerly aware of unlit craft, I nosed *Cappelle* out into the Straits. Though we spotted five fishing boats, Gary, with benefit of radar, pronounced the number nine. Once past Cape Gata, we sailed parallel, our boats transformed by their bobbing triangles of red and green navigation lights into Christmas trees on rockers. Bob and Mel took the 02.00 to 04.00 hrs watch. Steve and I, carrying out our nautical duties from 04.00 to 06.00 hrs, concentrated on checking the compass with fading torch batteries. Changing course to leave the Samian coast meant a constant scan for shipping. Steve, after declaring a distant light mass a coastal settlement, watched it, a cruise liner in all its glory, detach itself from its background, draw close and pass on.

Day had already wrapped itself round the night when the Captain's pencil line on the chart lead us, John "Longitude" Harrison style, straight to the heart of the tiny land-locked cove of Emborio. But where was *Golden Prospect*, fallen back after radioing her engine was overheating? Rowing out of the cove, Bob and Mel spotted her reconnoitring the coast. Out of sight of land, Julia and Gary had become disorientated. After relocating their position by Satnav they were at last making their approach. But within the steep-to embrace of Emborio we failed to pick up their radio call. Moved courteously over by fishing boats, evening was falling before, at Gary's insistence, we hoisted black balls indicating "yachts at anchor".

My first sight on waking was the tips of Wacky's ears as he crouched on the anchor bin, keeping a low profile while peeping at a man on shore beating an octopus. Riffling through Dilys Powell's *An Affair of the Heart*, I discovered that in 1954, representing *The Times*, she had attended Britain's first-ever sub-aqua archaeological survey in this very cove. I identified the villa where the dive party put up and the hut they made their headquarters.

The old lady in the general store patted our cheeks and give a dry spit to ward off evil spirits before waving farewell as we set sail round Cape Mastiko. When a sudden squall raced across the Cape, we saw *Golden Prospect* ahead heel abruptly on the deceptively flat sea as if in receipt of a playful tug from the Kraken. Twenty-six miles further on, where a fisherman's ούζερι boasted one-armed bandits, we abandoned our attempt to anchor stern-to on Volissos quay beside a sand-hill, a concrete mixer and a pile of building aggregate to come in bows on. A goat, a sick cat and an emaciated donkey approached. Wacky, maintaining his customary joie de vivre, pirouetted on the sandhill, while Julia rubbed away at her washing under the quayside tap.

In the seventeenth century, Scottish traveller William Lithgow, earner of the nickname "Cut-lugged Wullie" after dalliance with a lady whose brothers cut off his ears, escaped to Chios. He may have trudged inland, as we did, to the village on the acropolis. Stirred by sea breezes, the air smelt of coriander, pine and apricot-scented gorse. Pink mallow bordered the road. In the quattrocentro landscape before us, a Genoese fort surmounted a sienna-coloured hill. Reaching the village, we were directed to the baking ovens. A basement shopkeeper, having examined the contents of my shopping bag with unabashed curiosity, added his contribution of bantam eggs before taking the carnation from a bud vase on the counter to present to me «γιά την κόρι σου» ("for your daughter"), who was standing behind me.

On our way past the Tourist Board's monument to Homer (Volissos being one of seven ancient cities to claim his birth), a covered wagon powered by a pump engine skidded to a halt, its expressionless driver nodding us in. Hardly had we climbed aboard when the springless trailer bounced off, making me wonder how my eggs were faring – badly, it turned out – while willowy Julia tried to shield her head from the iron hoops supporting the tarpaulin roof. We fell out at the quayside, only to see the driver, not waiting for thanks, rattling back uphill. Julia, rubbing her head, sighed ecstatically. Chios was just how she had always imagined Greek islands!

We were awakened by the hooter of a fishing boat wishing to take on fuel, the driver of the diesel lorry in attendance letting us have diesel also. Later we explored the village of Pyrghi, the walls of whose houses, thanks to the unique Chiot art of graffito, were prettily pargetted like Victorian samplers in pastel-coloured plasterwork. Our journey across the island's mountain chain to its depressing χώρα was made by taxi. In the Great Massacre of 1822, Turkish forces had crossed the narrow foam-ridged channel from the Turkish mainland opposite to drive the islanders into the sea. It was arranged for the taxi driver's cousin (an alarmingly "no hands" driver) to bring us back, since most vehicles, including the village bus, only plied the precipitous route one way a day.

That evening fishermen ringed Volissos harbour, the waters outside too rough for handline fishing. Bob and Gary mounted the hill to view prospects. Here the skipper of a fishing boat assured them that by midnight the north wind would drop. If Chiots were so skilled in the laws of the sea that Christopher Columbus learnt the art of navigation from them, who were we to argue? To the keen interest of a patrolling battleship, we pulled away. Hauling in the anchor, the Captain let out a yell as a feather of fish hooks sank into his hand. Then, in falling over each other to raise sail, we knocked the anchor chain overboard. Once this was dragged in, *Cappelle* rolled drunkenly on a bed of hard lumps and holes as we executed a wide sweep to avoid charted shoals, a manoeuvre that had us all confused and argumentative. With the battleship hemming us in abeam as we veered off towards Lesbos, all four of us remained on watch, a pair of eyes to each corner of the compass. Frequent checks on the depth sounder and strict concentration had to be exercised to judge our distance from the rock-girt coastline. We revived our flagging energies with short-term hot-bunking spells, while Bob agonised over engine vibrations.

Dawn found us abeam the north end of Chios. When I looked back at the perfect proportions of Profitis Ilias (common name for a highest mountain), it reminded me so forcibly of the logo for Paramount Pictures I missed the ring of stars. We made mutual sighting with *Golden Prospect* as a cheerful Gary radioed, "Good Morning! Did you see the dolphins?" At times during the night *Golden Prospect* had made straight for the mountains, Gary relying on instruments to keep her off the rocks. At 09.00 hrs we sailed a glorious reach in sight of Plomari, a pyramidal prospect of coloured houses opening like a pop-up book as in a Mehmet Sonmez painting. Still the battleship gave escort.

Lesbos

Once in harbour, Wacky, who had been a demanding little so-and-so all night, orientated himself by leaping on and off the quay. Gary, meanwhile spotted a giant octopus on the sea-bed between our boats and set about its capture. Surprisingly the junior Kraken, with an elephant's hide and parrot beak, came up without a struggle. Plomarians, who gathered round, said we were not to touch it, for it was a Deep Sea Monster. Why had it been it so easy to catch? Was it sick? All the same the restaurateur asked to show it to his friends, leaving us to wonder if we had given away an epicurean delight.

When we rowed to a neighbouring bay to snorkel, I stayed in the dinghy in charge of the grapnel anchor. Swimming was abandoned when Gary observed from the scum that the bay was an emptying point for holding tanks: "Now we know why the Owl and the Pussycat's boat was pee-green!" he commented. Afterwards, as a favour, Stephen busied himself with a set-square, designing templates to stencil *Golden Prospect's* name on her stern. Under strict instructions to refrain from tampering with the masking tape until the following day, Gary crossed his heart, but only on a technicality, for, ever the enthusiast, at one minute past midnight he was seen peeling it away.

In the fearsome swell I dropped a tea-towel overboard. Stephen, leaning to retrieve it, overbalanced. Mel and I, each grabbing an ankle as he took a header, had to bust our guts to haul him back on board. For the gunboat anchored beside us, the whole incident was a comedy performance of the highest order. We expected a twenty-one gun salute. Even the seagulls waxed hysterical. From this moment *Cappelle* and the Greek Navy were buddies. No opportunity to barrack was missed. It was our turn to boo and cheer when the sailors were marshalled in line to dive from the ship's stern.

Mirsinia

Mirsinia was a classic anchorage, secret, remote, a fertile valley at its head, pink oleander, the "rose growing by the brook" of Ecclesiasticus, frilling the beach, the tinkle of goat bells lifting into the air. On the shore three buildings formed a harmony: a coral-coloured hull fronted a fisherman's cottage, a white chapel crowned a bluff, and the ruins of a small factory buttressed a cave-ridden cliff. When the resident fisherman rowed over, though we did get the message he had once visited Newcastle, the English he claimed was broken Spanish. Offered a drink, he requested *ούζο* and told us that the derelict factory, later an olive press and now a goat pen, was once a gravel plant set up by an Englishman (or was it a Spaniard?). There had been no rain in Mirsinia for four years. Of Chios he commented, «*Κλέψει! Κλέψει!*» ("Thieves and vagabonds!") It was ever the way to describe the neighbours.

Wacky, invited to tea on *Golden Prospect*, took fright when he slid down her sun-awning on his bottom. The trip home went well until, in order to turn the dinghy to bring it in alongside, Bob rowed past his ship, at which point Wacky panicked and took an unscheduled leap for home that might well have ended badly. Settling for the night, he chose the angle between the mast and boom where the mainsail folded thickest. The early sunlight shocked us by lighting up rocks scrawled with scurrilous graffiti, the artist having added a dagger dripping blood. Insults varied from «*Ρουφιάνο!*» (pimp or intriguer); «*Πούστι!*» (sodomite); «*Πυτανάς γιε!*» ("son of a whore") and a portmanteau word «*Βρωμοπάλιομάλακακαταραμένο!*», which is unspeakably filthy and, avoiding obscenities, might be translated as "disgustingly-dirty-cursed-old-sleaze-bag". The feud was likely to involve politics, money, sex, property rights, *φιλότιμο* (honour or face), or all five combined. It could be our fisherman friend was not popular...

Mitilini

When we put into Mitilini, capital of Lesbos, people were voicing concern about a minor undersea earthquake, which caused the harbour waters to suck back more than a metre before surging in again. On the last day of May gale force northerlies rendered the Levantine bazaar of Main Street more appealing than the waterfront. Here butchers, grocers, fish-mongers, pharmacists, jewellers, cheese-mongers, coffee merchants, pastry cooks, and carpet shops dealing in lurid mats depicting biblical scenes in fluorescent dyes, rubbed shoulders.

Mel and Stephen must return to work in London, while Julia and Gary were anxious to resume Cycling Round the World. If nothing else, a *FOR SALE* notice on *Golden Prospect* produced casual visitors. Getting his cycling muscles in trim, Gary reported white water off the north coast of the island. Then winter returned with a vengeance. The first week of June was cold enough for us to relight the Tilley. Time to tidy up too! We spring-cleaned the cooker and threw out battered saucepans, the leaky ice-box and old clothes. Wacky, who entertained passers-by with his habit of diving head-first down a port hole "like a rabbit down a burrow", took to hibernating under the duvet. In the cabin, driving rain forced unexpected leaks. «Πολύ χάλια!» ("Wretched weather!") nodded a shop assistant, selling me comfort chocolate when a rotting hulk moved in to block the view.

Following the magic sign "Launderette", Julia and I ended up at the back of the bus station where the treasure announced itself as closed "due to technical fault". While we deliberated, its owner appeared, assuring us he would endeavour to get the service going in a day or so. He was as good as his word. Our bundles were washed, dried and folded "as good as ironing", resulting in sheets, towels and shirts that positively sparkled. (Had we known how much bleach was put into them, we might have had second thoughts, for they rotted even faster than usual!) The owner of Our Beautiful Launderette described Lesbos as a prosperous and self-respecting island, with little inclination for tourism, despite official encouragement. Some Greeks, he averred, moved to islands where land was cheap, then could not survive without recourse to tourism. On Lesbos work was always available. Though a notice pinned to a tree outside the Post Office announced its staff as "helpful to foreigners" and a flag at the harbour entrance proclaimed it the "International Year of Tourism", most of the advertised attractions stayed shut. The Hellenistic statuary in the garden of the Archaeological Museum was weed-smothered, and I never did get to see the Matchmaker's Lamp in the padlocked time-warp known as "The Lesbos House". (In the nineteenth century the Matchmaker might be seen of an evening on her way to negotiate with the parents of some eligible boy and girl. Should a marriage be arranged she would return through the streets in triumph, her red lamp lit to signify to the townsfolk that nuptials were to be celebrated.)

When the gale veered SW, life was more comfortable off the boats than on. To the bemusement of a huddle of goats, we clambered into the castle precincts via the moat. The sprawl of vandalised staging was the aftermath of a long-ago pop concert. Down below a tree grew out of a pomander-roofed hamam. Traversing the tussocky hillside, I stumbled across an iron crucifix and bell bolted to a low-lying rock. Behind it, mysterious steps led down to a dark chicane and beyond into a pokey cave. Here colour smacked the eyes and the smell of must overlaid with incense assailed the nostrils. In an alcove, where Neolithic man had once crouched to pestle grain in a stoup, water dripped through a smoke hole. Now the sanctuary, its altar and benches draped in fiery tongues of mildewed scarlet satin, was dedicated to the Madonna of the Underground Cave. A vigil light burned before a curling print of the Panagia and hydrangeas sprouted from a jam jar. Moving quietly to disturb no spirits, I lit a taper before creeping up to the daylight. With conditions on board too boisterous even for him, Wacky awaited us on the quay.

As soon as the weather took a turn for the better, *Enchanted April*, bearing an elderly German couple, pulled in. As Bob moved to take the warps, the lady opened a gate in the bows to step graciously ashore. Afterwards the gentleman tendered his thanks in old-world English, saying that, since offers of assistance were rare in the islands, the gate had been put in for his wife's convenience. Each day, wearing silk pyjamas, her face protected with a wide-awake leghorn hat tied on with chiffon, the lady donned household gloves to carry out her domestic duties. Within the cabin a mechanical bird trilled in a sweet, watery voice of sobs and pauses. Wacky, usually content with a single by-rights inspection of a new neighbour, insisted on camping out on the new arrival's coach roof, his nose, to our embarrassment, pressed to her window. One morning, realising from billowing door nets that the Germans had gone shopping leaving the boat open, I climbed aboard and closed up, leaving a note. If Wacky ran true to form, he would not hesitate to investigate. Glancing inside, I saw a live nightingale hopping about with a splintered wing. So this was the Tweetie-Pie to which Wacky hoped to play Sylvester! Later the couple called to thank us. The gentleman, confessing to have, at one time, threatened Wacky (impervious, in this case, to insult) with a slipper, was mortified. "You see," he explained contritely, "we thought he was a *GREEK* cat...!" adding, "He had more reason for his interest than you know, for we have also on board his natural prey!" The couple were also giving sanctuary to a mouse.

Scala Mistegnon

13th June came in with its sails unfurled and swelling. With *Golden Prospect* in the lead, we lost no time in dream-boating down the Muslim Channel until, reporting engine trouble, *Golden Prospect* turned back. The pilot evaluated the minuscule harbour of Scala Mistegnon as navigable. But Bob, finding its waters fouled with floating warps, exercised extreme caution. Standing on the stern I cried out as the sea bed came up to meet us. Then a fisherman called out that, since he would be away for a few days, we were welcome to tie to his boat.

Golden Prospect failed to clear Mitilini until her third attempt. (Gary's neglect to reseat a gasket after solving an impeller problem was thought to have caused a leak, which in turn shorted the temperature warning light. It transpired the original trouble was nothing to do with the impeller, but was triggered by a plastic bag blocking the engine sea-cock.) As soon as *Golden Prospect* was sighted, we radioed warnings of shallows. But to no avail. For, in the light of the evening sun, she ran hard aground and stuck fast. Gary tried to reverse. We rocked her. Using both dinghies at once, we sweated blood to free her. Nothing worked. The silence was pregnant. The Pilot, while drooling over the village's "tranquil embrace", had omitted to mention how tight that embrace might be! We knew the eyes of the village were upon us. At last a caïque put out to draw *Golden Prospect* free with an almighty sucking noise, as a result of which Julia and Gary parted with their ready cash, a large denomination note comprising a whole week's housekeeping money, an act that made them Skala Mistegnon's most popular visitors for 1990. "Well," said Julia, "we could hardly ask for change!" Chastened, *Golden Prospect* distanced herself to anchor off. Julia, who was growing more superstitious every day, put it all down to the fact that, strictly against her wishes, we had left harbour on Friday the 13th.

In high heat we walked the five miles to Thermi to sample its spa, described as a cure-all "open from June to October". Lush grass carpeted the olive groves, but the coastal ravines bulged with garbage, including disposable nappies thrown out of car windows. We passed an αρχοντικό, one of the "gentleman's mansions" for which Lesbos is famed. Fronted by an overgrown knot garden bearing a serpentine edge of the shells of St James of Compostella, the forsaken homestead with lichen-covered coat-of-arms over its gateway and crumbling balustrade, exuded nostalgia, breathing of times lost. It was as if the house still echoed with the laughter of family summers of long ago.

At Thermi both the colonial-style hotel and bath complex were derelict. Gary pointed out that exotic-looking hoopoes had taken over the garden. Wheelbarrows and hardened bags of cement, evidence of a planned restoration, were dumped. We asked a woman when the baths would open. *"Το καλοκαίρι!"* ("In the summer!") she replied sweetly. But which summer? The lintel of a concrete chapel by the shore was marked with the restoration date 1950, while the fluted marble column that supported a door jamb showed the site sacred since pagan times. I ran into a field of poppies to examine a capital, a stele askew amongst yellow ragwort, and an ancient altar within a patch of tumbled stones sloshed with limewash.

As if paddling down the Orinoco, Gary, kneeling in the bows in his Foreign Legion Kepi, sculled over. Together we watched the moon's radiance suffuse the mountains before its orb appeared. Next morning Gary took charge of our joint departure. After making a careful survey, he put in his arm and lifted out *Cappelle's* anchor wedged upright in only a metre of water! How we had ever entered Skala Mistegnon in the first place was a puzzle.

I trained binoculars on the mountainous coastline seeking a white chapel at the entrance to Skala Sikinia to salute its patroness, the enchantingly named Παναγία της Γοργόνας (Our Lady Mermaid, Madonna of the Fisherman) on whom Stratis Myrivilis based his novel "The Mermaid Madonna". As if in answer, the breeze blowing in aft summoned me to exchange chopping salad for balancing the sails to take advantage of the Madonna's favour. Bob leapt to the helm and I caught my foot in the cat tray as *Cappelle* surged forward leaving *Golden Prospect* standing. After ten glorious minutes, the blow died as abruptly as it arose. (No doubt we had reached the limit of Our Lady Mermaid's territorial waters.) Giving furious chase, *Golden Prospect* hit the doldrums all-standing, her boom clouting Gary on the head. By the time law and order were restored, lunch was forgotten, for we were in sight of the Castle of Mithymna at the exit to the Muslim Channel.

It was then that ever-solicitous Gary spotted a paddle boat lying dangerously far out to sea and sailed off to render assistance. We circled, waiting. "Guess what?" shouted Julia merrily from *Golden Prospect* as soon as we were within earshot again, "They were *BONKING!*" The naked paddle-boaters, it seems, staging an away-from-it-all (except, in this instance, Gary) session of Love in the Afternoon, had failed to appreciate his intervention.

Petra

Facing us was a mile-long beach centred by a cube of rock topped by a sturdy little monastery reached by rock-cut staircase. Wings of the village of Petra extended each side. As the lemon clouds of evening barred an apple green sky corrugating with bands of cyclamen, the mountains receded, separating darkly. Flushed with alpine glow, the mica-pitted rock absorbed the last of the rufous light. As it did so, the monastery was reborn as the palace of a princess. Inhabited by nuns, it was dedicated to the Παναγία της Γλυκοφιλούσα, Our Lady the Sweet Kiss. Tucked below in a fifteenth-century chapel a series of frescoes portrayed the story of St Nicholas. His face was green as his boat tossed in heavy seas, sainthood no proof against the miseries of ναύτια (sea-sickness).

We tied up on the outer wall of the small fishing harbour. Following orders, I leapt for the quay to fend off, twisting in mid-air as I endeavoured not to catch my foot in the warp. Exasperated with my clumsiness, Bob roared, "Oh, for crying out blanketty loud!" Julia, meanwhile, battled with a broken mooring ring while trying to hang onto *Golden Prospect's* dinghy. When we took a dip to improve our outlook, fishermen beckoned us into an ουζερί (ouzo bar) to fill our hands with green cocktail plums, with bawdy cackles offering Julia a double.

Humping bags of garbage through the squabbling charms of goldfinches congregated at the side of the road where thistles seeded, Julia and I tramped to the village. Petra was an upmarket resort, its summer population made up of Germans and Scandinavians. A Medical Centre, the first amenity brought in by the Teutonic race, had been established. We lunched at *Το Τυχερό Πέταλο* ("The Lucky Horseshoe") and dined in *Cappelle's* cockpit, unpestered for once by mosquitoes, all of us experiencing a more prolonged bout of arrival inertia than usual. In fact none of us was in any hurry to leave Petra.

According to the pilot, an underwater reef about a mile offshore was "sometimes" marked by a stick and "sometimes not". This was a trick of the light. Close inspection revealed a stout iron pole, concreted in, that had done many years service as a reef marker. The day we hitched the dinghy to it, I underwent a snorkelling metamorphosis. All in a moment, I was lying above the Himalayas on a pneumatic plexiglas roof, everything below radiant and polished in an all-things-bright-and-beautiful world framed in mystery. Directly below me twin canyons opened. The underwater reef to which we had tied the dinghy made my stomach churn as, an aquatic bird in flight, I forced myself to peer over the edge.

These mountains were far from Nepalese, but refraction made an unreality of depth. The shock of raising my head into the world of air was explosive; lowering it again a transformation as rusty fronds of seaweed, coralline fans of lichen, sea urchins like balls of knitting wool and swerving shoals of fish sprang back into focus. Gary hovered without gravity on the edge of the picture, scissoring to the sandy floor. When he kicked up he was bearing the top half of a barnacle-encrusted amphora. Bob joined him to uncover a Pacific snail shell disguised as a sand wart. Thus began our routine of swimming off the reef before taking tea together, Turkish Apple, Earl Grey or Julia's latest discovery, "Winston Churchill".

We were roused for customs inspection early one morning by a uniformed officer from a patrol boat. Later another official arrived from Mithymna to examine our papers. Both treated us with friendly courtesy. Since Petra was not an official harbour there were no dues to pay. Stay as long as you like! Sunday afternoon found us back on the reef before collapsing in a row on the beach, blissed out, tourist fashion. We watched idly as another Harbour Patrol vessel, apparently enjoying Sunday afternoon leave, circled our reef. But, on zooming back to harbour, we found ourselves tailed by Λιμενικό Σώμα 125. As we tied up, so did it, and a combative-looking officer in plain clothes (meaning Hawaiian shorts and flip-flops) barred our way, arms akimbo, feet apart. Bob and Gary, both instinctively unhappy with officials in mufti, kept their cool, but informed him politely not to worry, for our credentials had been checked twice and we were cleared for indefinite stay. Speaking though an interpreter, the man demanded,

"What were you doing on the reef?"

"Swimming!" we chorused, surprised.

This truism was a red rag to a bull. It was plain we had much to conceal. Ratings were already turning over the contents of our dinghy without by your leave. When I explained that we "swam for pleasure", the man, incensing feminist Julia, pointedly presented me with his back. From the way the crew examined the reef marker, we were perhaps suspected of a drug drop. Or we might be political activists in enemy pay, for the area was a cauldron of distrust between Greece and Turkey over oil rights.

Summarily ordered to hand over our papers which, our skippers were told, would be taken to headquarters in Molivos, they both stood their ground, saying that where their ship's papers went, they went. Hot Pants then tried another tack, concerning money (the most likely reason for the detention in the first place). Meanwhile, reinforcements gathered behind us in the form of the Fishermen of Petra spoiling for an argument. A partisan voice hissed, "You NO pay!" in my ear. Pale with anger, Hot Pants ordered us to prepare to leave, flinging over his shoulder as he departed that we were to attend the police station within three days or suffer dire consequences.

We were not troubled further. A second disturbance to the peace of innocents in the form of a cargo boat wishing to unload was the signal for the champions of our cause to invite us to join them inside their cramped fishing harbour. This was an unexpected privilege. One of our biggest fans was a toothless old reprobate, the Greek island equivalent of Compo of *Last of the Summer Wine*. Though cheerfully unfazed on finding none of us smoked, his original aim had been to beg cigarettes. His themes were familiar. On every island other than Lesbos, it was «*Κλέψει! Κλέψει!*» ("Thieves and Vagabonds!") he chuckled, as he ambled about, hands in pockets to keep his trousers up, happy to do odd jobs and act as a butt for his mates. When he appeared in Baden-Powell khaki shorts held up with string, holey knee socks and open-toe sandals — as a compliment to us, we were sure — his compatriots found it a huge joke. Asking if we liked fish, he promised to bring us some «*πρωί πρωί*» (lit. "morning morning" meaning "very early"). Before the fish lorry arrived at six a.m. to collect the catch, a knock on the hull signalled Compo with a bucket of fish. I produced a bowl to select a few, but with a courtly bow, he indicated that the whole brimming quota of top quality *καλαμάρες* (squid), bass, sea bream, sardines and small fry were for our delectation.

Resolving to give the sea food its due, Julia and I consulted Claudia Roden's *Mediterranean Cookery*. *Καλαμάρες* were the most complicated: pull head from pouch; discard innards and ink bag (taking care with latter); pull out icicle-shaped cuttle bone; cut out eyes and cartilage at base of tentacles, peel off reddish membrane covering pouch, and cook with fresh herbs. Served as Sappho Suprême at a candlelit dinner on the cockpit table, the result was ambrosial! The Ship's Cat, too, gorged himself silly. Not to be wasteful, we made Greek-style Bouillabaisse. Our fish diet was inaugurated. A handline fisherman to whom Gary got chatting, telling him the eels congregated at the end of the mole at exactly ten o'clock each night, offered him a fishing lesson. At five to ten Gary, as excited as a schoolboy, departed for tuition and at quarter past was back with a handsome eel. Triumphalism filled the air the night we savoured L'Anguille à la mode.

We all had routine chores. Julia was quick to spot the woman at the grocery store was not on the level. Doubling single items as she totted up, she screwed up her scrap of paper. At the counter, Julia counselled me to *"WATCH OUT FOR CHEATING!"* We then gave the shop the cold shoulder. Within days the woman was wheedling at us from her doorstep. Thenceforward her addition was scrupulous. It was a sad day when brandy sours became a thing of the past, but Petra brandy, matured in ούζο barrels, tainted the sours with aniseed.

Only once on return from Mithymna did I stop the taxi to take an experimental short-cut over a wall in a direct descent to the harbour. As I humped my shopping bags down the rough one-in-seven slope while trying to negotiate thorn bushes, brick ends, broken glass and the carcass of a burned out car, my heels slid from under me, and I ended up sprawled at the bottom, shopping strewn.

Sixteen

Idyll in the Northern Isles

Gary knocked on the hull to show us a mini-tortoise he had found wandering and "wound up", for it pedalled its legs. Tortie haunted us, transfixing Wacky, who stalked it to venture a pat. Several times Gary relocated Tortie out of the way of the fish lorry. But it always came back. While Gary and Julia were discussing adoption – we had met live-aboards who kept a tortoise for a pet – Tortie was left to roam, until one day it failed to appear and we discovered its crushed remains on the track.

Although Tortie was lost to us, Artemis had another surprise up her sleeve. Julia detailed me not to pass down a certain street without glaring at the butcher and greengrocer whose shops faced. Above all, I was not to buy anything from either man, for she had caught them abusing a kitten. With World Cup fever in the air, the shopkeepers whiled away their time by aiming a football at the bony little thing as it sought refuge amongst packing cases. Julia instituted a glaring patrol. Finding the infamous game in progress one evening, she expostulated as only Julia could. At this the butcher disappeared into his shop to come out carrying a sack into which, scooping up the kitten, he dropped it. Then, tying a knot in the top, still without a word, he handed her the wriggling bundle. Having run out of steam, Julia was reduced to stunned silence. "Is give you! Is present!" a woman in a doorway urged.

Thus Soccer joined us. An old ball fender with the top sliced off was his basket. Worm pills and flea powder were supplied by courtesy of *Cappelle,* fleas leaving Socky in such droves Julia tried to drown them in a bucket. Gaining confidence with remarkable alacrity, he was soon growling at any alien approach to his fish saucer. After two days of jealous sulks during which Wacky snubbed Julia (whom he now regarded as his second mother), Wacky and Socky became inseparable, chasing each other over the yachts with the sound of stampeding elephants and playing "I'm King of the Castle" on the piled fishing nets, two sets of black and white rumps quivering with excitement as they prepared to pounce.

Gary became the butt of feline pranks. A tuft of his hair sticking up above the coach-roof as he relaxed in *Cappelle's* cockpit was enough to trigger Wacky into launching an attack on Gary's head as if it were a furry animal. When Gary sat chatting holding a mug of scalding Winston Churchill between his legs, Socky, pursued by Wacky, fell into it, feet first, scalding Gary in a sensitive place. This was funnier for everyone else than it was for Gary! We were kept provisioned by his fishing friend with prime fish "for the cats", who were later persuaded to share it.

Summer was personified by the metallic vibrations of cicadas winding their winches. The flowery parasols erected by the fishing boats saturated the seas around with prismatic tints. Ever since the Hotpants episode, our snorkelling had been confined to nearer home. When Bob brought up another giant shell, the fishermen advised us to leave it on the quayside, when its occupant would "go away" and we could make a lamp. I laid claim to a certain submarine Sun Valley knowing that, if Neptune sliced past me with his trident, it was only Gary with his spear gun. When I gazed into the water, fish looked up at me with enquiring eyes as if wondering what I was doing peering through their fanlight. Now that the end of June was in sight, sea bathing was official, for Greek tradition has it that water melons should not be eaten before the summer solstice, and that the sea is not fit for bathing until discarded melon seeds float.

At Efthalou on the edge of the Muslim Channel radioactive thermal water ran down a cliff to flow through a tiny Byzantine bathhouse. As red as Turkey cocks, we lay puffing in the steaming water before sinking into the warmed sea pools outside, our heads pillowed on smooth rocks, our bodies hammocked in the sea while shoals of small fry explored our fingers. Only the naked body of a Rubensesque German woman picking her way along the rocks above disturbed us.

Petra Harbour lacked sweet water, so we eked out supplies with the bottled variety. On hiring a car to visit Eressos, we piled its boot with empty canisters, thinking to refill them at the nearest pump. Forests of chestnut, oak and poplar soon gave way to a bare landscape dotted with rocky outcrops. Below us, the Gulf of Kalloni bit into the heartlands. In the valleys ribbons of foliage marked the beds of dried-up streams. At Lower Eressos, where, to a yachtsman's eye, the pocket-sized harbour looked not so much picturesque as hazardous to enter, we picnicked in sight of Sappho's Isle. Upper Eressos, the older village, welcomed us warmly, for visitors were in the habit of confining themselves to the award-winning beach of the lower town. All the same, we did not like to avail ourselves of spring water from the tap bolted to its Tree of Idleness.

High in the mountains we made a detour through a bleak and shadeless landscape via a shale track that dissected the creamy pall of lava leading to the petrified Forest of Hamadroula. A project had been put in hand to civilise and contain the valley, making it a profitable tourist attraction by the provision of toilet blocks, concrete paths and litter bins. But by the time of our visit the scheme had been abandoned. We scaled a wall beside padlocked gates. Not a drop of water serviced the toilet blocks. The crested larks that fluttered in the scrub were the only sign of life. A bench invited the visitor to sit and to admire the red and green silicone glints of a fallen trunk by the light of the westering sun. A few trunks stood upright. Sensory perception received a shock, for rings of age were clearly visible and realistic root sinews disappeared into the ground. That these were formed not of wood, but wood transformed to stone, could be established only through touch. Our final call was at a garage on the outskirts of Petra where the purchase of petrol entitled us to a single canister of water from the garage tap.

An Australian opening a Jet Ski School, eager to acquire Gary's windsurfer, extended an invitation to us to join a beach party, requesting Julia bring her guitar. At midnight, seeing a bonfire ablaze, we went along. As we approached, Julia recognised the voices of a group of yobboes seen piling out of camper vans earlier in the day, Julia noting with amusement the new in-word "mental" – as in "Men'al 'ot ain' it!" and "Mental f****** stoopid!" Put on guard by the sounds of heavy metal, Julia hid her instrument under a bush. Sunburnt bodies sprawled in the firelight, hands stretching out to grab our contribution of foil-wrapped prime octopus. No one offering a greeting, we squatted on a log.

An ageing Neanderthal, hailing from the Planet of the Apes and referred to by his mates as "The Animal", acted as Major Domo. Caliban's waist-length hair was tied with twine and he scratched compulsively at his matted chest. A sample of his non-stop party patter was, "'Oos comin' skinny f****** dippin'?...OK! OK!...'Oos comin' skinny f****** then?...Haw! Haw! Haw!" To say this for the rest of the party, Caliban had no takers. When he finished swigging beer, he waxed expansive about his prowess as an octopus hunter. Why! – only that morning a brute had grabbed for his eyeballs. But he'd got lucky by turning its "bleedin'ead" inside out! A youth spun Gary a long story about how he'd come all the way from London to trace jet skis bought on hire purchase and made off with. A right racket these days, he said! As soon as it was clear our absence would go unnoticed, we made our escape, retrieving Julia's guitar as we went.

Within the walled gardens of Mithymna's Genoese fort, where an archaeologist sorted sherds, tamarisk bushes stirred in the breeze. On looking down into the harbour, I recognised *Runner Bean* whose skipper taught Julia and Gary to sail ("If," as Julia put it caustically, "you call scrubbing the deck sailing!"), and hurried back to relay the news.

By now our bond with the fishermen of Petra had cemented into an "any-friend-of-yours-is-a-friend-of-ours" mutual benefit society. Addressing Gary as «Γιατρέ!» they appointed him medical consultant in situations such as what to do when Compo dropped a lobster pot on his foot (or someone else did, for he could be insufferable). Of a morning, trousers slipping, he wandered up crying, «Αλάτι! Αλάτι!» ("Salt! Salt!") holding out a pan of fish mess for Julia to put on her stove for his breakfast. I once presented him with his own packet of salt, but that was not the point. What he craved was the social exchange of scrounging. Seeing Bob patching our dinghy, the skipper brought over his torn oilies, at which Bob sat on the wall absorbed in making an exacting repair. Putting his hand on his heart, the Greek bowed his thanks and next morning four beautiful sea bass wrapped in newspaper appeared on *Cappelle's* deck.

Gary lost no time in cycling off to invite *Runner Bean* to join us. At the time he and Julia were playing host to Mary-Jo from a Gay Community in California, to whom Gary had given puppy chase, as he was wont to do on spotting anyone riding a mountain bike. So far Mary-Jo had failed to encounter a single soul sister on her pilgrimage to the Sapphic Isle. As she pedalled away in further, hopeful search, *Runner Bean* put in with Mike and shy Lindy-of-the-Long-Brown-Hair, who had answered his advertisement for summer season crew.

If Lindy hoped to learn to sail, she could think again, for, during his ten years as a single-hander, Mike had grown accustomed to taking women for granted. As far as he was concerned, Lindy was recruited to act as his domestic support. Like many a dedicated sailor, Mike made any excuse not to go ashore. He was therefore willing to teach her to row so that she could make herself useful fetching supplies. Julia viewed the relationship darkly, declaring it would not last. But the pair seemed fond enough of one another. I did question the situation myself, however, when, the couple invited to tea, Mike climbed across alone, blithely remarking that Lindy would be unable to join us since he had "set her to mend a sail".

Gary, exercising his stubborn streak, was determined Mike and Lindy should visit "our" reef. On a grey day, wavelets chopping, Lindy choked on her mouthpiece. And when I looked back at our bucking inflatable tied to a pole around which the heaving swells exposed bare rock, I prayed we would not have to swim ashore. Without the sun, the sea soon lost its charm. Beneath the surface visibility was poor. Even Gary chuntered about the lack of fish. For some days we were confined to harbour by a strong meltemi. A fishing boat anchored off rather than face manoeuvring within, and our friends were long-faced at the loss of a 1,000 metre fishing net.

Another of Gary's bumble-puppy bike chases brought further acquaintances, an American couple based with the US Air Force in Suffolk, who had joined a Thomson Villa Party. They stopped by on an evening when Mike was strumming his guitar. Faith was so impressed, she suggested we attend a party they were giving at their villa. We arrived to find Lloyd and Faith struggling in increasingly trying circumstances to host a Chalk and Cheese affair. Self-appointed life and soul were Stan, a nut-cracker face, not-so-funny Les Dawson, and his partner, Lil, who encased her rolls of salmon-pink flesh in mauve elastic covered in dolphin trinkets. (She had yet to set eyes on the live version.) The perfect Fat Lady of the Donald McMandy postcards, she did the rounds perching on men's knees – most adroitly avoided this by standing up – while carrying on about "me knickers", a ready source of a joke. Burly Stan, a paper napkin dangling down the back of his neck, was naked except for a G-string like a swollen finger-stall perilously attached to the underside of his belly. His party trick was to pretend (or, God Forbid, not pretend) to be constantly taken short. While he knocked over chairs in his efforts to get to the khazi, Lil held her nose, warning everyone not to go in after him.

As we appeared, Lil, instantly summing us up, broke off pawing knees to draw attention to us with, "Excuse me! I've got to talk to these toffs!" "Go on! Give us a knees up!" she challenged Mike. To keep the peace, he played "Rock Around the Clock" for her to jig about clutching her drawers. A song especially for West Virginian Faith split the proceedings, getting the bird and the drumming of heels from the Thomson group, while bored Lil lumbered about plucking men's beards and pretending to squeeze their spots, making it evident that our lot had not got what it takes. It was obvious something had to be done. Lloyd assumed control. Explaining he had invited Mike to play for his wife, he welcomed any interested listeners to gather round. At one end of the terrace, Mike brought tears to Faith's eyes singing Don McLean style, while, at the other, Lil orchestrated the slap-and-tickle brigade as they tucked into Faith's generous spread. Niko, the villa owner sat with us to express his concern over our plan to sail for Samothraki. We must abandon such a scheme, he insisted, for the island was unsafe.

Molivos Nautical Week culminated in the Festival of the Sardine. The silver tide's blessing by the Bishop on the night of the Summer Solstice was celebrated with free sardines and *ούζο*, followed by dancing competitions and a firework display guaranteed to last an hour. (Gary's comment was that it was amazing what could be achieved with four well-spaced rockets!) We jumped at Mike's invitation to attend the festival, especially as he suggested taking our water canisters with us since he was party to a secret hydrant hidden under packing cases in an obscure corner of the harbour. Arriving early to be sure of gaining a place, we picnicked on deck where I pointed out a casually dressed reveller clambering along the ballast, joking he might be a policeman. To our surprise, so it proved, for the man called out he had come to collect harbour dues. We were to launch the dinghy and pay him. Mike shouted back there was no need for this, since we did not intend to stay the night.

When the sunset fanned like a peacock's tail and the deep pink of the sodium lights turned to gold, we joined the revelry onshore. Faces in the crowd glowed in the firelight and the air was heavy with the odours of hot fish oil, citrus, alcohol, cheap scent, fireworks and barbecue smoke. To volleys of applause, children pranced on makeshift platforms set up before packed restaurants that spilled diners onto the quayside. Elbowing with the crowd, we grabbed sizzling plates of sardines and halved lemons. Paper cups of *ούζο* were forced into our hands and strangers slapped us on the back. Replete at last, we licked ice-cream as we slid about on paving stones slippery with fishheads and *ούζο*. If only every nation could celebrate the Summer Solstice this way!

Above us, beneath a velvet sky patterned with jasmine-blossom stars, floated the golden ingot of the Castle of Mithymna. A breeze, just strong enough to waft us home, billowed the sails. Through the speakers Mike had fixed to the coach roof to comfort his lonely voyaging, the strains of Beethoven joined the music of the spheres. "In such a night…" we would have sailed forever.

But our idyll must end, Julia and Gary to return to Mitilini to see if interest in *Golden Prospect* had prospered, *Cappelle* and *Runner Bean*

246

to cruise north. The time had come to say goodbye to the fishermen of Petra – though they would persuade us otherwise. Accepting the inevitable, they shook hands and wished us well. Compo, when I slipped the old rascal cigarette money, expressed the hope we would return one day "with many little ones". At 04.30 hrs we dragged ourselves out of bed. Our last sight was of Gary in his psychedelic tee-shirt and Julia with Socky on her shoulder, as they waved goodbye from the end of Petra mole.

Lemnos

Propelled by an inter-island breeze of F4/5 we sailed north on a close reach under full main and genoa. The first faint smudge on the western horizon proved the penal island of Agios Eustratios, popular for ούζο from the barrel at 50p a litre. Then, in the early afternoon, we sighted the Bay of Mudhros on the south coast of Lemnos marked by its "conspic" lighthouse. Penetrating so deeply, it almost bisected the island, the bay had formed the fleet anchorage from which the Gallipoli campaign was launched. Since the entrance appeared dead ahead, and we reckoned a one knot current to be affording us a lift, we were puzzled when this marine travelator slyly pushed us four miles west, obliging us to tack east for an hour. What we had failed to observe was a Caution Note in the Admiralty Chart: "An onshore current, the cause of many wrecks, usually sets strongly from the Black Sea via the Dardenelles." Passing *Runner Bean* anchored off just inside the bay, we pressed on, sustained only by apple tea and peaches for the last thirteen hours.

Over the wall of the fishing harbour a familiar catamaran was festooned with bedding. Tony's partner Annie from catamaran *Chaton*, ran up firing questions. Following us on board, she was still with us two hours later when a note arrived from converted fishing boat *Ros Arcan* inviting us for drinks. Wacky, it seemed, had already introduced himself to their Ship's Cat, Muffin, by chasing her round her own deck. That night the rumble of fish lorries sent him scooting home with a dead crab. Patience must be exercised, for Mudhros Post Office, our next poste restante address, was on strike.

The sun's white heat was well suited to the shadeless island of Hephaestus, God of Fire and Industry. But the names of natural features on the Admiralty Chart, were startling in their incongruity: "Lowestoft", "Blenheim Cove" and "Australia Pier" dated from the time of Gallipoli, while the names of the Gog and Magog hills, "Denmad", "Yam", "Yrroc" and "Eb" originated from the dislike of a British Survey Team for its ship's captain. (Spelt backwards they read "Damned May Corry Be!") I peered into waters that concealed so much history. Here a Scottish officer stretchered aboard a hospital ship, had watched helplessly as an orderly let slide his kitbag containing the twenty golden sovereigns saved from his Scottish childhood. Afloat off Mudhros, denied the benison of hot water, and never seeing English fields again, the poet Rupert Brooke succumbed to measles and blood-poisoning. But, according to Homer, Philoctetes, abandoned on the island on his way to Troy when incapacitated by snake bite, was cured by burying his foot in Lemniot earth, the celebrated Terra Sigillata of the Romans.

Runner Bean put in to Mudhros. So anxious were the Port Authorities to add her to their list of yachts officially recorded as visiting the town (very few) that, once sighted, a four-wheel drive was despatched to hail her in for tally purposes. Wacky, following our voices when we socialised, lay at our feet like a dog, while Annie from *Chaton*, with her exquisite knack for saying the wrong thing, launched into a diatribe against Lonely Hearts ads in yachting magazines. Mike and Lindy stared at their toes until Bob succeeded in changing the subject.

After its great days as an Allied naval base, Mudhros slid into untidy decline. Near the cathedral, the well-off queued with the poor and elderly to catch the drips from a wall fountain. Villagers, anxious to chat, hurried to commiserate with us, England having lost the World Cup semi-final to Germany the previous evening. But Bob was in a good mood since the ironmonger supplied brass hinges to fit our loo door. In fact we boat people were in clover, for, back on the waterfront, Mike and Tony, exercising their plumbing skills, had induced sweet water to flow from a moribund standpipe.

Once the Post Office was back in business, the Post Master could not wait to be relieved of a red-hot package across which, well versed in the ways of Greek islands, Mel had written in bold lettering, *"PLEASE DELIVER TO MY MOTHER IMMEDIATELY,"* a daughterly attitude entirely understood on a Greek island. (It contained two packets of M&S panties.) However, my mind was far from home. That afternoon I shot out of the golden net of Hephaestus on hearing the words, "I think the wind's getting up!" Only when fully awake, did I recognise the voice as that of the Wimbledon commentator on the BBC World Service.

We staged a farewell barbecue at the head of the bay, a bare two miles from the far coast. Ignoring the directions of Annie, who was given to organising things, our skippers dived to dig in their anchors in the lee of a narrow spit of land backed by a low sand cliff. Whilst it was still daylight we set up anchor lights and rowed ashore laden with barbecue fodder. Collecting driftwood, we arranged it beneath racks supported on stones, while Mike hammered in a stake to support a lantern. Side by side in the marram grass were twin chapels, the ruined version in use a boatman's store. When we pushed open the door of the other we found a vigil light burning and – just the ticket – wooden benches. Carrying three back to the beach we arranged them round the fire, an act in harmony with the outdoorness of Ancient Greece, temples designed as shrines, not as places of assembly, which took place in the open air.

A copper moon dispersed cloud tatter to lay the Golden Way, unrolled in ancient days for the feet of Artemis and now known as Christ's Path. Annie fidgeted as we finger-licked, making comments about Mike's guitar and offering to help him out with a comb. Only when he began to play did she fall silent. His recital included his own composition "Green Song" – "To see Nature's secrets unfurl...", the reason, he told us, for devoting ten years of his life to sailing alone round the world. Its rhythm, as in Lawrence Durrell's poem, "Out of the swing / Of the swing/ Of the sea", echoed the ebb and flow of the tides. Lindy-of-the-Long-Brown-Hair never took her eyes off the singer.

From being vaguely aware of the sea's increasing restlessness and of a night breeze tickling the backs of our necks, it suddenly occurred to us that the wind had risen. On standing up, we saw battalions of wavelets marching towards the pebbled shore. Though we could make out the shapes of all three yachts, on two of them the anchor lights had blown out. We tidied hastily, stamping out the fire and tumbling equipment and picnic remains into the dinghies. There was some suggestion of returning in daylight to put away the benches, but we hustled them back to the chapel where the oil dip still flickered in the friendly dark. When Bob found it impossible to row against the onshore wind, Mike put back to give us an outboard-powered tow.

On *Cappelle*, where we had left the sun awning and wind scoop in place, the noise of flogging canvas was frightening the Ship's Cat. We spent a disturbed night, but the anchors held. By morning in the diffused light from a sullen sky, a gale-force north easterly tore at us over the isthmus. Mike's anemometer registered forty kts. (Had we abandoned the benches, it would have been impossible to put them away.) Protected from the sea's fetch, we stayed put. As soon as the gale dropped, Lindy rowed Mike over to say that, after revising their original plan of crossing to Çanakkale (on a rumour that Turkey, in retaliation for Britain's imposition of visas on Kurds, was levying £44 per head, plus £5 sterling, on all UK citizens), they intended to sail for Myrina, capital of Lemnos, if we felt like going their way.

At 07.00 hrs we made passage parallel to the south coast of Lemnos in confused seas. For a nasty moment around Cape Tigani a NEL lines vessel was aimed straight for us. Pitching and rolling, we slewed round to follow in her wake. In Myrina's inner harbour. where he and Lindy were busy sorting empties, Mike waited to take our lines. The renowned wine of Lemnos mentioned in Aristotle was on tap in the supermarket (though it was best to deal direct with the wine factory, since the supermarket's tap-your-own barrels were frequently dry). Though Myrina's fishmongers and greengrocers were excellent, its Self-Service Launderette was not as we hoped. Entry to the washing machines was barred. "Self" referred to delivery and collection only.

Myrina, centrally positioned in the Aegean between mainland Greece and Turkey, acted as an international staging post for yachts cruising to and from the Black Sea. Sooner or later all the world turned up.

Our company included two magnificent Whitbread Swan 65s, a family from Budapest, and hearties from Odessa, who kept to themselves. An obese German couple sunbathed on the deck of *True Love*. When they flopped into *Tiny True Love*, their dinghy, its waterline dropped alarmingly. On the scrounge for whisky, Captain Pugwash, last seen at Yat Lift, paid us a call. Having given up on the Greek shipping forecast, he was now in the habit of telephoning his son in England, he told us, to find out what the Greek weather was doing.

Announcing her early departure for the Sporades, *Runner Bean* battened down. That night a fair-haired, blue-eyed Epirote from Northern Greece asked to borrow our dinghy for the purpose of rescuing a warp let loose by his inexperienced crew. After we had gone to bed he knocked on the hull to invite us for a British gin and tonic, which he was happy to change to "tea" the following afternoon, honouring it in the Greek tradition with φλιτζανάκια (little cups) of Greek coffee served with a glass of water and a spoon sweet. Addressing Wacky as «φιλούσα μου», "my little sweetheart" he declared cats best on boats. His adored Maltese terrier had broken her toe catching it in the scuppers.

News of strong winds from the north made us glad not to have sailed for Samothraki. Gale warnings followed and the constant roar of the meltemi made for irritability. I found myself plagued with headaches, sleeping better by day than by night when I awoke to fasten banging doors and investigate cat fights. A bucket of water flung at a caterwauler blew back to drench me. I tried sleeping in the cockpit, choosing a night when mosquitoes bit, and a French crew urinated into harbour with the splashdown of cart horses. I also gave up cajoling Bob to rouse himself. After all, Lemnos was once known by the classic name of "Animoessa" or "Windy Island". Common sense dictated delay.

Shopping in Myrina led to a welcoming, «Να σου πώ...!» ("Let me tell you...!") with invitations to chat over coffee and the family album. I was shown a photograph of three handsome brothers standing shoulder to shoulder. All three, following Lemniot tradition, served in the Navy. The island's yearning for the glory of its naval past was ill-concealed. At the Sunday Parade (which had Wacky scampering home in mortal dread of Big Boots) citizens stood to attention as the veterans marched past.

Mystery message

Mitilini's sister castle of Myrina occupied the summit of the acropolis behind the harbour which stuck up like a decayed molar, its castellated wall undulating along a volcanic spine. At night, illuminated in floodlighting, it drew the eye like a goblin palace. On Friday 13th July I left for the market, but, on impulse, instead of taking the way to the main street followed instead the sign to the castle. Marble blocks from an earlier age gleamed in its ruined walling. One bore an upside-down Greek inscription. An iron grille lay in the grass. At the far end of the chicane the high sun of Hephaestus hammered down. The atmosphere, pressing on the distended surface of the silence, seemed tuned to a different frequency. It crossed my mind that in the Mani this was the hour when ghosts walk. Light-headed in the fierce glare, I was aware that my padded slippers made no sound. I felt strangely disassociated as I glided up the incline of the triumphal way, alone and conscious of a heat-induced sensation of transparency as if I was made not of flesh and blood, but gossamer. The sky was bled of colour, the rocks shimmered, and the hush, framed in the anaemic rustle of dried grass and the dynamo thrumming of cicadas, seemed four dimensional. This trance-like state held an extraordinary tension, an expectancy, a waiting for something. It was strange how in such ringing emptiness one felt noticed. I put it down to the side-effect of what Nikos Kanzantzakis called "the immortal nakedness" of Greece.

Then I came to an abrupt halt, feet together, staring down. I had been following the broad carriageway, but, unconsciously, had veered off centre. On one of the slabs that formed spaced ridges of shallow step, penned in an elegant hand, were the words «Σε χαιρετώ παιδί του κάστρου – από το κάστρο σου» ("I greet you, Child of the Castle – from your castle"). I crouched to examine the writing. It was freshly inscribed and dust-free. Lost in thought, I stepped onwards to the brow of the hill where the force of the wind struck. Retracing my steps, I half suspected a glitch, for I reached the bottom of the triumphal way without finding "my" message. This was ridiculous, so I backtracked and found it, fourth ridge from the top to one side.

Back in the real world, I was tongue-tied. We climbed the acropolis at other times by other routes, looking out to sea from above the lighthouse. One day, from on high, we watched a couple, who had blundered in and tied cat's-cradles on every available projection, make their fourth attempt to leave the island. By the time we descended, they were back in harbour. Loveliest spot was a scooped corrie, a "bowery hollow crowned with summer sea" where, when shadows were long, we surprised a herd of deer grazing the chequered glade.

Eclipse

Postcards showed photographs of Mount Athos taken from Lemnos at sunset. This was hard to take, for Athos was thirty-five miles away in the Halkidiki, and visibility over the hazy sea normally no more than three to five miles. However, I was assured that it was indeed possible to see the Holy Mountain, usually in the clear air of January or February, though at other times just prior to sunset. On a day of low humidity we climbed the acropolis to sit on the bramble-covered wall of the sunken arsenal to await events. Along the horizon stretched the inevitable mist. Then, without warning, the black triangles of Holy Mountain's twin peaks appeared. Initiating a unique eclipse, they invaded the tight ball of the sun like wolf's ears. When the sun set and the peaks vanished all that remained was a band of purple haze in the afterglow. How awestruck must have been Neolithic man to witness his source of life swallowed up before his very eyes! The light was draining from the sky as we descended, and a γρι-γρί, a fishing boat with lantern and a rimbambelle of smaller boats strung out behind, was setting out. Mahler's Resurrection Symphony live from the BBC accompanied dinner in the cockpit. I raised my glass to the Hobbit Palace glowing in nimbus light above.

Our companions were not always as welcome as the γρι-γρί, Next day a giant ferry manoeuvred into the inner harbour, the outer too rough for safety. In stately dance, its flanks stretching skywards, it advanced on our trembling line-up. Judging its swing to perfection, it put down a ramp as wide as a road, then, with an unnerving clang of anvils, dropped stern anchors (one of which could have levitated *Cappelle* as easily as a fork-lift truck), as it prepared to take on two lorry loads of sheep, several charabancs of service personnel and a queue of motor cars.

Our desire to reach Samothraki looked increasingly hopeless. To go ashore we needed a settled period of at least forty-eight hours. So far no lull had lasted more than twelve. A demoralised Swiss family arrived. "Too much wind!" they groaned, draping oilies over the boom after enduring a night crossing of Force 9, their Ship's Dog so sick even his coat looked green. With the last of my energy blown away, I slept for thirty-six hours, after which Bob roused me to eat before I slumped back into unconsciousness.

Clipper ship *Meredith*, namesake of her captain's wife, became our new neighbour. Meredith had her gripes, complaining Matt considered her every moment not nautically employed should be dedicated to touching up woodwork. It was not long before Matt, inviting us aboard, said, "My wife envies you your cat." (Sadly, Meredith's Siamese had been run over on the eve of their departure from England.) I said I hoped they would not mind Wacky joining us, for he always did, invited or not! Needless to say, he immediately sniffed out the lobster under preparation in *Meredith's* galley.

Wacky excelled himself at getting noticed. Chartered by Greeks, a converted fishing boat drew in. In a cage in the wheelhouse that essential concomitant of Greek family life, a canary, was spotted at once by Wacky, who had no hesitation in trespassing. What Clevershins failed to realise was that the caïque was merely manoeuvring. Dissatisfied with his position, its skipper pulled away. The first we heard of the Wacky situation was an anguished wail. It was the *Boomerang* story all over again. Convinced he had been press-ganged by evil-doers, he was determined to avoid a fate to which death was infinitely preferable. When we turned to look, he was teetering wild-eyed on the alien cap rail with every intention of making a madcap leap. Vaulting the rail, Bob cast off the dinghy. But rescue came too late, for Wackster's brain cells had been working overtime. If he could not jump the gap, perhaps he could still make the quay?

The caïque's gangplank was in the vertical position, so, like greased lightning, he shot up it to look down on the ever-widening space between the caïque's stern and terra firma. Cries of, *"No! No! Wacky! DONT JUMP!"* attracted the attention of passers-by. But, pausing only to gather all four paws on the top rung, Our Hero flung himself into oblivion in a death-defying leap. We screamed. Strong men wept and the populace, "Ooh...oohed!" Paddling for all he was worth in mid air, squirrel tail streaming, Wacky kept going against all the dictates of gravity to execute a thudding four-point landing on concrete. Though the spectators cheered, he did not wait to savour the acclamation. In two seconds flat he was down the hatch airing four sore paws on the Captain's bunk, his eyes round with the horrors of what might have been. Of course, by this time the caïque had straightened out and was tied up, canary and all. Wacky did not venture aboard again.

Our Hero recovered fast. That evening, when we dined out under a vine-covered pergola with Matt and Meredith, Wacky, full of his own importance once more, followed, despite discouragement, hiding in flower beds and dodging boots and bicycle wheels. First he lay at our feet and then he climbed the vine above us. Husks falling on the table-cloth were an intimation of his presence. There was a chirrup and we looked up to see a pair of mischievous eyes a-twinkle amidst a tangle of leaves. The waiter was surprised to find his newly laid cloth in need of brushing. When he left hurriedly, Meredith, alarmed he had gone for a broom to dislodge the perpetrator, scraped back her chair to rush after him, "You mustn't!" she pleaded. "It's our cat!" Whatever the waiter was about to do, he desisted. But he must have thought her crazy, for foreigners, however eccentric, were not in the habit of taking cats out to dinner. When we left, Wacky nodded a cursory "Goodnight!" from a geranium bed. At almost a year old he no longer required a late pass.

News of his exploits spread. Gifts were laid at his door. A child brought sliced octopus «για το ψιψινάκι σου» ("for your little pussy cat"). And Matt, arriving for sundowners, called out, "Shall I come aboard? — *OR WOULD YOU PREFER I STAND AND RECEIVE!*" In one hand he held a box of chicken breasts (donor: unknown Greek) and, in the other. a plastic bag containing six party-wrapped sardines (donor: girl on the caïque).

Conversation raised the subject of where we planned to go next. Let's face it, from whatever vantage point we took, the Samothraki adventure could well end in trouble. We also realised that, in the rigidity of our aim, we were forfeiting elasticity of purpose, one of the pleasures of cruising being serendipity, the scope to make fortunate discoveries by accident. (The tourist doesn't always know where he's been; the traveller doesn't always know where he's going.) When Matt and Meredith told us they had found Dhiaporos the perfect desert island, we agreed that, at the first sign of a decent break in the gales, after a twenty-four-hour period of calm and with a good forecast, our yachts would leave together to part in separate ways; *Meredith* for the new marina in Istanbul and *Cappelle* for Dhiaporos. For us, Samothraki, the most mysterious island in the Aegean, was destined to remain so.

Waiting to waylay us on return from the wine factory hung around with bottles like disciples of Dionysius, was Matt with his camcorder. Such pictures fitted their view of us as "the most laid back couple they'd ever met". ("It's the saucers that do it!" cried Meredith. "Nobody on a boat uses cups and saucers!") Dining at a pizzeria that night, our farewell salvo came in the form of a blinding flash and an explosion that had us running out into the square. We were soon called back to find the dazed cook, a Lemniot Manuel with singed eyebrows, spreadeagled against the wall clutching a ladle: "Is orl right!" he gasped, "Is often happen!"

Farewell to the Castle

My final task was private. Taking a duster and a marker pen, I made my way back to the castle. On a slab adjoining that of the mystery message I wrote "Σ'αγαπώ καστράκι μου – από την Ούρσουλά σου" ("I love you my little castle – from your Ursula.") That bright and breezy morning no sorcery was abroad. But as I turned away, it closed in behind me.

Seventeen

The Halkidiki

Though we had dallied over two weeks in Myrina, a surprise was in store for Bob when he went to collect the transit log and settle harbour dues. The policeman roused at four a.m. had a smile; there would be no charge, for *Cappelle* would always be a "Friend of Myrina". As we parted company with *Meredith,* Matt shouted, "And if you don't start fishing for that cat, we'll report you to the RSPCA!"

Westbound with a favourable F 4/5 on the quarter, we encountered nothing more than a swathe of beach flotsam snaking in the current south of Thassos, and a silver tide of tuna fish splashing in the sun like animated ingots. In a temperature so perfect I stripped off.

The Halkidiki is shaped like a deformed lobster with three claws, or a three-pronged trident plunged from the mainland into the upper reaches of the Aegean. The prongs are the peninsulas of Athos to the north with Kassandra to the south and Sithonia in the middle. Our navigational plan, being careful to compensate for a southwesterly current flowing at 1.5 kts, was to make for the Singitik Gulf which lies between Athos and Sithonia.

In the haze on the forward horizon came an infinitesimal change, so subtle as to be felt rather than seen, a sort of suspicion of a thickening of the atmosphere. As time went by we were convinced this fragile density had substance. Only one thing could account for it, that Mysterium Tremendum, the Holy Mountain. What was more, approach to the Forbidden Peninsula was made not only by that anathema, a woman, but in this case δεόγυμνη, "God-naked" as the Greeks say. It was a miracle *Cappelle* was not struck by lightning!

As we drew nearer the face of Mount Athos we marvelled at cliffs rising sheer over 6,500 ft to its tapering peak. We could make out the remains of precarious bivouacs on inaccessible ledges where ascetics had lived out their lives under the strictest of monastic discipline. Despite the benign weather, no scenery, especially when viewed from sea level, was more savage than that between Cape Akrathos and Cape Pinnes marking the extremities of the triangular face of the Holy Mountain. Sidney Loch, a Scotsman who made his home at Ouranopolis on the borders of the Forbidden Republic, had once watched a boat containing two monks and a fisherman set off to round the peninsula. They never reached harbour.

In these brooding waters the fleet of Mardonius was smashed to pieces in 492 BC. Now would have been the time to sound our ship's hooter (if we had one) for, in triumphant memory of the destruction of the Persian fleet, it was the practice of passing ships to sound their sirens. Visible above was the ravine where the seventh-century St Peter the Athonite aspired to a state of grace by crouching without standing room for fifty years in a rock passage "fit only for a bow-legged toad". Distinguishable too was the Cave of St Athanasios, with a chapel in its maw, and the notorious Cave of the Wicked Dead, still foetid, they said, with the green and livid corpses of the excommunicated monks condemned to live and die within.

The afternoon light was fading when, twelve hours and fifty-four miles after leaving Lemnos, we nosed our way into the rock-girdled Bay of Sikias. A hail of «Ερχόμαστε απ' τη Μυρίνα!» ("We have come from Myrina!") brought an obliging fisherman to guide us into Port Sikias, a cluster of cottages patronised by well-to-do Greeks seeking the simple-life. A magnificent brass bedstead, complete with mosquito nets, occupied a terrace. Tents were erected for the children. Palomino blonde beaches, the sand coarse-grained, the rounded rocks as lickable as dollops of clotted cream, sloped beneath waters of thrush-egg blue. It was providential that Bob was conscientious about fixing the riding weight, for the night brought fierce gusts, with fitful lightning from the direction of Samothraki.

Port Sikias

Scattering the bellied reflections of the fishing boats so that they writhed like multicoloured snakes, I flopped into harbour. Round the corner in the bay we explored the channel between a natural fish hide and a sand cliff edged with shrines marking where vehicles had plunged from the road above. When I raised my head I was in a holiday world of water-wings; face down I was an interloper in a piscine habitat. Bob surfaced from the halcyon sea with a rainbow shell fit for a Cabin Boy "ichthyous and mer". Back in harbour I saw that what I had thought to be blue plastic bags floating beneath the surface were jellyfish shaped like frilly double-tiered kites.

That evening crooked stilts of lightning stalked the horizon. Alerted by a sudden rush of wind, I hurried to bring in the cockpit cushions as the storm broke while Bob scrambled ashore to attach extra lines. After the long dry heat the coach roof leaked. Though water splashed into every utensil we put out, it was impossible to keep pace with the deluge. Wacky hid under the table. At midnight the rain faltered and I snoozed upright beneath an overhang. Dawn broke on a harbour crammed with all manner of boats. Though the sky was clean-washed, the forecast was for F 6/7 with καταιγίδες (violent thunderstorms).

Wacky showed such keen interest in an old motor tyre on the deck of a neighbouring caïque that, with the departure of her crew, I climbed aboard to investigate, finding the tyre in use as a container for a sizeable turtle. With freezer lorries backing down the mole, their double wheels hanging over us, we were concerned not only for ourselves, mere lotus eaters, but with our invasion of commercial space. The fishermen showed no resentment, however. When a fishing boat expecting to pull onto the quay was obliged to tie to the stern of another on our account, we assured its skipper we would be leaving as soon as possible. But he only smiled and shrugged, saying, «Σιγά! Σιγά!» ("Gently! Gently!") At siesta time, planning each move so as not to interfere with the network of moorings, we wormed our way out hand-over-hand, stern first, inching *Cappelle* port and starboard from the decks of other boats, nervous over shallows, untying and retying warps stretched across our path until, motoring in and out of gear to turn the yacht around, we floated free.

Dhiaporos

Pointing at the skies, a fisherman called, «Ο καλός καιρός!» ("Good weather!") Even so, clouds piled up as we made our way along the coast of Sithonia towards Dhiaporos. Halfway there, we watched sunbathers scuttle as epileptic flashes jagged the skies and thunder claps reverberated along the hills. We were reefing down when ball lightning exploded. It grew deathly dark and the sea turned black, forked lightning driving a harpoon into the sea ahead. As we anticipated the end of the world, the storm bowled away along the hills leaving a bow of coloured light though which to sail until we reached the rainbow's end.

By the time we dropped anchor off Dhiaporos, soft zephyrs blew and the late afternoon sun flared on a headland calvary as if a vigil light burned within. Wacky, beside himself with the thrill of witnessing the rudimentary fishing tackle we had acquired in Myrina in action, glued his eyes to the nylon threads looped round our fingers. He preferred small fry when they squirmed and it was not easy to keep him from leaping at fish hooks. Ferried ashore, he immediately scuttled belly-flat for the undergrowth as if trying to hide from the All-Seeing Eye of the Sun. Persuaded to lie in the shadow of our upturned dinghy, he panted an anxious homing signal as if fearing abandonment. Panic set in at the sight of a beflippered Behemoth stepping out of the sea. Calm was only restored by the sound of his Captain's voice. Since the Ship's Cat resented being a member of the Expeditionary Force, we returned him to his ship. Dhiaporos, without sweet water, recalled Seferis's poem,

> "On the secret seashore
> White like a pigeon
> We thirsted at noon..."

Ormos Panagia on the mainland with its manicured lawns, sugar canes and blackberry bushes visited ten days later for water and supplies, was more verdant than anywhere we had lately put in. I was urged to look slippy, for the sea-bed was unsafe. Around the fountain profligate Germans spilt water. At the general store, where goods were sold in picnic bites, the manager disconcerted me by asking if I would like my bags "carried to my car". Twice I dumped provisions by the sea for *Cappelle's* shuttle service. Though Bob was expecting her to break free at any moment, I made a last dash down a motorway verge to a fruit stall. As I scrambled aboard, she abruptly raised anchor for herself.

Back on Dhiaporos we edged into a fiord that gave way to land-locked Porto Krifto, the Hidden Creek, a forest-green tarn. As the sun dropped behind a burning fiery bush, *Cappelle* rocked in rose-pink waters. While a fishing boat laid its nets, Bob repaired the dinghy painter's loop using webbing from an old life-jacket. It was so quiet we retired to bed leaving the sun awning and the wind scoop in place. But in the early hours a swirling wind broke a strut of the wind scoop and the anchor light caught fire. After putting the blaze out with a wet towel, Bob contrived a jury rig for the wind scoop with a chopped-up coat hanger, parcel tape and twine. Turning on the World Service as he worked, he learnt of Iraq's invasion of Kuwait. When the fishing nets were taken in next morning, not a single fish was gathered in. Porto Krifto was a dead, as well as hidden, creek.

Amouliani

From Porto Krifto we made passage to Amouliani, a holiday island patronised by industrial workers from Thessaloniki. Amouliani lay opposite the site of the canal by which Xerxes had hoped to forestall naval catastrophe by leading his fleet through the neck of the Athos peninsula. Behind the mole, already congested with fishing boats, it was difficult to tie up in a depth of only two metres. Visiting yachts were expected to keep to the weather side, their usual mission being to fill up with spring water. But our need was to secure shelter for the night. Twice hustled on by sour-faced fishermen, our unpopularity was made clear. But we found ourselves so hemmed in we could not extricate ourselves.

Wacky, having leapt into the hold of an unattended caïque was heard crying to get out. We requisitioned a prop as a gang-plank to help him. But, under the misapprehension that it was to clout him with, he executed a spring-loaded take-off to cling to the ship's rails and emerge trembling, leaving us wondering just how many lives he had left! I passed a dreadful night fretting over his fate "oot on the toot" in alien country, the heat stifling and Amouliani's mosquitoes as hostile as their fishermen. Drunken youths, who invaded a nearby parked ferry, spent the night tossing chairs at one another. At three a.m. a caïque made a noisy getaway. Another, loaded with clanking gas bottles, followed. When Wacky, to a background of feline altercation, arrived home at five a.m. refreshed and cheerful – which is more than we were – we attempted to move out. But, though we got away from the quay, nothing would budge our anchor. Inspection showed a caïque's hook placed so exactly on top of it, the act could only have been deliberate. Bob, already suffering a sore eye, dived to loop warp over the restraining anchor's flukes for me to haul up. Only good fortune and sustained effort brought about our release. Not in the best of tempers, we did not delay to take on water.

Athos

Outside Amouliani, the view banished all disagreeable thoughts. With the looking-glass sea lightly mist-veiled, it was the perfect monochrome dawn in which to explore the Athos seaboard. Cormorants increased the impression of gliding into the fluidity of a Japanese print. In the distance the sun rose behind the peak of Holy Mountain. We trickled past the settlement of Ouranopolis (Heaven City), built in 1923 by refugees from Cappadoccia, victims of the Treaty of Lausanne, who came humping bundles of ancestral bones. A passage between reefs brought us to the borders of the Forbidden Republic, two hundred autonomous square miles guarded by a private police force. Here the ravine-split mountain spine began its dragon's-back ascent until, twenty-five miles further on, it climaxed in the High C of Holy Mountain.

Conditions that day meant our sails required only minimum attention. As we puttered along, the Monastery of Zographou slid into view, then the buildings and dependencies of Docheiariou fanned out against a forest of walnut, mulberry and arbutus, its stout walls festooned with flowering creeper. Docheiariou's arsenals and defence walls were no mere ornament, for it suffered badly at the hands of the Saracens. Its dominating tower was staked round by dark cypresses as stiff as stalagmites; its aura was of tranquil desuetude and its ikon that of the Smoky Virgin. According to legend, a loutish monk, one Neilos, was in the habit of shambling along letting the smoke from his lop-sided taper drift into the ikon's face. The Virgin, taking exception, struck Neilos blind. Not until his third entreaty did she restore his sight. For this reason she was also known as the Ready Listener. There are stranger names (which may sound glamorous to non-Greek ears). The pretty Κουκουλίσσα translates as "The Virgin of the Peas and Beans", for she was the favourite of a monk known as "John Peas and Beans" on account of the flatulence brought on by his diet.

Next to appear as we trickled down coast, was the Monastery of Xenophontos, two storeys of jutting balconies crowned by Balkan domes and backed by sword blades of cypress. Further on, the mountains rising higher, the sea deepening to delphinium in the full light of morning, came the nineteenth century sprawl of St Panteleimon, commonly called Russiko, a monastery showered with Czarist wealth. Crimson-roofed, its gables embellished with lime-green onion domes capped with burnished gold and topped with golden crosses that flashed in the sun, St Panteleimon presented an extraordinary scene of Russian splendour in an Aegean setting, like a backdrop for a ballet by Diaghilev to be performed on a proscenium of golden sand. Built to house six thousand monks, its soul died with the Czars. Now less than a dozen Mongol-featured cenobites eked out their swan song amongst the spiders that inhabit haunted ballrooms, quarrelling in their second childhood over a pet cat or canary. From seaboard all we saw was romance.

The most spectacular sights, however, were as yet denied us. Beyond the small port of Daphni (little more than a quay) where accredited (male only) visitors were landed, submerged rocks no longer buttressed the shore. With our guide book describing the coastline ahead as "full of excitement", we might have been guilty of nudging fractionally inshore, though to no appreciable extent, for we had every intention of abiding by the rules, even the latest edition of the *Greek Waters Pilot* warning that a yacht with a woman on board might not approach the Forbidden Republic by less than five hundred metres. Confronted by a fast-moving launch bearing the insignia of the ecclesiastical police force, the double-headed eagle, I whispered jokingly, "Ought I to hide?" not for a minute thinking I might have started a police chase. But at that moment the launch caught up with us. Standing in the bows was a police officer who shook his fist angrily before gesturing us to stand off, spreading his fingers to indicate the statutory distance. Although sure we were already that far off shore, we stood obediently out to sea. Once the launch was out of sight we filtered discreetly back onto our original course.

Soon Simonpetra, most astonishing monastery of all, reared seven storeys high on the summit of a crag a thousand feet above the sea. There, guided by a star, Simon the Hermit was called upon to place the πέτρα, the foundation stone. Tibetan-style, its cantilevered galleries of warped wood swung dizzily out floor by floor over space. Beside it lay a disturbingly gloomy ravine. Centuries on, when the moon rises and the shrill cries of lynx and howl of jackal break the spectral silence, monks still report the shriek of demons by which the early hermits were pursued. Athos's religious lifestyle, needless to say, bred an unforced nature reserve known to stray beyond its confines. At Ouranopolis, as late as 1951, terrified women watched as two winter-hungry wolves emerged from the peninsula to tear to pieces a tethered donkey.

The four storeys of the white-washed cells of Dionysiou reared above an immense pier-like foundation wall surmounted by a square tower. We could see the crimson mob caps of its church within a walled court. Beside Dionysiou the bed of a torrent narrowed as it climbed into the glacial screes of Holy Mountain down which winter blasts whistled. But, in August, walnut trees overhung the terraced kitchen gardens where monks toiled, and in the oleander-bordered orchards the peach trees were heavy with fruit. Some say that when the sun sinks, the Virgin, blue-mantled in moonlight and surrounded by Nereids of another age, still wanders the myrtle-scented copses.

A gruesome story attaching to Dionysiou relates how a sea-bathing monk was swallowed up to his armpits by a shark. When his companions urged him to stretch out his arms in the sign of the cross, he did so, and the shark could not swallow, but neither did it disgorge its prey. The monk then received orders from the Abbot to clasp his hands above his head to facilitate his end. This directive too was obeyed and the monk vanished. After such a tempting snack, the shark continued to cruise the shore, while the monks debated the merits of sacrificing a goat on chains in a good cause. The bait was seized and the shark, monk and goat within, was hauled ashore to be buried with bell, book and candle.

I regretted sight was denied me of the fourteenth-century mural of the *Presentation of the Virgin* at the Temple. A timid little girl, the Virgin is depicted being presented to a hoary old priest by her gentle and dignified mother, St Anne (as a grandmother, an integral part of the Greek Holy Family) and her father, Joachim. It is said to be a very human painting. The seven glamorous handmaidens are not paying attention. Failing to hold their tapers upright, the girls gossip, letting beeswax drip on the floor.

Beyond lay "The Desert" where the sides of the Mysterium Tremendum reared from the sea in outcrops covered in heath and sun-baked myrtle. Here the Skete of St Anne, sixty cottages around a common church, was scattered down the mountainside. Beyond the skete the rocks were more hostile. None of this area was in any way safe for a small boat, except in this spell of exceptionally calm weather. Ahead straggled the Ladder of Heaven, perpendicular eyries known as The Karoulia or The Pulleys, up which monks were initially winched, chased by leather buckets of soil with which to fill pockets in the rocks. By this means they grew enough subsistence foods to support a life of prayer, only interrupted by the threading of forest seeds for rosaries and the boiling of deer horn for the moulding of crosses.

Further on came a settlement known as Kapsokalyvia or "The Place of Burned Huts", named from the practice of a fourteenth-century monk who, wishing to appear mad to discourage intruders, repeatedly burned his shelter. (The eremitic lifestyle must have suited him, for he lived to be ninety-five.) Apart from the pyromaniacally inclined, the monks who lived in this area must be deemed socialites, for the true solitaries inhabited the expanse between Cape Pinnes and Cape Akrathos on the awe-inspiring ramparts off which *Cappelle*, complete with naked anathema, had first arrived, and which we once more approached. At close quarters the mile-high rock was not grey, but layered puce, russet, olive and pink. Here the monks lived on roots, herbs, spring water and twice-baked rusk, with the occasional treat on a day like this gained by casting a rope to passing fishermen in the hope of charity.

Sidney Loch remembered the disquieting sameness of these solitaries, dirty, indifferent, negative and, above all, ordinary, as if poverty, renunciation and loss of all sense of time served to erase every trace of personality. For all his affection for Athos and admiration for the wisdom of its abbots, Loch was not blind to the faults of its relic-pedalling monks. One he knew collected splinters of wood and the bones of forest creatures to hawk (after laying them against the glass of a reliquary long enough to absorb sanctity) as guaranteed fragments of the True Cross or the bones of saints. On one of his protracted explorations of The Desert, Loch came across a sick and starving German theologian, who had saved all his life to visit Athos. Now he babbled for rescue. To his eternal gratitude Loch arranged for him to join a party of monks travelling from the Monastery of Grand Lavra to Ouranopolis across the border, and freedom.

An unobstructed view past the face of the Mysterium Tremendum meant that our marvellous day was drawing to a close. Hanging between earth and sky on the sheer flank of the mountain was the cave of St Neilos-the-Flowing-with-Myrrh, who lay entombed within. It was said that mariners scooped up the shining globules of myrrh that streamed down the cliff. It must have been on just such an afternoon as this, for the late sun glinted on the rock face and struck gold from the wavelets.

Like all prudent boatmen we crossed ourselves beneath the Cave of the Wicked Dead before allowing our sails to draw us away from the Holy Mountain, our eyes fixed on its cloudless summit as it receded in a sky grown pale. Then we hoisted the blue cruising chute to take advantage of the summer breeze while we recrossed the mouth of the Singitik Gulf. As we neared the beaches of Sithonia, a Hobiecat flying a hull put out and a smiling couple circled: "You looked so lovely out there, we've come to say 'Hi!'" So saying they were off, flying the other hull.

Porto Koufo

Closing the cave-ridden headland, where Greek holiday-makers were engaged in fishing sessions, we turned into the Gulf of Kassandra to enter the cliff passage leading to the deep anchorage of Porto Koufo (The Deaf Harbour), so sheltered that what conditions were like outside was anybody's guess. As soon as we tied up against a fishing quay, Wacky leapt ashore to make friends. Since *Cappelle's* deck had a magnetic attraction for indiscriminately tossed fish hooks and cigarette butts, the night was far from peaceful. Next day an English family, Paul and Hilary from Germany with their two sons, who kept a boat in Holland and appreciated the circumscription of our lives, offered to ferry Bob and his fuel canisters to a garage and to give me a lift to the hill village of Sikia.

As soon as a vacant slot appeared among the boats on Porto Koufo's yacht quay, we made our move. These Thessalonikian yachtsmen did not patronise the seasonal restaurants established to fleece tourists, but brought their supplies from home to supplement the fish they caught. From an early age Greek children are brought up to the art of fishing. Korina, the three-year-old namesake of a yacht we helped tie up, was already a proficient fisherwoman. For Korina and Wacky it was love at first sight. Each evening little parcels of fish would be delivered. Xristina, Korina's mother, spoilt us too, bringing bowls of freshly washed fruit from her garden in Thessaloniki.

Yachts piled in, their skippers reporting rough seas outside. Leaving

Bob resting behind drawn curtains, for his eye was increasingly painful, I climbed the cliff path to look down the coast of Sithonia. Camp sites, alternating with car parks, stretched as far as the eye could see. Pavilions advertising "TV Games" were as popular as the beach. We knew we must leave soon, for Porto Koufo lacked sweet water. But next morning Bob woke with blurred vision. A Greek neighbour kindly sought him an introduction to a prominent ophthalmologist, who happened to be holidaying on the quay. His examination resulted in Bob's referral to the Eye Hospital at Polygiros. He was to lose no time in seeking treatment.

Hospital

I was advised to telephone Polygiros for an immediate appointment. The nearest telephone was situated about a mile away in a mini-market whose owner sat sipping alternate tumblers of ούζο and Metaxa. Although he burst into a shaky rendering of "I Give My Heart to You" when I entered, he failed to offer assistance with the telephone directory. I understood from a hospital spokesman that it would be closed next day, but not the reason given: «δεκαπέντε Αυγούστου!» ("15th August.") Our alternative was to take the long-distance bus to Thessaloniki. On arrival I was to buy the local newspaper, the Μακεδονία, where, under "Public Announcements", I would find hospitals listed, together with departments open to out-patients. The word to look for was «Οφθαλμολογικά», the Eye Department.

Bob spent a wretched night. By 4.45 a.m., mosquitoes still out in force, we were standing by the roadside, together with two fishermen, awaiting the early bus. By six o'clock we were more than restless. But it was 7.15 a.m. before the bus pulled up, the fishermen berating its driver with a lively stream of «Μαλακά!» ("Wanker!") and «Αι γαμίσου!» ("Go fxxx yourself!") Three hours later in Thessaloniki I bought a copy of the Μακεδονία. Although its front page was taken up with a full-colour painting of the Virgin lying on a bier, the penny did not drop.

The relevant department of the Hippocratia Hospital was listed as

268

open. But all banks were closed. Then the silence of the streets struck home – no traffic, no people, shops barred. I banged on doors. Bob was reduced to leaning on a wall holding a handkerchief to his eye, when, as in all the best stories, along came a Good Samaritan. "I think you do not know today is Public Holiday!" he told us. 15th August, as everyone but us in the Old City of Thessaloniki, knew, celebrated the Dormition of the Virgin, a major Holy Day in the Greek Orthodox Church. Assuring us that the Hippocratia was a most excellent teaching hospital, he offered to fetch his car and take us there. But since the hospital was not too far away, we elected to walk. All the same, pointing out every pot hole and pavement edge to a blind man, it seemed a long way.

A woman, sensing our destination, gestured us towards a building site. Here we were nodded beneath scaffolding into a tree-lined court to enter French windows. Sole occupant of the room within was an old lady with a cabbage leaf on her head. A starched nurse lead Bob away. Without enquiry as to his name or means, he was given powerful analgesics, atropine, and a cortisone injection directly into his eye. After a wait, a nursing sister, accompanied by a doctor, motioned me to sit. (My impression was that they were as much bothered about my reaction as about the patient!)

"What a shame when a holiday is spoiled!" the nurse soothed. When I failed to lose control, she visibly relaxed: "The condition of the gentleman's eye is serious. He could lose his sight! It is vital he be admitted to intensive care at once!"

However, saying he had a boat to look after, Bob was refusing to stay. Of course, I gave assurances I was perfectly capable of looking after the boat myself. On our subsequent trek through the hospital corridors, the nurse, who had trained in Canada, chatted away. Did I know the Hippocratia was a teaching hospital attached to the University of Thessaloniki? Did I know Greek medical students had to pass an examination in English as part of their training? The trouble was they rarely got the chance to practise. Now here was the Κύριος sent by the Παναγία herself on the very day of her Dormition! As Sister-in-Charge she would be rounding up her trainee doctors to practise their

269

English. The trouble with people today was lack of effort, etc, etc, so essential in the learning of a language, as she herself knew. We are all one country now, she declared, *"WE ARE EUROPE!"*

Bob, wearing striped pyjamas, awaited me in an airy ward. I was told treatment would be administered around the clock every two hours for five days and nights. Then a trolley was wheeled in bearing a complimentary three-course meal for both of us. Turning out our pockets, we counted just enough money to get me back to Porto Koufo, where I promised to run the engine. My troubles were not over, however, for back in Porto Koufo the motor refused to switch off. It was left to a Greek neighbour to abandon his dinner guests and burn his arm silencing it by unconventional means.

No one can have too many friends, but news of our predicament spread and I was soon overwhelmed. Small rivalries developed about who should do what for us and when. The English family offered their Mercedes and cat-sitting. Paul drove me to a bank, and then on to the hospital where Bob, young doctors queuing up to chat, was receiving blood tests. On asking an old woman with winter-apple skin the way back to the hospital after taking Paul and Hilary out to lunch, clasping my hands, she searched my face eagerly for signs of distress: "Your children?! Your children?!" she gasped.

One of Bob's ward companions was a dear old grandpapa, hot favourite with the nurses, who, addressing him affectionately, called, «Πού πάς, Παπού?» ("Where are you going, Gran'pa?") as he doddered about. Mostly, he sat propped up in bed like a potentate surrounded by his entire family who picnicked on his counterpane. The ward's other occupant was a whey-faced paper-hanger with a head injury in the care of his faithful pet of a teenage wife in a chador. Moslems from Northern Greece, the couple spoke Vlachika, a language not understood by the hospital staff. At night, though I felt she would prefer to curl at her master's feet, the girl occupied the empty bed between her husband and Bob, who whispered to me he had woken early to see her hajib had slipped. Blushing, she had made haste to draw it on again. As it was second nature to her to wait on men, as a matter of course, she waited on Bob too. Differences apart, and without a word in common, the couple went out of their way to be kind to him. Having no money, he declined to be escorted to the canteen until, each taking him by a hand, they marched him off between them. I imagined this ill-assorted trio crossing the hospital gardens, eye-patched Englishman in ill-fitting pyjamas halfway up his calves flanked on one side by a girl shrouded like a black crow and on the other a bandaged youth.

The luxury caravan Paul had trailed from Germany was as big as a cottage. Parked amongst beachside trees, it occupied a private camp-site with a vertiginous approach down a cork-screw sand piste. (Paul swore he had only ventured down to look, but been too scared to drive out again.) Since the rationing of the thick yellow well-water was of major concern, the camp-site owner maintained a presence with a shotgun across his knees to make sure no outsiders stole his asset. We swam together and shared German sausage and ice-cream.

Korina's family also took me swimming. Wearing a Parisian bikini under a miniature life-jacket, Korina was completely at ease, so busy steering her plastic Happy Boat while her brother dived and somersaulted, she never noticed whether she was in her depth or out of it. Nearby a teenager, fresh from holiday in England, taught her mates to say "bum" and "bugger". A fishing crew pulled their caïque onto the beach to show off a tiger-striped sea-serpent with a battery of ferocious teeth caught in its nets. Stavros, in his role of pater familias, extended to me the same tender concern he showed for his wife, patronising us both rather like older children, who were not yet quite responsible. All the same, I was aware that Christina, in return for the public deference that was a Greek husband's due, knew just how to wrap him round her little finger.

We returned to *Korina* for the midday meal. Stavros was served first, with myself next, urged by him to take much φακή (lentil soup) because it was good for me. When the children's heads drooped onto the table, I excused myself for the μεσιμεριάτικο (the midday sleep). If enough fish were caught that evening, I was to go to supper.

An atmosphere soon developed between Stavros and Paul, contenders for who should collect Bob from hospital. Paul won. As we drove into the hospital courtyard a woman banged angrily on the bonnet of the

Mercedes shouting, "No parking for tourists! This is hospital!" With Bob still weak and our water situation now critical, Paul and family elected to sail on with us to our next destination. As we nibbled honey cake and sipped German wine, we let the Boukadora, the favourable afternoon breeze, waft us the eleven miles up the coast of Sithonia to Porto Carras.

Eighteen

The mad woman of Neas Marmaras

Porto Carras

Based on the Languedoc-Roussillon marinas, Porto Carras was an artificial yacht basin excavated out of coastal flats. Entry was via a canal running alongside a hotel on stilts whose balconies provided a grandstand view of the ebb and flow of luxury craft.

Ali Baba jars decorated the quay and an arched bridge spanned a backwater. On being assigned Berth No 67 over the VHF, we felt like film stars: "A dream come true!"; "A masterpiece of modern planning!"; "An amazing luxury resort!" cooed the brochure tossed on deck as we passed. The whole scene was unreal in its charm. It was as if *Cappelle* was taking up residence at the Boat Show or became part of a glossy double-page spread, her fragile existence dependent on when someone flipped the page. From Berth No 67 to Berth No 69 the yacht names read: "*Cappelle, At Last, Aegean Mistress.*" Appropriate enough! (A shame about *Bar Bar* and *Megabux* to follow.)

Next morning we awoke to birdsong from the ornamental trees on the quayside. Wacky devoted his days to sitting beneath one, willing a bird to drop on his head. The dry-stone wall behind supported a wild garden from whence he returned pawing at the ticks embedded in his face. Charter yachts were lined up nearby under the management of a tall Californian working his way round the world. Glyn invited us to drinks on *Heart of Gold* to meet his Irish wife and small daughter born in the Pacific islands. His introductory information was unsettling: the first thing to remember was that Porto Carras water was undrinkable. While plutocratic yacht owners purchased over-priced water by the bottle, the alternative for such as us was to cross the bay to Neas Marmaras where, jostling with ferries and fishing boats, a yacht might replenish its water tank from the standpipe beside the fifth lamp-post from the end of the commercial quay. The reason *Heart of Gold* was anchored out in the yacht basin was that boats were regularly boarded by the hotel guests given the run of the marina. There was no launderette, the showers operated only two hours a day, and the supermarket sold its tea bags in singles at 20p each and its eggs hard-boiled.

I sat at a café table to watch the world go by. A glance at the opposite skyline revealed the staring-eyes of half-built chalets. A Japanese girl from the Summer School tripped past carrying a cello. Next, holding the arm of a dumpy and perspiring fellow countryman, came an English girl dressed à la mode for a Miss World contest: big hat, big hair, cut-away swimsuit and white stilettos. Finally the gross figure of a German, his feet splayed in flip-flops, a reverse baseball cap on his bullet head, promenaded his paunch with his shirt hitched up..

Bob had been instructed to attend Out Patients at the Hippocratia every five days. Since the early bus to Thessaloniki left Neas Marmaras before the first ferry from Porto Carras arrived, his trip started with a three-kilometre walk along the beach. From his initial appointment Bob brought news of two depressions meeting over the Sporades to bring chaotic weather conditions. That evening Glyn lounged bleary-eyed on the quay, wine bottle in hand, awaiting the return of his flotilla. Apart from cleaning and reprovisioning the boats when they did put in, he had explanations to make to newly arrived punters whose flights were due, as to why their yachts were missing.

The Sporades

As soon as the Flying Dolphins were reinstated, we settled in the fore compartment of an inter-island hover-craft for the thirty-five-mile passage to the Sporades to collect poste restante. Beyond the sheltering arms of Sithonia and Kassandra the ferry met the residual swell left over from the depressions. Rising and falling like a lift, it slammed into each trough with a thud, making it impossible for seat-belted passengers to remain attached to their seats. The distress of the Scots family behind us increased. Then came an ominous sound from the teenage daughter, followed by indignant protests from her young brother, and his mother's placatory murmurs,

"But, Mummy! She's been sick all over my tee-shirt!"

"Hush dear! We'll buy you another when we get there!"

"But Mumme -ee – ee! It's in my *HAIR!*"

Father and mother were next to succumb. The agonised retching emanating from Father met with anguished appeals from his son and heir, "No! No! No! Daddy! Don't get up! JUST CONCENTRATE ON STAYING ALIVE!" There was a poignant silence. Then Alistair could not resist a triumphant, "I'm not sick! Aren't I good?" There was no reply.

Though we experienced a strong desire for ear plugs, it seems unduly unsympathetic that neither of us had ever felt better. Somewhere in the background a Greek orchestrated an overture of operatic moans before emitting a waterfall of vomit. After delivering her glib departure spiel in three languages, the smartly uniformed Hover Hostess had urged passengers "not to hesitate to ask should they require assistance". Now she was nowhere to be seen.

Our first port of call was Patitiri, capital of the low green island of Alonnissos. Boats awaited their turn to manoeuvre into harbour through the swell. Unable to enter the main harbour at Skopelos because of deteriorating conditions, we made an unscheduled stop in heavy seas at Agnonda on the sheltered side of the island. In Skiathos the Hover Hostess reappeared to recite her mindless arrival patter, trusting we had enjoyed our trip on the company's "wonderful ship". The state of the fore-cabin as we filed out with the grey-faced did not bear thinking about. Sticky paper trailed everywhere, the Hostess's last caring act being to lob in a multi-pack of toilet rolls.

Skiathos of the golden beaches and flowering trees vibrated in wind and light. We picnicked in a square beside an aged tree which slanted obliquely across the pretty nineteenth-century birthplace of Alexander

Papadiamantis, the island's literary son. As charter flights brought in waves of tourists, it was reported that our return *Flying Dolphin* was held up at Volos by engine trouble. This was interpreted by us to mean the Pilot deemed it sensible to wait for the swell to die down. We were given the forecabin all to ourselves. In the brilliant light of evening I caught sight of the Scots family at Patitiri, where they had sensibly disembarked. They looked better, and young Alistair sported a new tee-shirt.

By the time of Bob's next appointment, the air was autumn tart. After we had tracked down copper piping for a repair to the greasing feed of the propeller's stern gland, it was almost time for the last bus home, but we hurried up precipitous streets to the Basilica of St Demetrios, everyone's favourite saint, not least on account of his Little Summer. On Thessaloniki falling to the Turks in 1430 his shrine alone remained undesecrated, although every other church in the city was converted to mosque.

On the roof of the marina office, Time-Share Dollies waved champagne glasses for a photo shoot before invading the concourse to offload apartments at the Village Inn. I gave short shrift to the pair who straddled my path. A more welcome encounter was with Michaelis (with a taste, he told us, for a certain fifteen-year-old single malt!). Owner of *Aegean Mistress*, he was arriving with his valet in preparation for her end-of-season passage to Thessaloniki. In the course of conversation Bob passed on our tetracycline tip and in return Michaelis took us to lunch at the Sailors' Rest. Here he related the history of Porto Carras, the broken dream of his friend, ship-owner John Carras, who had envisaged another Costa Smeralda. Under the regime of the Colonels, John Carras had put up a personal fortune of £3 million, doubled by government grant, to create the marina project. But, with the overthrow of the Junta, permission was withdrawn for the projected casino, and the rot set in. Carras had recently died. Aware that, of his two sons, one was a beach bum and the other an asset-stripping spendthrift, he had divided their inheritance between them, but arranged for his trusted friend, who managed the marina, to be granted its leasehold in perpetuity. Now all parties were at each other's throats; the brothers endeavouring to muddy each other's pitches, the marina manager in the hot seat. The hotel-owning brother operated the hotels as two-star, booking Italian car-workers to precede the German blue-collar brigade, while the British ("not 'rough', you understand, but 'undiscriminating'," said Michaelis tactfully) took up the beginning-and-end-of-season low-cost accommodation.

If we intended to go home for Christmas, Michaelis's advice was to leave *Cappelle* where she was for, whatever its faults, Porto Carras's isolation had so far rendered it immune from theft. With Bob's discharge not yet granted, we therefore took out a one-year marina contract (which worked out cheaper than September through March at the monthly rate).

Few hotel guests troubled to explore the deserted coves of the Porto Carras estate. Striped like green corduroy, the hillsides rolling down to the sea were publicised as the "largest privately-owned vineyards in Europe, producers of the luxury Chateau Carras". A short walk, occasionally disturbed by a "Fun Bus", brought me to my favourite cove. The wavelets rippling the silver sand into corrugations on the bed of its water garden were reminders of the Legend of the Nereids, who tied the rays of the moon into bundles and with these silver brooms swept the sea bed in radiating strokes ready for a new dawn. We swam with red-finned rainbow wrasse.

The Metéora

On arranging to visit the Metéora, the Monasteries of the Air, so-called by St Athanasios because they hung between heaven and earth, I was not surprised to be told to "dress soberly", for St Athanasios was of the same persuasion as Tertullian, who defined women as "temples built over sewers", dubbing them "the affliction" and "the sling" for hurling sin into men's souls.

Each monastery, set on a pudding-stone pinnacle formed from the conglomerate that once swirled in primeval rivers, was an ark set on its own Ararat. Not for us the reception Rousanou gave to traveller Robert Curzon in 1834 when two half-mad crones, shrieking curses, refused to let down the only means of ascent, a rope ladder. Since the 1930s a dizzy bridge has linked Rousanou's approach path to the pike that forms a snug base for this red-roofed dolls' house. When I remarked on the beauty of the surrounding flowers a sweet-faced nun raised her hands in abrogation. "It is the air!" she said.

The original entrance to St Varlaam was an eaved belvedere jutting over a precipice like the fo'c'sle of a galleon, its grappling anchor clasping a bunched net. Restricted now to raising stores, the net had been designed to accommodate visitors "like a joint of meat suspended from a bottle-jack", which was how the Rev Henry Fanshawe Tozer put it, spinning in space in 1853 as he was winched aloft. Ascent was now by rock-cut staircase. Attitudes had changed in other ways too. Perched on a prayer table in the 1950s as the Abbot read the litany at four in the morning in the presence of Patrick Leigh Fermor was Marigoula or "Little Mary", the mate granted Makri ("Big Boy"), the monastery cat.

Our way home took us past the awesome massif of Mount Olympos, Home of the Twelve Gods and germinator of awesome thunderstorms. The gods' frown trailed us all the way to Porto Carras. Next day damson-hued clouds gathered over the hills and temperatures fluctuated. Out in the forest I watched two Scandinavian girls abandon their backpacks to step, naked as Nausicaa, down to the waters of a cove marked "PRIVATE – Entry by invitation only". At the back end of the year all was deserted. As the gods quarrelled, the sun disappeared and I took to my heels, soaked to the skin by shawls of rain as lightning forked from an angry sky.

On a wet evening one of Wacky's trophies was causing him concern. He fussed until I inspected a six-inch millipede he had laid on deck. Geckoes remained his firm favourites, and I once rescued a tiny bundle of tossed feathers. The long-beaked thing feigned dead, but winged off straight as an arrow when I opened my hands. In the woodlands Wacky and I had a scary encounter with a Doberman Pinscher. Wacky sensibly fled up a tree and did not venture in the woods again. He also fell in. I was out shopping when Bob was confronted with a dripping apparition too shocked to miaow. Wet paw marks showed Wacky to have clambered out of the water via the dinghy and made his way back across the deck of *Aegean Mistress*. We suspected him of overbalancing when indulging in his injudicious habit of nodding off while gazing down at fish.

As autumn drew on, the ferry service to Neas Marmaras was reduced to a single fishing boat. One morning, as I waited for it, two children discovered an octopus at the foot of the sea wall. The little girl promptly pelted off for a fish hook, while the boy flung himself into the sea and swam to his father's boat for tackle. Both arrived back together, the girl calling excitedly, «Μία σακούλα, γρίγορα!» ("A bag, quickly!") Another trip found me surrounded by Geordies intent on return to the hotel. Beside me an obese woman repeated, "Flippin''eck whaur's bluddy bo-at?" while the reprise of the bucket-and-spade boy clutching his father's hand was, "Wha's time, Da-ad? Ah want me dinnuh!" Chat centred on the power cuts, not the only inconvenience, for an απεργία (strike) now paralysed both the post office and the telephone exchange.

Before Bob left for a short break in England, he ferried fresh water back to *Cappelle*. Left to rub down, mask and repaint the scuppers, the westerly swell made my life a misery. I must clamber on and off the boat several times to load provisions since I needed both arms to haul myself onto her wallowing bows. I was also forever checking the chafe preventers. Now that the marina was unsupervised, a fishing boat with a rough-looking crew entered. Glyn's advice was to bolt myself in at night. (Not so easy as the door needed tying open to give free access to Wacky.)

As soon as conditions were bad enough to rule out further boat maintenance, I took the early bus to Thessaloniki to view the treasures discovered at Vergina during a road-building operation. Exploring side streets on my way to the Archaeological Museum, I came across the fifth century Basilica of the Mother of God squatting in a sunken square surrounded by high-rise apartments. In Tsimiski Street, Thessaloniki's Bond Street, whose patisseries displayed enough jewel-like crystallised fruits and marzipan fancies to satisfy a harem, I watched the urbanites in black stroll the pavements, pooches on leashes. A Greek visitor curious, like myself, about an intriguing bell dangling above paving fenestrations in a rubble-filled open space, persuaded me to join her in investigating a rock burrow which led into the undercroft of an Early Christian chapel. My companion kissed the curling print of a saint and we wrenched on a hideous brass tap over a font. Calling me by the affectionate diminutive «κυριάκι μου» ("my little Mrs"), she cried out with pleasure as we splashed our faces in the water and drank from cupped palms, before creeping about χέρι χέρι (hand-in-hand) searching for tapers to light sentinels to our visit with her cigarette lighter.

Back at the bus office there was no sign of life. To my enquiry about bus times, the girl at the desk shrugged, «Δέν έχω ιδέα!» ("I've no idea!") Candles were being set up in shop windows, for power cuts were now scheduled to last six hours out of twenty-four. Before our bus reached the city limits, the traffic lights failed. With power "on vacation", the villages en route were blacked out. At the marina the supermarket had been forced to empty its deep freeze, while groans arose from the Sailors' Rest whenever the electricity "took a holiday".

At least Greece had one thing going for her. She was to host the Centenary Olympics, sure to issue in another era of fame and fortune. The natives were so convinced of this that postcards were already on sale in Thessaloniki where a street banner proclaimed, "GOLDEN OLYMPICS – ATHENS 1996". When the nation learned that Atlanta had stolen her prize, her citizens wept, and Glyn seriously kept his head down.

In Porto Carras British pensioners sat outside the hotel wearing an air of resignation. Hands clasped in laps, they rested poor legs hillocky with varicose veins. While gathering scented honeysuckle, I heard one remark, "Well, what I always say is, coming here saves on heating bills!" When the last charter flight left and the ferry went back on fishing duty, we had to admit that winter was upon us. In the village my popularity blossomed. I was a sharer of winter – one who belonged!

In the footsteps of Alexander

Sailors had particular cause to be grateful to Alexander the Great for his prototype lighthouse, the Pharos of Alexandria. I was up before dawn one morning to follow his footsteps in Northern Greece. Raised in the marsh lands of Pella and schooled under the tutelage of Aristotle at Mieza near Edessa, Alexander, was not the product of a happy home. His mother, Olympias, was a witch, while his lecherous father, Philip II of Macedon, surrounded himself with under-age concubines.

At Vergina, whose treasures I had viewed in Thessaloniki, Philip's palace was sited on a terrace overlooking the theatre into which Philip led the wedding party of his daughter, Kleopatra, to be joined in marriage to her mother's brother. Trumpets flashed in the sun and banners fluttered. Led by a champion bull, flowers around his dewlaps, his lyre-shaped horns gold-foiled, the animals for sacrifice, one for each god, were paraded. Mounted on a white charger, Philip, resplendent in a scarlet tunic, on his head a golden wreath, spread his cloak of Tyrian murex across his stallion's haunches. Then, with an imperious wave of his ceremonial sword, he dismissed his guard to enter the parados alone. In collusion, no doubt, with the vengeful Olympias (for Philip, who had seven times married the daughters of local kings, had taken unto himself yet another nubile bride), a traitorous bodyguard lay in wait. Philip of Macedon, all unprotected, was stabbed to death with a short knife. It was a dramatic succession to the throne for twenty-two year old Alexander, last of the Homeric heroes.

A small boy at my side clutching a Bugs Bunny from Edessa scuffed his toe in the dust:

"What are we here for?"

"I don't know!" snapped his mother. "But just you listen! We didn't keep you off school for nothing!"

As I slaked my thirst at a spring of sweet water indicated by our guide beside the tomb of one of Alexander's generals in a peach orchard, someone whispered, "Why does she think we want to drink *WATER*?" More mutterings:

"What's this all about, then?"

"I dunno...some bloke or other. I'm glad Dad didn't come!"

End-of-Season Porto Carras

Porto Carras emptied. President Karamanlis's helicopter no longer landed at weekends.

Aegean Mistress sailed off to winter quarters. And two Germans, supervising the lifting of a small boat, brought cat biscuits "for the little cat who is like a dog". To exit the concourse, I was now obliged to play hide and seek with Wacky, who chased after me, believing, like A A Milne's James James Jonathan Jonathan Willoughby George Dupree, I should "never go down to the end of the town" unless I went down with him.

In Neas Marmaras inertia set in. Shops were left unattended or entrusted to the womenfolk. The butcher's wife, stitching at drawn-thread embroidery, laid it lovingly aside in snowy tissue before picking up the bloodied meat cleaver to slice me pork chops. The obsession of the girl at the gas exchange was with florid Golbein tapestries. After Bob was obliged to remove the empty gas canister from the cockpit locker in his pyjamas (Sod's Law having it that the gas always ran out before the kettle boiled for early tea), we paid her a visit. While we were admiring her latest handiwork, the electrician from the Village Inn offered us a lift home – if we would wait till he had finished work. This gave me the opportunity to stock up with canned dog food (all that was now available for Wacky) in a nearby shop. But an anxious child ran to fetch her grandpa, who questioned me closely. Being but a destitute boat person, it was feared I intended to eat the dog food myself!

The pharmacy put up its shutters. Firewood mounted under the eaves. «*Χειμόνας!*» ("Winter!") said the old lady, padlocking her περίπτερο (kiosk). But the village hardcore remained. Butcher, baker and candlestick-maker rounded down prices and waved aside small change. Faced with the beach walk to buy fresh food, live-aboard life became real and earnest. But I had friends. I left the greengrocer in the upper village till last. After I had paid him, he always crammed every nook and cranny of my shopping bags for όχι δραχμές "no money", as he put it in pidgin Greek. Judging me about to prepare a stew, he would push in celeriac, a bunch of broad-leaved parsley or some newly dug winter vegetable, with an extra apple or pear to fill a gap. Then followed a pantomime. In my best Greek I told him he was «Ενος καλός Κύριος!» ("A good gentleman!") We shook hands laughing, and I staggered off on the long trek home. At the back of the beach, a tethered donkey straddled the track in front of a pink-painted Chinese pagoda (derelict disco), waiting for the apple it knew I brought it. (I could have done with that donkey, for it was the perfect form of transport.) The trudge round the perimeter of the marina was a drag. One rainy day a workman turned his car without a word to drive me back to the boat. The days grew short. The temperature dropped. Drowsy wasps invaded the cabin.

When Glyn tested his engine and filled his water tank on the eve of his departure for Athens, he suggested we accompany him to Neas Marmaras to fill our water canisters. Beside the quay a farmer's market was in full swing. After a granny, adding extra tomatoes, had handed me half my money back, I persuaded Glyn to try his luck. Not only did she refuse any money at all for his tomatoes, but made him the gift of a fine pomegranate to go with them! Like all experienced sailors Glyn's passage-making preparations were meticulous. For his last night he moved *Heart of Gold* to the front of the Village Inn to facilitate his departure should the forecast be good. When we awoke, we were alone with the silence. Only a military jet reminded us of war in the Gulf.

After days of downpour, we were yet to be blessed by St Demetrios, who saved his Little Summer for Hallowe'en. Temperatures rose twenty degrees, the streets of Neas Marmaras baked dry and kitchen chairs were set outside front doors once more. The light had drained into the opalescent sea before I reached the beach. Across the water Kassandra lay soot-black against a red-hot poker sky. It was horribly eerie under the hotel where moisture dripped through cracks in the concrete onto the deserted shopping mall. Next day St Demetrios still held sway, so we abandoned *Cappelle* in favour of a last swim in the Garden of Thalassinous Delights. Sea sapphires sparkled, the jellies had sunk with the rain, and pipe fish flicked among the marine grass. In the warm shallows the low-tracking sun shone through onto the sand. But in shadows the water held a tremulous hint of cold to come. Bob hovered over a shoal of big fish he swore were fogging the water to confuse him.

The time came to double up on duvets. Though we were under contract not to use our Baby Blake, of the two toilet blocks in the marina, one was grilled and locked, while the condition of the other was unspeakable. But we hit a lucky streak. Bob's investigation of an outbuilding led to his discovery of a defective water heater left to gush forth a perpetual stream of hot water.

What to do about Wacky?

Our perennial Christmas problem loomed. What to do with Wacky? To investigate kennel business, and hoping for Bob's discharge from hospital, we left for Thessaloniki. Since the darkness at 5.15 a.m. was Stygian, we were anxious not to step into the river, which now extended onto the beach. The information we had gleaned about possible cat kennels bore no fruit. And the girl at the airlines office implored us with tears in her eyes not to consign our pet to an address in the Yellow Pages, saying she had visited her cousin's little dog there to find him imprisoned in a filthy cage in a cellar and "when I see him I cry!" In the end we purchased a single air ticket for me alone. (A break would give the salt water rot that disfigured my fingernails a chance to grow out.)

Darkness was closing in when we boarded the bus home. As we swerved up through chestnut forest to the oak-covered ridges of the Halkidiki's central massif, we entered ancient lion country. Soon all we could see were our own reflections in the bus windows. The driver, haloed in hazy light, votive offerings clinking round the windscreen and chrysanthemums in his dashboard vase, slipped cassettes into the stereo. Ignoring the "No Smoking" rule, he puffed away as he swung his vehicle, tooting the horn when its headlights caught the red eyes of night creatures. No one spoke, not even when alighting at some godforsaken spot where the driver dispensed luggage from the hold. Only his assistant called «Πάμε!» ("Let's go!") as he swung onto the step on one leg. When we pulled up outside a καφενείο, passengers fell out for a stretch and a smoke. One well-dressed youth (probably a wedding guest) fell out literally, rigid as a ninepin. Not until the bus was on point of departure was he hauled up, bundled on board and stuffed uncomprehending into his seat.

Before the bus reached Neas Marmaras rain slashed the windows, the swish of the windscreen wipers emphasising our insulation from the outside world. All too soon we were catapulted into reality to make a dash for the taverna. Bob asked to phone for the village taxi. But it never came. Suddenly the inn-keeper, shaking a pan over the fire, banged it down, wiped his hands on his apron, and, with a grunt to his customers, grabbed the keys of his gangster Cadillac and marched us off, complaining that the taxi driver made so much money from tourists in the summer, he could not be bothered to turn up when really needed. In no time the Home Alone cat was wrapped round our legs, and the inn-keeper, refusing βενζίνη (petrol) money, was off back to his interrupted cooking.

Pale winter faces greeted my return from England. Thessaloniki wore a cheerless air. Although Bob had made every effort to find Wacky a temporary home, nothing had proved worthy of consideration. In Porto Carras the heavy rains continued. Spreading across the beach in an ever-widening stream, the river burst its banks. Bob grew accustomed to wading it in sea boots. Then, after a storm, he was forced to brave water thigh high to make a telephone call. Now was the time to seek alternative accommodation.

Land Base

Bob took up the first offer, a self-contained flat over a garage belonging to Dimitri Koutanos and his wife, who lived on the premises. "Catherine's Apartments" were sparsely furnished, but clean (though, according to their owner, in need of redecoration). Bob was welcomed with open arms for he provided the perfect solution to a dilemma. Mrs Koutanou was English and wished to spend Christmas with her family in Manchester, but was concerned about leaving the property unsupervised. It was arranged that Bob, as caretaker, should stay at low winter rates (unspecified) until the worst of the winter weather was over and he could move back to the boat. To make the flat comfortable, he requisitioned the village taxi, piling into it bedding, soft furnishings and home comforts such as radio, pressure cooker and kettle. The couple were quick to pack up and go, Mrs Koutanou notably failing in her promise to curtain the French windows.

Shortly after Bob and Wacky moved in, the temperature plummeted to ten degrees below and the blizzards started. Wacky soon found his bearings, climbing down from the balcony to cross the snowy track and returning to feed from his blue bowl before crawling between duvets. His greatest mistake was to fall into a bucket of slaked lime while exploring out-buildings.

Meanwhile, Greek neighbours, seemingly anxious about Bob's welfare, invited him to their New Year party, telling him about the Koutanous' weird habit of activating a hooter alarm on their roof every time the neighbour's little dog barked. With the intention of keeping tabs on *Cappelle*, Bob took up Dimitri's offer of a pedal bike in the garage – "If you can mend it," Dimitri had said. Swiftly abandoning the bone-shaker as beyond repair, Bob was forced to trek to *Cappelle* via the main road, for fast flowing estuarial waters now dissected the beach.

Warning me, on my return, that Mrs Koutanou had developed "a funny look in her eyes", Bob advised me not to go out of my way to speak to her. In the event I never did set eyes on her. Though the washing machine was on at all hours, Bob's enquiry as to whether he might have sheets and towels laundered had met with no response. And Dimitri had waved aside his request to settle the account, though he did invite Bob to watch TV one evening, but cancelled at short notice. In the early hours (the time heavily underscored), a note from Mrs Koutanou was pushed under the door explaining she was still occupied with housework. I passed the time of day with Dimitri and his son, harried in all weathers to build a wall and hose down the outside staircase. When twice I saw them engaged in the latter in pouring rain, only adding to the lake of mud at the bottom, I remarked to Bob, "It's mad!"

We had no desire to be away from *Cappelle* longer than necessary, and I did not unpack. As soon as razor-red anemones burst through the piebald lattice of snow on the cliff-top and from the balcony we caught sight of the exuberant leap of a dolphin, it was time to go. We arranged the room as Bob had found it. And I was careful to wash the marble floor, polish the formica tops and straighten the pile of unused horse blankets in the wardrobe while he went to settle up. I was giving the sink a final rinse when my ears were assaulted by the sound of altercation, including a woman screaming, "Filthy Pig!" I in no way connected this with Bob. Then I heard his angry retort that he had "never been so insulted in my life". He returned visibly shaken. Dimitri had looked shifty when asked for the account. Then the deranged Mrs Koutanou had burst in with, "GET OUT! GET OUT! YOU EFFING FILTHY, EFFING PIG!" Seeing fit to ignore this outburst, Bob told Dimitri he would pay nothing that was not written down.

We were awaiting our taxi when Dimitri came in, flinching nervously, figures pencilled on the back of an envelope. The amount was preposterous. Far from the "winter rate" the Koutanous promised in return for care-taking, Bob was to be charged high-season holiday rate, added to which was an exorbitant sum for electricity, for dry-cleaning the untouched horse blankets, and for complete redecoration of the entire apartment, requiring, according to Dimitri, five days' labour at overtime rates. The final insult was £5 a week for "hire of bicycle". It was absurd. It was also, as Bob pointed out, a rampant rip-off born of Greek greed and Mancunian insanity. A full-scale row ensued. Dimitri held his ground, Bob threatened to call the police. At this the Greek's lip curled, saying that was fine by him. Bob would need to fetch them from Thessaloniki, for the local police station was closed out of season. Had he, Dimitri, not forborne to throw Bob into the street? He would permit him to leave, but would see to it that he got his money first. At this Bob's fists clenched. "As for you!" said Dimitri, wheeling on me, the soft target, I was "no lady" for I had failed to introduce myself to his wife. (What she had been doing, I now realised, was assiduously avoiding me.) I replied that he knew very well Mrs Koutanou was mentally ill and the sooner he got her to a doctor the better. He did not reply. Outside our taxi waited. Our one desire was to get out of this madhouse. Moreover I was seriously concerned that Bob was on the verge of fisticuffs. We paid, not what Dimitri demanded, but triple the amount we had reckoned, using up three of our precious Eurocheques.

With Wacky struggling in my arms, our only satisfaction was to encounter on the stairs a Swedish golf pro who, arriving to prepare for work at Porto Carras Golf Club, was seeking accommodation. Making sure the couple heard every word, we advised him on no account to consider "Catherine's Apartments", for the woman was plumb crazy and *"BOTH OF THEM ARE CHEATS!"*

One thing I had never imagined was vacating a Greek apartment to demented howls of *"Bastards!"* issued from an upper window – soon, I suspected, to be followed by pots and pans hurled by a wild-eyed Mrs Rochester. The taxi driver, sitting so impassively, had seen it all before. At the sight of yacht masts, Wacky scrabbled at the taxi window to get out. None of us, whatever the discomforts to come, had ever been so glad to be back on *Cappelle*. Wacky rushed about trilling at the rediscovery of all that was familiar. As for us, we collapsed with a stiff drink.

Nineteen

Farewell to Porto Carras

Winter in Porto Carras

The deserted marina was home. With a pan to collect rain water pooled in its cover, we clambered aboard a neighbouring motor cruiser. And, by trial and error, Bob mapped out a middle distance approach to Neas Marmaras — along the river bank as far as the road bridge, then via a cut-back to the beach beyond the river bridge past a deserted tuna-smoking factory. Soon the estuary, shifting course through quick sands, drained sufficiently to ford with caution. My marketing routine became to remove shoes, socks and jeans to tie round my neck before wading into the bruisingly cold water. On the return trip I held the shopping on my head. It was vital to watch my step. In the time it took to market, the fast-flowing stream could alter from two thigh-deep channels with a sandbank between to a sickle-shaped lagoon with a wide outfall of shallow rapids.

Porto Carras opened for spring conferences. Tailor's dummy men and pin-heeled women from a Hair Products Convention aired themselves on the concourse. Soon the Village Inn welcomed golfers. Back in London I had lost no time in despatching a Christmas parcel containing a fan-heater, a plum pudding, books, puzzles, chocolates and cat goodies. Learning before leaving there was no sign of the parcel's arrival, I asked the GPO to put a trace on it. The package was located languishing in a sorting office in Thessaloniki. Thus we had Easter treats.

There is a Greek saying,

"Dry Epiphany and pouring Easter weather
Bring us Happiness and Plenty both together."

In which case we were in for a splendid summer. The rain fell in curtains. Intrepid golfers might be out under striped umbrellas, but we sat in semi-darkness beneath our coffin cover listening to the drumming of the rain on the coach roof. Warmed by our new fan-heater, collecting rain water to top up our tank, stitching deck shoes, binding carpets, reading and doing odd jobs, we were not discontent, for we were well situated in comparison with the Kurdish families the BBC World Service reported as driven into mountain snow on the Iraqi borders. In Neas Marmaras there were smiles and Easter greetings. «*Καλό Πάσχα!*» called a granny from her doorstep, and a papa side-slipped across a precipitous street to pat me on the head when I responded, «*Αληθώς ανέστι!*» to his «*Χριστός ανέστι!*»

As soon as the longueurs of winter were at an end, a spangled carpet of marigolds, crimson trefoil and purple irises splashed the grass in the floral patterns of a Turkish carpet. In the village wisteria trailed from pergolas and lilac hung heavy. Hottentot fig and winged lavender veiled the rear of the beach, while the coves were invaded with jelly strandings like plumed cherries. Outside an abandoned villa where *πιθάρια* (giant terracotta jars) lay broken, a smoked honey scent led me to beds of wallflowers. Spanish broom brushed the headlands and everywhere Judas blossom exploded like pink popcorn.

I sewed three of Yener's ill-fitting spare cockpit cushion covers into two, sacrificing a towelling bathrobe to make the third. Heel-trodden jeans were chopped into clam-diggers. Then there were the snags in the genoa's sacrificial leech to make good, since one of Wacky's cantrips was to use the furled sail as a scratching post. Bob bound a wire coat-hanger to a boat-hook to contrive an implement to poke out limber holes, and we touched up the stanchion bases with silver Hammerite. After relaunching the dinghy, Bob dived to scrape the propeller. With perseverance, he managed to obtain a new engine battery, but nowhere, though we were loath to set sail with our storm-tattered edition, could we replace our Greek courtesy flag. (Not that the Greeks cared!) News filtered through that the marina had been left in limbo. The Carras brothers' law-suit had ended in favour of the hotel-owning brother and the marina manager had disappeared taking with him all records and staff.

It was a thrill when people told us that we had already travelled more extensively in the Aegean than most Greeks. It was said that the majority of yachts in Porto Carras were Someday Boats (as in "Someday we shall go to the islands!")

Tax avoidance required us out of Greek waters by 3rd May. But on the day we planned to depart, we awoke to an adverse change in the weather The sky was an ominous grey and a brutal wind whipped in from the east. As often, when a weather bulletin was vital, the forecaster failed to turn up at the radio station. We took her absence as our cue to remain in harbour. In the time I took to shop, the estuary changed course, angry waves making fording treacherous. Despite looking out for the tell-tale shine of quick-sand, I missed a patch, feeling my foot sucked in and having to lie half-down in the icy water to wrench it out. When the marina filled with fishing boats, we knew we were in for a hard blow.

That weekend the hotel opened for package holidays. On the concourse two little girls, bare feet in flip-flops, hugged themselves to keep warm. St George's Day (sacred to brigands and Englishmen) brought fearsome squalls. When Wacky returned from hunting minus his Evil Eye, Bob was quick to fit him a spare from the ship's emergency supply. Searching for the lost amulet between the woods and the water, I came across a bank whereon wild orchids blew. Picking seven blooms, I took them back to *Cappelle* where they thrived in a Greek vase, remaining as fresh on the day we left Porto Carras as on the day they were picked. *ORCHIDS FOR APHRODITE!* Tying their stalks with ribbon, I dropped them overboard in votive offering to Aphrodite of Fair Sailing, watching as they fanned out on the water before drifting towards the exit canal.

We vacated Porto Carras without a backward glance, Bob writing in the log of that "desolate winter". Though we planned to make our way south and west by first crossing east, our immediate intention, taking a leaf out of *Heart of Gold's* book, was to proceed to Neas Marmaras to test the engine and fill the water tank. We would then make the short passage to Porto Koufo from which, assured of a favourable wind, we would light off for Myrina, nearest Port of Exit.

Though caïques blocked our way to the hydrant, a fishing smack crewed by swarthy ruffians in red bandanas, as like pirates as I ever wish to see, were quick to pull *Cappelle* in amongst them. While Bob fitted the water hose and Wacky complained loud and long at being snatched from The Enchanted Place, I ran to the bake-house. On my return, the grimy finger of a ringletted Captain Hook beckoned. His other hand was not missing, for it was holding out a patched colander of sardines. When I proffered coins the pirate did but laugh and flash his gold teeth. Of course the fishermen were anxious to know about such as us with our Red Ensign and Ship's Cat out and about so early in season. When we told them we were on our way to Myrina, we were "bravoed" for the exploit. As we headed down coast, Wacky prowled the deck in a bad temper.

Porto Koufo was a different scene out of season, devoid of yachts, but with caïques belching fumes as they reloaded their nets. With the fishing fleet's departure, peace descended and, except for ourselves and the hawks that hovered over the greening hillside as if hung out to dry, there was no sign of life. Fresh crusty bread, Athos wine and succulent sardines made a splendid supper. Likewise, sardines plopped into a washing-up bowl soon revived Wacky's flagging spirits. In a few glad moments, stalking back periodically to see if more had spawned, he emptied the lot.

All too soon the fishing boats returned and the loading of lorries started up inches from our noses. From midnight to two a.m. came a lull and then the activity began all over again as a second fishing fleet arrived. Fishing boats queued up, while a shuttle service of lorries hooted its way down from the road above to back down the mole. Men hollered, engines roared, doors slammed and I lay awake fretting over the Ship's Cat until I heard from the chomping of cat biscuits he was home. The following day, an increasingly unfavourable wind failing to dispel a wet mist, a fisherman approached. Wagging his finger, he said in English, "No you go! Stay Porto Koufo!" which was nice of him, since *Cappelle* was out of place taking up room amid so much industry.

On the third morning, though the forecast was for rain and thunderstorms, we cast off. This time we were in for a big send-off for, on exiting the red cliffs, we met Captain Hook and his Merry Men making their way in. Calling, «*Καλό ταξίδι!*» they saluted us with high fives. Mount Athos soon emerged from the cloud-cover. On passage due east we maintained a steady 4.9 kts. After twelve hours, when we were making our final run along the path of the westering sun as the islets, hills and cliffs of Lemnos unfolded like a Chinese box, a patrol boat put out from Myrina to escort us into harbour, signalling us to tie alongside a disused caïque. The harbour might be empty, but the fishing fleet was due. Meanwhile Wacky, shut in for the mooring procedure, demanded freedom. I watched him as he crouched on deck looking about him as he revived his cognitive map before leaving for old haunts. *Cappelle* was third boat out, so he practised going back and forth to the quay a few times to orientate himself before departing for the evening. Stars were peeping as we fastened on the sail cover. At three a.m. heavy rain and the clatter of the fishing fleet woke us.

Lemnos

The islanders joked their climate was "just like England" for rain had scarcely ceased for a month. On May Day Lemnos concerned itself more with homage to its veterans than garlanding the prow. But its song was still for the brave. Hats held over hearts, the citizens paid their respects to the old campaigners. When we checked out there were no dues to pay. A cormorant, a fish across its beak, stared at us as we left the "fishingboat bobbing" harbour. Off the south coast, the water wine-dark, the low sun picked out every intricate fold of cliffs so convoluted it was a puzzle to match their indentations with those on the chart. Bob, in anticipatory mood again, worried we might have slipped past Mudhros Light, our landmark for changing course. But, to prove us wrong, up it came tucked beneath a promontory.

Here we bore south, heading for the Muslim Channel. Perhaps it was not sensible to undertake the fraught business of crossing the shipping lanes of the Dardenelles by night. But this decision weighed against our preference to make landfall on an unfamiliar stretch of the Turkish coast in daylight. The silhouette of a ship crossing our bows appeared to have a slow-burning brazier on deck, but, as it moved on, the brazier stayed put, rising and metamorphosing into a copper moon. We both remained on watch, all senses alert, until at 02.15 hrs, with no more shipping in sight, Bob knocked off. When the "white-winged forerunner of the sun", ice-cold Phosphorus the Morning Star, blazed forth, I entered the log and woke him with soup, reporting the lights of Asia Minor ahead.

By the time of my second watch, the sun had risen and *Cappelle*, beating into tossing seas, was attempting to force entry into the Muslim Channel. Bob admitted to having had his moments while I slept. Aiming, in order to avoid semi-submerged reefs on the Turkish mainland for what he thought was a red navigation light on Cape Molivos, he had found himself closing with the port light of a caïque, an encounter neither skipper relished.

It took all Bob's skill to bring *Cappelle* between **Baba Burun** in Asia Minor, notorious for gusts, and Cape Molivos on Lesbos in a head sea roughened by a Poyraz, a cold north-easterly that can blow all day in spring and is strongest along the coast around the Turkish resort of Ayvalik, for which we were bound. Though the sun shone brightly, it was bitterly cold. With a longing glance towards Efthalou and its thermal bath, I dragged on enough layers to turn me into Michelin woman. Rolling heavily, we made gruelling progress, the sea slopping the deck first one side and then the other. Rounding Cape Korakas in tiresome waters, fatigue playing havoc with his appreciation of distance, Bob agitated over the non-appearance of the elusive islands of **Güneş Adası**. I assured him there were still two more labial capes to pass before we might expect to see this landmark. Only after putting Cape Faros and Cape Tsakmaki behind us did we recognise the island group's steely promise far out on the horizon.

Soon after we turned out to sea, we lost the coast-seeking wind and the waters calmed. When the light structure on the cluster of Egg Island west of Güneş became conspicuous, the channel through the Ayvalik archipelago opened up. South of Porsolene a dolphin cavorted, a descendant, perhaps, of the ancestor of which Pausanias wrote, "I have seen the dolphin at Porsolene showing its gratitude to a boy who cured it when it was wounded by a fisherman. I have seen it answer the boy's call and carry him wheresoe'er he wishes."

Our excuse was that neither of us, after sailing a difficult passage for twenty-three hours, was at our best. But this was no reason for not treating the information in the pilot with circumspection. Besides which the author's covering note: "Many of the reefs and shallows are not shown on this plan" was a clear incentive to check with a more reliable authority. Foolishly swallowing the bait that the route was "straightforward", and that "once up to the central beacon"(again vague) marking the buoyed channel, it would open up, we also foolishly took for granted that the direction of the pilot's approach to Ayvalik matched our own. The result was that hook, line and sinker, in mid channel, we ran aground under full sail, impetus driving *Cappelle* into the mud before we could drop canvas. As with *Golden Prospect*, the classic solutions, revving the engine in reverse, rocking the hull and tugging with the dinghy, proved useless.

It was an unpleasant situation, for we were out of sight of civilisation and had encountered no one since before daybreak. It would be nice to report a dolphin came to our rescue. But that was left to German resident, Otto, unusually late back from a fishing trip in his powerful speed boat. With warps attached, he hauled us free, manoeuvring *Cappelle*, uttering appalling cranking noises in a churn of mud, back into deep water. She was by no means the first yacht, he assured us, to run aground at this spot. (In fact the whole Muslim channel was notorious for reefs and shallows, as *Olinda*, the Russian tanker disguised as a Turkish trading vessel, discovered during the Aegean war.) Slowly and humiliatingly, Bob certain she had damaged her engine mountings since our progress was now accompanied by ominous knockings and scrapings, *Cappelle* limped up the two-mile channel to Ayvalik's inner lagoon, where Otto indicated us to tie up beside a fresh-water standpipe.

Ayvalik

It was not without misgivings we were revisiting Turkey, not only because of the Gulf War, but because of recent sensitivities between Britain and Turkey over the Kurdish question. Turkish newspapers were thundering "foreign soldiers" would do well to remember the Turkish military were in charge on the Iraqi border! Moreover, the BBC was reporting the expulsion of journalist Robert Fisk for citing the theft of food relief by Turkish soldiery. We were relieved when the people of Ayvalik welcomed us with unabashed enthusiasm.

When we traipsed round town on duty visits to Customs Patrol, Passport Police and Health Department, officials applauded our small Turkish courtesies. Bob, document case in hand and spit-smart as always on official business, was informed the Chief of Police wished to consult him on an important matter. This was the deterioration in the tourist situation. As everywhere, concerns were purely local. In the summer of 1990 Ayvalik had entertained 26,000 foreign visitors, most of them British, whereas in 1991 it was already May and seasonal bookings amounted to a mere 3,000. What had gone wrong? The police chief sent for a tray of tea. Settling back, fingers steepled, he waited for the oracle to pronounce. Bob spoke of the onset of the Gulf War affecting holiday plans. At this the police chief expressed amazement. Surely the British knew that Turkey was a NATO country, and that in any case the theatre of war was so far south as to be of no concern to Ayvalik? We knew this, but many at home did not. Bob then spoke of the recession, saying British people could no longer afford holidays abroad. The police chief was more understanding, looking somewhat mollified when Bob assured him that the warm-hearted citizens of this altogether delightful town were in no way to blame, giving his personal guarantee he would do his best to reassure those at home. We left with Bob informally assigned the post of diplomat without portfolio.

The weather closed in. Otto, paying us a courtesy call, explained that we might have avoided running aground had we consulted the Admiralty Chart, for this marked the shallows west of the beacon. We had been lucky. It was by sheer chance he had witnessed our mishap.

(Hearing this, I was more than ever glad of my act of propitiation to Aphrodite Euploia and her miraculous intervention!)

Ayvalik was Wacky's first experience of the Islamic umbrella. Whenever the Muezzin sounded he raced home convinced that Allah Himself was after him. When the rank stink of tom-cat began to permeate the air, he stayed below, ears pricked for the sound of alien paws invading his sovereign territory. Saddam the Nasty, a marmalade tom, proved the invader. We once caught him on deck in broad daylight standing foursquare over poor Wacky, who lay on his back in surrender. Driving Wacky incoherent with fury, Saddam then committed the ultimate insult of defecating in the cockpit. Despite threats and dowsings, we were never entirely successful in frightening him off.

On the recommendation of the Police Chief, we ate at "The Fifteen Brothers". But, when at the fish market I purchased fresh sardines, these, followed by the luscious strawberries just into season, were established as our evening meal. A sardalye (sardine) spin-off also brought sporting moments for the Ship's Cat when Bob devised a double plastic-bag insulation system to dangle over the side to keep the fish fresh. The sardines in the inner bag attracted scores of inquisitive small fry that somehow became trapped in the outer bag filled with water. When tipped into a washing-up bowl, Flash Paw gloried in the catch, doing it in style, whiskers bristling, water splashing, continually beating his own record. It was the beginning of his bucket and bowl fetish. Ever afterwards he was addicted to peering into sinks and nosing lids off buckets.

The damage sustained to *Cappelle* by running aground was to her bilge pump. Our sad-faced neighbour, with no charterers in the offing, introduced Bob to his chandler cousin. But he had nothing to offer of suitable dimensions. Meanwhile the wind blasted in from the north east to circle the corners of the compass before dropping as a prelude to torrential rain. Once again we retreated beneath the coffin cover and lit the Tilley. Though Bob's feet froze, he refused to wear socks, declaring they only made it rain more. Anxious to please, our friend promised there would be no more bad weather after 6th May, the first official day of summer. When the forecast for that day was the familiar one of gales and precipitation, he felt he had let us down.

Pergamum

An eager taxi driver chased the Pergamum bus on our behalf, shoving us on board with, "You pay later!" Soon afterwards the bus screeched to another unscheduled halt for an old woman to be hoisted aboard. At the next village, poking the business man beside her in the ribs with a coin, she demanded, "Ekmek!" (bread). Obligingly, he disembarked to buy her a loaf. Passengers, obeying the no-smoking rule (though the driver did not), resorted to telling their tespihs (prayer beads) as we rattled across the Caicus plain.

In Bergama's stepped alleys artistic licence had run riot. The pavement outside one sky-blue hovel was edged with a jaunty lilac border, while the façade of another had been given a wobbly red frame like a child's painting. Beyond the River Selinus the elegant minaret of Ulu Cami pointed to the gleaming ruins of Pergamum. We chose the direct route through pine woods. If I remember Pergamum for nothing else, I shall remember it for Homer's "blossoming meadows" tricked out in the flowers of early May, wild roses that tore at my legs, rampant daisies, jostling poppies, loosestrife, campanulas and baby-blue forget-me-nots. In this Garden of Eden it was no wonder the women of Pergamum held torchlight processions in honour of Persephone.

Higher up, the breeze pinned us against the mountain. Scaling a dry-stone wall, we at last achieved the site that had inspired so much dramatic confidence. It was easy to see with the eyes of a Delegate General of Alexander as he surveyed the about-to-be-conquered panorama stretching south. Everything about Pergamum went one better, the rake of its amphitheatre the steepest in the Ancient World, its Altar of Zeus so commanding Hitler chose it as his model for his 1936 Olympic Stadium (thereby, perhaps, confirming it as St John's "Throne of Satan"). Near the Temples of Trajan and Athena bushes dripped with votive ties, as if the city, described by architect Léon Krier as "probably the most beautiful ever built in the Western Hemisphere" still found favour with those wishing to evoke the sacred strands of the cosmic net that binds heaven and earth. I shied a coin over columns that glistered as white as the parchment once manufactured in Pergamum. Forsaking the Triumphal Way, we followed goat paths through domestic foundations, discovering here a section of fluted column and there a sarcophagus encircled with scarlet poppies.

Back in Ayvalik our friend was eager to show Bob the bilge pump he had been to Izmir to procure. Bob devoted a day to its installation. But before we could be on our way again, depressions closed in. A British yacht arrived, its captain long-faced after being required to settle a £600 tax bill in Mitilini before being permitted to exit for Turkey. (The cause was his thoughtless two-week over-stay on Aegina.) Wacky (presumably discovering the salt slabs in the fish market) returned in the middle of the night with a thirst raging enough to induce him to knock lids off saucepans, slurp sink water and stick his head in the milk jug.

Mitilini again

After a round of rubber-stamping and fond farewells, heedful of all the navigational advice we could get, we crossed to Mitilini. Bob was busy bleaching the cross-bench with oxalic acid while lending half an ear to Dave Lee Travis chairing *Jolly Good Show* on the radio, when his brush halted in mid-stroke. Over the air waves came a request from Julia and Gary ("I Wanna Break Free" by Queen) penned under a tree in a rain forest in Borneo. A year ago the four of us had been together in this very spot.

The weather forecast grew so repetitive we knew it by heart: "Cloudy with rain and thunderstorms throughout Greek seas". Wacky's desire to revisit Sappho's garden was deterred by political processions accompanied by loud-speaker vans and heavy-booted soldiery. When the strengthening south-westerlies forced *Cappelle's* bows crosswise, we pulled up on the stern anchor and put out bow fenders. By the time the blow had increased to gale force, bringing a heavy swell through the entrance to the inner harbour, we had left it too late to get off the exposed North Quay. There was nothing for it but to spend the night in the cockpit, the engine ticking in reverse, the "infuriated tomato" set to buzz every fifteen minutes to keep us awake. In a dawn lull we moved across to the Town Quay.

Wacky's vulnerability was underlined by his encounters with the runny-membraned Saddam. On the day his booster injections fell due, I took him, making a terrible fuss in a holdall, to Mitilini's small animals' vet. No introduction was necessary, for when the vet saw from Wacky's WHO certificate that he had been a client of his old friend Adrianos Liberopoulos of Rhodes, he was charmed to make his acquaintance. A few hours after his injection Wacky showed signs of allergic reaction and I lost no time in bursting into the vet's surgery as he was about to operate on a dog. Abandoning his patient, he loaded a hypodermic, showed me how to inject the cat, and sent me scampering home. When, after an anxious day or two, Wacky was back on form, his energy levels nearly provoked his undoing.

The position of our new berth was somewhat dangerous. A through-route for traffic, the waterfront sported three zebra crossings. All were routinely ignored. The cognoscenti, waiting anywhere, made a dash for the centre of the road where they stood stock still, shaved on both sides by fast-moving vehicles until venturing a hasty sprint to the far side. Although I did my best to leave the boat while Wacky's attention was directed elsewhere, one evening I returned to find Bob in a tizzy, a fisherman having told him he had seen the cat follow me across the road. Horrified, we searched a public garden and the doorways of the now closed shops. But there was no sign of Wacky, and no answer to our calls! Sick at heart, I steeled myself for the worst as I listened to the traffic's whirl. Around midnight circulation ceased. As it quietened down it occurred to me that, in Wacky's position, I would wait until then to return. As if in answer to my thoughts, there was a chirrup at the forehatch and there he was, as pleased as Punch to be home. (Perhaps he had lain doggo under the newspaper kiosk opposite until the coast was clear. We never knew.)

Dodging rain showers, I let myself loose in the Aladdin's cave of Mitilini's main street. My favourite street-seller was the Orchid Man, who, issuing his cajoling street cry, «*Ορίστε παιδιά! Ελάτε,*» (loosely parallel to, "Come buy my sweet orchids!") strolled along with his wicker back-pack of the flower that the *British Herbal Guide* of 1653 advised should be treated with caution as it was under the dominion of Aphrodite. An artist had set up easel before the cathedral. Fish slabs gleamed with heaps of the pink prawns soon to supersede sardines for supper. With few Mitilinians speaking English I plunged into transactions without hesitation, making up in fluency for what I lacked in grammar. This often resulted in the bringing out of the family album.

Weatherise, the Canadian family whose charter yacht we were tied alongside had had a disappointing fortnight. When the wife fulfilled the cruising custom of handing over their remaining stores when they left for home, I was aware she acted with a certain disdain. Once we stopped laughing on unpacking the carrier bag, we fell into a discussion of just when such a favour failed as a compliment! The Canadian contribution set the seal – a two litre wine bottle containing little more than the dregs, half a cut tomato, one onion (peeled), a margarine carton with the scrapings and two small potatoes! I even wondered if we had been given the scraps by mistake, but the bag was neatly packed and Bob had seen the garbage taken away.

An art gallery in a nearby country park was dedicated to the celebration of two sons of Lesbos; Theophilus, a naive artist of maddening charm, and Tériade, publisher of the prestigious hand-made Grands Livres to which he persuaded luminaries such as Picasso, Chagall, Matisse, Giacometti and Bonnard to contribute. Beyond the gallery lay the tower village of Taxiarxes. No islander could care less whether a stranger liked anything as amorphous as Greece, for his interest was restricted to his own island. In the case of Taxiarxes, however, its people were not concerned with what we thought of Mitilini, let alone Lesbos, but only wanted us to admire their village. A woman promised the boarded-up taverna would open shortly – when we could see it was never likely to open again.

As soon as the wind dropped, we moved back onto the North Quay to be nearer the water hydrant, whose key was held by the Port Police. But poor weather returned and it was another week before we were happy to put to sea. The day's early promise dissipated. The sky turned to watered silk. With storm clouds boiling on the southern horizon, we turned, close-hauled, into Mirsinia where "The ghost of a garden fronts the sea". But now it offered no idyll. In Plomari our lines were taken by an old sailor with a West Country burr from *Stay Young,* whose wife, parting bloodshot geraniums, peered curiously at us through a port-hole. We awoke to cloud-cover and rain (responsibility for which the Port Police placed squarely on the Iraqi oil fires) and a gut-awareness of the notorious "Plomari swell". *Stay Young* had vanished, and the fishing boat next to us plunged about like a sick cow. Wacky, faced with judging his moment to leap ashore, was both pleased with the familiar setting and vexed with conditions. Wedging myself in the cockpit, I washed my hair in our bucket of Mitilini water before it spilt.

Psara

As we sailed towards the tiny island of Psara ten miles west of Chios, Plomari blurred into the multi-coloured triangle on a conical hill first seen on our approach the previous year. (Odysseus, homeward bound after the Trojan War, had "hesitated to choose the long passage outside the rugged coast of Chios and, by way of Psara, to keep that island on the left" as we did.) By 14.15 hrs, Bob positioning *Cappelle* within a cocked hat of sightings of Profitis Ilias on Chios at 133 deg M, Cape Agios Nikolaos on Psara at 175 deg M, and Psara's highest point at 235 deg M, we had made 26.2 NM. At 18.45 hrs, after a passage of forty-eight miles, we entered the harbour which had played host to the Round-the-Aegean Race. A fisherman tied us up. «Εχουμε ησυχία!» ("No news! All is well!") we told him.

Dotted along the coast, white rocks like scattered lumps of feta cheese jutted through black basalt. To the south, one of Nikos Gatsos's windmills that "patched his rotted sails, alone, with a needle of dolphin's bone", brandished bare spokes. There was an abiding air of melancholy. Psara, whose fireships harried the mainland, was one of the first islands to revolt against their domination by the Turks, whose retaliation failed, usually on account of poor weather. But in June 1824 a Turkish force, after succeeding in making a landing, drove the entire population of Psara off the cliffs. The tragedy was commemorated in a celebrated poem by Solomos:

> "On the blackened ridge of Psara
> Glory walking alone,
> Recalls the gallant young men.
> On her head she wears a crown
> Made of what little grass
> Remained on that desolate earth".

Local names for the winds – "Wind of Melons", "Wind of Grapes", "Wind of Aubergines" and "Wind of Bitter Apples" – proved the island not always barren. Its hospitality was legendary from the time of Ceres who, exhausted and thirsty, reached Psara in her search for her daughter Persephone. Through a cottage window a widow handed her a bowl of honey-water sprinkled with barley. But the widow's son, one of those razor-headed, snotty-nosed little urchins familiar in the islands, cheeked Ceres, not knowing her to be a goddess, at which she changed him into an ancestor of the bright-eyed lizards seen darting about to this day.

Our sleep was broken at 1.30 a.m. when *Rita of Berlin* tied up. Fairy lights blinked on outside the taverna. In the morning the crew handed us a bucket of fresh-caught sea bream. This was followed by Wacky arriving home loudly demanding that sticky burrs from the waste ground be pulled out of his fur. And a white egret joined our company. As exquisite as a bird in a Chinese painting, rapier beak to match, it stepped about on fragile ebony legs with the precision of a ballet dancer, its pure white feathers and summer nape plume lifting like thistledown in the light airs. Under the trees a Papa in a tall hat, his soutane green with age, sorted nets. In the shade of a quay-side tree encircled by dry-stone walling, I was startled to find I had disturbed the siesta of a Great White Pelican. Opening an albino eye, it regarded me with all the scorn of its forty-million-year ancestry.

On mounting the headland I discovered a clumsily restored chapel, the date 1956 on the lintel. Instinct told me I was standing on the μαύρη ράχη, the infamous "black ridge". At its edge I found a memorial stone to the "Heroes of Psara". It was a haunted place. Discarded doors and building materials lay strewn on the soured grass. Playing a hunch, I heaved aside rolls of rusty wire-netting and scavenged among brick ends until I came across evidence of a classic temple. From beneath chunks of broken plaster peeped a snowy Ionic capital.

Twenty

The Cyclades

Andros

Exchanging salutes with an entering fishing boat as we left harbour, we were away to the Cyclades by 05.00 hrs next morning on the forecast of a smooth barometric field. Wacky, curled up like a doughnut in the forepeak, thrust aside the whole disagreeable business of passage-making. It was calm and slightly misty for the Andros crossing with little current running in the Doro Channel. The first boats encountered were idling in the declining sun that struck the mountains of Euboia with surreal clarity. Once we had pin-pointed the lighthouse on Cape Fassa, the haul to the deep inlet of Gavrion on the far side of Andros seemed long drawn out. But, by the time the light faded, we were carrying out the last of our arrival chores. The additional task of Odysseus, whose path we followed, was to make sacrifice: "And many a bull's thigh we laid on Poseidon's altar after spanning that weary stretch of water."

A katabatic southerly, which dropped as suddenly as it rose, awoke us next morning. The first Flying Dolphin, followed by three car ferries churning the waters with twin screws, had us out of bed. Pneumatic drills started up and soon lorries and coaches were filling the waste ground. Emerging from slumber at the sound of sails being handed, Wacky had reared up, paws on the cockpit rail, to give this new port of call a pert once-over. Now he lost no time in getting acquainted. His favourite spectator sport was hand-line fishing, his head following every toss and flick of line.

Our eyes were drawn to *Rogue*, a neat Swan 36 flying the Stars and Stripes dicing with departing craft as she entered harbour. Soon we were shaking hands with Hugh and Danielle from Portland, Oregon, who told us that all they could extract from the wall fountain was a dribble. We explained that water was a platinum resource. This lesson had been taken to heart by Geoffrey of *Jackdaw* moored beside us, who, with his partner, Annette, had left San Remo in Italy with 100 gallons of water, only to squander every drop. Geoffrey was now an expert on water brokerage, his solution being to beg or buy small quantities wherever he went to replenish the water canister he kept in his back-pack.

The Cyclades consist of some thirty islands encircling Delos, the hub of the Cycladic wheel. Andros, the most northerly, is known as "The Sailors' Island". My *Guide to the Cyclades*, addressing me as "You fervent lover of long trips", invited me "to partake of a divine 'Good Morning!' where the water is diaphan blue", urging me not to miss the "different but simple Dorian habits", which, after a glass or two with Danielle, had our imaginations running riot! While assuring the reader that "Any kind of art either peaceful or warrior has been flourish", the *Guide*, however, remained short on fact.

All enquiries about bus times to the χώρα the other side the island meeting with "Watch the ferries" or "Ask the driver", we joined forces with Danielle and Hugh to hire a taxi. From the heights, the sunken harbour of Paleopolis, the old capital, manifested itself through "diaphan" seas. The marble streets of the new capital, Andros, shone with sea-spray and sunshine. A bridge extended to Agia Thalassina, Our Lady The Sea, a white chapel perched on a harbour rock. In a strong meltemi the turquoise waters crash above it. Discreet behind wrought iron gates, marble lions after Canova snoozed on the steps of the imposing mansions built by sea captains and shipping magnates. We were lunching on potato and sausage omelette, an Andriot speciality, when, to the amusement of the locals, the village idiot, clean-barbered and well-turned out, attached himself to us as unsolicited guide. Soon we were obliged to rouse our driver, for we had promised he should be back in Gavrion in time to meet the evening ferries.

According to single-handed sailor and travel writer, Ernle Bradford, the squalls that whipped down around Gavrion were every bit as bad as he had been led to expect, the surrounding seas "baffling when the wind is moderate and heavy when the wind is strong". By 5.00 a.m. next day, strong winds had caused the cancellation of ferries. A fishing boat stood off, its skipper, waiting patiently for Bob and Geoffrey to untie their hastily fixed extra lines to let it in, insisted they be retied behind him.

Tinos

In the next lull we pulled out. As we passed the narrow Steno Strait between Andros and its sister island, Tinos, a swordfish rocketed into the air directly in front of our bows. It could not have startled me more had it cried "Excalibur!" We hovered in an ever-changing aspect of weaving islands, barren kingdoms that form the quintessential spirit of the Cyclades. Set beneath Disney skies in a sea of heartbreak blue, they are the Platonic essence of all natural shapes and forms. This like-it-or-leave-it landscape with no hiding place offers no αγάπε (or friendly love), as sailors do well to remember. Its psychology is Jungian. Down below lurks the id.

The town of Tinos scintillated like the white foam of a tsunami that had crashed and crystallised. In its background reared the improbable cockscomb of Exoborgo, site of the ancient Venetian capital. Possessing the miracle-working ikon of the Tiniotissa, Tinos is the Lourdes of Greece. Thus, two months before Italy declared war in 1940, an Italian submarine's gratuitous torpedoing of the Greek battleship *Elli* as she lay at anchor in the roadstead, dressed overall in honour of the Tiniotissa, was an unpardonable act of aggression.

Tinos's wedding-cake bell towers were silver-painted. The leaves of the trees on the waterfront revealed silver undersides as they trembled. The presence of a water hydrant meant we had reached Eldorado, for Tinos boasted the sweetest drinking water in the Cyclades. Hopes were dashed, however, with the news that Tiniot water was not available to yachts! Moreover, lifting the hydrant cover beneath a marble pediment

307

carved with sailing ships and fishes, exposed a manhole swarming with cockroaches.

Lined with booths, the Marble Way rose directly to the Tiniotissa's magnificent church. *Τάματα* (votive discs) were on sale: eyes, hearts, body parts, each a pressed-tin ex-voto. Among them were baskets of Evil Eyes. When I seized the opportunity to stock up for Wacky, the old man who took my money hobbled off to add his personal gift of a tiny crucifix. All Greeks, with their long perspective of supernatural belief, sense the relevance of paganism, even, in the islands, its dominance. They find nothing inappropriate in paying simultaneous court to both it and Christianity. The one serves as ballast for the other, or to link broken threads. We sailors need all the protection we can get!

Since guests on neighbouring *Rachel Jane* were anxious for an introduction to our Ship's Cat, Wacky aka Wackster, whose name they mistook for "Webster", P G Wodehouse's redoubtable moggy, we were invited to drinks. Hearing the excitement of a crowd, we climbed onto the coach roof to watch a priest carried by on a palanquin. Candle-sellers importuned with cut-price offers. "Two for the price of one!" "Taki is never undersold!" "Buy my bargain candles!" All were grist to the Tiniotissa. Wacky, getting bored meanwhile, and taking a shine to the sophisticated night life around us, crossed the waterfront to the restaurants. Thus it was that he almost lost the rest of his nine lives under the wheels of a speeding car, for, wondering where he was, Bob called him. At the sound of his Captain's voice, without a moment's forethought and saved by a miracle, Wacky dashed back through the traffic. After Bob got over the shock, we decided that in future it was safer to leave Wacky to his own devices.

It was to be hail and farewell to *Rachel Jane*, due to leave for Athens. But the gods were merely pausing for breath. By morning gale force winds blew. Reefed down, *Rachel Jane* left anyway, for her guests had a plane to catch. She was soon back. Her crew had been unable to stand upright. By midday white water forced its way into harbour. A tremor of excitement swept the quay when, with the gold-braided Harbourmaster standing to attention, a motor launch made its approach requesting permission to land "distressed" passengers. Photographers elbowed through the crowd, a gangway was lowered and a VIP party disembarked. Of the three yachts that attempted to leave, all returned, the last to make it careering off to be pinned against a corner of the mole, where, grating her hull, she remained for days, impossible either to cushion or dislodge.

Caught in the wind triangle of Tinos, Mykonos and Delos, we experienced siege conditions. In wind-laundered air the carmines and Peking yellows of efflorescent bougainvillaea radiated against the eye-hurting white of the walls. The meltemi, blowing away the atmosphere, afforded no defence against the sun's glitter, leaving a lens-like vacuum which rendered all objects emphatic. On the Marble Way I tripped over a woman crawling bare-legged to the cathedral. She was not "for the fairground", as they say of the mad, for such acts of penance or entreaty were an everyday occurrence. The ikon of the Tiniotissa had been discovered by a nun, Sister Pelagaea, on the very day, as it happened, in 1823 when the Greek standard was raised against the Turks. Donations from diaspora-scattered islanders poured in for the construction of a church to glorify her. (In the perennial way of things Greek, the site chosen was over a wonder-working spring dedicated to Poseidon. As Lawrence Durrell said of her, "All power to her elbow and Poseidon be with her!")

We waved to *Jackdaw,* anchored off in the inner harbour. At teatime on the day the meltemi set in in earnest, Geoffrey and Annette put in a shame-faced appearance loaded with provisions. For all that *Jackdaw* was but yards from the quay, it was impossible to get back to her. After we had witnessed the windage on the largest of the inter-island ferries, leading to her being winched to shelter on enormous steel hawsers, boat movement ceased altogether.

While I went into a shop to buy a postcard, Bob stooped down to pick up a row of books blown to the pavement outside. In return the old lady presented me with a strawberry bon-bon, together with another for the kind Κύριος. Then came a free postcard for me and a pebble with "Tinos 1991" painted on it. I had hardly vacated the shop with sweets, pebble and postcards, when she hurried after me with another pebble for the Κύριος, plus a box of matches.

When we climbed the long staircase to the cathedral, we mingled with families bearing candles taller than themselves. Hung with thuribles and ecclesiastical banners the church's interior, if a little sinister, was infinitely alluring, its perfumed, soupy darkness filled with arpeggios of Gregorian chant, murmured prayer and shuffling feet. We joined a queue to pay homage to the Tiniotissa. Each pilgrim kissed her ikon in the presence of a deadpan priest, who moved to disinfect the glass that covered her blackened plaque. Her image was unclear, for it was smothered in some of the precious jewellery bestowed on her; milk-white pearls, an important bracelet and diamond brooches all flared in the candlelight. Trance-like pilgrims genuflected and pressed their lips to shadowy paintings. The "silver harvest", a scintillating sky of ex-voto offerings formed from silver sailing ships, a silver miner's lamp from Lavrion, silver silhouettes of islands, silver cutlery, hearts, animals and body-parts, gleamed from above in the flicker of guttering thickets of candles.

When we looked out across the spume-filled sea from the cathedral heights, the sun smote like an axe. In a precinct backed by sky-needling cypresses, an illustration familiar to me from photographs sprung to life, the curl of a balustrade embracing a dangerously pink bougainvillaea framed against the graceful curve of a blinding white marble staircase. Back on the Marble Way I made enquiries about a small Γλυκοφιλούσα (Madonna of the Sweet Kiss) ikon gone missing from a bijouterie window. This was located, wrapped in gold-embossed tissue paper and pinned with a spray of flowers. "Only for you, my lady! She is guarantee!" said the shopkeeper. But whether he meant her provenance or her protection I never knew.

On the quay trouble had erupted. *C'est Si Bon* was towed into harbour trawling her anchor. Skippers voiced protest, for she could have us all loose. "Watch out for that anchor!" called one. Back came the tense voice of an American woman, its control fragmenting, "Shut…your…mouth! *WE DON'T CARE!*" Shocked silence fell. It seemed *C'est Si Bon* had left Mykonos in a lull only to meet the full force of the meltemi. First her sails were blown out. Then her engine broke its prop-shaft. It was, allegedly, only prevented from leaping out of its housing by being sat upon bodily by the four-man crew. We never saw such blanched faces.

When we made enquiries about visiting Mykonos and Delos the clerk in the Tourist Office, mistakenly believing we meant to set sail in our own boat, gripped the counter declaring, "Certain disaster! Catastrophe! Whatever the forecasters say, the meltemi strengthens!" While Bob waited his turn at the barber's we watched the hairdresser practise his art on a curly-headed Greek. His assistant giggled, for an off-the-hook telephone emitted a stream of instructions from the Greek's wife, monitoring her husband's hairstyle in absentia.

The aerial views of Tinos from the bus to the village of Kalloni showed a landscape as rounded as risen dough, the cleavages in the hills delineated by lines of oleanders that crayonned the stream beds pink. The ubiquitous chapels once built by every prosperous Tiniot family speckled the hills like stray sheep. Clumsily plastered and decorated with crosses and wobbly pepper-pot towers, they presented a chunky, plaything charm. Omnipresent among them were the Venetian pigeon houses for which Tinos is famed. Busily patterned, some as high as twenty feet, these miniature limestone fortresses stood solitary or in groups, as if the gods had engaged in a game of chess using castles as pieces. With holes cut in the whimsical shapes of wheels, stars and diamonds, each pigeon house sported four corner turrets from which sprouted two or three triangular slates (decoy wings to attract birds) stuck upright like ice-cream wafers. On the hills above Kalloni's flower-throttled streets wild lupins and violet-flowered Salvia Triloba flourished. Beside them sparkled rills of Tiniot water channelled for irrigation – but denied us yachtsmen. Cupping our hands, we gulped thirstily.

Leo, *Rachel Jane's* skipper, asked me to settle an argument he was having with his guests. He was insisting he had met a pelican in the supermarket. Refraining from pointing out that, rather than browsing the aisles, the smelly old bird was patrolling the pavement outside, I confirmed I too had met the pelican. The islanders were possessive about their mascots, law suits not unknown. It was whispered that in order to uphold their reputation of living forever, certain pelicans were miraculously reborn when the sad moment came. Later Leo demonstrated his newest acquisition, a hand-held, battery-operated Magellan GPS obtained via his son serving in the Gulf. It was the first global positioning gadget any of us had seen and we were most impressed!

If this was the future it could save a lot of trouble.

Delos

Faced with more unpredictable weather, we took the first ferry to leave for Delos. At the focus of Aegean trading routes, the island was destined to become the religious centre of the pagan world. Here Leto gave birth to Apollo of whom the poet Shelley wrote,

> "I am the eye with which the Universe
> Beholds itself and knows itself Divine".

Assailed by Apollonian light, one could understand why this exposed land claimed the birth of the Sun God. Like Athos, Delos underwent "purification"; it decreed in 543 BC that the island should be defiled by neither birth nor death. These days a different sort of purification had been imposed to counter pollution, vandalism and theft. A curfew fell mid-afternoon, by which time all yachts must clear.

Reddish-brown and low-slung, set in a painted sea, the spring flowers superseded by poppy, statice and spurge, Delos smelt of scorched herbs. The periphery of the eye caught the shimmy of lizard and the spring of hare. Looking across the Sacred Lake (a drained mosquito breeding-ground) at the palm tree planted in Apollo's memory, we turned to face the lean and large-pawed Mycenaean lions perched on their haunches amid the sere grasses of the Terrace of the Lions. Staring east towards Apollo of the Dawn, as they had done for 3,000 years, five lions remained out of a possible fourteen. I crawled along a ditch to frame an archaic beast with yellow spurge growing beside him, angling my camera so that a stone canon ball lay at his feet to play with when the crowd was gone. Around us, earnest groups of French, eyes down, ears trained to officious guides, scribbled in note books.

We made an ankle-twisting approach through thistle and thorn bush to Mount Cynthus where Neolithic man established sun worship in a creepy cave. The light of the Sun God, first flourishing in the days when the Minoans held sea power and the threat of piracy did not exist, was long-since dimmed. By the advent of Christ, the Light of the World (who inherited his halo from Apollo's sun-spokes), its power was on the wane. But Delos was proof of long periods of peace and prosperity. Art thrives on happiness, which encourages the creation of such touchingly beautiful things that their immediacy reaches out, stretching time to breaking point. Water trapped in Cynthus's limestone layer enabled the peristyle houses on the slopes to be built with fountain courts. Dust was quickly dispelled from mosaic flooring with a sprinkle of water, bringing birds and panthers, flower vases, a sea-wet beribboned trident and entwined dolphins to life.

Back on Tinos, yachtsmen were dismayed to find the price of diesel forty per cent higher than on the other islands. But it was the arrival of the superb 120 ft sailing yacht of William Simon, Treasury Secretary to President Nixon, that really roused their ire. Fists were shaken as she was hosed down with copious draughts of the drinking water denied the rest of us! A military-style protest from Leo to the Harbour Master resulted in a special dispensation to *Rachel Jane* and *Cappelle* to replenish their tanks.

Mykonos

Cappelle was the first yacht to leave for Mykonos after the meltemi. The hush of afternoon was our signal to explore its cluster of blunt, contour-hugging alleys evolved from passages between rocks. A pelican waddled past and, in appreciation of the removal of a plastic beer-can ring from around its muzzle, a dog appointed itself our escort. Among frost-white cottages squatting like snowmen, every yard or so a plump chapel weighed down with flowers and Prussian-blue shadows, we were alone in the ancient wynds, as frame after frame of impossible prettiness, so age-old as to be unselfconscious, confronted us. In the prismatic light, I felt myself sucked into the vortex of passage-ways like a nautilus into its shell. Expelled into the open at last we found ourselves in Little Venice beside a terrace of houses with their feet in the sea.

The ridge beyond supported Mykonos's trademark windmills. The sails of the corn-grinding windmills of Greece are triangles of canvas attached between eight or ten thin wooden struts reefed according to wind strength. Which came first, sails for boats or for windmills? On moving on to Ornos Bay on the south coast of the island we were rewarded with a back-copy of the *Observer* for boat-sitting a British yacht. Here we awaited *Rachel Jane,* for Leo was throwing a party to celebrate the inauguration of his new custom-built barbecue designed to slot onto the lee of her cap rail. That smoke enveloped everyone "contrary to guarantee", annoyed Leo, but added to the fun!

Paros

With a forecast of W/NW variable F 4/5, we set sail for Paros where Vassili, Paroikia's harbour-master, operated a nice little earner supplying water from the well in his back-yard. Suddenly a figure emerged from our Lavrion past, Aussie Jack, more wizened and sparrow-like than ever, his eyes wet pebbles in a crackle-ware face, his taste for blonde goddesses willing to dive for his false teeth undimmed. But chain-smoking Jack no longer smoked and the tube in his hand was non-alcoholic. A wreck we had failed to recognise was his motor-cruiser *Shampee*. Left to winter in Paroikia when Jack was operated on for pancreatitis, hurricane-force winds had ripped the roof off her deck-house, after which human hands systematically stripped her of everything useful from radio direction finder to binnacle. Nevertheless, Jack was doing his best to act his old cheerful self. Bringing fresh croissants for breakfast, he stayed all day.

When we passed an incense-perfumed alley on our way out to dinner that night Jack pointed out *Το Τσαγιερό* ("The Teapot"), a but and ben with crooked stair. In there, he told us, lived a Scots girl who sold the best curry in the islands. (Jack should know, for his cooking repertoire, I recalled, began and ended with chicken curry.) If I mentioned his name, he said, I would be sure of a discount. Janet, a fresh-complexioned white witch with a bush of red hair, reigned inside her mysterious hovel dispensing curries and concocting her own blends of cooking herbs with oregano from Paros, thyme from Larissa, basil from Naxos and θρούμπα, a mixture of herbs and lemon zest used in curing the olive. On purchasing curry and rocks of jasmine incense, I noted that among her speciality teas was a guaranteed remedy for "Headache, Sickness and *Madness*".

At dawn boats piled in. A bareboat charter with blown sails wedged itself athwart our stern. In a series of short spurts, dodging the aproning waves I made my way to the harbour-side museum to view the Parian chronicle, a marble slab recording Greek history from pre-Homeric times. Museum security was minimal and, as it was a Sunday, there was no custodian. (The following winter a major robbery took place here.) In a street adorned with wall fountains, where to raise the eyes brought a vision of a blue-domed chapel framed in bougainvillaea, a notice pinned to a door down basement steps acted like a magnet. In careful capitals the English version read *"I GIVE LOVELY BABIES PUSSYCAT MIAOWING GREEK"*. Before we left Paros, I was glad to see the four kittens on offer reduced to one.

Ios

Paroikia operated as a ferry junction for back-packers. Its nights vibrated to a disco beat, its beaches bristled with needles. After Wacky had come home one night soiled and frightened, we pulled out next day just as the Cycladic dawn was breaking The sea was a silver negative, the air warm and windless. At Jack's instigation, we planned to take the "Fourteen-foot Passage" to Ios. Since Commander Graves of the Admiralty Chart's day, the Anti-Paros Channel had silted considerably and was not to be attempted by yachts of deep draught. In Jack's opinion, *Cappelle* would get away with it with an eye on the depth-sounder (though he advised not looking over the side in case it brought on heart attacks!). Sailing between the Vouves (Vulva) and the Peponas (Melon), to port the low-lying Bad Rocks, we saw ahead our landmark for the Anti-Paros Channel, the dawn-suffused chapel of Agios

Spiridhonos at the summit of an off-shore rock. (The French frigate *Superbe* was wrecked here in 1832 with the loss of all hands.)

Turning inside the Mavros Tourlos, the Black Mounds, we entered the channel. Opposite a stalactite cave visited by Lord Byron, islets sprinkled the fairway, but our progress was charmed. After correctly lining up with the light on Salango Island (a Summer Isle named from the cry of the herdsmen) we inched our way past the Remmatias (Islands of the Rapids), the depth sounder registering less than ten feet. By midday, in sight of Dhiakoft (Twin Blades) islet, landmark for Ios, we had completed the twenty-six-mile passage.

Wacky, shut in the forepeak throughout the Fourteen-Foot Passage, was off like a bullet, the Island of the Goddess Io with apron quay and raised flower beds, his cup of tea. ("Good cat country," wrote Bob in the log.) Scandinavian hippies with a baby and dog bade us welcome, the girl leaving off wringing rags in a bucket on the rotting deck of the makeshift house-boat they called home. A voice called, "Almost a year ago today!" On point of departure was *Ros Arcan*, last encountered in faraway Lemnos, cat Muffin still a member of crew.

Ios, taken over by the back-packing fraternity, publicised itself as the "Party-Island-Where-Anything-Goes". A handout exhorted us to, "Go wild, keep high, hang on the bar and get stoned!" or, should a quieter life be desired, play video games at "Sweet Irish Dream". The daytimes were quiet, but the nocturnal revelry continued until householders got up at dawn to freshen lime-wash. Up a mule track was the χώρα, a neat bowl of piazzas and houses, a unifying church at its centre. White chapels, dotted at random like sugar lumps rolled downhill from a split sugar bag, sweetened the slopes beyond the Red Lion, the Fun Pub and the Flames Bar. Posters caught the eye, "Have an Orgasm tonight – Try Tracey's Cocktail" or "Watch the sunset to Pink Floyd!" A banner announced "Mighty Slammer from Midnight til Early", while a gut-buster breakfast was advertised as "Bacon and Eggs, Coffee, Toast, Free Sex – Ask for Paul". If "mental" was the in-word in Petra, "shit" took precedence in Ios. Tee-shirts and cushion covers celebrated it. A photographer's studio displayed prints of a juvenile yobbo, fingers up his nose in various rude gestures. "Same shit, different day. Get yourself a shit pic," said the caption. Hesitating to visit a snack bar for fear of shitburgers, we went into a bakehouse, where the startled baker ventured to enquire what such as us were doing on the island. When we told him we had a sailing boat, he nodded understanding, for Ios was the traditional safe harbour for crews wishing to visit Santorini.

We set the alarm clock for 03.00 hrs, Wacky chasing after us as we left to catch the night ferry from Athens. Running back, I popped him down the hatch. The hard day's night was drawing to a close. Back-packers headed straight from bars to ferry. A lad retched over a wall. *Rothante* came in fast sending a stern wave swirling down the ramp to inundate intending passengers in no fit state to nip out of the way. (I never saw what happened to the couple stretched out on the pavement in mutual embrace.) On the ship service was refused to a skin-head who chucked his filthy gear on velvet upholstery before thumping the bar. With φλιτζανάκια, little cups of coffee, we sat in the lounge next to a Greek family on a seasonal exodus that had all the drama of moving house. Grandpa gripped his canary's cage as if for security.

Santorini

Delos and Santorini formed the point-counterpoint of the pagan world; its birth in light, and its destruction in fire and darkness. Plato's Atlantis, once Kalliste ("The Most Beautiful"), was a supervolcano, the island of Thira, shaped like a fingernail clipping, part of the rim of its crater. Oia, and the smaller Thirassia opposite, formed other sections of its breached circumference. Palaia and Nea (Old and New) Kammeni, the Burnt Islands, smoking plugs at the centre of the caldera, presented a reminder that Santorini sits on a thermal plume, an upswelling of molten magma from the centre of the earth.

The human mind cannot grasp the scale of the explosion that sent skywards so much solid material to hollow out the depths of the lagoon, though a physical sensation of the nano-second before the paroxysmal eruption of 1470 BC clutched at the gut. Since the cataclysmic event was at least as powerful as that of Krakatoa, it is reasonable to assume it effectively destroyed life on Crete sixty miles away. If further evidence is needed, the advanced civilisations then existing on Kalliste and Crete both ended around that date. By the time "the bull from the sea", the tsunami, travelling at 100 miles an hour, reached Crete, its height must have measured forty metres, enough to swamp the coast of an island whose exposed buildings were already flattened by blast. Pyroclastic fall-out followed.

The name Santorini was born of the customary usage of the prominent church of Saint Irene as landmark. To reach the island was an adventure, but to arrive within its great caldera at dawn was doubly so. Apprehension tickled the soles of the feet. One could not but be aware that the liquid mantle of the sea cloaked a fiery gateway. Nature had allowed no plant growth nor softening of the cliff edge to survive the impact of the geological calamity. In peachy auroral light the thousand-foot cliffs, their multi-coloured strata as clear as the marbling on end-papers, seemed sundered only yesterday. One sensed the next seismic event could be imminent.

Six o'clock in the morning was the perfect hour to explore. The fatal finger of disaster had pointed arbitrarily. A derelict Italianate mansion, victim of the 1956 earthquake, faltered on the brink of an acrid-smelling precipice, while its neighbour, with piazetta and hanging gardens, remained in a state of grace. A placard swung from a rusting balcony, «*MHN ANEBAINETE!*» ("DO NOT CLIMB!"), the scene a reminder that the ice-blue basilica on the further headland was an ephemeron. The evanescence of this world of contrast put a keen edge on its beauty. In the centre of the silver-lidded caldera the curséd heaps of the Kammenis told of the ineffably powerful monster that lurked beneath.

From our bird's eye view of the descending terraces of asbestos-white houses it was clear that no property on this crowded escarpment enjoyed the luxury of self-containment. Ladder-like steps and tunnelled walkways interlaced. No one bothered us. A man in a bathrobe drinking coffee on his patio nodded us on as we crossed it. We paid a premium for the view from a café balcony and left because of the whirling breeze and a pop rendering of the "British Grenadiers" put on for our benefit.

Finding nothing in the square except tourist shops selling the regulation oxidised Priapus (made in Taiwan) with penile corkscrew, we came to rest on the steps of the Ghizis Mansion, one of the rare old family houses to survive.

At ten o'clock, the curator, opening the door with a clumsy iron key, welcomed us in. An *Illustrated London News* of 1873 showed drawings of the surfacing of Nea Kammeni, while the toppling belfries of the 1956 earthquake were recorded in the stark black and white of press photography. A translation into modern Greek of the legal documents framed on the walls was pressed upon us. The stories were simple. In 1636 a νεαρός, a "young man" on holiday with the Ghizi family, had sickened and died of natural causes. Much was made in his death certificate of the last rites. The dowry documents of The Lady Katerina affirmed the monies settled on her in 1732 by virtue of her marriage, and the names of the nuns at the monastery were listed.

When we encountered Geoffrey and Annette they were complaining of rip-offs. With only ten minutes to descend the 900 ft of slippery cobbles (conveniently padded with dung-caked straw) to catch the boat to the Burnt Islands, we kept running, though muleteers shouted after us. It was touch and go, the boat about to cast off when we jumped aboard to find the advertised fare increased by 500 drachmas "for inflation". No breeze stirred the water. But the harbour was exposed in the direction of Crete. If a yacht must sail into the thousand-foot depths of the caldera, it was accepted practice to tie bows-to with a stern line to a mooring buoy, a tatting-reel of warps. The pilot described Port Thira as "fantastic chaos" when a yacht wished to leave. This time we did believe the author.

The fascination of the approach to Nea Kammeni, a contorted heap of spiked and glittering scoriae, impossible to moor to or clamber over, cast aside regret. In an inlet where the sea turned a poisonous lime green and the submerged weeds were the colour of red lead, two brightly painted fishing boats, not to be outdone in garishness, were tied to a short quay. Bravado might have found us mooring here, but for Nea Kammeni's infestation with a very large and very bold breed of rat that would not hesitate to board even in broad daylight.

A hotel proprietor once recorded a description of an imminent eruption. According to him, for two or three days before the event the waters around the Kammenis became curiously discoloured in patches of sulphurous yellow, black, white and crimson which, as the eruption developed, brightened as they altered and swirled in kaleidoscope patterns. On the eve of the 1886 event that extended Nea Kammeni threefold, the sea round the islets turned milk white. This pallor, morphing to lurid green and violet, heralded the eruption.

Granted one and a half hours to cross the island, we scrunched along a cinder track through anaemic grasses and clumps of yellow daisies. Skirting the rim of small craters, each a reeking devil's punch bowl, we paused to empty our shoes of ash. The igneous rocks spray-gunned by a spaced-out junkie with slogans in praise of his drug, were as smooth and glossy as melted chocolate. Such a setting demanded black wind-flowers. It was a landscape to breed strange tales. Santorini's inhabitants report vaporous apparitions of vampires haunting the countryside at night. Though the sun doused their brightness, flames flickered in the shadows, while wisps of the methyl-tainted smoke curling from crevices caught at our throats. On Nea Kammeni's far side, where we felt the heat of the ground through the soles of our shoes, we looked beyond a narrow channel to Palaia Kammeni. Here a seemingly new-minted swathe of pitchy lava was arrested in 197 BC as it bubbled.

Back on the quay, I splashed my cinder-caked feet in the creek's abnormally warm water. At the mouth of the cove the sea changed colour, darkening to emerald. Far away across the caldera, Thira's lace edging of white houses trimmed the thousand-foot cliffs streaked with pale cascades of fall-out.

An Athenian who leased café premises ribbed us for being wealthy yachtsmen, but sat with us as we awaited the bus that was to make its air-brake-pumping descent to the main harbour, explaining how much in rent and tax a summer season in Santorini cost him. Orchestrated by a battery of camera clicking, our sight of the celebrated sunset off Oia was from the deck of the ferry. Three school-leavers were developing cold feet about stopping off at the Party Island. A youth offered advice: "Enjoy yourselves! Let it all hang out!" He did, however, add that it would be best for the girls not to linger in the streets after the bars closed.

Back in Ios, we found the doors of the OTE blocked by teenage back-packers sitting cross-legged on the floor awaiting collect calls to request, they said, "more money from home". Provisioning turned into a riot at the greengrocer's when Bob, asked how many children he had, muddled his Greek numerals to name such an astronomical figure he was clapped on the back until he had a coughing fit, and a γιαγιά sat down backwards in a box of tomatoes.

When we met Annette again, the stars in her eyes were reflections of the outrigger island of Amorgos. Her view corroborated what a native of Santorini told me – if we wanted to visit an island that was "beautiful, original and unspoilt", we must backtrack halfway to Turkey to the most easterly of the Cyclades.

At 03.30 hrs Wacky catapulted into the cabin, his latest offering a giant moth to which I administered the coup de grâce with the fish slice. By 05.30 hrs *Cappelle* yawed in the decayed swell of a southerly. Rounding the coast I scanned a legendary site of Homer's burial. (The, wrongly supposed, washing up there of Homer's body was once Ios's chief claim to fame.) Here we changed course to 084 degrees, north of east, on a dead run for Amorgos.

Twenty-one

Amorgos to the Mani

Amorgos

At 14.40 hrs we recovered the log on approach to the magnificent bay of Port Katapola. At 15.00 hrs, after circling twice, we drifted bows-to onto the quay. It was time to combine lunch and tea. Afterwards I slept, awaking to find Wacky taking photo calls. Enticed by the prospect of economic wealth, Amorgos girded itself for tourism. A brochure advertised accommodation "with all the synchronous expectations".

The Monastery of Khozoviotissa on its wild eastern coast was said to hang on a thousand-foot sea cliff like a wind-hovering bird. Given an official seal in 1088, its legend was the familiar one of two halves of an ikon floating in from the sea as a sign of where the Panagia wished her house built. She took good care of Khozoviotissa's economy, for, during three hundred years of Turkish occupation, it prospered as a pirates' lair. Taking advantage of their position at the centre of trade routes, wrecker monks placed strategic lights to lure passing vessels onto the rocks. By this means the islanders grew rich enough to buy their religious liberty from their overlords and to deck their women in the celebrated "island jewellery", yellow gold, some of which survives to this day in the Benaki Museum in Athens.

Khozoviotissa's floorboards and tie-beams were of the original juniper, while its door arches displayed Venetian influence in the use of limestone from Milos. However, natural causes, looting and pillage, indifference, gross ignorance, wear and tear, philistine alteration and overpainting destroyed much historical evidence. When an iron spike in an inaccessible part of the cliff fell out in 1952, it was taken as a bad omen, and in that year the monastery was dispossessed of its estates. This meant that a self-supporting religious house, equipped with wine presses for the making of wine from its own vineyards, and oil from its own olives; with a trough carved from a single tree trunk for the kneading of dough prepared from its own corn; and with beehive ovens fired by brushwood carried home on the backs of its own fishermen monks, could no longer call upon its produce to fill its cellars, storerooms and granary. In other words, Khozoviotissa was reduced to a cipher. However, it is claimed the Panagia still protects her property, for the monastery remained undamaged during the earthquake of 1956, whose epicentre lay under the nearby sea-bed.

Although, in days past, Khozoviotissa was said to be worth the four-hour hike from Port Katapola, the route was now served by a village bus, which deposited us near the edge of a thrift-covered cliff to follow a goat track. It was not an approach to appeal to those suffering from vertigo. A tethered donkey moved into our path. But my pockets contained no titbits. Around a headland came the first sign of habitation in a high boundary wall. With strict attention to convention (so I believed), the white veiling similar to that worn by Turkish women that covered the chins and foreheads of Amorghian women persuading me loose trousers were in order, I had dressed in full-length culottes so wide they were almost a divided skirt. But here a notice gave monastery regulations. Its list of embargoes included "women in trousers". Then I knew I should have paid heed to the old saying that "in a skirt the Panagia protects you". According to ancient tradition, trousers brand a woman "loose-living" and "low-class". It was too late now.

The path curved upwards. Khozoviotissa, still in hiding, lay in wait. Then there in front of us, rightly described as "gleaming like a dragon's egg", shimmered its white profile suspended between heaven and earth in grim cliffs. Like an outgrowth from the dark rock, the buttressed elevation reared unadorned. The monastery presented itself as a Byzantine painting in a cliff frame. A walled allée ran through terraced herb gardens to a narrow side entrance. Bent double, we negotiated a high threshold at the top of a steep flight of steps to enter a vestibule furnished with a lidded well. At a higher level ahead, at the top of another flight of steps, was the original monastery entrance, a rock fissure edged with limewash once connected to the ground by rope ladder in the days when divines occupied cavities in the cliff.

Here a pair of black-robed, tall-hatted monks, awaited us, hands clasped. Though the Abbot's eyes shone warmly in a wise and humorous face, his side-kick, a rubicund, pious young man in the role of beadle, regarded me dubiously as an advancing Jezebel. I had been practising the Madame Butterfly shuffle, pressing my knees together, but this was impossible when mounting treads. Gravely the beadle barred my entrance and shook his head. At my extreme disappointment he and the Abbot then exchanged pertinent glances, the latter indicating that the hussie might attempt to demonstrate her modesty by ascending a few further steps under close scrutiny. I rose as chastely as I was able. After a pause long enough to make me rue my wicked ways, the Abbot solemnly gestured his permission for me to accompany Bob to the glare of the bell tower.

In the chapel he sat between us, captivated to hear about the two of us and a Greek cat on a small boat we planned to sail home to England. Repeating «Πω, Πω, Πω,» he raised his hands in holy amazement. Then he busied himself to show us the Deesis of Gennedios, a painting that commemorated a storm at sea on 1st November 1619. While the upper third depicted the Virgin with the Christ Child flanked by saints, the lower two-thirds were a lively representation of a close-hauled ship in difficulties. Stylised Byzantine waves foamed round her, her foresail ballooned and she was about to be swamped. The helmsman and crew fought to hold her while, in the middle of the boat (the steadiest spot), a green-faced Papa, lifting his hands in earnest prayer, beseeched Heaven for deliverance.

From the recognisable crags of Kinaros and Levitha it was evident that the tempest had taken place north east of Amorgos. Though November was late in the year to be at sea, there was an oral tradition of the reciprocal appointments of Abbots between the monasteries of Khozoviotissa and St John Theologian on Patmos. The voyage would have been occasioned by preparations for the Panagia's Festival on 21st November. At any rate it could be no coincidence that, after 1619, close links between the two monasteries were discontinued. At Khozoviotissa the festival, however, is still celebrated, the islanders bringing food and wine on which to feast at the ancient refectory table.

In the room below the beagle offered us λουκουμία (Turkish Delight) with tiny cups of lemon liqueur, a local speciality, and glasses of spring water to go with it. I endeavoured to bring a twitch to his lips that was almost a smile when I purchased a book, refusing the change. Afterwards, we bought loaves, stamped with the double-headed eagle hot from the ecclesiastical ovens, to eat for lunch.

Next day our intention was to leave at an early hour, but our departure was delayed when the Ship's Cat went missing. It was too much to think he had followed Amorghian precedent and stowed away on a fishing boat (as had a cat from a French yacht). I thought I remembered catching the sounds of nocturnal caterwauling, but we called and called to no avail until, round the corner from the direction of the bramble marshes trotted Wacky, late for a date, giving anxious voice. With scratches on his nose as souvenirs of a night of Amorghian adventure, he was curled up fast asleep by the time we raised anchor.

Skhinoussa

When the gravity swell died we sailed on a beam reach in the lee of the Agrilios Islets. Here Theseus had abandoned Ariadne, who lived among the stars in her red-gold bridal coronet as the Corona Borealis. We intended spending the night at anchor at Mirsini on the island of Skhinoussa eighteen miles west. But this was an area for which we had no charts. Moreover, it was difficult to make out where Skhinoussa ended and Iraklia began. Over the "never silent sands" of Naxos cumulus clouds were building and thunder threatened. But Dionysus's dancing satyrs soon encouraged the West Wind, which enabled us to pin-point land-locked Mirsini by means of its insignificant light structure, our concentration on the location leading us to make the foolish error of forgetting to take in the Walker Log whose cord snapped and tangled round the propeller.

Vacating an anchorage next morning was speedy work compared with leaving harbour. Within half an hour we had raised anchor, washed the deck, streamed the log with its spare cord, hauled up the mainsail and taken a bearing on Iraklia light. Wacky was none too thrilled to be back on dog meat, but I was saving the last of the cat food for a treat.

The light that shone that day was truly Cycladic. The north face of Sikinos seemed too precipitous to support its frosting of chapels. Its crest, marked by ruined windmills, looked close enough to touch, its apparent proximity as shocking as is the sudden confrontation with distant detail viewed through a telescope. I could pick out individual bushes in the ground cover with the naked eye. With every impression heightened, we felt singularly aware, as if the light of Apollo had quickened the senses.

Pholegandros

In the five-mile channel between Sikinos and Pholegandros lay a string of islets. Until we altered our angle of approach, we had trouble identifying the arthritic arm of the reef that formed a natural mole to Port Karavostasi (Port Shipwreck). It was wise to give it a good offing, for it extended far out under water. Ernle Bradford, defeated by the heavy scend setting into Shipwreck Bay, had failed in both his attempts at entry, but for *Cappelle* Pholegandros assumed the status of Mary Rose's "Island-That-Wants-To-Be-Visited"— though I hoped it would not swallow me up! Extreme care had to be exercised around the Dhio Adelfia (The Two Brothers), round-headed rocks offset to resemble a conversation-piece. Between them and the northern reef was a patch of shallows, while the curl of the southern reef was buttressed with below-surface rocks. But once past these hazards we were free to sail into Port Karavostasi's Bristol-blue depths. A yachtswoman regarded the spirited little Wacky with envy.

"Don't you worry about him?" she asked.

"Yes, all the time!" was the answer.

But he had his own life to lead and it was unfair to restrict it.

Though the Phoenicians gave the island the name Phelekgundam, meaning "dry and rocky place", its χώρα was a green oasis, its houses interspersed with chapels before which women crossed themselves, even doing so, I noticed, when passing by in the village bus. As we stood on the rim of the acropolis beside the citadel whose walls encircled a grid-pattern mediaeval housing estate, our breath was forced back by the meltemi, known here as the Καμπάνατος ("The Scold"). At the foot of the 750 ft cliff a seething cauldron of water stretched north as far as the eye could see. With NW F6 increasing, seas rough, it looked as if the Καμπάνατος was setting in.

A few days later, with NNW F6 forecast for the South Eastern Aegean, for the South Western area it was predicted to moderate to F5. Pholegandros lay at mid-point. We gambled therefore on sailing west into quieter conditions. It was difficult to back *Cappelle* off the quay. But, circling within harbour, we made all secure and raised sail. The confused seas around Cape Katergo gave Bob problems holding course but after an hour of nervous concentration he was able to settle the ship. Then, under full main and genoa, we made passage west at 4.5 kts on a beam reach while the Ship's Cat gobbled a fricassee of chicken chopped with sardines. At 18.30 hrs the highest mountain on Milos (an island described by Lawrence Durrell as "damnably dull", Venus de Milo notwithstanding) reared up against a ginger-pink sunset.

At 20.00 hrs we closed bun-shaped Paximadhi Islet, only slightly more dense than the heavens, in order to steer clear of the Ananes (The Pineapple Islets) to the south whose Group Flashing Light was not working. The night soaked up the sky like blotting paper. For a moment I thought the Milky Way, light as mousseline, had fallen into the Mirtoan Sea. Then, looking up, I saw it was merely xeroxing itself on the water in phosphorescent tinsel flare. We took two-hour watches. "Remembering Gaidharos!" I fastened my safety harness and wound the infuriated tomato to ping at regular intervals to keep me awake.

Cape Malea

I was off watch from 04.00 to 06.00 hrs, but Bob woke me to tell me we were on course after sailing 72.4 nm. "Come up and look!" he exclaimed excitedly. Five miles ahead in the warm early light reared the Formidatum Caput Maleum – Cape Malea in all its glory! Had I been Odysseus, I could not have been more awestruck. Here the Peloponnesus ended in a gargantuan dinosaur's foot, elephant grey, steep-to and six miles wide. At 06.20 a.m. a jazz-age orange sun sprang onto the crinkly horizon, bouncing as it pulsated like a yo-yo on a string. Ships were trooping down the coast towards the important shipping lane between the island of Kithera and the Peloponnese. Keeping a sharp look-out, for there was no separation zone, we set course beneath the cape, black squalls off the heights ruffling the water.

With no other yacht in sight, let alone a small wooden one, we sped on under full sail on a high of elation, *Cappelle*, slotted into the groove, answered to the finger touch. I longed to be in two places at once, both at the helm and high in the eyrie above where an anchorite once mortified his flesh, to bear witness to her progress. Before we entered the Malea Channel Bob made a half-hearted remark concerning the prudence of getting a reef in. But, spirits soaring, we had no truck with timidity. Then, after we passed Cape Zovolo, gusts of F 6/7 hit us. ("Bend, if you can, to the dark sea…") This was marginal. "Too much sail!" yelled the Captain. But there was nothing to be done about it now. In sight of Elaphonisos (Deer Island) Nemesis waited to punish vainglory with the full force of a blistering north-easterly out of Vatika Bay.

Grim-faced, Bob fought the helm in an experience that paralleled that of Odysseus: "I might have made it safely home but, as I came round Malea, the current took me out to sea, and from the north a fresh gale drove me on past Kithera." If I had not yet learnt the value of a stout ship with four tons of ballast, I knew it then. "We've GOT to get a reef in!" Bob hollered. "Take the helm, put her into wind and HOLD her there!" Painfully slowly, battered by the elements, I endeavoured to keep my streaming eyes on the tell-tales while screwing

Cappelle round to face the Donkey's Jaws (the old name for Deer Island) as Bob winched in the genoa and recovered the log. Then, effort peaking, I clasped the helm with my left arm while hanging onto the mainsheet with my right, striving to keep the sheet steady as the sail was lowered so as not to swipe him off the coachroof where he lay supine tying reefing points. The strain gave me ague and it was at this point that the Ship's Cat emerged to see what the palaver was about. As he crouched to spring onto the streaming side deck, I momentarily let go the wheel to hook him with my toe and throw him up to clamp under my arm. The next action was to fling him into the cabin with such a murderous yell he would not dare show his whiskers again.

After an eternity the sails ceased to flap and the tumult and the shouting died. If the gods were kind, *Cappelle* would make it into the Gulf of Lakonika. Shaking like a jelly, I was left with the memory of that exquisite distillation of living, that sexy moment on the edge. Perhaps a sailing boat's greatest gift is that it restores to modern life the precariousness of the past, providing the zest that gives buoyancy to meaning, while validating the tension between adversity and joy. Danger is a life enhancer and there is a secret joy in peril. Now whole populations are brought up with ease and security as their goal. In seeking to enlarge our lives, we had to accept we had endowed it with a special dimension that meant it might not always be under our control.

With a reading of 96.3 nautical miles on the clock, we reset the log and commiserated with the Ship's Cat, who was philosophical over his callous treatment. There was a moment to look back at that breathtaking gateway where the Parnon rolled down to the Formidatum Caput. What a dramatic way to exit the Aegean World! The isolation of the islands, seen from a distance like puffs of smoke on dark water or solidifications of heat, had forced them to develop as cultural microcosms. In the Aegean, the past remains so tangible and so rich that no one who enters is set apart in time. There is an urge to record oneself in the archipelago's annals of coloured fragments – CAPPELLE WAS HERE!

Outside the Malea Gate, both climate and atmosphere underwent a sea-change. The outlines were no longer adamantine and the light no longer drove the viewer "half blind with violet frenzy". The subdued seas turned ashen, the curdled clouds almost English. I knew now why sailors coined the phrase, "Round Malea, forget your native land!" Beyond the gateway was another country. I also understood sailors' respect for Malea. Of the six generalised depression tracks that converge over Greece, three congregate here, with the consequent possibility of a rapid deterioration in the weather.

Gulf of Lakonika

With 101 miles on the log, one reef in the main and half a genoa, we sailed west at 270 degrees across the unpredictable Gulf of Lakonika, which measures some twenty-five miles across at its southern end and lies between the heavily indented arms of Greece's most redoubtable mountain ranges. To the west the 8,000 ft palisade of the Taigetos was fretted against the skyline of the Mani, while to the east lay the inhospitable Parnons. At this point we were uncertain as to our best landfall. Diesel might present a problem, for since leaving Paros there had been nowhere to refuel. It seemed best, therefore, to take advantage of the favourable winds and cross the Gulf to Porto Kaio on the opposite shore, a pirate redoubt affording good shelter. Its disadvantage was that it offered no supplies, no water and no fuel. At the head of the Gulf, on the other hand, some twenty miles inland, lay the town of Gytheion with full facilities. But to reach it we must beat to windward for four hours. Moreover, Gytheion, little visited by yachts, could be uncomfortable, if not untenable, with the blow in its present direction. We decided, therefore, to continue west.

In less than an hour the wind abated to F 4/5 before, little more than half way across the Gulf, dying altogether. Encountering the seam where two seas meet and take a dislike to each another, *Cappelle* was chopped by white water from all sides. In this disagreeable environment we staggered about measuring diesel, finding enough left to motor, if necessary, for thirteen hours. Anything seemed better than being churned about in a washtub. Then, as if in answer to a prayer, in came a westerly to head us. Shaking out the reef as the wind backed south, we altered course to 334 degrees for Gytheion. The condition of the sea, described by Bob in the log as "appallingly confused", was our tribulation, for it was as hard and lumpy as a field of moguls. The swell created by the north-easterly still blowing from the Parnons slammed us, while rotating winds turned the water into a maelstrom.

Only when the variable breeze veered north east and steadied, before dropping to light airs, did we resort to engine power. At first the engine refused to fire. Then, when it did, we crashed and lurched as *Cappelle* heeled when water resistance fell away. Tired and disorientated, the daylight fading and the only point of reference the distant *chevaux de frise* of the Taigetos, we conserved battery power by restricting the use of the light over the chart table. Then the breeze backed once more, first west and then south west, increasing to F4, which was our cue to hoist full main and genoa and charge up and down troughs while endeavouring to study the Admiralty Chart by torchlight.

The intervening bays were too distant to distinguish. Without a Commander Graves's silhouette of the Taigetos, my best judgement was that the darker land masses had to be obtruding capes. By this means we identified Cape Kolokithia ("Vegetable Marrow") and, further north, Scoutari, beyond which the land fell back. A particularly dark projection must be Mavrovouni ("Black Mountain"). As usual, our eyes sought landmarks long before it was possible to see them. (I suspected Bob was beginning to doubt even the existence of Gytheion.) But then a tall octagonal lighthouse materialised from behind Mavrovouni – and we knew we had made it! After twenty-seven hours and 121.85 NM at an average speed of 4.6 kts (not bad in the circumstances) our lines were taken.

Gytheion

It was still not quite dark when we doubled the warps, had a meal and went to bed. Wacky, delighted to be well placed for shore leave, hopped off to be nice to children fishing. The prize he brought back was a gecko, which he lost. (I discovered it three days later, carpet-fluffed and minus its tail, but lively enough for release.) In the morning, refreshed and cheerful, we continued to be amazed at the difference a good night's sleep makes.

The butter-yellow houses along Gytheion waterfront formed an aquarelle of themselves in the harbour, Bob wrote in the log, "Town is non-touristy and a great relief." It boasted a park with trees and flowers, grass watered by sprinklers and an aviary of the small brown Maniot quail over which much historical blood has been shed. We were made welcome, prices were half those of the islands and the abundant sweet water was free.

A pair of fisherlads laid off from a caïque took root alongside *Cappelle*. Shaded by Maniot hats as wide as parasols, their rods balanced on supports, they competed over the size of the fish they pulled out. «*Ετσι είναι η ζωή! Δέν πειράζι*» ("And such is life! Never mind!") they commented equably when scattered, much to my annoyance, by a hubristic Britisher. On board *S/Y Arrogance*, as I sniffily dubbed her, was Oily Charles, his desiccated spouse and a hard-pressed young Cambridge factotum. They were waiting for the latest depression to clear before tackling Cape Malea. Molly told me they had sought shelter in Porto Kaio, but that the tales of mythical caves were rubbish. (I thought her one of those people who know how to make little of much, and still wanted to see for myself!) We lent Charles our hose and in return, grandly distributing largesse, he ripped pages from his Livre de Bord, marking anchorages in the South of France, endeavouring, I thought sourly, to compensate for flattening our dinghy on his way in. When we devoured poor man's *μουσακά* (mousaka) at a restaurant that night, Oily Charles (who, in Molly's temporary absence, oozed at me in such a practised way I was certain he was not safe in yachts) ordered rich man's lobster. *Arrogance* passed in the night. Then the Maniot fishermen took up stations again and normal life resumed.

"Moored" to the mainland by causeway, boat-shaped Kranai Island, where the runaways, Helen and Paris, spent their first night of love, provided a grandstand for the voluptuous sunsets of the High Taigetos. When the mountains soaked up rose-pompadour from the declining sun their limestone caps glittered pinkly. Poor Menelaus, King of Sparta

– not only was his wife, Helen, abducted, but his ship was dashed to pieces at Malea.

As I passed the restaurant of the previous night, my arm was taken. With «*Ορίστε παρακαλώ!*» ("Come! Please!") I was led to an outside table and served coffee by the owner and his son. The restaurant was empty and, as the men's eyes darted to the road. I realised that, in the nicest possible way, I had been kidnapped as a decoy for passing trade. When they ran to bag two car loads of Italians, seeing my function fulfilled, I slipped away. Bob devoted a day to the engine. The generator was welded, the starter motor serviced and the battery (pronounced "asleep" by the local garage) replaced with a heavy agricultural version. An ignition fault led to my initiation into the mysteries of hot-wiring to bypass the starter switch in case of emergency (a skill I prayed I would never be called upon to practise).

On a day off we took a trip to the fairy-tale Caves of Dirou, discovered in 1895 by a fisherman on the far west coast of the Mani. A Papa alighted from our melon-scented bus at Areopolis to sit at a café table and comb his white beard. From their seat here the Mavromichales (Black Michaels) once ruled over the inhabitants of the Mani, refugee descendants of the Spartans with a touch of Slav.

In the caves we found that strict rules applied – no filming, no bags, no noise and, above all, no breaking off of stalactites, the penalty for taking "even the smallest piece" being *"TWO YEARS IN PRISON!"* Here we stepped into the fragile ecology of the *Tales of Hoffman* to glide through this world of speleological fantasy. Rowed with muffled oars Charon propelled us wordlessly as if to the strains of a barcarole. Submerged in the limpid depths, varying from shallow to "unfathomable", giant waterlily lights rendered reality indistinguishable from reflection. We sculled through grottoes devoid of crustaceans and through echoing caverns whose cupolas hung with stalactites, glimpsing apses glistening with marble lace or side aisles as yet unexplored, their walls streaked with Taigetos red, green, blue and toxic yellow. Charon whispered names – a stalactite in frosty foam was "The Fox" in his winter coat. As we glided through banqueting halls floored with liquid obsidian, he indicated "The Dragon's Lair", "The Pink

Apartments" and "Satan's Palace". A galleried arcade revealed "The Shipwreck", a fearsome prehistoric roof-fall where marble spokes jutted from the surface of the water like the broken masts and spars of a foundered ship.

Back in Gytheion a German yachtswoman waylaid us to describe our Ship's Cat's pursuit of their Ship's Cat "Lady", which her owner found highly amusing. Young Lothario, taking a leaf out of Paris's book, it seemed, was keeping nightly vigil on *Excellente's* coach-roof warbling songs of passion. The Lady Helen in question, however, not only old enough to be his grandmother, but several times over, persisted in disdaining the attentions of so juvenile an admirer.

The Deep Mani

With no new depressions intervening, we exited the stone horns of Gytheion at 05.00 hrs into a millpond sea to explore the Deep Mani. Its mountainous hog's back, angular in form, stark in aridity and the colour of molten lead, rose inland near Sparta before plunging sixty miles through wild ravines to the infernal Kakovounia, the Bad Mountains, and the Mouth of the Underworld where Hercules, protected by his lion's pelt, descended into Hell to drag to the light of day the triple-headed wolf-dog Cerebus.

Cut off from civilisation by Mavrovouni, we were soon rewarded with dazzling visibility. After rounding the hook of a cape on which once stood a classic temple dedicated to "Violet-crowned Aphrodite", we encountered the first of the grim villages of Dark Age peel towers that backed onto screes formed by snowmelt and spring torrent. Doorless and windowless below the top floor, each family home was a squared off, flat-roofed, defence tower with gun slits. Together they resembled a colony of giant mushroom stalks. Though grouping meant safety in numbers from outside attack, a villager's traditional enemy was his neighbour. The trick was to build your tower house, by constant addition if necessary, higher than his, thus putting him at a disadvantage from your musket, cannon and hurled rocks.

A Maniot once said that when God finished the world, having nothing left but stones, he created the Mani. Feuding was explained in terms of a necessary cull, there being no room nor subsistence for more than a limited number of inhabitants. The smallest left-over crumb of παξιμάδια (twice-baked rusk), collected and wrapped in a kerchief, is still kissed in memory of the Last Supper, an act of frugality old enough to have taken on religious significance. Violent death resulting from a blood feud was the spice of life. Quarrels were picked on the slightest pretext, from the infringement of property or animal grazing rights to the entitlement to quail or the defiling of women. As late as the 1920s so much as a glance at a woman could sound a death knell.

In the Mani a woman's life was on a par with that of a donkey. Both were worth killing for, but, like a beast of burden, a woman was of insufficient status to warrant a funeral. Despite the fair sex being of so little account that the Queen Bee was accredited with masculinity, on occasion they gave as good as they got! It is recorded that an enraged bride, who had recently given birth and was in trouble with her in-laws over the non-payment of her προίκα (dowry), found the strength to hack off her father-in-law's head and kick it down the mountainside.

By midday the mountains reverberated in a brassy glare. After cruising the coast for eighteen miles, we recovered the log to enter steep-sided Porto Kaio. Contrary to expectations, the redoubt was not so much sheltered as exposed to the west wind, which whistled across the saddle from the opposite coast less than a mile away. Dark ripples splashed our faces as we inspected holding. Ashore, two ruined tower villages and a forsaken monastery menaced the hill-side. But, with her anchor dragging, we could not abandon *Cappelle* to explore. The land seemed full of the ghosts that stalk at midday, a road scar indicating not so much the ability to open up Porto Kaio as the means to flee from it.

With slaves in demand from Spain to the Caucasus and Egypt to India, Porto Kaio, the slave trade its mainspring, played the part of a fair-weather refuge for pirate ships. Maniots, acting as middlemen, raided the islands and sold captives to the Venetians, who, along with the Genoese, were the great slave merchants of the Levant. (A master stroke was to make off with your neighbour's wife and sell her into slavery. Such an act could keep a whole village dodging fusillades for months!)

As the redoubt lay within striking distance of the strategic sea-gate of Malea, Maniots were well placed to trade in loot. On the look out for laggards belonging to Turkish and Venetian convoys coming up from Crete, their ships would ambush and relieve them of their cargoes of lime (necessary in building tower houses), spices, incense, silks, precious metals, perfume and opium. Good company was kept, for reputable enterprises had a priest in tow to absolve the crew in advance for any misdemeanour its members might commit in the performance of their duty. In return the priest received his cut of the spoils to display alongside his votive offerings. Having raised his voice in prayer, he would gird his habit, grab his cutlass, whet its edge, spit on his hands and join in the fray. He had a further service to perform for, if, after a week, no ship of booty hove in sight, it was his mandate to intone a deckboard litany entreating the Almighty to deliver.

My sleep was shallow and, with Wacky in the curl of my knees, I remained aware of the whine of the wind, my rest disturbed by dreams of anguish. Although a critical consciousness told me the visions were nonsense, under the skin of the dream they were impossible to shake off. I had lost my purse and was distraught, though it contained little of value. My mother, also in travail, wrung her hands and wailed in the background, an attitude alien to her. Then the scene changed to Dickensian London. In a murky saloon Bill and Joyce sat sobbing, for they too had lost something irreplaceable. We tore our hair and scratched our cheeks. Just before dawn I jerked out of sleep paralysis in a cold sweat, overwhelmed with relief at being back in the real world. As I struggled to get a grip, a voice from the opposite bunk said, "Let's get out of here!" Without stopping for early tea, we sailed to deliverance out of the mouth of Porto Kaio into the bleeding wound of the dawn. I later learned the refuge had a curse on it. A Temple of Poseidon, where traces of human sacrifice were discovered, once occupied the site of the abandoned monastery.

The sea outside was so calm and the low sun so pleasant, we felt safe to explore Asomato Bay where, five steps ashore, lay the Gate of

Hell, a grotto once stacked with smugglers' spoils now adopted as a fishermen's store. That "unimportant morning" there was no storm to rouse the Hell Hound Cerberus from his deep down slumbers, which was just as well, for we had no honeyed sops of barley bread to satisfy his slavering jaws.

As we drifted south in a dimensionless reverie, *Cappelle's* bows forged a silk cut. The rocks of the shore replicated themselves upside down and the rising sun illumined the eastern aspect of the Mani bringing distant objects into co-existence with near. This rendered everything momentous, as if isolated in its own essence. Cape Tainaron (Cape Matapan), the legendary Mouth of Hell on the end of the pinched-head cape where the Taigetos petered out, crouched like a grey wolf. Haunches raised, nose extended on paws, it might as well have been the end of the world for us, as it was for the ancients. We rounded the lighthouse, hugging the shore, but, unlike as in the days of Patrick Leigh Fermor, who passed so close the keeper threw him a pear, no one acknowledged *Cappelle*. Within yards, as if the shutter of a camera lens had descended, our world was transformed. This side of the cape, the wolf's hackles were ink black, their silhouette razed with sun spokes. To the Messenian Gulf the south west wind bequeathed a swell that tumbled us horribly. Unless conditions eased, hard graft lay ahead.

Twenty-two

We exit Greek waters

Cape Tainaron to Kalamata

It was a roller-coasting eternity before we drew level again with Porto Kaio. Here the Evil Mountains, not yet breasted by the sun, soared higher. In the shadows I made out the village of Vathi, a miniature tower-house Manhattan. Below it, the Mani widened into the fissured bastion of Capo Grosso whose mucous-dripping rocks gaped with black holes. To port waves broke on a reef we failed to locate on any chart.

Tucked in beside Capo Grosso, whose 200 ft sides were squat in comparison with the Bad Mountains behind, but whose face had all the elements of "the rifted rocks whose entrance leads to Hell", was the small port of Yerolimena where an eighteenth-century French doctor described seeing the entire population, among them priests and young children, gleefully engaged in wrecking. By tradition there were several entrances to the Underworld. On Capo Grosso the likely candidates were an upper swallow hole and a cave where the sea slobbered. Perhaps it was appropriate that, even at close quarters, my eyes failed to penetrate the gloom of these Gateways to Hades. Nothing would have induced me to swim inside to investigate, as did Patrick Leigh Fermor. But, according to Walter Pater's poem, Aphrodite sent her bondmaid, Psyche, on such a mission, coins in the poor girl's mouth to pay Charon the Ferryman, and instructions not to return without the mysterious casket that would restore her mistress's beauty.

We trundled on, no place to be, but unable to move faster, given time to study every inch of Capo Grosso's toad-slimy walls. After more than five toilsome miles the blunt-nosed cape began to fall away, its near-perpendicular slopes displaying the remains of ancient cultivation terraces. Above us, sparse golden thistle sprouted on boulder-strewn table-land. As the light reached them, the molten lead of the sky-high Kakovounia beyond turned to champagne. It was a landscape heavy with time. Such fighting folk as John the Dog and Black Michael to whom this stamping-ground belonged lived on a diet of lupin seeds, vetch, a modicum of gritty oats, a few wild figs, prickly pears, carobs and stale cistern water, with pig and quail to feud over for festivals and a handful of almonds and olives on hey days.

We worked our way past Cape Tigani. Here salt was gathered. Fifty years ago Isabel and George Millar had taken shelter in the tiny frying-pan of a fishing harbour, until, instinct warning them that Tigani's smooth-tongued fishermen had designs on their motor sailer, *Truant*, they made their escape in the middle of the night. Altering course out to sea in the hope of catching some wind, what we met was the swell from the Ionian. But at 11.43 hrs, still only fourteen nm from Porto Kaio, the wind filled our sails for an hour before failing altogether, leaving us plunging. It was not until we were within the shelter of Cape Akritsas, outer arm of the Messenian Gulf, that the sea smoothed. Picking up light airs, we glided past Kardamili set low on a coastal proscenium in a mise-en-scène of black spruce and jagged rocks, home to scholar-gipsy Patrick Leigh Fermor. Here we were hailed by the crew of a fishing boat. And when an Italian day-sailer crowded with children circled *Cappelle*, I held Wacky up to wave a paw.

Kalamata

After rounding Cape Kitries we set course due north for Kalamata (Place of Reeds), making so much better progress than expected, the Captain concluded that *Cappelle* was lightened by a north-flowing current. Seeking a white building and a flour mill described in the Pilot as lying east of the harbour entrance, we peered through the haze ahead. It was the usual story of an "easily identifiable landfall" which, seen for the first time, is anything but. But by 16.45 hrs we were nosing into a backwater where a Frenchman from a catamaran helped us tie to a broken bollard. Rising from the coastal flats the awesome wall of Mount Taigetos reduced the rusting in-harbour hulks to abandoned toys.

To go ashore meant balancing on the taffrail and dragging myself up onto the mole. Climbing back on board with provisions was impossible without assistance. But a glance at the filthy water below made for extra caution. After settling in, it was time for a sundowner. An old man tried to tempt Wacky with toffees, which, needless to say, were rejected, whereupon Papou dropped the packet on deck as a conversation starter. All I knew of Kalamata was that it was famous for olives and that the Kalamatianos was a stately dance in chain formation. The earthquake of 1958 was the reason for the town's lack of distinction. More than thirty years on, rubble lay uncleared. In the pitiful shells of waterfront mansions rafters dangled from ornate plaster ceilings and cornices crumbled, while broken doors creaked eerily off hinges. Shoddy shop fronts and ferro-concrete apartment blocks gradually replaced the old earthquake fodder. Athwart a side street an homuncular church of ancient origin formed a road-block between two graceless multistoreys.

In a life of inattention to the days of the week, we had succeeded in perfecting the art of reaching civilisation after the banks closed. A thin weekend was in prospect. Bob spent an exasperating Sunday morning tightening the pump-action sink tap with no wrench to fit its bolt, the idea of having to remove the sink itself firing him with sufficient strength to tighten the tap with a loud roar and his bare hands. Afterwards we squeezed through a barbed wire entanglement surrounding factory gates to gain access to a grubby beach and flee across the scorching sands to wallow in sea water with the consistency of warm consommé. Under an umbrella a pretty girl recuperated from a motor-cycle accident, the stump of her leg, torn off above the knee, a lurid mess. We queued for the beach shower. But by the time we were home again its benefits had evaporated.

The backwater was deserted except for a wiry old guy bouncing up and down like Zebedee. Bob was the answer to his prayers, «Καπετάνιο! Καπετάνιο! Βαρκάκι! Βαρκάκι! ΓΡΗΓΟΡΑ!»

("Captain! Captain! Dinghy! Dinghy! QUICKLY!") he shouted. Grasping the old man's predicament in a trice, Bob bundled him into the dinghy and rowed for dear life after a sizeable fishing smack drifting out of harbour. Grandad, meanwhile, now well on his way to having the situation of his own making saved, was doubled up with laughter. It seemed, after a drink or two, he had attempted both to untie his caïque from the height of the quay, and board it. Not surprisingly, the offshore breeze won. Hero of the hour, Bob caught up with the escapee and shoved the old salt aboard, still cackling merrily.

Mistra

To my enquiry about Mistra, a travel agent replied that, if supported, a tour coach would leave the following Thursday. Not having encountered a single tourist, I knew, as did the agent, who knew I knew, that no coach would run, so we planned to go by local bus. The following Monday, though advertised as opening at 07.30 a.m., the doors of the harbourside Bank of Greece stayed shut. By the time we had panted stickily uphill to the main branch we were obliged to hail a taxi to get us to the bus station to catch the bus to Artemesia, where we would take the Lakonia bus to Sparta. There we hoped to pick up a connection for Mistra.

With Mistra in mind, I had paid no attention to our route, so it was a thrill to cross the Langhada Pass, the most spectacular in the Peloponnese, through terrain Lawrence Durrell described as "the nether end of Tibet". Rising from the calamus plain, the bus ground in low gear up into the High Taigetos whose empty crags were once the haunt of buck-skinned Artemis in her guise as Keeper of the Wild Things. Above the gorge of the Nedousa the hairpin bends quadrupled. Langhada, its soil red, its rock bleached, burnt, frosted, blown and gnawed with caves, its air cool and fresh, was a formidable combination of peak and chasm. So fascinated was I, I ceased to care a Frankish fig whether we ever reached Mistra or not.

After edging along a precipice, the bus was swallowed by a tunnel cut through an unstable headland. As we emerged, the driver pulled up beside the blue shadow of a bottomless ravine to gulp spring water gushing from a rock. I could see its source, a tiny electric-green alp high on the hill. «Πάρα πολύ ενδιαφέρον» ("very interesting"), said my guide book, referring to the view. Though the French section translated this as "plus que très intéressant" ("more than very interesting"), it was left to the English translation, "much too interesting" to take the biscuit (especially if another vehicle should come round the corner!). A sweeping descent into an asteroid crater floored with the cushion heads of chestnut trees delivered us to the oleander-edged terraces of Artemesia.

The scents of genista and mignonette blew through the bus windows as we ascended the further rim of the crater, hummocky with camomile. A road sign reading "Top of the Taigetos" heralded the unfolding below of the shimmering mulberry and orange groves of the Plain of Evrotas. The Spartans developed into a master race whose life style was geared to the military efficiency summed up in a mother's enjoinder to her son on the eve of battle, "Return with your shield – or on it!" Unwanted babies, and boys who reached the age of seven without outgrowing a disability, were committed to the gods by being flung into a ravine from which there was no escape. Spartan girls were subject to as rigorous a training as their brothers.

When we sped past a pyramidal foothill carpeted with the ruins that had to be Mistra, backpackers on board attempted to halt the bus, but the driver putting his foot down, chortled, "No Mistra bus! – Sparta bus!" A Spartan bus driver/taxi driver conspiracy was in operation, obliging Mistra passengers to hire taxis in Sparta to take them back to Mistra. With only two hours to go before our return connections to Kalamata, we must look slippy.

Guillaume de Villehardouin, born at the fortress of Kalamata, had established the city of Mistra with the building of the castle that remained his favourite. To his credit also was the famous School of Chivalry from which a thousand horsemen were wont to stream down to the silvery plain, trappings a-jingle and pennants a-flying beneath the tight-rope crest of the mountains where horses were once sacrificed to Apollo. Sad ghosts of the ruined palaces were the wives of Greek despots, foreign princesses trained in the Courts of Love, all of whom died young. More recent blood was spilt in the Civil War, the Metropolis becoming home to squatter families who survived on rusks and the water from its fountain court.

Following footpaths between walls of intricate *cloisonné* brickwork we gazed beyond the cornelian clusters of mob-cap roofscapes. Ruined churches nestled amidst roses and the slanting brackets of century plants. Everywhere the prickly pear branched in tangles of barbed ping-pong bats. It was easy to believe the cruel sun had driven you mad and that the high voltage dynamos of the cicadas whirred inside your head.

Having learned my lesson in Khozoviotissa, I had donned a long skirt to visit the six-domed Pantanassa, Monastery of the Queen of the Universe. I need not have worried, however, for sight-seeing had been monopolised by bum-bagged French teenagers in Lycra hot-pants showing fleshy half-moons. Professing to understand nothing of the nuns' appeals, they wielded sharp elbows. The honeyed-olive of the Byzantine murals was well preserved and I enjoyed the depiction of the Passing of Lazarus in which a bystander held his nose ("by now he stinks" : John 11.39), but the sun had climbed too high in the sky for light to penetrate the enchanting little church of the Peribleptos ("That Attracts Attention from All Eyes") tucked half under the hillside where we peered at frescoes of fairytale knights. Holy vandals had symbolically disembowelled the stomach of a Panagia. But, high out of reach, a winged tetramorph reigned undesecrated.

After the mountain air, the humidity of Kalamata was stifling. The streets were deserted except for an illegal immigrant who could only repeat, *"Albanya!"* My head throbbed, my sight blurred and my body, its thermostat failing, felt at bursting point. Seeing the world through the wrong end of a telescope, I urged my feet to keep walking. As we plunged towards the heat haze obscuring the harbour I had the sensation of being inside my own shadow, understanding now how, in the hinterland between the conscious and unconscious, Maniot women discovered dazed in the mad-dog sun, believed themselves victims of the Makrynas, the Faraway One, the Great God Pan. Buying a watermelon each from a gipsy, we hugged their cool green globes.

There was no better destination than within the curtained shade of *Cappelle* tied up against the dank quay wall.

At dawn, our eyes endeavouring to strain a miasma of fog as palpable as cotton fluff, we crossed the Gulf of Messenia. Emerging from mist, how tame seemed those unambitious hills the other side! I took a despondent view of the beckoning land's vapidity. It emphasised how I missed the astringency of the Aegean World, that loss compounded with *nostalgie de la sauvage* for the Wild Mani. Beyond Venetiko Island we homed in on the pepper-pot Tower of Bourdzi to anchor in the outer harbour of Methoni, a salad of fishing boats, yachts and pedalloes. Bourdzi occupied an offshore shoal joined to the shore by a four-arched bridge so Chinese willow-pattern I missed the stylised lovers and blue birds. But, not even against the almond-blossom sky of evening, could such a sight lift my dulled spirits. There being little point in lingering in Methoni's sand-churned waters, we pressed on next morning into the Ionian past the dark cliffs of Navarino Bay, site of the last major battle between sailing ships. By it Greece gained her independence.

Katakolon

As the Peloponnese receded, we sailed a close reach on a heading for Katakolon on the northern arm of the Bay of Kiparissia. We knew nothing of this peninsula, except that it was shaped like the cross-section of an aeroplane. It was disconcerting when this appeared not ahead, but well to starboard. But for good visibility we might have passed by. A check on the autohelm showed a slipping drive band. Turning east, we closed the coastline. A speed boat circled, its driver removing his cigar long enough to shout,

"Splendid sail?"

"Rather!"

Down-at-heel Katakolon, nearest safe harbour to Olympia, home of the ancient Panhellenic Games, was built in 1857 to service the currant trade. Now its waterfront was lined with cruise-liner bait. Despite being a Port of Entry, it lacked both a fuel station and a bank, meaning we should be out of funds for the third weekend in succession.

We joined the smaller craft on an apron quay fronting the waste ground. It was pulsatingly hot. A procession of heavy-bellied Canadair sea planes swooped repeatedly over the bay scooping up water to bomb forest fires. (In 2007 the whole area, along with much of the Western Peloponnese, was devastated by wildfire. The village of Artimeta, where a mother perished with her four children in the burnt-out wreck of their car, gained the name of "the crematorium".)

As the evening breeze rose, the chatter of the sea muffled the pumped out renderings of the current popular songs, «Σ'αγαπώ!» ("I love you") and «Καλό καλοκαίρι!» ("Have a good summer!"). Along the waterfront paraded a *Lederhosen* band sponsored by the Austrian State Tourist Board. A light aircraft above trailed a banner advertising the imminence of a Beer Fest. We planned departure for its eve. A Taiwanese ketch flying the European flag (making it either Belgian or Dutch, for the larger European nations did not fly this flag alone – "Europe" not recognised as a country of registration) tied up. On my apologising in advance for Wacky who, according to form, would pay the ketch a night visit, I learnt he had met his match, for on board *C. Brieze* were four cats and two dogs, all uncertificated and undeclared. Dutchman Willy did not hold with pet regulations.

Monday morning found me outside the post office waiting to collect poste restante and cash a Eurocheque. An ambiguous notice pinned to the door announced the office either open or closed (it was not clear which) for two hours before midday. By one p.m. the door had remained locked all morning. Cars and motorbikes pulled up. People drifted away in disgust. What had happened to the local post master was anybody's guess. In the afternoon I mingled with an angry crowd blaming the late arrival of the unfortunate post-office clerk despatched from Pirgos to deal with the emergency. Besieged, he flung me a sheet of postage stamps, indicating I was to tear off what I wanted and pay later.

Dumping two bags of potatoes to rest my arms, I was vaguely window-shopping for a birthday gift when joined by a polite young man who, seizing potatoes, ushered me into a bijouterie to meet his father. In no time I had succumbed to the purchase of minute gold earrings, paying over the odds (though by just how much only time

345

would reveal) by credit card, a usual method of transaction in Katakolon, but unusual for me. Quickly escaping the overblown attentions of both father and son, I backed out of the shop.

Olympia

Across the Elysian Fields lay Olympia. The coachload of tourist ladies giggling over a site once alive with naked Chippendales, was a reminder that this was the height of the season. Despite Olympia's vulnerability to natural disaster, a banner declared, *"WE PROTEST TO RETURN OF OUR ANTIQUITIES FROM LAUSANNE "* in what looked like blood. At first the Olympic Village appeared little more than a woodland park filled with rubble and truncated columns. A German father marshalled his brood at the original fourteenth century BC sprinter's starting line, a ridge of grooved limestone. Gradually the Sacred Grove asserted itself. The air was heavy and dark clouds threatened. When Pheidias the Sculptor asked for a thunderbolt as a sign of Zeus's approval of his statue of the Lord of the Lightning, he was not seeking too outlandish a favour, for the area is prone to thunderstorms.

We arrived home to find *Cappelle* lying in the shadow of a Ferris wheel and Wacky much agitated by marching bandsmen. Realising that, in my haste to rescue my potatoes and vacate the jewellery shop, I had failed to pick up the receipt for my transaction, I returned. But its premises, a temporary trading post set up to service cruise liners, were emptied and padlocked. Though I did not know it then, I had been conned a considerable sum. Moreover, the studs were worthless. As the Greeks say, «*Τα παθήματα, μαθήματα!*» — "We live and learn!"

Zakynthos

Although I could now carry out my departure chores half asleep, I was wide-awake on leaving for Zakynthos after stepping out of bed on a wet fish deposited by Wacky. Like the bloom on a grape, the island soon appeared. By midday we were searching the chalky waters of the harbour approaches for marker buoys. A dredger driver gestured us to the north east quay where we were pleased to see yachtsmen filling water bottles direct from a standpipe. After we drew the curtains to keep out the heat Wacky flopped into the darkest corner of the cabin, and I crossed to a white sand beach to collapse into the sea. Each morning, I virtually woke up in it, but my new-found friend, Antigone, was always in first.

Although the coast of the Peloponnese was still visible as a faint harebell-blue line on the horizon, the town of Zakynthos with its campanile and piazzas, was Italianate enough to give the impression we had already left Greece. I paid only one visit to a warehouse supermarket papered with fly posters where I cut my hand on a broken jam jar. Back home, bloody fingers wrapped in a handkerchief, I discovered dead cockroaches in my shopping bag. Transferring our custom to the bright little shops off Solomos Square, we fared better. It felt good to be a sailor, especially after viewing the exhibition of crashed motor cars (two with GB number plates) on the waterfront. We were preparing to leave when yachts piled in reporting northerlies of F 6/7. On deck at two a.m. to fend off *Sea Chariot*, a motorised cocktail cabinet under delivery by what appeared to be a bunch of waiters, we sensed the wind abating.

Kefalonia

In contrast to low-slung Zakynthos, Kefalonia presented a barren height. Another of Homer's "pointed isles", it had supplied pine trees for Odysseus's masts, Zakynthian tar from its tar pools being used to preserve their wood. When Cape Skinari bore 270 degrees, we forced ourselves out across uneven furrows of water, speed dropping. To starboard a flock of edge-dancing shearwaters squabbled over a shoal of fish. Optimistically, we had persuaded ourselves the wind would free. But by midday the nor' nor' wester, known here as "The Maestro", lived up to its name. After we had given Kakova shallows a wide berth, the Maestro drove us further and further into the lee of the steep-to 5,000 ft bulk of Kefalonia's Mount Aenos (a brooding mountain possessive enough to make me feel it was aware of us), which plunged steep-to for a stretch of eight miles. Our aim was to make passage round Cape Pelagia into the Gulf of Argostoli. But the Maestro had other ideas, both heading and forcing us towards Thionisi, a mighty molar on which once stood a Temple of Zeus.

According to the Admiralty Chart, it was essential to enter the Gulf dead centre, since its vase lip was fouled on both sides with underwater rocks and reefs. Forced to approach too far east, we tacked away to the south west at a 100 degree angle, pointing back towards Zakynthos, with no plan as yet to admit defeat. Low-lying Vardiani Island formed our western hazard. From the level of the tumultuous sea we could make out neither the island itself, nor its identifying lighthouse. Binoculars were impossible to handle. ("Poor vision in filthy head sea," the Captain wrote in the log.) Turning ninety degrees, we tacked north west again, but were unable to hold course. I was not sure which bothered me most, the invisible island on one side or the jagged spike of Thionisi on the other. During three disagreeable hours (less ten minutes) in the lip of the Gulf, hemmed in by obstacles and averaging less than one knot forward progress, *Cappelle* held her own. But from whatever angle we tried, the wind zapped us, the seas as hard as willow bats. (I did not read until later the pilot's warning that in this area the Maestro "can be hair-raising".)

By 18.00 hrs we acknowledged with relief that Thionisi was now slightly aft. To starboard instead reared the Aspra Vraska ("The White Rocks") of the cliffs of St Nicholas Point, where the saint surely reigned in his aspect of Blue-bearded Poseidon. Since we were now over the edge of the very shoal we had been trying to avoid. I prayed he was not in a malevolent mood. Once round the point, we should be within the rim of the gulf, with Cape Akrotieri and Vardiani Island breaking the fetch to the west, which would give the Captain breathing space to fix our position. At last, with only six miles to go, the Maestro dropping and westering, we fired the engine.

At 19.15 hrs the entrance to Argostoli, two miles behind a wooded spit, hove into sight. With yacht handling demanding total concentration, we had been without sustenance all day. Much of the stowage was on the floor. And I could not find Wacky in the forepeak. His instinct had been to climb, and he was discovered, wild-eyed, in the cubby-hole above the wet wardrobe. Feeding him titbits, I tidied up and fastened burst lockers while Bob set the autohelm so that he could study a plan of Argostoli harbour, which George Sandys, visiting in 1616, called "capacious enough for a navie".

When we looked back across the blue-black sea, Golden Zakynthos, an island that had taken us all day to escape, seemed near enough to touch. Too soon it was time to pay attention, for ferries were crossing ahead to Lixouri. At 20.15 hrs we took in the log before wheeling to starboard around Cape Theodorus, whose pretty Palladian lighthouse glowed tea-rose in the sunset. As Bob handed the mainsail, spotting an orange float, I yelled,

"Nets!"

"Cut engine!" bellowed Bob at the same moment.

Fatigued or not, it was as well to keep our wits about us. A ship is no slave, as Joseph Conrad pointed out. You owe her your total involvement. Of the celebrated Smeetons who rounded Cape Horn at the third attempt, Beryl said she always worried when Miles was not worried "because on a boat someone has to worry". On this occasion we both worried.

Once inside Argostoli's bottle-neck, we negotiated beacons to avoid patches of shoal. As darkness was falling, we moored on the Customs Quay among quarantine-flagged arrivals from Italy. Our welcome, as we squeezed past *Wild Mood,* was cordial. The Essex couple on board, waving bottles of Gordon's gin, explained that, arriving exhausted from Italy that morning without strength enough to relay it, they had dumped their anchor ten metres off the quay. With only one mooring ring free, the crew of a cabin cruiser kindly fixed our second warp to the hawser of a laid-up ferry. Wacky danced off meanwhile to be greeted with a cry of delight from *Wild Mood* whose Ship's Cat, Pudding, was brandished aloft. In the log Bob wrote:

"Very tired and frustrated by the failure to make satisfactory progress into the headwind coming out of the Gulf of Argostoli at about 15.00 hrs. Tacked reasonably past Thionisi

Island, but wind increased off the entrance to the Gulf and progress to windward with engine and main was pathetically slow. Our inability to recognise Vardiani Island (low-lying, so much as to be invisible in afternoon sun and choppy sea) meant that we could not be sure of our position and, with a reef on the east side of the Gulf, our ability to sail was severely handicapped. Altogether a very unsatisfactory afternoon and evening, proving how difficult it is for this boat to make directly to windward in a Force 6 (or more). ALSO PROVING HOW EASY IT IS TO REDUCE THE SKIPPER TO FOUL INCOHERENCE IN THESE DAYS OF HIGH SUMMER HEAT!"

Sharing the Customs quay with *Cappelle* were *Lady of the Wind*, *Aphaian Aura* and *Coq de Mer*, a fanciful line-up brought up by *Dragonera*, a classic sloop with shining brightwork. Of the two night birds on board, the blonde favoured bronze chiffon with floating panels while the Posh bird modelled a white satin mini with ropes of pearls. Together with their dashing partners, the foursome were waited on by a liveried couple. Out-classed, my tentative greeting met with icy stares. When the Port Captain asked *Dragonera's* skipper to make way for a launch, he refused, with the practised excuse of engine trouble.

VIP Greeks awaited their motor cruiser *Christolfi* with impatience. Headed by Force 7, she arrived a day late, her skipper crossing himself. Her owner's wife took a fancy to Wacky. (Cats were Top-of-the-Pops in the Ionian that year with a song called «Η γατούλα μου μικρή» – "My Little Pussy Cat"). Soon the Κυρία was knocking on *Cappelle's* hull seeking introduction. But Wacky would not allow himself to be picked up. "It is you he loves!" she cried, enchanted, reminding me with the utmost seriousness that should he ever mislay his Evil Eye, it must be replaced forthwith for «Αυτό είναι πάρα πολύ σημαντικό!» — "It is most important!" Wacky might well need its protection, for his new admirer told of witnessing his nightly jaunts up the ferry's gang-plank. He also indulged in many a Pudding chase.

An anxious Greek questioned us as to whether we had seen "my friend" single-handing *Blue Moon of Skye*. I had grown jaundiced about the word "friend", since it so often referred to someone who owed money. An Italian motor cruiser tied to our stern. The Love Boat companions of the two youths on board flashing gold Rolexes were North Country British girls with ever-changing bikini wardrobes. In charge of *Wet Dream* was the Contessa, an elegant Madame with greying hair. With quiet authority, she made sure *Cappelle* was well treated. One of the girls took to playing with Wacky until led inside by a boy.

With the arrival of a dart-shaped Magnum 70, generators purred all night. Forever polishing her picture windows, her American skipper unburdened himself. He had been persuaded, he said, to skipper his company's latest model "for a couple of weeks", to show her buyer how to handle her. As well as being bored stiff, for the weeks now stretched to six, Gene was heart-broken over the fate of his baby. He pointed out an elderly Greek, his trap-mouthed wife, her sister and a yappy dog unaccustomed to sailing, with the bitter words, "That old goat's supposed to be *LEARNING!* For Chrissake, he's not even *INTERESTED!* All he'll do is hand My Sweet Baby over to some young fool! Mark my words, by this time next year she'll be *RUINED* and he'll be off-loading her for the next model!..." Gene was not seeing life through rose-coloured glasses. "Europe? You can bloody keep it! You know what these goons wan' me do in Italy? Anchor off some bloody cliff!" (We guessed Anacapri.) What he really enjoyed was setting up party boats in Mecca (Fort Lauderdale). The memory had him dewy-eyed. "Europe! You can bloody *KEEP* it!" With *Blackeye's* mind-boggling fuel consumption, I was beginning to learn what the big timers cost to run.

Advice from *Wild Mood* was to provision well, for the cost of living in Italy was high. Perilously laid over during the crossing, they had been unable to vacate the cockpit for twenty-four hours. Their conviction that a smaller craft would have capsized did not augur well for *Cappelle*, though we were sure she was stiffer than the Moody. Κυρία *Christolfi*, as excited as a child, called with the news that they were "off to Zakynthos" in the morning! On hearing the rattle of chains, we rushed on deck to shout, «Καλό ταξίδι!» truly believing it was the last we should see of the party. Lined along *Christolfi's* rail the Greeks blew kisses. We could scarcely credit it when they shouted, "See you tomorrow!" For all the hassle of farewell, they were only to be away one night.

Christolfi's slot was quickly bagged by a converted Scottish fishing boat, *Seagull of Kefalonia*. We paid close attention to our fenders, for the local lads under training as crew were having trouble manoeuvring. The English girls recruited as hostesses were bored stiff with making preparations for charterers. Full of themselves and still wound up, three American couples were duly piped aboard to flop into basket chairs and unload their mental baggage in penetrating tones. Phrases such as "base rates", "pre-tax profits" and "specific loan provision" sounded strange on a Greek island. A hostess asked Blue-rinse if she might serve him a drink. "No dice!" he said. "But, believe you me, Honey, when I drink, *I DRINK!* So, when I give the word, jest you batten down the hatches!" At that moment the girl caught my eye and we exchanged winks.

Ithaca was on my mind. Ithaca had given me my marvellous voyage. As Cavafy said, "Without sea-girt Ithaca I might never have started." Happy am I, for, like Ulysses, I had travelled far and wished to pay my respects to his birthplace. Choosing a weekday, for "this bus does not create on a Sunday", I looked down from the mountain tops at the fabled island lying flexed and rounded like a Henry Moore pebble, its waist linking two ash-hued peninsulas. Cavafy went on…"Rich with the experiences you have gained, do not expect Ithaca to give you riches." But sight of the sea-girt island was satisfying. Homer described it as a land "with no wide courses, nor meadow land at all". While none of the ancients questioned this austere kingdom as Odysseus's homeland, it became fashionable for academics to argue the toss. But the Odyssey is a seafarer's story, and the sailor's instinct should prevail.

Bob concerned himself with how best to obtain a reliable weather forecast for the passage ahead. In the event, a circumnavigating yachtsman from Moorhead NC (whose wife had become so possessed by ocean malaise she had lost the power of speech) sent over a Navtex print-out. In stultifying heat we hauled up the dinghy to scrape, scrub and pack, before struggling to replace our torn genoa with its reconstituted original. With the sun in our eyes, we made mistakes as the halyards twisted in light airs. But in a command performance that nearly had me overboard obliterated in flapping canvas, we raised sail seven times. At last the sitting of the replacement genoa met with the Captain's approval. At which point *Seagull's* skipper despatched his lads to scrub and bag the other one. Donna of *Aphaian Aura* (she of the exquisite Janet Reger underwear packed in polythene she showed me!) lent Bob her folding bicycle to transport *Cappelle's* gas canister to the exchange, together with her shortwave radio to check the Austrian weather forecast (the most reliable). On *Aphaian Aura's* thirty-seven-hour crossing from Italy, whose waters reportedly teemed with oil-drum rafts full of Albanian illegal immigrants, she refused to be drawn.

On our last night on *Seagull* Captain Stamati donned his entertainer's hat and business talk was superseded by the clink of glasses and air of relaxation. Alone on deck, Stamati sang to himself as he cradled his mandolin, the syncopated refrain etching itself into my head.

Our last morning was the Greek island mixture as before. The greengrocer showed me photographs of his son at University in Bristol, and the local doctor (stroking my arm) called me a "polyglot". (It turned out he thought I was a Frenchwoman, who spoke English rather well!) The woman in the postcard shop told me her name was Kalliope and gave me her address, for when I returned to Argostoli (if I and my children were spared), we would meet (if she and her children were spared) for the purpose of speaking Greek. When Bob collected our exit papers, he discovered *Venturer* on the Town Quay, the fourth time in hundreds of miles our path had crossed. Again it was a familiar story, for *Venturer* was parked over the sewer outfall. There was time for a last book swap and for her crew to renew their acquaintance with the "little rabbit", who long ago in the days of his youth shot down the port hole in Mitilini.

An hour later, giving Vardiani Island, fully visible this time within its turquoise coronet of shallows, a good offing, we turned between

Kefalonia and Zakynthos out into the Ionian. At first the waters were confused, but from mid-afternoon they settled down, allowing *Cappelle* to sail steadily at four kts on a close reach. After we had cleared the light on Cape Yerogambos the wind freed. Setting course due west, I gave in to the demands of the Ship's Cat for a cuddle. Did he but know it, like so many of his compatriots, he was joining the diaspora. Bob adjusted course for leeway. The land behind faded and the open sea began its rhythmic roll.

Depending on circumstances and the attitude of her crew, a small boat is either a prison or freedom. Though the uninitiated believe the live-aboard life affords time to think, more frequently it does not. Now, however, I had the leisure to indulge in a sentimental yearning for what lay behind. From Greece our parting was threefold; first from the Aegean World; second from the wild places of the Mani, and finally from the Greek waters themselves. Off Paxos to the north in the time of Tiberius sailors swore they heard the death cry of the Great God Pan when vanquished by a new religion. But we knew Pan was alive in the High Taigetos in that parallel Golden Age where the trees of the forest speak, the waves of the sea sing, and man has not forgotten how to listen.

With the coming of sunset and the brief rise and fall of a crescent moon, the wind from the Adriatic continued its dependable blow. Promising each other to clunk, click, I pulled on sea boots. We established two-hour watches as *Cappelle* forged a groove. From the Straits of Otranto came a rumble of thunder. So bombarded were we with shooting stars we attended their splash and fizzle, Bob remarking that, if this was not a natural phenomenon, it must be a rehearsal for *Star Wars*.

Riding the yacht's pneumatic movement as she bounded forward on an even keel, her bit between her teeth, I was to all intents and purposes alone while the captain slept. With the sails well balanced, I did as Odysseus who "never closed his eyes but kept them on the Pleiades". By comparison, the infinite distance of the constellation rendered the protean waters shallow. To the Ancient Greeks the Pleiades were the seven daughters of Atlas and Pleione the Sailing Queen, so-called because their helical rising in May initiated the navigational year.

They have been described as a "tea-tray in the sky" and as a "badminton racquet". Tennyson, going over the top, declared them a "swarm of fireflies tangled in silver braid". To me, going right over the top, they were diamonds swathed in gauze.

I was alone then, looking up at planets so three-dimensional, I peered into the spaces behind them. This was the world of understanding, not counter-intuitive, but functioning by the geometry of common sense. *Cappelle* was the axis of an earth around which the universe turned. The heavenly bodies that circled, designed in due proportion and keeping their relative positions, were her satellites. When we chose to make landfall, we would make it by applying the pragmatic truths of mathematics in a world of perfect logic. Palpably not emptiness, the void above shimmered with the energy unmanifest that Democritus described as a "dynamic state of rest", the Uncreated, the About-to-Be.

Astrophysicists write of the "sighing of the sun". Analysing my relationship to the order of things, my ears caught the strains of a perfect chord and the ringing of the spheres. My identity weakened. For a fleeting moment the sea flowed in my veins as I glimpsed the reality of a unified field in which there are no edges and all life, both animate and inanimate, shares the same energy. The vanishing points that disappeared into the boundless spaces between the vagabond stars would never meet. The further I gazed, the further back in time. Out there in the open sea at night beneath an exuberant sky, space-time could not be but an aspect of a simultaneous dimension. Pushing reductionism further, I could lay no claim to the role of observer, for I was of the essence of the creative energy all around me. Consciousness was limitless and my mind expanded into it, its relationship with the universe beyond the symbiotic. Infinity was everywhere and I was part of it. *I WAS STAR-DUST!*

Lost in star-gazing, I turned to listen, as clear into my head floated Captain Stamati's recitative, an echo of Greece following three live-aboards to whatever the future held.

Epilogue

Wacky's distinguished career as Ship's Cat continued in Italy, in the Aeolian Islands, in Corsica and in France. Despite his predeliction for uninhibited adventure he never once missed the boat. His obligatory six-month incarceration in quarantine kennels on reaching English shores cast a shadow but, made the darling of the staff during this period of enforced confinement, he survived. After rejoining *Cappelle* on the River Arun in Littlehampton he was soon putting the fear of God into the river-bank moggies and even some of the dogs. By the time we sailed on to Gillingham his fame had spread.

Wacky's crowning moment came with an invitation to appear as a guest star at the National Cat Club Show at Olympia, alongside such feline luminaries as Arthur of Spiller's Cat Food, who demonstrated his talent for scooping up cat food with his paw. Here he was awarded a champion-of-champions red-white-and-blue rosette inscribed *TO WACKY FOR HIS LOVE OF ADVENTURE* in gold lettering. During sojourns in both the Cotswolds and Aldeburgh in Suffolk, he adapted well to the life ashore before we moved to our permanent address in Scotland, where he was able to take up his duties as Ship's Cat once more during the summer months on the beautiful West Coast.

Although Wacky took to the comforts of life ashore, including spacious accommodation, a big red Aga and a garden, he never lost his sea-awareness. When the wind howled, fearing his home might slip its anchor, his instinct was to climb. (I once found him clinging to the shelf over a doorway when gale force winds threatened.) His town garden he saw as his deck. He ran to the railings to greet passers-by with whom he had become friends, and was immediately alert at the click of the gate in case some stranger was about to invade his sovereign territory.

Though affectionate and ebullient, he remained an alpha-male, who even tried to exercise his bossiness over me in Bob's occasional absence. At night he left the house via his cat-flap to circumnavigate the block via garden walls or cross the street to parley back-of-the-buildings with his dustbin friends. On sunny days he loved to sniff the catmint and loll among the periwinkles.

His happy and eventful life was seven times longer than that of the average Greek feral cat. When he finally fell asleep it was, oddly enough, Hallowe'en. So now, on dark nights, I sometimes catch a glimpse of him out of the corner of my eye riding his broomstick among the stars. His remains were cremated. Maybe one day I will scatter some of his ashes on Samothraki, the mystery Aegean island we never visited, or have them made into a blue diamond as a φυλαχτό to wink on my finger.

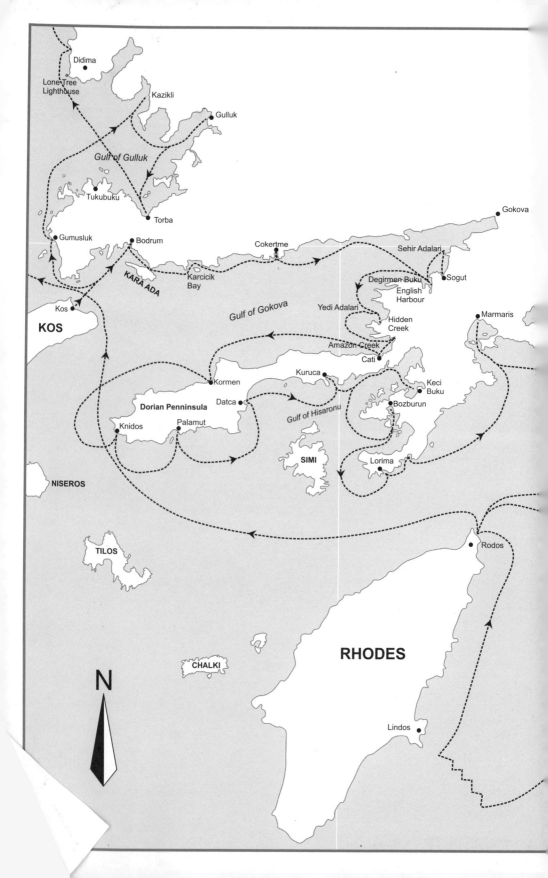